ACCOUNTS OF INNOCENCE

Joseph E. Davis

ACCOUNTS OF INNOCENCE

Sexual Abuse, Trauma, and the Self

The University of Chicago Press
Chicago and London

Joseph E. Davis is research assistant professor of sociology at the University of Virginia.

The University of Chicago Press, Chicago 60637
The University of Chicago Press, Ltd., London
© 2005 by The University of Chicago
All rights reserved. Published 2005
Printed in the United States of America
14 13 12 11 10 09 08 07 06 05   5 4 3 2 1

ISBN (cloth): 0-226-13780-5
ISBN (paper): 0-226-13781-3

Library of Congress Cataloging-in-Publication Data

Davis, Joseph E.
    Accounts of innocence : sexual abuse, trauma, and the self / Joseph E. Davis.
      p.   cm.
    Includes bibliographical references and index.
    ISBN 0-226-13780-5 (cloth : alk. paper) — ISBN 0-226-13781-3 (pbk. : alk. paper)
    1. Sexual abuse victims—Psychology.   2. Victims of crimes—Psychology.   I. Title.
    HV6625.D38   2005
    362.76—dc22

                                     2004009714

For my mother, and in memory of my father

CONTENTS

ACKNOWLEDGMENTS

This book, long in the making, has benefited from the advice and support of many people. Colleagues have read and commented on chapters, shared ideas in informal discussion, allowed me to try out ideas in their classes, and in general been a wonderful source of support and encouragement. In alphabetical order, these include Charles Bosk, Beth Eck, Carl Elliott, Jennifer Geddes, Steven Jones, Ian Hacking, John Herrmann, Richard Horner, Daniel Johnson, James Nolan Jr., Kimon Sargeant, Jeffery Tatum, and Robert Zussman. I presented drafts of material in this book at a meeting of the "Working Group on Bioenhancement and Identity" (sponsored by McGill University) in Charleston, South Carolina, in 2001; at a meeting of the "Working Group on Narrative" at Harvard University in 2002; and, the same year, at the workshop entitled "Crafting Narrative Analysis for the Social Sciences," held at the Massachusetts Institute of Technology. My thanks to Carl Elliott for the first opportunity, to Francesca Polletta and Marshall Ganz for the second, and to Susan Silbey for the third. A much earlier draft of this book was presented as a doctoral dissertation at the University of Virginia. James Davison Hunter, chair, and Sarah Corse, Krishan Kumar, and Charles Mathewes served as the examination committee. For their generosity and mentoring, I am deeply grateful. Finally, special mention must be made of Arthur Frank, who, in his capacity as one of the reviewers for the University of Chicago Press, raised important questions and made many helpful suggestions. The final product, whatever its other faults, is greatly improved because of his careful reading and counsel.

In addition to intellectual help, I have also benefited from strong institutional support. The Institute for Advanced Studies in Culture at the University of Virginia provided me with both a doctoral and postdoctoral fellowship. I further benefited from the ongoing support of the Center on Religion and Democracy. Together these institutions are my intellectual home at Virginia and provide an interdisciplinary work environment that is always collegial and stimulating. Special thanks to James Davison Hunter, colleague and friend, as well as to the other faculty and staff. I worked on portions of this book during two summers at Macalester College. Brooke Lea and Jack Rossmann of the psychology department made that happen, and, as in the other summers I have been there, were most gracious hosts. A remarkable year in residence at the Institute for Advanced Study in Princeton provided the opportunity, with yet one more rewriting of the introduction, to finish this book.

Doug Mitchell, executive editor at the University of Chicago Press, provided the steadiest and warmest encouragement possible. I cannot thank him enough for taking an interest in this project, offering timely advice, and shepherding it through to publication. I also want to acknowledge the always cheerful help of Kristine Harmon, former research associate at the Institute for Advanced Studies in Culture, who provided editorial assistance with earlier drafts and helped track down hard-to-find materials. For my wife Monica, there are no adequate words of appreciation. She was always patient, always kind, and always forbearing of my preoccupation with this project.

°☯°°☯°°☯°

Earlier versions of chapters, or parts of chapters, appeared as follows, and the publishers are gratefully acknowledged. Chapters 1 and 2: in "Social Movements and Strategic Stories: Creating the Sexual Abuse Survivor Narrative," pp. 107–25 in Wendy Patterson, ed., *Strategic Narratives: New Perspectives on the Power of Personal and Cultural Narratives* (Lanham, MD: Lexington Books, 2002); chapters 6 and 7: in "Not Dead Yet: Psychotherapy, Morality and the Queston of Identity Dissolution," pp. 155–78 in Joseph E. Davis, ed., *Identity and Social Change* (New Brunswick, NJ: Transaction, 2000), © 2000 by Transaction Publishers. Reprinted by permission of the publisher.

On December 13, 2002, Bernard Cardinal Law, the Archbishop of Boston, resigned his office. His resignation followed eleven months of unrelenting media attention and public furor over the issue of child sexual abuse among Catholic clergy. The scandal erupted when the *Boston Globe* published a two-part investigative report into the Cardinal's handling of John J. Geoghan, a former priest, who was then facing two criminal trials and multiple civil lawsuits for child sexual abuse. Cardinal Law, according to the *Globe* reports of January 6 and 7, 2002, had known of Geoghan's long history of pedophilic behavior as early as 1984 but did not remove him from ministry. Geoghan continued to abuse young boys, despite repeated stints in treatment, until he was finally defrocked in 1998. Since then, the *Globe* reported, the archdiocese had settled fifty lawsuits filed by Geoghan's victims and had another eighty-four pending, many of which named Cardinal Law as a defendant (Rezendes 2002; Pfeiffer 2002a).

The *Globe* report brought an immediate outcry, and two days later, on January 9, Cardinal Law issued a public apology—to all those abused as minors by priests, those abused by John Geoghan, and "particularly those who were abused in assignments which I made" (Law 2002). The apology, however, did little to stem the tide of criticism, as other cases began to come to light in the following weeks, including the highly damaging case of former "street priest" and advocate of "man-boy love," Fr. Paul Shanley (Pfeiffer 2002b). Shanley, who was subsequently arrested, was accused of the rape and molestation of boys over several decades. More lawsuits followed, along with intensified charges of a Church cover-up and calls for Cardinal Law's resignation.

What began in Boston quickly spread nationwide. In the following months, the details of past abuse by scores of priests (and a few bishops) in dioceses around the country hit the papers. The articles showed that Catholic bishops and religious superiors, at least until the early 1990s, when changes were instituted in virtually every diocese, not only knew about past infractions but also continued to reassign offenders and allow them to minister without supervision. Moreover, Catholic leaders had often rebuffed parental complaints and, when exposure was threatened, negotiated quiet financial settlements. The records of court settlements were almost always sealed. Observers, both in and outside the Church, found the revelations of the bishops' actions and their failure of oversight astonishing, and in every type of public forum they expressed disbelief, betrayal, and moral outrage. Protests were organized, new legal strictures were discussed, new lay advocacy groups were formed, and a vigorous debate broke out over the causes of the scandal and the appropriate responses. As the scandal grew, the bishops moved to institute new policies aimed to both prevent future cases and deal with priests and brothers who had abused in the past. At their June 2002 meeting in Dallas, the bishops passed the Charter for the Protection of Children and Young People, which specified the removal of any priest involved, past or present, in the sexual abuse of a minor. They mandated the establishment of a national Office for Child and Youth Protection, which would issue an annual report on the implementation of the charter and would be "assisted and monitored" in its work by a lay National Review Board. They pledged to report every allegation (unless "canonically privileged") of sexual abuse to the public authorities and to redouble their efforts to reach out to victims (see Davis 2003).

Cardinal Law's resignation in December, occasioned by yet further revelations of priestly misconduct drawn from Church records made public by the Shanley prosecution, effectively brought the Catholic "annus horribilus" (Dinter 2003) to an end and moved the scandal off the front page of the newspapers. It was far from over, however. The Boston Archdiocese alone was facing abuse-related claims by more than five hundred people; hundreds of lawsuits were in the courts elsewhere, and more were forthcoming. Prosecutors, judges, and attorneys general, angered by the bishops' actions, were convening grand juries, opening Church records, and generally making it their goal to crack down. Victim groups, their ranks and coffers swelled by the scandal, were vowing to keep the struggle alive. Lay Catholic groups, such as Voice of the Faithful, which were formed in response to the scandal, remained restive. The effects of the crisis will be playing themselves out for years.

The Catholic scandal is but the latest in a steady stream of activism, public concern, and conflict over the issue of sexual abuse. Although the scandal first made national news in 1985 and received ongoing media coverage into the early 1990s as new cases arose, the decade of the 1990s was dominated by a different public drama, the so-called memory wars. Over that decade, concerns about recovered abuse memories inspired an immense body of popular and academic writing, million-dollar lawsuits, and extensive press coverage. It also spilled over into television docudramas, confessional talk shows, soap operas, and novels. In this acrimonious debate, the central issue was whether or not it is possible to "repress" memories of sexual abuse. On one side were psychiatric researchers and adult survivor therapists who sought to defend psychological understandings of sexual abuse as a form of trauma that can lead to complete amnesia with respect to the traumatic events. Spearheading the effort on the other side was the False Memory Syndrome Foundation, an initiative of parents who claimed to have been falsely accused of abuse, and allied mental health professionals and academics. The foundation, together with many other psychologists and psychiatric researchers, argued that genuine victims seldom, if ever, lose all memory of their abuse. Drawing heavily on memory research and seldom straying too far from a narrow focus on empirical truth claims, the critics charged "recovered memory" therapists with implanting false memories of abuse in the minds of vulnerable therapy clients, causing untold damage to the lives of thousands of these clients and the innocent parents they accused.[1] The targeted therapists reacted to the foundation as a politically motivated "backlash." The FMS Foundation and its professional allies, they argued, were using their academic status and power with the media to protect perpetrators of child abuse and to perpetuate the sad legacy of blaming the victim and denying the harmful effects of sexual abuse.

The Catholic scandal and the memory wars or, to back up even further, the concern with sexual abuse in day care centers and preschools that dominated in the 1980s, highlight the influential place that sexual abuse has had in American public consciousness in recent decades. Indeed, it would be hard to find another social problem that has commanded such continuous attention or a form of social victimization about which more has been written. At least with respect to the personal sphere, it seems fair to say that sexual abuse has become our paradigm case of victimization (on a collective level, genocide is probably the paradigm). It is a common problem, it concerns children (the most vulnerable social members), and the terms in which it was formulated are consistent with the framing of many other types of victimization. The sociologist Joel Best (1997), for instance, surveying the discourse of different types of victimization, identifies a core set of common propositions (an ideology) about how it is publicly described. First, victimization is very widespread but largely unrecognized, both socially and often by victims themselves, who must therefore be taught to recognize their experience for what it truly represents. Second, victimization—including even a single, brief incident—is consequential, potentially causing profound and long-lasting psychological aftereffects and impaired functioning. Third, victimization is morally unambiguous—victimizer guilt and victim innocence are straightforward and unassailable. Fourth, and finally, claims of victimization must always be respected; anything less would amount to blaming the victim. The definition of sexual abuse, as will become clear in the following chapters, follows these propositions point for point. Beyond this ideological correspondence with other forms of victimization, the central place of the concept of trauma in characterizing the effects of sexual abuse is also significant. In recent decades, trauma has emerged as *the* principal model for thinking about the interpretation of psychological injury in many different campaigns on behalf of victims.

In ideological and psychological terms, the case of sexual abuse captures key features of the contemporary understanding of victimization and its consequences. The case recommends itself for study both in its own terms as an important and publicly volatile social problem and as illustrative of the wider cultural phenomenon.

REAL VICTIMIZATION

At its most general level, this book is an effort to understand why in our cultural moment we place such causal and explanatory, that is, psychological, significance on victimization in people's lives.[2] Naturally enough, I took up this topic in part because of dissatisfaction with previous answers. The literature on "victim culture" which began to appear a decade ago turns a critical eye on the proliferation of victimization claims, therapeutic programs, and mental illness categories and theorizes what this proliferation means for American society. These works, including such well-known titles as *A Nation of Victims, I'm Dysfunctional, You're Dysfunctional,* and *The Abuse Excuse,* typically look briefly at many forms of victimization and emphasize the multiplication and often trivialization of victim claims. They focus not on institutional arrangements but on the victim claims themselves and their consequences. They identify the key dynamic as an evasion of personal responsibility and see the proliferation of claims as a sign of a declining sense of responsibility in society. The result, these works maintain, is a weakening of Americans' bonds of social solidarity and common citizenship.

These critiques make some valid points, but within a narrow ambit. They typically avoid discussion of "real victimization" and draw their conclusions instead from egregious claims, unusual cases, and folk diagnoses—for example, the recovery movement with its ever-growing number of addictions. This strategy has important limitations. It necessarily leads to an overemphasis on victimization accounts as excuses or justifications for personal misconduct or failings. It leaves out of the picture the specifically *moral* logic that informs the discourse of victimization and its appeal as a sense-making framework for personal experience. And it takes for granted the contemporary "regime of the self," to use Nikolas Rose's (1996) term, with its burden of autonomy and self-invention, that is such a potent source of anxiety, disappointment, and moral unease in our times. Further, minor or manufactured slights and folk diagnoses are not independent of forms of more serious victimization but derive their meaning and rhetorical force from them. Understanding the discourse of victimization requires that we begin with concepts and categories of *actual* victimization.

Sexual abuse is actual victimization, though, as already noted, the topic of sexual abuse has not been free of public controversy. Children's allegations against parents, day care providers, and teachers have often been bitterly contested and publicly debated. The memory wars were launched in the early 1990s when parents began publicly charging that their adult offspring's incest allegations were based on a condition, "false memory syndrome," induced in therapy. These public controversies, however, have seldom been about sexual abuse *in itself*. Rather, they have focused on the veracity of abuse allegations in some circumstances and the role of professionals (social workers, therapists, and others) in eliciting allegations. While such challenging of abuse claims can become an interrogation of whether sexual abuse really happens very much or can lead to the conclusion that many if not most victim claims are not to be believed, the basic wrongness of sexual abuse, both morally and as a legal matter, and its potentially deleterious effects on the victim are seldom directly questioned. So while there have been controversies, they are generally not about whether adult-child sexual contact is a consequential form of victimization.[3]

The concern with actual victimization does not preclude attention to the issues at stake in the memory wars. Indeed, they could hardly be avoided. The treatment books, both professional and self-help, in the period under study here take it as given that some clients will have complete amnesia regarding their abuse history. Since recovery involves disclosing and working through the abuse experience, the books lay heavy stress on "memory work" and suggest various techniques and practices, from hypnosis and guided imagery to reading survivors' published accounts and journaling, for stimulating (if possible) memory recall. The FMS Foundation and other critics dubbed these techniques and practices, when used with a client who has no previous memory of being abused (they are also used with clients who have limited recall or are prone to denial), "recovered memory therapy" and subjected them to a withering critique. Though the memory wars are now fairly quiescent, at least as compared with the mid- to late-1990s, the nature and dynamics of traumatic memory remain a point of debate within psychology. It is not my aim to take a position in these debates. Still, tracing the discourse of sexual abuse through its psychological formulations and therapeutic applications sheds some light on the search for buried memories by highlighting the value of a sexual abuse account for making sense of confusing and troublesome experience and for restoring the basic goodness of the self. The social authorization and sense-making power of the account, I will argue, helps to explain how a survivor identity might become an object of desire.[4]

The memory wars are also relevant here for another reason. A key argument of this book is that if we wish to understand the significance of the psychology of victimization as an "account" for troubled lives, we need to attend to the nature of the subjectivity—the ways of understanding and relating to ourselves and to others—that this psychology creates. I trace in detail the historical and institutional trajectory of a single case, the adult survivor of childhood sexual abuse, as a means of discovering the basic moral coordinates that constitute the self under the victim description. As noted above, this case makes a strong claim to be representative of victimization accounts more generally.[5] Interestingly, the FMS Foundation and allied critics of recovered memory therapy also frame a victimization argument. In their formulation, unwitting therapy clients and the persons they falsely accuse of sexual abuse are both victims of a condition, "false memory syndrome," induced by a therapist. What is striking is that in this instance too the implicit psychology at work constructs subjectivity around essentially similar moral coordinates of an innocent and harmed victim determined by external events. The foundation and others criticize the ideology of victimization and yet reproduce it. Even this conflict points to the presence of a common normativity and regulative ideals for formulating troubled identities.

Exploring a discourse of real victimization as a window on how the victim self has been socially constituted is to enter a minefield of potential misunderstandings. We might have no problem thinking of such condition-categories as "shopping addiction" or "compulsive vulgarity disorder" as "constructed."

They reference problematic habitual behaviors, to be sure, but characterizing shopping as an addiction or cussing as a disorder is obviously a new way of thinking and talking about them. Over the past two decades, we have become accustomed to many problems of living being redescribed in psychiatric terms, especially within the culture of "twelve-step" and other self-help groups. But we know them to be redescriptions, new formulations—"constructions"—for problems that were hitherto understood differently. The categories of "sexual abuse" and "adult survivor," however, seem quite different. It is hard to imagine them as new concepts and even speaking about them as constructed feels wrong. Talking about changes in *concepts* and *categories* can easily be misread as doubting or downplaying the reality of adults having sexual relations with children, questioning the personal suffering of victims, or introducing a moral relativism toward the practice. But even if we avoid conflating concept (sexual abuse) and object (actual sexual behavior), isn't the point of social constructionism to challenge the taken-for-grantedness of an idea or state of affairs? Referring to a long list of books with "social construction" in the title, the philosopher Ian Hacking observes that

> in almost every case the aim is not to refute an idea, but, to use Karl Mannheim's words, to "unmask" it, and often to show its "extra-theoretical function," with the hope of "disintegrating" the idea. Or at least to undermine its authority, showing that an idea or a present state of affairs need not have been the way it is. (1997:14)

Given these possible aims, I want to be clear from the beginning about what social constructionism as a theoretical strategy means, and does not mean, in the context of this book.

SOCIAL CONSTRUCTIONISM

Social constructionism has become an important theoretical approach within many subfields of sociology and well beyond. As this case study explores how new knowledge was developed, transmitted, and deployed by the activities of victim movements, psychological experts, and psychotherapists, it touches directly on three of these areas: social problems, social movements, and mental health/medicine. While social constructionism is not a single, unified approach, differences are less important here than similarities. In each area of inquiry, social constructionism engages "ways of worldmaking" (Goodman 1978), the cultural and symbolic processes that constitute meaning and underlie action in social life. It begins from the assumption that experience, behavior, things, and people are complicated and heterogeneous; what they mean to us is not pregiven or fixed. Sense-making and action require perception, interpretation, and formulation, for which we create images, types, categories, kinds, concepts, rationales, stories, and other forms of knowledge and acts of cultural production. In social constructionism, the constitution of meaning is made the *object* of study, along with the particular historical conditions, cultural symbolisms, and institutional arrangements under which it emerges and is negotiated.[6] A brief look at what constructionism entails in the subfields noted above, concentrating on key elements relevant to this study, will help make this more concrete.

In the study of social problems, social constructionism targets the process by which problems are socially discovered and socially defined. The focus of study is not on the condition that is claimed to be a harmful problem. Such conditions—environmental degradation, racism, child abuse, Internet pornography, homelessness, and so on—have little in common, being united by neither their causes nor their effects. Rather than conditions themselves, researchers study the complex social process by which a condition is defined or redefined (whether successfully or unsuccessfully) as a public problem, concentrating on the "moral entrepreneurs" and constituencies who make the problem claim, on the interests of these "claims-makers," on the types of resources they marshal, and on the rhetorical devices and political strategies they use to make their case.[7] From this perspective, social problems are configurations of moral meanings that are the achievement of the individuals, social movements, special interest groups, and others who succeed in bringing public attention to putatively harmful conditions.[8]

Claims about harmful conditions also involve claims about the types of persons who "inhabit" the conditions (Loseke 1993, 1999). Two person-categories are often preeminent: those harmed by the condition, or the victims; and those who cause the condition, the villains or victimizers.[9] In formulating these categories, claims-makers commonly "typify" the victims and victimizers as having certain moral characteristics, based on the designation of responsibility for injury (see Holstein and Miller 1990; Loseke 1993; J. Douglas 1970). These characterizations, in turn, provoke certain emotional responses and require corresponding remedies or sanctions. The victim, innocent of responsibility or fault for the harm suffered, is worthy of sympathy and concern and should be helped or compensated. The victimizer, by contrast, who intended harm, deserves condemnation and should be sanctioned or punished. As a definitional practice, then, victim and victimizer types not only name categories of people implicated in a harmful condition (e.g., "deadbeat dads," "battered women," "adult survivors of childhood sexual abuse"), but also formulate a reality about those people.

Social constructionism in social movements research, generally called the "framing perspective," shares a similar emphasis on the definitional practices—the "signifying work"—that collective actors engage in to draw atten tion to particular social conditions and provoke social change.[10] Scholars, borrowing from Erving Goffman, use the term *frames* to describe the systems of meaning that movements construct to inspire and legitimate their activism, both in terms of the need for such activism and the desirability of undertaking it. Social movements, according to David Snow and Robert Benford, "frame, or assign meaning to and interpret, relevant events and conditions in ways that are intended to mobilize potential adherents and constituents, to garner bystander support, and to demobilize antagonists" (1988: 198). Like social problems claims, these ways of understanding do not exist *a priori*, but emerge through an interactive and negotiated process as a movement group consciously fashions its grievances, strategies, and reasons for action by drawing upon and modifying existing cultural beliefs and symbols.[11] Here too, constructionism includes an emphasis on the way that person types are formulated in the definitional process.[12]

In the sociology of mental health and medicine, social constructionism makes medical knowledge, including the origins of professional beliefs, disorder classifications, diagnostic techniques, and healing rationales and strategies, the objects of study.[13] Particularly in psychiatry, classifying illness symptoms and making diagnoses are interpretative acts because they always involve the assignment of meaning. Mental illness symptoms and the diagnoses that order them are contingent readings of experience, rooted in therapeutic rationales that are shaped by language, cultural and institutional values, considerations of political and social status, taxonomies of pathology, and rules of interpretation.[14] As a result, scholars observe, symbolic healing practices display wide variation and change over time and across cultures. The distinction between health and impairment, the meaning of symptoms (signs of disorder), and the diagnostic categories and theories of etiology that are used to define and classify symptoms and symptom patterns both vary and change (Blum 1978; Ellenberger 1970; Kleinman 1988). New categories of disorder arise (e.g., attention deficit disorder, post-traumatic stress disorder, sleep disorders), while others disappear (e.g., hysteria, neurasthenia, neurosis). Social constructionism, along with the similar cultural approach of scholars working at the intersection of anthropology and psychiatry, seeks to understand shifts in medical knowledge and diagnosis and how they play out in the practices of healing and health care.

Social constructionism in medicine and mental health also includes exploring the expansion of the jurisdiction and boundaries of medicine, a process called "medicalization."[15] Medicalization, according to a leading sociological theorist, Peter Conrad, "consists of defining a problem in medical terms, using medical language to describe a problem, adopting a medical framework to understand a problem, or using a medical intervention to 'treat' it" (1992: 211). Although medicalization includes all conditions that come to be defined in medical terms (e.g., epilepsy), in practice, research has focused primarily on the process by which previously nonmedical problems—either "natural life processes" such as childbirth or menopause, or behaviors considered deviant, sinful, or criminal—are given medical meanings. In the latter category, the list is long, including such problems as alcoholism, opiate addiction, school misbehavior, overeating, undereating, compulsive gambling, and physical child abuse. As these examples suggest, medicalization is not an all-or-nothing process but one of degree. Some problems may be almost fully medicalized (birth), others only minimally so (alcoholism). In exploring the dynamics of medicalization, scholars observe that the medical profession does not always take the leading role. In many cases lay activists or social movements play a significant part, and in some cases medical professionals are virtually absent. Scholars also typically explore how medicalization transforms a problem and brings it under new controls and with new techniques. These outcomes (guise of moral neutrality, domination of experts, individualization of social problems, and so on), they argue, are independent of the question of medical efficacy.

As this study progresses, the definitions of the social problem of sexual abuse, the categories of victim and victimizer, movement action frames, psychiatric diagnoses, healing rationales, treatment models, and medicalization will all be under discussion. As my concern is with the constitution of the victim self, I trace an internal moral logic that informs these categories and models and so pay much less attention to broader cultural and structural factors that would otherwise be important in a conventional constructionist analysis. What I want to emphasize here, though, is that displaying the social and cultural production of this new knowledge does not necessarily undermine it or imply that it is wrong. As Conrad observes, "It is important to distinguish between the sociological investigation of how knowledge is developed and sustained, and how the knowledge is to be evaluated" (1992: 212). Social constructionism in sociology contributes to understandings about social processes involved in knowledge production. It need not be used in the hope of "disintegrating" that knowledge or undermining its authority. I stress this because, as Hacking notes, the phrase *social construction* has been widely deployed in the service of consciousness-raising efforts. Such unmasking is not my purpose. I do, however, offer some evaluation of the medical/psychological knowledge I discuss. I took up this project because I had an ethical concern with the way that people, in their victim stories, represent who they are and who they can and should be. In exploring how psychological knowledge about victims has been produced, I hope to contribute in some small way to a rethinking of our representations of victims, suffering, and selfhood.

Such a rethinking is necessary. Languages of victimization—developed, refined, and reproduced in social movements, the mental health professions, human service agencies, recovery groups and websites, self-help books, and other locales—have brought into existence new ways of conceiving of personal troubles and troubled selves, and new norms and techniques for acting on that self. These forms of subjectivity (and their integrated norms and techniques) have significant consequences for the way that other people think about and act toward victims and for the way that victims understand, experience, and evaluate themselves and their lives.[16] Many of these consequences, as in the case of adult survivors of sexual abuse, have been salutary, directed to reducing stigma, countering self-blame, encouraging victims to disclose their experience, encouraging others to believe them and recognize their suffering. But there have been other consequences, some unintended by responsible activists and clinicians, but real and deeply problematic, nonetheless. These consequences are plainly and continuously visible, as the regular flow of victim talk attests, including that arising from the recent Catholic scandal. Large numbers of people have come to define themselves in terms of woundedness, and very often other people also see them that way.[17] They describe their lives as determined in significant part by external events. And they understand healing and self-realization to consist in searching for and living in moral accord with a "self" conceived as inwardly generated.

Notions of the self as (1) externally determined and as (2) autonomous, free of external constraints and obligations, are not, of course, limited to discourses of victimization. They are poles within our contemporary regime of the self and take various forms in social and psychological discourse. What is arresting and perhaps unique about discourses of victimization, as the case study illustrates, is that they bring these two seemingly contradictory models of subjectivity together, linked, as I will show, by a moral logic of establishing innocence. Neither model, sociologically and philosophically, is adequate as an account of how persons achieve self-definition. And neither model, in my view, is compatible with a morally rich view of persons, one that sees a potentially meaningful role for suffering and recognizes our dependence on and obligations to others. As those who suffer and as moral agents, we need a different picture of whom we can and might be.

SOCIAL SOURCES OF THE SELF

The social shaping of human subjectivity is an old and continuous theme in sociology. All the great classical theorists—Karl Marx, Max Weber, Emile Durkheim, Georg Simmel—addressed from different vantage points how social arrangements influence categories of cognition and the types of human beings that participate in those arrangements. A long stream of work, some of the more recent spurred by the writings of the philosopher Michel Foucault on the "constitution of subjects," continues this tradition to the present day. The general tendency in this writing is to focus on particular social processes and to view mentalities, forms of personhood, and conceptions of selfhood/individuality as determined by these processes, whether capitalism, the division of labor, urbanization, bureaucracy, technological change, late modernity, or some other process. Much the same tendency is evident in the large corpus of writing on postmodernism and on identity politics, both in sociology and well beyond (see Dunn 1998). In addition to the general critique of the rational Enlightenment "subject," postmodern theorists have argued that the individual's sense of identity and biographical continuity are increasingly superseded by fragmentation amidst the endless flow of images and sensations encountered in consumer culture. In identity politics, writers have emphasized power relations and how dominant groups impose on marginalized people, or the "other," the very frameworks by which subjectivity and self-understanding are experienced and known.

The approach I take is different. Rather than seeing victim subjectivity as the outcome of some more fundamental social process, I want to ask how understandings of victims have been shaped by specific ways of thinking about and acting upon persons with troubled identities. In other words, and paraphrasing Nikolas Rose (1999: xvii), I ask how persons have been conceptualized within therapeutic practices, how these conceptualizations came about, what kinds of techniques for acting on victims have been linked to these conceptualizations, and, as already noted, with what consequences. In the context of the case study, this means investigating how a new system of beliefs about the sexual abuse victim came into being and how that system is deployed in healing practices with adult survivors. Drawing on an image from the work of the psychiatrist/anthropologist Arthur Kleinman (1988), I conceptualize this flow of meanings as having an "upward" movement into public culture and therapeutic rationale and a "downward" movement, through therapy, into the lived experience of those seeking help.

The upward movement had two major phases, which blended into each other. It began with social movement activism in the 1960s and 1970s. Given the publicity devoted to sexual abuse in recent years, it is hard to believe that the term as it is commonly used now only dates to the 1970s. It is hard to believe that prior to the 1970s sexual offense victims did not talk about their experience in public forums. Sexual offenses and incest were certainly a topic of public and professional concern earlier, but the stranger offender, rather than the victim or the family, was the predominate focus of attention. Movement activism, however, brought a sea change that not only increased the concern with the victim and incest but also fundamentally changed the terms in which victimization was understood. The new terms were not built on some progressive accumulation of knowledge, either clinical or produced by research. Rather, as I will show, they followed a sharp break with received professional knowledge, a break based on a new *moral* orientation and commitment to the victim. The existing sexual offense research and clinical literatures, movement activists argued, were deeply biased against the victim. These literatures, they maintained, reflected and legitimated a broad social pattern of minimizing victims' harm and compelling their silence. Activists called for a new approach that defined all adult-child sexual encounters (touch or nontouch) as forms of pure victimization, and made the victim's fundamental innocence and a corresponding recognition of injury the touchstone for legitimate interpretation.

The second phase of the upward movement, then, begins with the disqualification of much of the older clinical opinion and findings. Movement activists and allied mental health professionals, along with early victim-activists who publicly shared their experiences and personal struggles, demanded new efforts to survey and theorize the long-term effects of sexual abuse, and in terms that rigorously avoided any hint of "blaming the victim." To deflect any fault or weakness from the victim, the professionals held that adult-child sexual encounters were *in themselves* determinative of long-term psychological aftereffects and social disabilities. Sexual abuse, they argued, was a traumatic violation of the self and one that, unresolved or untreated, could spawn a wide range of serious problems in adulthood.

These problems they theorized in terms of a new psychology of trauma/dissociation—a form of the officially recognized diagnostic category created for the Vietnam veterans, post-traumatic stress disorder. In this psychology, the effects of trauma are conceptualized as forms of coping. Rather than signs of weakness or disability, trauma symptoms—such as overeating, anxiety, memory loss, marital conflicts, flashbacks, and many more—are represented as normal, perhaps even creative responses to intolerable experiences. Framing symptoms as coping mechanisms locates the onus of pathology outside of the victim and so preserves the victim's innocence even in the face of what might otherwise be considered "morally contaminating characteristics."[18] In this way, blamelessness for the victimization itself (i.e., responsibility rests exclusively with the adult, or older adolescent offender) is extended to blamelessness for a wide variety of possible personal problems tied to the victimization as aftereffects. Trauma psychology, in turn, became the basis for adult survivor therapeutic rationales, both professional and self-help.

In the downward movement, therapists (individual practitioners but also groups and books), on the basis of the rationales, redefine client experience and persuade clients of its validity. In adult survivor therapy, the pattern of intervention follows precisely the "consensus model" of the healing process drawn by Kleinman from the large cross-cultural literature on such practices. To influence a change, the healer redefines the problem from which the "patient" is suffering in terms of an authorized system of cultural meanings (or therapeutic rationale) that organizes the patient's experience and makes it intelligible. The redefinition is a kind of translation, a reading of the patient's experience in light of what it signifies within the healing system. But more than interpretation takes place. Healers also use various rhetorical devices to persuade the patient that the redefinition is valid. As this takes place, the "patient's experience comes to resonate with, or is conditioned by, the symbolic meanings of the healing system," and both problem and patient begin to change (1988: 133). In the therapeutic interaction, shaped by the mutual expectations of the participants, the healer also guides, via the symbols and rituals of the healing system, change in the patient's emotional reactions. He or she also confirms the transformation of meaning through specific techniques or rituals of change and affirms its success.

This upward-downward movement is a storied process, and I draw heavily on the concept of narrative. Narrative study, which has recently flourished in many fields of human inquiry, is part of a renewed emphasis in these fields and beyond on human agency and its efficacy, on context and the embeddedness of human experience, and on the centrality of language to the negotiation of meaning and the construction of identity in everyday life (see Hinchman and Hinchman 1997; Davis 2002a). Research has proceeded along several different lines. In the approach I draw on, researchers study how stories are socially constructed—the "manufacturing process," to use sociologist Arthur Frank's (1998) phrase—and how they function to mediate action and constitute identities. This approach derives in part from the work of scholars who have argued that representations of identities/selves have a basically narrative character.[19] We construct a self, "tell" our lives as stories, drawing, in the words of psychologist Jerome Bruner, on the "narrative models" that our culture "makes available for describing the course of a life" (1987: 15).[20] These socially approved "ways of being" constitute the categories of meaning that mediate the way individuals understand their experience and its significance, and how they orient themselves in relation to others. From this perspective, then, narratives and narrative models are crucial to the constitution of subjectivity. Thus, with respect to each of the ways of worldmaking I will be considering—social problem condition and person categories, movement frames and identity fields, diagnostic categories, and therapeutic rationales—I pay particular attention to the institutional stories they embody and express.[21]

NARRATIVE MODELS

When social movements and social problems claims-makers construct a person-category and assign characteristics to it, they also formulate a narrative about the category.[22] Sociologist Laurel Richardson (1990) calls this category narrative a "collective story," while Donileen Loseke (2001), drawing on the narrative concept of "formula," uses the term "formula story." According to Arthur Asa Berger, a narrative "formula" is a "highly conventional scheme ... involving stock characters and recognizable plot structures" (1997: 65). The collective or formula story "displays an individual's story by narrativizing the experiences of the social category to which the individual belongs" (Richardson 1990: 128). Specifically with regard to victims, scholars emphasize the oppositional "counter-narratives" (Steinmetz 1992) or "subversive stories" (Ewick and Silbey 1995; cf. Nelson 2001) produced for and by those who have been abused, discriminated against, silenced, or marginalized. In a like manner, narrative models are also constituted when mental health professionals construct or recast diagnostic categories. Problem/disorder categories are aggregates of and generalizations about the "illness episodes" of many individuals occurring through time, episodes that are "stories of personal failures and successes, of social and personal relationships" (Staiano 1986: 16). These categories, too, produce a "possible self" that one might be or become, as well as a possible "consciousness" and public identity around which individuals can galvanize.

Collective stories and psychiatric categories create institutionalized patterns for and legitimate the replotting of individual life experiences. As narrative models, they both constrain and enable what can be said and directly affect how individuals understand, describe, and feel their experience. But narrative models do not, I want to stress, *determine* the self-narratives that individuals tell. They are not "rubber stamps" and they do not, as sociologists James Holstein and Jaber Gubrium remind us, "predictably cause us or others to become who or what we are" (2000: 99). How we come to understand ourselves and narrate our experience is an artful and interactional process, shaped not only by the available narrative models but also by our distinctive experience, social context, and personal aims. At the same time, narrative models of the kind I am discussing are not like cafeteria offerings, more or less equivalent and simply available for the picking and choosing. The process by which we identify with and narrate our experience in their terms is complex, often not fully conscious or deliberative, and heavily influenced, directly or indirectly, by others. Selection is influenced by institutional pressure from above, so to speak, as well as by our needs and desires for explanation from below.

Some narrative models are virtually demanded by specific cultural and institutional contexts. In adult survivor therapies, the therapist employs what I call a "mediating narrative" to authorize and structure the client's rejection of old self-understandings and the appropriation of new ones. As described in the therapy textbooks, the therapist takes the client through a guided telling of her experience in contrasting languages of external determination (the false self) and authenticity/self-determination (the true self), with the aim of helping her to renarrate her past, refeel and redescribe her suffering, and reorient herself toward a new future. In this narrative process, aided by various therapeutic techniques, the therapist leads the client toward specific frameworks of meaning for her experience and herself, and measures therapeutic success by the degree to which the client has embraced these frameworks. In any given client's account of her experience, there is certainly room for interpretive divergence from the model. Real life seldom fits the neat categories of a textbook. Still, a specific narrative framework of subjectivity is mandated, and clients are expected to learn it and learn to govern themselves by it.

Further, narrative models carry different moral and cultural valences as "accounts" for personal experience and thus differ in their explanatory appeal and acceptance. The stories that we tell about our lives matter to us and to others, and the concept of accounts is important because it helps to specify the remedial and biographical work those self-narratives can effect. There have been two different traditions of research on accounts, and they emphasize somewhat different account functions. One tradition, the social interactionist, defines accounts as types of explanation that social actors (individuals or groups) invoke to avoid or resist undesired responses in circumstances (a "social predicament") where they have been accused of behavior that is in some way unsuitable, disturbing, or deviant. The key categories of accounts within this tradition are excuses (e.g., an insanity plea for a crime) and justifications (e.g., a plea of self-defense).[23] Their primary functions, according to theorists, are to preserve the self-image, status, or relationships of the actor who uses them (Scott and Lyman 1968; for an overview, see Davis 2000).[24]

A second tradition of accounts, the social psychological, defines accounts more broadly. In this research, accounts are not so much explanations of deviance or blameworthy conduct as a particular type of self-narrative, one that arises as individuals retrospectively work through the "whys" of negative life events and adapt to them (though, theoretically, account-making may also follow positive events, such as the start of a relationship).[25] In this tradition, researchers emphasize the positive psychological role that accounts play for the individuals who tell them. Accounts are "storylike constructions," with a plot structure that ties together attributions of responsibility, reported memories, description, and emotional expression. Like stories more generally, they reconfigure the past, endowing it with meaning and continuity and projecting a sense of what might or should happen in the future. Their principal functions, according to researchers, include promoting a greater sense of control, facilitating coping and closure, and enhancing hope for the future.[26]

Both traditions of accounts research emphasize the importance of narrative models for shaping and constraining the accounts that individuals give of problematic personal experiences. The remedial and biographical work of accounts depends on their recognition or honoring by other people, and so others must understand a proffered account and view it as valid. Especially in the second meaning of accounts, it is also crucial that the account-giver see his account as explanatory, as fitting. At any given time, the available narrative models vary in their public and institutional acceptance, their interpretative and explanatory scope, and their moral and cultural resonance. These dimensions also influence which models will be adopted, what stories people will tell about themselves to whom and under what circumstances. The collective story of the adult survivor, I will show, and the psychiatric trauma model underwriting it score high on every dimension. The powerful work of this account helps to explain the demand for and openness to it as a framework of meaning for a troubled self.

ORGANIZATION

Following the upward/downward movement of new meanings and then exploring its implications, the book is organized into three parts. The first part is historical and traces the origins of the new psychology of adult survivorship. Specifying the change in ideas that began to take place in the 1970s necessarily involves comparing professional understandings before and after the break. I begin, therefore, in chapter 1 by examining the legal and clinical approaches to sexual offenses and the offense victim over the decades prior to the social discovery of sexual abuse in the mid-1970s. I ask why no adults molested as children were publicly sharing their experiences before 1971 and begin to answer this question by arguing that the existing constructions of the categories of sexual offense and offense victim neither warranted such a public telling nor provided the narrative framework—for both victim and audience—in which to do so.

Next, I turn to the new approaches that began to be formulated in the 1960s, and the social and therapeutic movements that were the principal claims-makers. Chapter 2 focuses on the family therapy and child protection movements, chapter 3 on the antirape movement and on the role of adult survivors as public activists. Since each of the movements built its meaning frames on preexisting models, I concentrate on these models and how their adaptation shaped new condition and person categories, and led to a rejection of the old. The various movement framings had many differences, but as noted near the end of chapter 3, it is possible to identify a significant core of shared representations about abuse and a collective story about the abuse victim.

Having traced the emergence of the collective story through movement framing activities in the 1960s and 1970s, I consider in chapter 4 how it became the basis for a new psychology in the 1980s. For the mental health professionals (many associated with the feminist and child protection movements) who took up the problem of finding a unified theory, the challenge was to locate a model that preserved the innocence theme of the collective story while making a causal connection between sexual abuse and a large number of disturbances and disabilities correlated with adult survivors. Post-traumatic stress disorder (PTSD), which had already been applied to rape, suggested itself, but initially the fit between PTSD and victim experience was loose. A concerted effort was made to tighten the fit, however, and professionals formulated a dissociative-type trauma model to do so. This effort, I argue, was pulled by the conceptual advantages of this diagnosis over others for enshrining victim innocence and pushed by legal battles for compensation.

The second part of the book traces the downward movement by exploring how the collective story, through the new trauma psychology, is particularized in the lives of individuals in psychotherapy and to what ends. As the recast trauma model took shape, so too did a therapeutic rationale, with both self-help and professional variants, for diagnosing and treating adult survivors. In chapter 5, I begin by outlining the central propositions of the rationale and then briefly discuss its early application in two treatment modes—self-help books and self-help groups. As a conceptual prelude to the detailed discussion of individual therapy that follows, I conclude the chapter by exploring the persuasion process of psychotherapy.

Over chapters 6 and 7, I present a detailed analysis of adult survivor therapy, in composite. A "mediating narrative," which unfolds in three stages, or "stories," about the past, the present, and the future, structures the therapy, as well as the therapist's techniques and the self-transformation that is the goal of treatment. In chapter 6, I describe the therapeutic relationship and its aims and then explore the first stage of therapy in which the therapist leads the client to give a victim account of her experience. Chapter 7 continues the analysis by examining the "survivor" and "thriver" stages of therapy and the narrative requirements of each. When successful, the whole process yields a "fit" between the stories of the mediating narrative and the individual client's new account and identity. Chapter 7 ends with a recap of how narrative fit is accomplished and how contrasting descriptions of true and false self are employed to this purpose.

In the third part of the book, I draw out implications of the case study. In chapter 8, I return to the "memory wars" and interrogate the countermovement and the terms in which the debate over recovered memories of abuse was cast. This debate makes remarkably little reference to the larger moral/political claims that shaped the concern with child sexual abuse in the first place. I ask how the moral logic that infused the definitions of the abuse victim and victim trauma had unintended consequences. Some of these consequences bear on the issue of false memories. Others touch on larger issues, and I turn in chapter 9 to the moral and political implications of the trauma model and the mechanistic view of mental life that it embodies. I then return to the overarching issue of the causal and explanatory significance of victimization in contemporary culture. I appraise the therapeutic language of the "true self" and the cultural problem of moral accountability for understanding the meaning that accounts of innocence have in our society.

METHOD

Consistent with a constructionist approach, my method was inductive. The types of data on which chapters 1 through 4 are based are listed near the beginning of each chapter. In the methodological appendix, I describe the method of their selection. My presentation of the adult survivor therapeutic process in chapters 6 and 7 was built on an analysis of professional and self-help treatment books, using the "grounded theory" method developed by Glaser and Strauss (1967; Strauss 1987). I used books because these provide models for the whole sequence of steps that make up the treatment process. The self-help books constitute a form of therapy (bibliotherapy) in themselves. They are also widely used as an adjunct to professionally provided psychotherapy. The professional textbooks recommend models for mental health practitioners to use in individual therapy. Obviously these do not cover the entire range of clinical practices and are likely more applicable to therapists who see many adult survivor clients ("survivor therapists") than to those who see only a few. Further, these models may only imperfectly represent what therapists actually do with their clients, especially older practitioners, since these treatment approaches are relatively new.[27] However, my concern was with the basic structure of survivor therapy and not with all the nuances and approaches of individual therapists. The treatment manuals, many of which were written by the recognized experts in the field, provide the normative accounts of this structure, the texts for training, key reference sources for clinical questions, and so on. I list the textbooks that were used as data and the procedure for their selection in the methodological appendix, where I also describe the method of their analysis in more detail.

A NOTE ON LANGUAGE

Tracing the construction of new categories of persons and conditions raises the problem of what to call them. To adopt the names for the categories given to them by activists and claims-makers is effectively to adopt the very constructions that are under discussion. While no labels are completely satisfactory, I have tried, as far as possible, to use certain terms generically. In speaking of adult-child sexual contacts, I either refer to them descriptively, as contacts, experiences, and so on, or as instances of "child molestation." About adults victimized as children, I use either the phase "adults molested as children" or "adults sexually victimized as children" or simply "adult survivors." The last term, of course, is one of the new categories I am exploring, and it came to have a very particular meaning in the treatment literature, as one who was overcoming his or her past experience, but I saw no easy way around its use.

A second language difficulty concerns gendered terms, and to this difficulty I likewise saw no completely satisfactory solution. Much of the research and clinical literature, especially until the mid-1990s, is concerned with victims who are girls or women, and so uses female pronouns. Since most offenders are believed to be male, male pronouns are typically used for the offender. For the sake of simplicity of prose, and because these understandings have shaped the gender dynamics of the literature, I follow this practice. The reader should be aware, however, as the discussion will indicate, that victims include males and offenders include females. To avoid the constant use of the plural or the clumsy he/she when discussing therapy, I refer to therapists in the singular as "he" and clients as "she," except when I am explicitly referring to a male client. Again, of course, clients can be either male or female. Numerically, the majority of survivor therapists are almost certainly female. Most of the treatment books considered here were written by women, and anecdotal (Haaken 1996) as well as survey data suggest that women predominate as providers of survivor therapy. Moreover, women now numerically dominate the mental health professions, except in psychiatry, but that too is changing (Philipson 1993).

PART ONE

Defining a New System of Meanings

CHAPTER ONE

Incest and Sexual Offenses before the Social Discovery of Sexual Abuse

There were many remarkable features of the Catholic scandal, but perhaps the least commented upon was the role that past victims themselves played and the understandings of sexual abuse that informed the crisis. The representatives of a victims' support and advocacy group, the Survivors' Network of Those Abused by Priests (SNAP), formed in 1989, became the de facto voice of victims.[1] In the daily flow of coverage, hardly any new development was reported that did not include some commentary from a representative of this group. SNAP Executive Director David Clohessy and three other past victims delivered emotionally charged speeches to the assembled bishops in Dallas, and SNAP President Barbara Blaine led a victims' delegation in a private meeting with the episcopal conference leaders. SNAP leaders wrote op-ed pieces, spoke at symposiums and conferences, issued press releases, held press conferences, led protests, appeared on talk shows like *Oprah,* and were in every other way a ubiquitous public presence. Following the scandal in the press, one might easily have gotten the impression that such a high-profile role for victim-survivors was nothing new.

Yet even more taken-for-granted was the psychological perspective on offenders and victims. The very focus of the scandal on the Catholic leadership and the public demand for a "one strike you're out" policy toward priest offenders reflected in large part the widely shared view that sexual acts of any kind with children or adolescents are symptoms of a compulsive psychological disorder unlikely to respond to any limited or short-term therapy. That bishops sent offenders to treatment centers or made new ministry assignments on the basis, as Cardinal Law put it, of "psychiatric or medical assessments" was widely derided precisely because it contradicted the view that offenders cannot help themselves and are seldom cured.

With respect to victims, virtually every commentator shared the view that sexual abuse leads to long-term suffering. There was some question raised as to whether such suffering was inevitable, and occasionally articles quoted psychologists or psychiatrists who insisted that abuse victims are not *necessarily* permanently scarred. "Unfortunately," according to one such professional, "there's this sense that everyone who is sexually abused as a child is doomed for life, which is not true" (quoted in Boodman 2002). There was also an occasional quotation from a clinician suggesting that the degree of harm may be related to the type of abuse that took place. But the idea that sexual abuse of whatever kind or degree typically causes enduring harm informed every aspect of the scandal. The victims who made public statements were outspoken on this point. Mark Serrano, for instance, a board member of SNAP, in an op-ed piece that appeared in *USA Today* shortly before the Dallas meeting, wrote, "Every day, I relive the sexual terror committed against me as a child nearly 30 years ago. . . . My memories of my sexual abuse are as real today as they were when I was a child" (Serrano 2002). The four victims who made presentations to the bishops vividly described their childhood abuse and its effects: shame, guilt, promiscuity, substance abuse, and mental illness. In interviews and appearances, many other victims did likewise, describing current problems as the enduring consequences of abuse. The weight of professional opinion was certainly on their side. It seems hard to believe now, but it has not always been so.

A NEW STORY

On April 17, 1971, at Washington Irving High School in New York, Florence Rush, former staff member of the Society for the Prevention of Cruelty to Children and a member of OWL, Older Women's Liberation, took the podium at the New York Radical Feminists' (NYRF) first conference on rape (Rush 1974). The rape conference and the "speak-out" that preceded it in January were concerned with analyzing rape from a radical feminist point of view, giving victims a chance to give a public account of their rape experiences, and fostering the formation of feminist consciousness-raising groups. Rush was unlike the other speakers. She was older—fifty-five with three grown children—and she addressed not adult rape but child molestation, and told her own story of being molested and fondled on various occasions as a child and adolescent. She also briefly quoted from and editorialized on five prominent studies of sex offense victims or offenders (Burton 1968; De Francis 1969; Gebhard et al. 1965; Kinsey et al. 1953; Tormes 1968). Her central point was that each of these studies, with the partial exception of De Francis, was fundamentally morally flawed. These studies were marred, she argued, because they treated most sexual offenses as minor and as having few adverse consequences for the victim. But worst of all, they "blamed the victim" by treating the victim as one who participates in, perhaps even initiates, the sexual encounter. They also implicated the mother. What was needed, in Rush's view, was a new approach to "sexual abuse" that did not blame the (female) child victim, but treated such offenses as part of the broader subjugation of women in a male-dominated society. In a set of recommendations for victims published with the conference proceedings, Rush bid all feminist movement groups to encourage women and young girls to tell their experiences and to identify and expose their offenders.

In 1971, standing up in public and telling a personal story of childhood molestation was a revolutionary thing to do. While anonymous survey respondents had answered direct questions about childhood sexual experiences at least as far back as the 1920s, and psychiatric clinical papers had reported molestation and incest cases for decades, first-person public accounts of such experiences outside a legal context were nonexistent. There simply were no public "adult survivor" stories, to borrow the later designation, before the 1970s.

Why not? For the activists who followed Rush in the 1970s and beyond, it became an article of faith that a "conspiracy of silence"—society-wide but spearheaded by mental health professionals—explained the dearth of public victim testimonies. Yet public attention and the issue of abuse were not new. In 1937 the opening page of a widely cited article announced that "the seduction of children by adults is a recognized social problem" (Bender and Blau 1937: 500). The authors noted a recent Parliament Commission investigation in England and the broader legislative attention given to the problem "in all civilized countries." In 1938, Illinois, in response to a perceived "sex-crime wave," passed the first "sexual psychopath" law.[2] By the early 1950s, twenty states had passed similar legislation. These laws provided for the confinement of certain sexual offenders, including those found guilty of incest and child-molesting, in a state hospital for the insane until such time as they were officially declared "cured" or "not dangerous." By the early 1950s, additional states had also dramatically increased their penalties for persons convicted of indecent or immoral practices with a child.

In fact, sexual offenders were a topic of a great deal of public concern again during the late 1940s and 1950s, a concern described by Alfred Kinsey and his colleagues in one of their now famous studies of sexual behavior as an "hysteria over sex offenders" (Kinsey et al. 1953: 121). Articles decrying the rise of sex crimes and theorizing about the psychology of sex "fiends," "perverts," "psychopaths," and so on, appeared in a wide range of popular publications, including *Collier's, Saturday Evening Post, Time, Better Homes & Gardens,* and *Parents,* to name but a few.[3] J. Edgar Hoover, director of the FBI, wrote two such articles, lamenting the rise in sex crimes and the lackadaisical attitude of both public officials and ordinary citizens.[4] In response to a concern with sex crimes, New Jersey set up a State Commission on Habitual Sex Offenders, the New York legislature commissioned a sex-crime inquiry, and Michigan convened a special session of the State Mental Health Commission to take "immediate measures" and seek long-term solutions to the sex-crimes problem. Many other states did likewise (Sutherland 1950). Specialized institutions were created to treat sex offenders, and states appropriated funds for research. The California legislature, for instance, allocated $187,000 between 1950 and 1954 for research in sexual deviation, including, importantly, research on the child victims of adult sex offenders. Several influential studies funded by this initiative were published in subsequent years (e.g., Bowman 1953; Mangus 1952; Weiss et al. 1955). In professional circles, a host of studies of incest and other sexual-assault offenders and victims appeared in the psychiatric and sex crimes literature from the 1930s to the 1970s.

However, despite the popular concern with sex crimes, the public testimonies that began with Rush were indeed a new phenomenon. What accounts for the previous "silence" of abuse victims, and what changed to bring about such public storytelling? I want to argue that individuals did not publicly share their "sexual abuse" experiences before the 1970s because no socially recognized story of victimization existed that would warrant such a public telling or provide the terms in which to do so. Stories are always produced and told under particular social conditions. The social norms and conventions operating in various cultural and institutional contexts govern when stories are told (expected, demanded, or prohibited), what kinds of stories can be told (rules of appropriate content), and how stories are told (rules of participation; see Ewick and Silbey 1995). The pre-1970s understandings of sexual offenses and offense victims neither compelled nor justified public tellings (i.e., told to strangers). Nor did they provide a narrative framework by which victims could formulate a public account of sexual molestation or incest that both they and their audience would find intelligible, believable, and relevant. There were no public victim stories, in short, because there was no collective victimization story.

Which brings us back to Florence Rush. What changed in the 1970s, what led to the massive outpouring of victim testimonies, was precisely the construction of a victim-centered collective story about sexual abuse. This construction, I argue, was the strategic work of two social movements—child protection and antirape—and the uniqueness of Rush, indeed the experience that made her testimony possible, was her activism at the intersection of these two movements. In her address at the NYRF rape conference, Rush did not simply share childhood experiences; she also proffered, in schematic form, the plot for a new collective story. In so doing, Rush drew upon the child protection and antirape movements' attention to the victim of abuse and emphasis on victim innocence and injury. Together, these concerns laid the groundwork for a new definition of the victim person-category and its collective story of the experience common to the persons in the category. The collective story became the framework around which adult survivors could interpret their experience and narrate it, including publicly. By means of a new collective story, the repressed returned. A cascade of victim testimonies followed, both ratifying and reproducing the new narrative.

The creation of a new, victim-centered story altered the existing formulations of sexual offenses, offender, and victim. I begin, therefore, by examining the older understandings from which the new understandings would depart. Using every major study, I identify the definitions of offender and victim, incest, and sexual offense used by researchers and clinicians before 1977, and the interpretative paradigms that inform these definitions. Because the characterization of victims is directly related to the question of their harm, I explore how the effects of sexual offenses and incest on the child, both in the short and longer term, were understood. And, because the definitions of deviant behaviors are directly related to how much of those behaviors there are, I also review the understandings of the incidence of sexual offense and incest victimization. The next two chapters describe how all these understandings—of sexual offense/incest, offender, and victim—changed and why. Because my concern is with the movement *away from* the older definitions, I do not explore the social processes and practices that led to their construction. However, the reader should be aware through these three chapters that the old categories also reflect and reproduce specific institutional, cultural, and political conditions. They too are historically contingent and morally constituted.

DEFINITION AND PREVALENCE OF INCEST AND SEXUAL OFFENSES

The literature on adult-child sexual relations produced before the mid-1970s is large and diverse. Early writings in anthropology were largely concerned with the incest taboo and its explanation. Biologists studied the effects of inbreeding and posited various theories of biological disturbances as causative factors in sexual offenses. Sociologists produced a small but influential number of research studies on incest. The psychiatric literature, by contrast, was large, with one strand concerned principally with incest, especially father-daughter incest, and another strand concerned with a much broader range of sexual offenses. The criminological and legal literatures, too, were considerable, and focused on a wide range of legally defined or socially proscribed sexual offenses, contact and noncontact, in and outside the family. Similarly, there were many general studies of sex offenders and a number of general studies of sexual behavior, the latter often including information about preadolescent sexual experiences with sex offenders. Over the decades, both the incest literature and what might collectively be termed the sexual offense literature focused on the pathology and background of the father/adult offender and causative factors of the offense. The number of studies that considered the role of and outcomes for the child victim was much smaller, though it began to expand in the 1950s.

In the period I am concerned with, the definition of incest in most research and clinical reports, both sociological and psychiatric, was strictly limited. In cross-cultural studies, anthropologists had found a seemingly universal prohibition on father and daughter, mother and son, or brother and sister having sexual intercourse or marrying (Murdock 1949). Following this understanding of the prohibition, researchers and clinicians typically defined incest as genital intercourse between blood relatives. Relatives included all members of the nuclear family, grandparents, aunts, and uncles, but never cousins. Some clinicians, especially after 1960, broadened the range of sexual contact in their incest definitions, adding such sexual behaviors as sodomy, oral-genital contact, genital fondling, mutual masturbation, and attempted coitus. They also extended the range of relatives to include those by marriage. But whether they defined incest narrowly or more broadly, researchers and clinicians treated incest as its own category of deviance. Influenced by the anthropological studies and Freud's theorization of its role in mental life, they treated incest as the violation of a uniquely powerful and developmentally significant taboo. Incest, therefore, was not simply an expression of or reducible to other types of sexual deviance, and writers in the incest literature made little reference to the broader sexual offense literature.

Researchers and clinicians—even those with the broadest definitions— believed incest, absolutely and relative to other forms of sexual deviance, to be rare.[5] As part of their polemic against the older literature, writers in the 1970s and beyond routinely asserted that the annual incidence of incest was earlier believed to be less than 2 cases per million in the United States (e.g., Butler 1978; Forward and Buck 1978). But this low figure refers to the incidence of incest *in criminal statistics*. Kirson Weinberg, for instance, in his classic study, *Incest Behavior*, reported that U.S. average rates of incest conviction were 1.2 cases per million persons in 1910, 1.9 cases per million persons in 1920, and 1.1 cases per million persons in 1930 (1955: 39). Robert Masters reported in 1963 that in no U.S. state was the annual rate of convicted incest offenders greater than 2 per million (1963: 63). Criminal statistics on incest reported for other countries were similar (see Greenland 1958; Maisch 1972: 86–90). In Sweden, for example, only about 30 cases per year came to the attention of the courts (Riemer 1940). Virtually every author, however, was quick to point out that the actual incidence of incest must far exceed the rate of detection by law enforcement authorities (cf. Meiselman 1978: 29; Weiner 1962). Some even thought that incest was common in certain social classes (Riemer 1940: 566), between brothers and sisters (Klein 1932), or among certain specialized subgroups, such as prostitutes and sex delinquents (see studies in Weinberg 1955: 147–48). The more general agreement, though, was that incest was rare, even when underreporting was taken into account.

There was good reason for thinking that incest was rare. It was highly stigmatized behavior (except perhaps in some subcultural groups). Clinicians apparently came across few cases. Charles Wahl reported in 1960 that "it is quite a rare thing to encounter an actual, verifiable clinical example" of incest (1960: 189).[6] Most cases reported in the research literature were accessed through court referrals, prisons, and social agencies, sources hardly representative of the general population. Moreover, there were no prevalence studies of incest. The closest thing to survey data comes from general studies of sexual behavior, but these studies are not concerned with incest per se and therefore do not separately define or report it. The only reasonably representative survey of the general population that speaks directly to the issue of incest was the Kinsey study of sexual behavior in the human male (Kinsey et al. 1948). In that study, the number of men who indicated that they had been approached sexually by an adult female relative while a pre-adolescent was extremely low. The authors note that in most of the reports of a pre-adolescent sexual approach the offender was an adult male, but they indicate that the prevalence found was low and present no data that would allow one to ascertain if some cases were incestuous. In their study of females (Kinsey et al. 1953), the Kinsey team found a higher prevalence, perhaps 2 to 4 percent, of respondents reporting a pre-adolescent "sexual approach" by their father, grandfather, uncle, or older brother.[7] But since they do not separate contact from noncontact sexual experiences and do not specifically identify cases as incestuous, there is no way to determine what percentage of cases constituted incest.[8] Finally, two other studies, though little cited in the incest literature, also suggested a relatively low prevalence in the general population. In a study of male sex offenders by Paul Gebhard and his colleagues, none of their noncriminal control group ($N = 477$) reported coitus with a daughter, and just 0.2 percent (one case) with a sister (1965: 572, table 63). A study of 2,439 letters to an advice column dealing with sex and courtship matters in a popular British magazine found only seven letters that reported actual incidents of incest (Greenland 1958).

While scholars, clinicians, and, almost certainly, the general public thought incest was rare, the same is not true for other forms of sexual offenses against children, especially girls. As noted, there was a second sex crime panic in the late 1940s and well into the 1950s. Popular circulation magazines carried articles publicizing a rising rate of sex crimes against children, reporting on the views of psychiatrists who believed that detected offenses were but a fraction of the actual incidence, castigating a general "hush-hush" attitude toward sexual deviance, and arguing that sex offenders come from all walks of life. The New York Society for the Prevention of Cruelty to Children told *Collier's* magazine in 1947 that the "carnal abuse" of children accounted for 25 to 35 percent of all of its cases, and that in the previous year it had handled 528 such offenses. In a 1950 article, *Collier's* featured efforts to address sex crimes in St. Louis, where, it reported, parents had come to recognize that their children were no longer safe: "In alarming numbers, the little ones were becoming hunted game, stalked by the molester, the sex psychopath and the despoiler." More broadly, popular magazines, as well as new children's books, child protection programs, and educational films—such as *The Dangerous Stranger* and *Strangers*—told parents that children were at risk and offered advice on "how to protect your children from sex offenders." One expert referred to such protection efforts as the "do-not-speak-to-strangers movement" (Deutsch 1950: 63), a designation that captures the pervasive popular assumption that offenders were strangers.[9]

While professionals disputed the popular view that sex crimes were on a dramatic rise (Guttmacher 1951; Karpman 1954; Sutherland 1950), professional studies of sexual behavior consistently found a considerable minority of women who reported at least one sexual experience with an adult (or older adolescent) during their childhood years. In a study of marriage published in 1929, Gilbert Hamilton asked the following question of 100 married men and 100 married women: Before or after puberty, "were you ever frightened or disgusted by the sexual aggressions of (persons of the opposite sex)?" (1929: 334). He did not define "sexual aggression," and the reported range of experiences and offenders was fairly wide. Of the 100 men, 22 reported a total of 32 prepubescent incidents. Some 20 percent of these incidents were with little girls, the balance with older girls or women. Most incidents involved sexual suggestion, exhibition, or (apparently) single incidents of touch. Of the women, 20 to 25 percent reported some form of aggression, before or shortly after puberty (calculated from table 279, sections B.B, C, and E, pp. 336–40). About one-third of the incidents reported were with small boys, and two-thirds with older boys or men. Most of the incidents involved exhibition, (apparently) single incidents of touch, and attempted rape. In another marriage study, published in 1938, Lewis Terman asked 752 married women a question similar to Hamilton's: Had the respondent had a sexual incident before age 15 that "shocked or greatly disgusted" her at the time? (1938: 250). A total of 32.4 percent reported a "sex shock" (calculated from table 74), though the nature of the shocking/disgusting incidents was not reported. In another study, published in 1951, Terman asked the same question of 556 married women deemed "gifted." Of that sample, 24.6 percent reported a "sex shock" (calculated from table 5, p. 136).

Similarly, in a 1940 study in New York City, Carney Landis and his colleagues (1940) asked 295 women, married and single, "normal controls" and psychiatric patients, about any prepubertal "sexual aggressions" (undefined) they had experienced. Some 35 percent of the study subjects reported a total of 107 incidents with older males.[10] Kinsey and his colleagues (1953) found that 24 percent of their general sample of 4,441 white adult females reported a preadolescent sexual contact with an adult (or adolescent at least five years their senior). Of these respondents, 80 percent reported a single incident, while 5 percent reported 9 or more incidents. Exhibitionism and verbal approaches accounted for nearly two-thirds of all reported incidents, with fondling (no genital contact) and manipulation of the child's genitalia accounting for most of the rest. Three percent of respondents reported an experience of coitus. In a study of 1,800 middle- and upper-middle-class university students in Berkeley, California, conducted between 1951 and 1954, Judson Landis (1956) asked both men and women about experiences with a "sexual deviate." He found that 30 percent of the men and 35 percent of the women reported at least one such experience, though these percentages include experiences in late adolescence and adulthood. About 70 percent of the girls and 45 percent of the boys had their experience before the age of fifteen. As with the earlier studies, a majority of reported experiences involved no contact, being either verbal only or with an exhibitionist (almost 90 percent of reported male experiences, 55 percent of female experiences). John Gagnon (1965), in an analysis of more extensive questions asked of 1,200 of the 4,441 women in the original Kinsey sample, found 28 percent reporting a sexual experience with an adult before age thirteen. Based on his study and earlier ones, he estimated that "between 20 and 25 per cent of children reared in a middle-class environment will experience a victim experience in childhood and that the bulk of these will be minimal in character such as exhibition and genital touching" (1965: 191).

Though few in number and suffering from a variety of methodological problems, these surveys were widely known and frequently cited in the professional literature on sexual behavior and deviance. They indicated that childhood sexual experiences with an adult or older adolescent, at least for girls, were by no means rare (very little was known about boy victims). They even indicated that in at least a significant minority of cases the offender was known to the child victim, often being a friend, acquaintance, or family member. But the comment made by Gagnon about the minimal character of most experiences is crucial to understanding how these findings were perceived. While many professionals believed that sexual offenses against girls were not rare, they also believed that the majority of these offenses were essentially nuisance experiences, including no-contact and fondling incidents, and rarely involved the use of physical force or threat of force. In themselves, they argued, such experiences need not be particularly traumatic for the child victim and, especially if responded to without hysterics by the child's parents or the authorities, need have no enduring effects (Guttmacher 1951: 118–19; Kinsey et al. 1953: 121; Landis et al. 1940: 211). Further, researchers with child samples often found a correlation between repeat sexual offense victims and distressed family backgrounds. In these cases, they believed that personality disturbances already present in the child might predispose him or her to cooperate with the offender. Thus, even when a child displayed emotional and behavioral problems after the offenses, researchers did not necessarily view these problems as effects of offense trauma. The problems may have been present before the offenses took place, even predisposing the child not to resist the offender's advances.

SEXUAL OFFENSES AND THE CHILD VICTIM

A variety of studies were conducted that bear on the question of the effects of sexual offenses for the child victim. Some of these studies were done with children, ranging from shortly after to several years following the offense.

Others, such as the surveys discussed above, involved retrospective accounts by adults of their childhood experiences. Some studies were concerned only with shorter-term consequences of the victimization experience, while others focused on the longer-term effects on adult adjustment. Excluding incest, where the findings are somewhat different, the various studies consistently reported that the majority of victims suffered little if any serious injury from their experience. The studies, however, also report a recurring minority for whom the offense appears to have brought a negative outcome, especially in those few cases where physical force was involved or in cases where the child was forced to give legal testimony. Yet the dominant theme is one of a relatively minor effect in the majority of cases, and this theme shapes the tone and conclusions of most studies.[11]

Rasmussen, in an influential 1934 Norwegian study (reported in Bender and Blau 1937; Burton 1968), attempted to ascertain the long-term effects on 54 women of a sexual assault that had come before the courts 20 to 30 years earlier, when they were between 9 and 13 years of age. Depending primarily on the judgment of their doctors, Rasmussen concluded that all but 8 of the subjects were well adjusted, and she did not link the later personality disintegration of these 8 with the sexual assault. In a 1937 study of 16 children (5 boys and 11 girls, ages 5–12) admitted to a hospital following a sexual assault (all but 2 referred by a court), Lauretta Bender and Abram Blau (1937) found some general behavioral problems with the children but concluded that / of 16 showed no apparent acute emotional or behavioral reaction to their sex experiences, and that all "showed less evidence of fear, anxiety, guilt, or psychic trauma than might be expected" (1937: 510), though some delayed guilt reactions were observed (see below on the 4 cases in this study that involved a parent). In a follow-up study, 14 of these subjects were interviewed again in 1951 by Bender and Alvin Grugett (1952). Now into adulthood, 9 of the 14 were judged to have adjusted satisfactorily, though apparently measured only in the sense of adequately performing adult roles. Of the 5 whose adjustment was "generally unfavorable" 4 were intellectually deficient, and the other was an incest case (see below). None of the study members, they noted, "again needed social correction or attention because of sex activities" (1952: 836). In both of his samples of married women, Terman (1938, 1951) found little relationship between an experience of "sex shock" as a child and the ability to have orgasms as an adult.

Carney Landis and his colleagues (1940) reported that 56 percent of those who experienced prepubertal sex aggression found the experience emotionally "unpleasant" or "extremely unpleasant" (1940: 279), "but in only rare instances could they [sex aggressions] be considered traumatic" (1940: 125). They found that women who experienced sex aggressions were more apt than those who did not to have feelings of guilt or disgust toward sexual matters and to give evidence of a homoerotic orientation. However, they also observed that the sex aggression had virtually no discernible effect on other women and apparently does not predispose the individual toward the development of mental disorders in adulthood. Kinsey and his colleagues (1953), based on their large sample, reached no general conclusions as to the significance of adult-child sexual contacts for the child's subsequent development (see also Gebhard et al. 1965). They noted, however, that while some subjects reported their experience favorably, 80 percent said they were emotionally upset or frightened by their contacts with adults. Yet only a small proportion had been seriously disturbed. In most instances the "reported fright was nearer the level that children will show when they see insects, spiders, or other objects against which they have been adversely conditioned" (Kinsey et al. 1953: 121). They also reported that "some of the older females in the sample felt that their pre-adolescent experiences had contributed favorably to their later socio-sexual development" (1953: 121). In his university student sample, Judson Landis (1956) found that some 77 percent of the girl victims said that initially they were frightened, shocked, or otherwise emotionally upset. However, he concludes from the respondent's self-reports that the "great majority of victims seem to recover rather soon," especially when the offender is a stranger and the offense minor, "and to acquire few permanently wrong attitudes from the experience" (1956: 108). He also noted that 5 percent of respondents said they were more shocked by their parents' reaction than by the experience itself. Lindy Burton (1968: 100–111) reported on four French studies of child victims published in 1961. In each study, the authors emphasized the lack of subsequent disturbance in child victims. From his survey data on adult women, Gagnon reported that the "overwhelming majority of the subjects reported that they reacted negatively to the victim experience" (1965: 184), with reactions ranging from simple fright to more extreme responses. In terms of adult adjustment, however, Gagnon determined that "only" 5 percent could be considered to have been severely damaged for whatever reason. The overwhelming majority showed either no apparent adult maladjustment or only "slight difficulties." Finally, in a study based on 41 child victims (6 male, 35 female) whose cases came to police attention in England, Burton found little evidence of trauma and suggested that the "sexual assault of children by adults does not have particularly detrimental effects on the child's subsequent personality development" (1968: 169).

In the sexual offense literature, then, researchers viewed the majority of sexual offenses, excluding incest, as minor in nature, and the effects on the child victim of such offenses as relatively slight and short-lived. In cases where more significant disturbances in the victims were observed, either immediate or long-term, researchers were typically quite cautious about making a causal connection between these disturbances and offense trauma. The studies of known victims—as opposed to the general surveys of adults that asked about victim experiences—drew from cases identified by the police or by social agencies. In these studies, the children, especially the children who had more than one victim experience, came preponderantly from troubled homes. In assaying the background of victims, researchers found some who showed personality disturbances before the offenses. Such disturbances, they believed, could affect both a child's vulnerability to being sexually approached and his or her reaction when the offense attempt occurred. Personality disturbances, therefore, might not only predate a seduction but even contribute to its onset or course. Thus, the relationship between a sexual seduction and emotional or behavioral disturbances later observed was not simply one of cause and effect.[12]

Beginning at least with Rasmussen in the 1930s, many sexual offense researchers categorized the different victim responses that they observed and attempted to correlate those responses with features of the victim's personality or family background. Working from a distinction first theoretically articulated by Karl Abraham (1927) in 1907, virtually all researchers classified victims into at least two general categories, distinguishing those who participated in the sexual experience from those who did not. The nonparticipant was the "accidental" victim. This type of victim was a victim in the pure sense; there was nothing, at any time, mutual about the encounter with the offender. While they did not use standardized definitions, researchers in general classified as accidental victims those who had had one or at most a few ("multiple accidental") entirely isolated sexual experiences without any buildup of social interaction with the offender (most often a stranger). The accidental victim, too, was one who typically reacted strongly and negatively to the offense and promptly reported it. Different researchers, using somewhat different definitions and different samples, reported varying numbers of accidental victims. In a study of 73 girl victims referred by district attorneys, Joseph Weiss and his colleagues (1955; see also Rogers et al. 1953) classified only about one-third as accidental (they also noted that the children in their study may not be typical of sex victims in general). Judson Landis (1956) classified more than one-half of the female victims in his college sample as accidental. And Gagnon (1965), based on self-reports by adult women in the large Kinsey sample, classified 77 percent as accidental and another 13 percent as multiple accidental.

The second broad category of victim was the "participant" or "collaborative" victim. Researchers classified victims as participants who were involved in any way, passively or actively, by a provoked or mutual desire, in the initiation or maintenance of the sexual experience. Participant victims, as contrasted with accidental, typically knew the offender, had more than one sexual experience with him, often received some type of reward from the offender for her participation, and kept the relationship a secret. Different researchers reported varying percentages of participant victims. In their sample of sixteen cases, Bender and Blau (1937) found some degree of victim participation in every case: "The history of the relationship in our cases usually suggested at least some cooperation of the child in the activity, and in some cases the child assumed an active role in initiating the relationship" (1937: 514). Weiss and his colleagues (1955) treat two-thirds of the victims in their study as cooperating participants, while Landis (1956) puts almost half of his sample in a "possible participant" group. Gagnon (1965), by contrast, using victim self-reports of participation, classifies only 8 percent of his sample as collaborative. Varying degrees of victim collaboration are also emphasized by many other researchers.[13]

In contrasting the two general categories of accidental and participant victims, researchers were seeking to identify predisposing factors in a child's personality and background that might favor his or her participation in the offense. Did the personalities and backgrounds of the two groups differ and, if so, how? Might such differences, if any, help to explain why some victims got caught up to varying degrees in sexual relationships with adults and some did not? In fact, the sexual offense literature reports differences between the two types of victims. Accidental victims were found to have no personality or family background characteristics in common (e.g., Weiss et al. 1955). They were in all essential respects a random group. Participant victims, on the other hand, displayed certain personality traits in common, and researchers identified these traits, for the most part, as arising from personality disturbances grounded in broader deprivations in the child's family life.[14] The child's participation in the sexual offense, including any "seductive" or "provocative" behavior, they argued, was a form of "acting-out" of unconscious personality needs.

Bender and Blau described the victims in their study as having exceptionally attractive and appealing personalities and showing "an abnormal interest and drive for adult attention" (1937: 515). The authors noted that the children had other behavioral difficulties in their histories, and some seemed "more susceptible to adult seduction because of emotional deprivation in their earlier years" (1937: 513). Weiss and his colleagues (Weiss et al. 1955; see also Rogers et al. 1953) were also impressed by the attractive and appealing personalities of the "participant victims" and their strong demand for adult attention and approval. They viewed these children's disposition to sexually act out as related to more basic problems in family life, particularly daughter-mother conflicts—almost all of the participant victims "felt deprived by their mothers and resentful toward them" (8)—and unintentional sexual stimulation of the child by one or both parents. For some victims, they argued, the sexual acting out is but one expression of a pattern of emotional and behavioral disturbances (e.g., extreme mood fluctuations, nightmares, phobias, truancy, self-damaging behavior) that are rooted in home situations characterized by continuous parental neglect and cruel and inconsistent treatment. For these participant victims, they theorized, the sexual relationship might represent a way to achieve some consistent affection. When Landis (1956) compared the "possible participant" group in his study with the accidental and control groups, he too found family problems. While the control and accidental groups were similar, the girls in the "possible participant" group had significantly poorer relationships with their mothers before age fifteen. The possible participants also came from families with significantly lower levels of marital happiness.

In a study of two samples of child victims that came to the attention of courts and a social agency in London, T. C. N. Gibbens and Joyce Prince (1963) argued that a distressed family background and involvement in sexual assaults are closely connected. Stranger assaults were most common with children from "apparently respectable homes" (and who subsequently tended not to show any overt disturbance), while the victims of nonstrangers were typically from already disturbed homes. Gagnon (1965) did not report on family background, but he did find that "collaborative victims" were significantly more likely than accidental victims to have engaged in prepubertal heterosexual play with other children before the experience with the adult. Burton (1968) found assault victims more dependent, affection seeking, and afraid of rejection than the nonvictim controls. She thought the child's affection-seeking behavior suggested a "real deprivation of parental affection" (1968: 162), especially in the youngest years of life, and that the child's need may have predisposed her to sexual involvement. Vincent De Francis likewise reported extreme emotional deprivation in the lives of many victims and suggested that "[t]hey hunger for, and crave, affection and are likely to accept it from any source, under any condition and almost at any price" (1969: 61).

In these various studies of sexually assaulted children, researchers suggested that some percentage of victims participate in the sexual seduction,[15] and that they do so to meet unconscious needs.[16] Early theorists, such as Abraham (1927), argued that the child's need is a sexual drive, a theory followed by Bender and Blau (1937). In a follow-up study, however, Bender and another colleague revised this view, arguing instead that the child's behavior was symptomatic of interrupted individuation and not really genitally sexual at all (Bender and Grugett 1952). With improved opportunities for individual fulfillment, they found, the children abandoned their sexual preoccupations and practices. Gagnon observed the higher incidence of prepubertal sex play in collaborative victims but also found that "[t]he notion of the sexual or erotic child who is provocative of sexual contacts is not demonstrated by this data" (1965: 188). In the victim studies, rather, the sexual experience was believed to principally gratify an emotional need for attention and affection or a desire for independence. Researchers theorized that such need satisfaction may in part account for a child's cooperative behavior.

Later critics have argued or implied that these researchers believed that the needs of the child, in whatever form they might take, were the *only* factor accounting for a child's participation in maintaining or concealing an offense. But this is not strictly accurate. While researchers addressed very narrow and specific questions about differential victim participation and injury in these studies, they also noted that children are conditioned to trust family friends, teachers, and other acquaintances, and that offenders use luring tactics and assurances to induce the child's cooperation (Bender and Blau 1937; De Francis 1969; Gagnon 1965; Landis 1956: 103). Moreover, these studies were part of a larger literature that was principally focused on the pathology of the adult offender. In this larger literature, the strength and social status that the adult offender possesses over the child, his premeditation of the sexual offense, and his bribes and luring techniques are recognized as features of sexual victimizations (e.g., Gebhard et al. 1965; Weinberg 1955). Further, most of these researchers seemed to see their work as balancing a misperception, at least in the general population and court system, of the exclusive role of the offender. Their argument was that the offender's character and intimidation are not the *whole* story. Some victims, too, they argued, by not resisting, or by remaining silent, or by returning to the offender, play *some* role and are, therefore, not "innocent" of involvement in the way that the purely accidental victim is. The psychoanalytic theoretical assumption they were making—and some used victim self-reports and court testimony as evidence—was that children too are psychologically complex, and thus their behavior must also be considered. As Bender and Blau wrote, "Within recent years, since the progress of child psychology, it has become evident that the child is not a negligible psychological creature in either an intellectual or emotional sense" (1937: 513).

In the sexual offense literature, the issues of victim participation and pre-existing personality disturbances complicated the question of offense effects on the victim. When victim disturbances were observed, were they the result of the offense, a consequence of the victim's cooperation in the offense, or a manifestation, perhaps exacerbated by the offense, of problems present before the offense? For researchers, disturbances discovered after the offense might have been caused by the trauma of the experience, or, at least in some cases, such as victim guilt, the disturbance might have been an effect of the victim's cooperation.[17] On the other hand, researchers also believed that disturbances might have been caused by parental deprivations or family disorganization that long preceded the seduction, and in relation to which the offense stands more as symptom than as cause. Writers in the offense literature, then, to the general conclusion that the majority of sexual offenses—again, excluding incest—had little traumatic effect on the child, added the view that when disturbances were found, they might not be causally linked to an offense trauma, but might represent effects of cooperation or a preexisting condition.

INCEST AND THE CHILD PARTICIPANT

While the majority of sexual offenses were believed to be minor experiences having little traumatic effect on the child victim, the same is not true for offenses within the family, including incest. As noted earlier, the general sex offense literature does not single out incest cases for special treatment or discussion. However, a number of studies did report a pattern in their findings on victim effects when the offender was a family member. In these studies, sexual contact with a relative was found to be more disturbing for the victim than sexual contact with a nonrelative. With a relative, the offenses were typically of greater intrusiveness and more frequent repetition, and likely to disrupt the victim's relationship with her family.

In his marriage study, for instance, Hamilton reported that "[i]n the 8 cases where the aggressor was a family male [father, stepfather, brother, uncle] no woman escaped either serious difficulties in effecting an adequate marital sex adjustment or a marked degree of personality imbalance during adult life, or both" (1929: 342–43). There were four cases of seduction by parents in the Bender and Blau sample, and they noted that these were among the cases where the victim showed immediate harmful effects: "Anxiety states with bewilderment concerning social relations occur especially in children who are seduced by parents" (1937: 516). In the follow-up study, they found that fifteen years later, one victim suffered from chronic psychosis, while the other three had attained "moderately successful adjustment" (Bender and Grugett 1952: 827). Carney Landis and his colleagues found that "[t]hose sex aggressions in which a member of the family [father, brother, or uncle] was the aggressor were more likely to be of strong emotional value to the child and were apt to have such sequelae in adult life as poor sex adjustment or certain symptoms of psychosexual immaturity" (1940: 200). Without providing specific details or the percentage of cases that involved family members, Judson Landis (1956) reported for his large sample that experiences within the "primary group" tended to be more serious offenses and to have longer-lasting effects. In about one in five of the cases in the Gibbens and Prince (1963) study the offender was the father. They argued that "[g]enerally speaking, the nearer the relationship [between offender and victim], the greater the subsequent overt disturbance" (1963: 14). Other studies also showed more significant disturbance when the offender was a close relative (see De Francis 1969; Peters 1976).

In general, the incest studies also reported a pattern of at least short-term disturbances in the child. In surveys as well as case studies, researchers and clinicians found that "child incest participants" (incest studies virtually never use the term *victim*), notably the daughter, since most studies focused on father-daughter incest, expressed a large variety of neurotic, psychosomatic, and behavioral problems. A few studies found gross psychopathology. Wahl (1960), for instance, in a report on two cases of the rare phenomenon of mother-son incest, found both sons suffering from schizophrenia. He argued that his cases supported the view that incest may play a role as a stressor and precursor in the genesis of schizophrenia. A year earlier, Stephen Fleck and his colleagues (1959) had argued, on the basis of several case studies, that "incestuous preoccupations" were not simply a symptom of schizophrenia as previously recognized, but that chronic sexual seductiveness by a parent (with or without actual incest) may be a contributing factor in the development of the disorder.

Most incest studies, however, found less serious forms of disturbance. In a study of five cases some years after the incest, Paul Sloane and Eva

Karpinski, for example, argued that "incest in the post-adolescent period leads to serious repercussions in the girl" and reported that in only one of the cases had the girl "worked out a satisfactory adjustment" (1942: 673). While specific reactions varied, they found guilt toward the mother and the working out of anxiety by "indulging in promiscuous relationships" to be common problems. Weinberg did not provide precise data on long-term effects, but, in an undisclosed number of interviews with daughters a few years after the incest, observed that some experienced sexual problems and some required psychiatric attention (1955: 147). In a 1960 Norwegian study by Vestergaard (reported in Cormier, Kennedy, and Sangowicz 1962: 205), sixteen daughters were followed up ten years after the incestuous relationship. The author argued that the relationship and the reaction of the family to it had been almost invariably damaging. While earlier behavior problems did not continue, the daughters tended to be anxious, depressed, overfearful, and intensely angry toward their fathers. Some of their marital histories showed evidence of sexual conflict. John Rhinehart (1961), in an analysis of four incest cases, variously reported depression, dependent character personalities, and unsatisfactory relationships with men ("father-surrogates") in the former child participants. In a study of three families, Pavel Machotka and his colleagues (1967) reported depression and marital problems. In a 1972 Northern Ireland study, Narcyz Lukianowicz found "no apparent ill effects" in just six of his twenty-six father-daughter cases. In almost half of these cases, he reported, the child participants were promiscuous and delinquent as adolescents, choosing adult males as sexual partners rather than other adolescents. While there was little evidence of gross personality disorders, neurosis, or psychosis, he described many daughters as manifesting "character disorders" and found some reporting sexual frigidity (Lukianowicz 1972).[18]

A number of incest studies of children done shortly after the offense also reported negative effects on the child participant. In a study of eleven girls referred to a guidance center, Irving Kaufman and his colleagues (1954) reported that all were depressed, displaying symptoms ranging from mood swings and psychosomatic complaints to suicide threats. After the detection of the incest, all but one showed learning disabilities, despite normal intelligence, and guilt over the disruption of the home. Some sought to deal with their anxiety, guilt, and depression by a masochistic "searching for punishment" and compulsive sexual promiscuity. Many expressed homosexual inclinations as well as anxiety about future heterosexual experiences (see also Fleck et al. 1959; Karpman 1954; Wahl 1960). David Raphling and his colleagues (1967), studying a single case of intergenerational incest, reported deleterious effects on the daughters, including depression, somatic complaints, and anorexia. Based on sixty-six father-daughter and father-stepdaughter cases, Herbert Maisch (1972), in a West German study, reported that more then 70 percent of the daughters manifested some form of personality disturbance. Some of this disturbance was antisocial behavior and somatic complaints that "were no more frequent after the start of incest than before" (1972: 169). But more than one quarter of the daughters were depressed, including some who made suicide attempts, and another 12 percent suffered from anxiety, phobias, or compulsions. These latter disturbances, Maisch believed, might be directly linked to the incest trauma. Overall, he estimated that the incest stress probably caused personality disturbance in 35 percent of the cases, exacerbated preexisting symptoms in 27 percent, and had no traceable relation to personality problems in the remaining 38 percent (1972: 215). Many other studies also reported detrimental effects on some percentage of the child participants, such as negative self-image, depression, sexual acting out, sleep disturbances, and running away from home (see, for example, Eist and Mandel 1968; Lustig et al. 1966; the review in Meiselman 1978: 188–89; Tormes 1968; Weinberg 1955).[19]

The clinical picture in the incest literature was of disturbances, both long-term and short-term, in some, though not all, child participants of incest.[20] What researchers and clinicians did not find, however, was a consistent pattern to these disturbances. As Maisch argued in his late study, "the psychopathology of female incest victims is completely non-uniform" (1972: 160). The difficulties identified in the lives of incest participants varied widely depending on their social circumstances and preexisting personality characteristics. While sexual problems—promiscuity, frigidity, sexual orientation confusion—were frequently hypothesized as aftereffects of incest, they were typically only found in a minority of cases, as were other disturbances. The trauma of incest was not found to cause specific psychiatric disorders or even consistently to predispose individuals to particular disorders. The incest literature identified many disturbances, but no "incest syndrome" or stable pattern of "symptoms" linked to childhood incest experiences.

The finding of heterogeneous disturbances in the lives of incest participants was consistent with the observations made by early psychoanalytic theorists about the role of sexual seductions in the etiology of mental disorders. In an 1896 paper on the etiology of hysteria, Freud "put forward the thesis that at the bottom of every case of hysteria there are *one or more occurrences of premature sexual experience,* occurrences which belong to the earliest years of childhood" (1962a: 203; emphasis in original). In 1897, he revised this view, arguing later (in 1924) that he had earlier "attributed to the aetiological factor of seduction a significance and universality which it does not possess" (Freud 1962b: 168). This revision was necessary, Karl Abraham (1927) argued in 1907, as it became clear that not all children who experienced a sexual seduction later suffered from hysteria, and not all those who suffered from hysteria had experienced an actual seduction. An actual seduction, therefore, could not be the cause of *every* case of hysteria or, in Freud's even broader generalization, of all "psychoneuroses."[21] In light of the non-universality of actual seductions in the etiology of the psychoneuroses, Freud expanded the seduction theory into his oedipal theory, which, as Gagnon later noted, "served to broaden and extend the scope of the theory and to give it greater generality since the adult disorder no longer depended upon the presence or absence of a specific seduction" (1965: 177). In the oedipal theory, not actual seductions but unconscious incestuous interest was of universal etiological significance for the psychoneuroses. Later writers on sexual abuse would charge that Freud abandoned his seduction theory due to political pressure and a personal inability to face its implications, thereby initiating a long-standing cover-up of the reality and effects of sexual seductions on children. I discuss this charge further in the next chapter. My point here is simply to note that early psychoanalytic theorists, like the later incest researchers and clinicians, did not identify any particular mental disorder as always arising from actual incest experience.

In the incest studies, even more than in the sexual offense studies, the question of cause and effect was made problematic by background factors. For the most part, writers viewed family disorganization as virtually a prerequisite to the genesis of parent-child incest (e.g., Cavallin 1966; Maisch 1972; Weinberg 1955). Thus, for incest researchers, it was difficult to isolate the possible effects of the sexual events from the larger family pathology that surrounded them, even after the disclosure of the incest. As with the sexual offense researchers in their "participating victim" category, these researchers did not find the pathology of the father/offender by itself adequate to explain all features of the initiation and typically lengthy maintenance of the incestuous relationship. They too considered the possible role of preexisting personality disturbances in the child participant, as well as predisposing factors in the "incestuous family." In order to sort out these background factors, I briefly consider the evolution of theories about the etiology of incest and the resulting formulations of the categories of father, mother, and then daughter in the incestuous family.[22]

INCEST EFFECTS AND THE FAMILY BACKGROUND

The Father (Male Offender)

A wide variety of different theoretical perspectives informed the research and clinical effort to explain why the powerful incest taboo gets broken. Especially in the early decades of the century, biologically oriented explanations of the incestuous father were common. Writers attributed incest to causes such as mental illness or subnormality, a particular congenital character defect, and hypersexual impulses (see reviews in Maisch 1972: 94; Weinberg 1955). A concern with inhibition-removing factors, such as alcoholism, was also popular, along with explanations for incest that might be described as environmental. Among factors considered decisive in the different formulations were overcrowded living conditions, social isolation, poverty, and the sexual inaccessibility of the wife.

By about 1940, however, the effort to identify a single cause for violations of the incest taboo was progressively abandoned, and psychiatric and psychoanalytic approaches emerged as the dominant paradigms. In these multivariate approaches, incest, like other sexual offenses, was treated as a form of sexual psychopathology, and writers focused on the personal conditions that affected sexual disturbances and eroded mental inhibitions. Working from the Freudian theory that adult sexual psychopathology is based on early childhood experiences and traumas, researchers and clinicians studied the personality and background of fathers (and occasionally brothers and mothers) involved in incest with a daughter or son (or sibling). On the basis of this research, several efforts were made to classify the male incest participant into personality types and psychiatric diagnoses (e.g., Apfelberg, Sugar, and Pfeffer 1944; Gebhard et al. 1965; Guttmacher 1951; Karpman 1954; Weinberg 1955). Since the personality disturbance of the incest "father" was seldom a sufficient explanation in itself, they also sought to identify various social predisposing factors for the genesis of incest.

The probability of incest was increased, researchers and clinicians argued, when certain psychological and environmental factors were present, but there was no single profile of the incestuous father. Some were ineffectual, passive, and dependent men, while others were highly authoritarian husbands and fathers, tyrannically dominating their families (Cavallin 1966; Cormier, Kennedy, and Sangowicz 1962; Gebhard et al. 1965; Lukianowicz 1972; Lustig et al. 1966; Maisch 1972; Raphling, Carpenter, and Davis 1967; Weinberg 1955). Many incestuous fathers had histories of maltreatment and emotional deprivation, though some did not (Cavallin 1966; Cormier, Kennedy, and Sangowicz 1962; Gebhard et al. 1965; Kaufman, Peck, and Tagiuri 1954; Weiner 1962). Psychological disturbances ranged considerably, from no diagnosable disorder to severely psychotic conditions. Studies variously found, among other disorders, mental subnormality, "endogamic personality," pedophilia, and paranoid personality disorder (Cavallin 1966; Gebhard et al. 1965; Maisch 1972; Peters 1976; Weiner 1962). In some cases incestuous fathers were described as "oversexed" or pathologically obsessed with sex, while in other cases researchers detected no apparent history of adult sexual perversion (Cormier, Kennedy, and Sangowicz 1962; Lukianowicz 1972; Maisch 1972; Raphling, Carpenter, and Davis 1967). A minority of incest offenders were alcoholics (Apfelberg, Sugar, and Pfeffer 1944; Gebhard et al. 1965; Kaufman, Peck, and Tagiuri 1954; Maisch 1972). Researchers also identified overcrowding, poverty, social isolation, an external stress (loss of job, financial setback, injury), or subcultural values (in some isolated subcultural groups incest is viewed tolerantly) as a factor in some incest cases, though no consistent pattern covered all cases (Gebhard et al. 1965; Lukianowicz 1972; Riemer 1940; Weinberg 1955).

In sum, researchers reported considerable variation in the profiles of males involved in incest, and incest offenders were not restricted solely to the typical categories of alcoholic, moral degenerate, intellectually defective, or "sexual psychopath." Their social locations, moreover, varied as well. Contrary to the findings of the earliest studies, they were not restricted to the lower classes, to the inadequately housed, to rural areas, or to incest-tolerant, "Tobacco Road" subcultures. However, in the majority of cases, researchers reported that the father's personality disturbance predated the incest, and manifestations of his disturbance began long before the incestuous relationship was initiated.

Beginning in the 1950s, researchers began to extend the analysis of predisposing social factors to incest to include the family situation. Issues of interfamilial strain, conflict, and role confusion became focal points of investigation; thus, questions about the personality and behavior of the mother and daughter were added to the concern with the pathology of the father. Further, the scope of investigation was also expanded to include not only the factors predisposing toward the initiation of incest, but also those affecting its maintenance and termination. This turn to the dynamics of interaction within the family gained great momentum with the emergence of family therapy and the renewed interest in overt incest that it brought in the 1960s.

The Mother

In the period I am studying, the research and clinical literature was unanimous in the finding that mothers were rarely directly involved in incest. However, as scholars turned to the issue of the family situation prior to the onset of father-daughter incest, the role of the mother came to be seen as important, both in her relationship with her husband and with her daughter(s). While no single clinical or environmental picture emerges, the literature reports a number of findings on the mother's role in the incestuous family.

One set of research questions concerned sexual estrangement in the husband-wife relationship that might help to explain the husband's turning to the daughter. Most researchers, though not all (e.g., Lukianowicz 1972), reported that some mothers in incestuous families were frigid or sexually rejecting toward their husbands (Cormier, Kennedy, and Sangowicz 1962; Kaufman, Peck, and Tagiuri 1954; Lustig et al. 1966; Maisch 1972; Weiner 1962). Some studies, echoing an earlier observation (e.g., Riemer 1940), also reported that in some cases the incest was initiated during a period when the father did not have sexual access to the wife. In some cases a lack of access resulted from a divorce or the mother's death, but much more commonly it was the result of her physical absence or incapacitation due to work, alcoholism, illness, or childbirth (Cavallin 1966; Kaufman, Peck, and Tagiuri 1954; Maisch 1972).

The mother's absence or incapacitation was also related to a second set of questions raised by incest researchers about the family environment. These questions centered on the seeming failure of the mother to take effective action that might prevent or terminate the incest. Researchers treated the presence or absence of a "restraining agent" (Weinberg 1955: 67), the mother or perhaps another family member, as a variable in explaining the onset of incest. One reason, they argued, that the mother might not function as a restraint is that the incest only took place when she was physically absent or incapacitated. The literature presents cases in which the mother simply did not know the incest was taking place (and sometimes reacted strongly and decisively when it was discovered). In other cases, however, and for various reasons, the incestuous relationship was not a very well-kept secret. Why did the mother fail to intervene? Why, as writers on incest asked, might the mother be tolerant of incest, or so emotionally submissive to her husband that she could not or would not restrain him? As with incestuous fathers, no one type of mother was found. Many mothers were described as dependent, passive, and extremely submissive, even masochistic, in their attitude toward their domineering husbands (Cormier, Kennedy, and Sangowicz 1962; Eist and

Mandel 1968; Kaufman, Peck, and Tagiuri 1954; Tormes 1968; Weinberg 1955). Other mothers were described as themselves sexually promiscuous or contributing to a "loose sex culture" within the home (Kaufman, Peck, and Tagiuri 1954; Lukianowicz 1972; Maisch 1972; Weinberg 1955). Still other mothers were described as actively hostile to their husbands, deserting their sexual and household roles (Lustig et al. 1966; Machotka, Pittman, and Flomenhaft 1967; Weinberg 1955). As with fathers, researchers explaining the mother's behavior concentrated on features of her personality and background. Various forms of emotional deprivation in the mother's childhood and, in some cases, a history of incest were the most consistently reported features (Eist and Mandel 1968; Kaufman, Peck, and Tagiuri 1954; Lustig et al. 1966).

The mother's disturbances were in turn related to another set of questions about dysfunctional patterns within the incestuous family. Researchers asked about the mother-daughter relationship before the onset of incest and if a troubled relationship with the daughter might predispose her to participate in the incest. They also asked if the mother might consciously or unconsciously encourage a role reversal with the daughter to get free of domestic responsibilities and the demands of the father. I take up the question of a daughter's predisposition to incest below when discussing the child-participant category. On the second question, concerning role reversal, several studies presented a description of one particular mother-daughter interaction pattern prior to the incest (Eist and Mandel 1968; Kaufman, Peck, and Tagiuri 1954; Lustig et al. 1966; Machotka, Pittman, and Flomenhaft 1967; Raphling, Carpenter, and Davis 1967; Rhinehart 1961). In this scenario, the disturbed mother initiates a role reversal with the daughter, slowly pushing her into adult responsibilities and a position of "little mother." Initially favoring this daughter, often the oldest, the mother grows increasingly dependent on her and eventually turns hostile and ever more demanding. As the mother is typically sexually estranged from the father by this time, incest writers theorized that the role reversal in domestic responsibilities is intended, consciously or unconsciously, to include a role reversal in the sexual relationship with the father as well. In this way, many incest writers saw the mother in these types of cases as "colluding" in the incest by tacitly encouraging or giving unconscious consent to the incestuous behavior. In support of this view, they also reported that after the incest began, the mother used "massive denial" to protect herself from facing up to what was obviously happening, including her part in bringing it about.

The notion of the colluding mother was primarily the product of the family therapy movement. This movement, steeped in concepts drawn from general systems theory, first appeared in the mid-1950s, and initiated a wide-ranging and influential reinterpretation of problems that in the dominant psychiatric and psychoanalytic orientations had been the focus of individual therapy (Haley 1971a; Sturkie 1986). Rooted in a more interactional theory of pathology, family systems theory includes but goes beyond "an individual model of diagnosis and treatment to focus also on the other family members and their context as well as on the feedback loops that connect them" (Mrazek and Bentovim 1981: 167). Families, in this model, represent a symbiotic system that struggles to maintain a dynamic equilibrium that serves the members' unconscious needs. Because family roles are interwoven, the psychopathology of one member cannot be understood apart from the functioning of the other members and of the implicit family rules, injunctions, and communications and behavior patterns of their family system. For family therapists, individual psychopathology is contextualized intergenerationally and is both a symptom and cause of family "dysfunction." No one, in this view, gets or remains sick alone (Rice 1996: 59). Hence, in family therapy, the family, rather than the individual, is the treatment unit (Satir 1964, 1965).

Following from their concern with family systems, when systems theorists began to study incest in the 1960s, they treated it as a "family affair." In father-daughter incest, they argued, an "incestuous system" was formed by a collusive "interpersonal triangle" (Machotka, Pittman, and Flomenhaft 1967), in which not only the father but the mother and daughter played crucial roles. In fact, without denying the pathology of the "incest-prone" father (Machotka, Pittman, and Flomenhaft 1967: 110), for some systems theorists it was the mother who, despite her formal innocence in the sexual events, actually served as the "cornerstone in the pathological family system" (Lustig et al. 1966: 39). By effecting the role reversal with the daughter, by refusing sex with the father, and by denying the incest, the mother "set up" the incest and made its perpetuation possible. In the family systems model, the daughter was seen to play a complying role in the incest behavior. She returned hostility, theorists argued, to her overly demanding mother and helped to reverse their roles by assuming a pseudo-maturity in domestic and sexual matters. Like father and mother, she too was preoccupied with maintaining the integrity of the dysfunctional family unit and so kept the family secret.

Daughter (Child Participant)

The family systems emphasis on the complicit daughter was an extreme position in the incest literature on the question of the child participant's behavior. More generally, incest researchers asked questions about the daughter's preexisting characteristics that paralleled the questions asked in the sexual offense literature in the case of the "participating victim." These questions, as we saw above, were of two kinds. Were there preexisting characteristics that might make the child more vulnerable to being sexually approached? And were there preexisting characteristics that might affect her reaction when the incest occurred? The two questions were interrelated—except in the matter of certain ascribed characteristics that were sometimes correlated with heightened vulnerability, such as the daughter's physical appearance, birth order, or intelligence level—but the second was more central. In the majority of cases, researchers reported, the father did not use force or threat of force, and daughters neither actively resisted his sexual advances nor provoked or initiated them (Gebhard et al. 1965; Maisch 1972; Riemer 1940; Sloane and Karpinski 1942; Tormes 1968; Weinberg 1955). Rather, the most common response by daughters was one of passivity, at least at the beginning.[23] Accounting for this passivity led researchers to ask if, at least in some cases, some type of gratification-seeking or personality disturbance might explain why the child allowed the relationship to begin and (or) to continue.

Most of the larger studies in the incest literature portray the environmental circumstances surrounding the incest as distinctly unfavorable to all but passive resistance by a young daughter (Gebhard et al. 1965; Maisch 1972; Riemer 1940; Weinberg 1955). The father was found to be the active seducer in the vast majority of cases, and while he seldom used physical force, he resorted to bribes (including material rewards and "special-child" treatment), threats, elaborate rationalizations, and false information ("We'll put you in a home") to win the child's cooperation and silence. Given the relative position of the two parties, some writers found assessing the extent of a young daughter's cooperation unfeasible. Writing of daughters under twelve years of age, Gebhard and colleagues observe that "the authoritarian position of the father makes the differentiation between threat, duress, acquiescence, and willingness almost impossible" (1965: 207). Intimidation, fear, and dependence, but also love (Cormier, Kennedy, and Sangowicz 1962: 215) could account for much of the child's behavior.

At the same time, like the sexual offense researchers, psychiatric writers on incest did not typically view the child's behavior as entirely determined by the actions of the father. Some evidence was adduced to suggest that the child was not simply in the grip of the father's will. This evidence included the frequent repetition of the sexual acts over long periods of time, the presence of siblings who successfully resisted, the failure to terminate the relationship when clear opportunity arose, the absence of any complaints, daughters' accounts of pleasure and reciprocation in the relationship, and a lack of guilt about the sexual activity itself. In cases presenting such evidence, clinicians often inferred that the child was cooperating at some level. They suggested that certain disturbances before the incest might have heightened the child's vulnerability and explain her receiving some gratification from the experience.

Some authors reported affectional deprivation of the child prior to the onset of the incest and believed the child's cooperation was motivated by an effort to secure some expression of parental interest (e.g., Kaufman, Peck, and Tagiuri 1954; Rhinehart 1961). The fact that some daughters engaged in antisocial behavior and (or) sexual acting out prior to the incest was similarly interpreted. A number of studies, including the family system studies noted above, reported a preexisting tension in the daughter's relationship with her mother (e.g., Kaufman, Peck, and Tagiuri 1954; Woodbury and Schwartz 1971). Given the daughter's feelings of resentment or open hostility toward the mother, some clinicians interpreted the child's compliance in incest as satisfying a conscious or unconscious rivalry with the mother (e.g., Cormier, Kennedy, and Sangowicz 1962), or a desire to get revenge against her (Gordon 1955; Sloane and Karpinski 1942). Some suggested that some girls might have "even enjoyed their role of the 'little mother'" (Lukianowicz 1972: 304). Some studies found the daughter to be passive, dependent, and perhaps masochistic before the incest. Researchers and clinicians theorized that such personality traits and behavior might have made it more likely that the father would succeed in establishing and maintaining the sexual relationship.

Incest versus Family Effects

Since so much about the incestuous family situation was disordered prior to the incest, researchers and clinicians in this period found it difficult, if not impossible, to separate the effects of incest on the daughter from the effects of other aspects of her family background. As noted above, the daughter was typically exposed to considerable deprivation before the incest began. The father was disturbed, and his disturbance long predated the incest. The mother, too, may have been disturbed and in a hostile relationship with the daughter. The marital relationship was often strained and emotionally barren. The incest, in sum, was but one expression of a broader pathology within the family. This broader pathology, researchers reasoned, could certainly be a source of difficulties for the child quite apart from the sexual event or series of events. Karin Meiselman, based on her review of the literature, makes this point quite clearly: "The kinds of disturbed family backgrounds that are conducive to the occurrence of overt incest are almost certain to produce developmental difficulties, even if incest never occurs" (1978: 195).

Further, once the incestuous relationship began, additional and detrimental disruptions in the family often took place, and researchers believed these disruptions could have effects of their own on the child. They argued that the consequence of disrupting the family by reporting the incest could have negative effects on the child, as could the reaction of family members and the larger community. Some researchers, for instance, found guilt that was related not to the sexual activity but to the child's role in breaking up the family, and in some cases children were more disturbed by the reactions of adults than by the sexual events. For incest researchers, then, the incest and the other features of its social context were tightly intertwined. They could not isolate the many consequences of incest for the child participant from this context.

•☙• •☙• •☙•

In the period I have been discussing, legal and psychiatric frameworks were dominant among professionals. These frameworks, with their emphasis on sexual deviance and sexual perversion, focused on the adult offender rather than the child victim. In the legal context, the focus was on the offender as a criminal; in the psychiatric context, the offender was regarded as sexually deviant and mentally disordered. In the legal context, the question of the child victim was not problematic. For the various categories of sexual offense, the adult was held responsible, regardless of the actions of the child or adolescent. In the psychiatric literature, however, the issue of the victim was different. Here the legal model, with its sole focus on the guilt of the offender, was found inadequate because it ignored the psychology of the child. When psychiatrists explored the psychology of the child, they raised the question of possible participation: Were children always victims in the legal sense, or was the picture more complex? Working from the psychoanalytic model, psychiatric writers took the view "that the child is not a negligible psychological creature in either an intellectual or emotional sense" (Bender and Blau 1937: 513). Children's behavior, too, they argued, is determined by complex conscious and unconscious drives. Thus, while researchers did not dispute representing children as victims in a legal context, they viewed the implication of unconditional innocence as too clear cut, psychologically, for all cases. Innocence of cooperation or collaboration, scholars argued, could not be assumed. In fact, some held that the child could be the instigator or the more sophisticated participant.

I began this chapter by asking why there were no public "adult survivor" stories before the 1970s. In considering the findings on victimization presented in the early research and clinical literatures, we have seen that they provided no basis for viewing victims of molestation and incest as composing a uniform category of persons. Not all victims, legally defined, were considered innocent of cooperation or collaboration in their victimization, and most victims were believed to suffer little direct harm from the experience. Combined with the offender's pathology as the explanation for sexual offenses, the possibility of cooperation and the unlikelihood of direct harm worked against any collective victim narrative, especially for adults. No common experience of actual victimization and no common experience of harm tied all the persons in the category together; nor did the cause of victimization, which was rooted not in some larger social pattern but in the unique acts of individual deviants. Victims had no collective story and thus no rationale for public disclosure and no framework by which a public story could be formulated and understood.

All of this changed in the 1970s. The old literature builds on what came before it, testing hypotheses generated by earlier studies and comparing their findings with it. As the 1970s progressed, however, the approach to the victim that informed the older literature came under an increasingly harsh *moral* critique, independent of and prior to any new scientific findings. Critics from social movements concerned with violence toward women and children, like Florence Rush, asserted that the old psychology and legal approaches were biased against the child victim. These critics promoted a radical break in perspective rooted in changed theoretical assumptions about both the offender and the victim. After about 1977, sexual abuse researchers no longer worked from hypotheses generated by the old literature or reconciled their findings with it.[24] Indeed, as treatment books for and articles about adult survivors of incest and sexual abuse poured off the presses, the moral critique of the old psychology became a fixed element of the new knowledge about sexual abuse.

In the next two chapters, I turn to the redefinitions that occurred in the 1970s. The construction of a new social problem, sexual abuse, and the redefinition of the offender and victim categories *did* generate a collective victim story, and they further suggest why the pre-1970s understandings did not.

CHAPTER TWO

Constructing Sexual Abuse 1
Family Therapy and the Child Protection Movement

Read twenty-five years after it was first published, "Incest: Sexual Abuse Begins at Home," seems unremarkable. But in April, 1977, when freelance writer Ellen Weber published the article in *Ms.* magazine, alongside the story of "Mary C.," an incest victim, it was explosive. Widely cited and reprinted, the Weber article captured and popularized the growing conviction among some child advocates that sexual abuse was rife in American society. It began with the words: "One girl out of every four in the United States will be sexually abused in some way before she reaches the age of 18" (64).[1] But even more significantly, as the title suggests, it classified incest as a form of sexual abuse and sought to dispel the notion that strangers commit most abuse. "In a full 75 percent of the cases," Weber claimed, drawing on a late 1960s survey conducted in New York City by the American Humane Association, "the victim knows her assailant," and in about one-third of the cases, the "molestation takes place in her own home." Moreover, Weber argued, sexual abuse is not a lower-class phenomenon, but "occurs in families of every social, economic, and ethnic background" (64). In comparison with the public attention focused on the battered child, however, "the sexual abuse victim has been virtually ignored" (65), despite the fact that "many professionals" have seen a correlation between sexual abuse and later behavior problems, including drug addiction, prostitution, and sexual dysfunction.

The inattention Weber noted was not to last much longer. Already building for several years prior, 1977 was to be the year that sexual abuse was "discovered" as a public problem. Articles in both the popular press and academic journals began to appear in earnest (e.g., Herman and Hirschman 1977; Rush 1977; Weber 1977), with the tide continuing in 1978 (e.g., Armstrong 1978; Butler 1978; Forward and Buck 1978; Meiselman 1978), and 1979 (e.g., Brady 1979; Finkelhor 1979; Justice and Justice 1979), and increasing exponentially thereafter.[2] Not only did these publications represent a massive quantitative increase in the incest and sexual offense

literature, but they collectively signaled a break with the theoretical orientations that characterized the earlier literature. They articulated an emerging
perspective on childhood sexual victimization and its consequences under a
new principle of victim innocence and psychological harm and in a new
condition category: child sexual abuse. These publications sounded the
themes that would be elaborated in the years following, both in psychological research and in victim-treatment programs. They launched a veritable
movement.

To identify more clearly why such an outpouring of literature and public
attention occurred, I turn to the new understandings that emerged in the
1960s and 1970s as social movements took up and redefined the problem of
sexual offenses under the new classification of sexual abuse. For these movements, victimization was their central concern and they began—as suggested
by Florence Rush's speech at the NYRF rape conference—with the moral
rejection of the victim characterizations in the sexual offense literature previously produced. This break, I argue, is the conceptual key to the subsequent
emergence of a new person category and victim-centered collective story
about the adult survivor.

In this chapter and the next, I consider the work of three movements and
how each came to break with the older psychiatric/legal perspective of the
sexual offender and child victim. These movements were the direct forces
behind the new collective story, but, of course, they did not operate in a cultural or institutional vacuum. The new categories of sexual abuse and adult
survivor were framed and received in the broader American social context of
the 1960s and 1970s.[3] This context was shaped by a large number of events
and changes in social attitudes relevant to the emergence and public recep-
tion of the new categories. No list can be exhaustive, but among these developments the following are all apposite: the sexual revolution and the new
openness to talk about all matters sexual; the growing popularity of the
human potential movement and its expansive formulation of psychological
and emotional health; the rapid growth of the fields of psychology and social
work; changing views of children and the growing emphasis on children's
rights, including the landmark 1967 *In re Gault* Supreme Court decision
declaring juveniles to have constitutional rights; the interest of legal scholars
and criminologists in the study of "victimology," which grew throughout the
1960s and 1970s, and a related emphasis on survivorship and life under
extreme circumstances; the shift, beginning in the late 1960s, from a func-
tionalist or consensus model of society to a conflict perspective in the social
sciences, and the subsequent rise of family violence studies; and, even more

broadly, changing gender roles, family patterns, and new levels of parental concern about the socialization of children. Each of these developments created the social environment in which a whole variety of new claims about sex, psychological injury, children, and the family were framed and publicly selected, including the concerns with sexual abuse and adults victimized as children.

In this chapter my line of inquiry is limited to the immediate engines of change: the movements that framed new collective representations of molestation, victim, and offender, and the content of these categories. My data includes the books, magazine and newspaper articles, documentaries, first-person victim accounts, legislative hearings, government documents, and research literature on child and sexual abuse that appeared from the early 1960s to the early 1980s.

REFRAMING CHILD MOLESTATION

In the pre-1970s literature, social problem claims were framed in terms of sexual offenders. As discussed in the last chapter, in two periods—the late 1930s and the late 1940s/1950s—sex offenders were the subject of public outcries and legislative action. In both of these periods, psychiatrists were key claims-makers in defining sexual offenders as suffering from mental disorders, and in calling for legal responses aimed at rehabilitation and treatment (Freedman 1987; Sutherland 1950). The role of psychiatrists reflected their growing professional stature, and the definitions they proffered of both problem and response necessitated their expertise (Weisberg 1984). In the psychiatric definitions of child molestation in both time periods, the agents of harm were sexually disordered individual offenders, and these definitions shaped the various sex offender statutes enacted in response to public concern, including the sexual psychopath laws of the late 1930s and the "dangerous" or "mentally disordered" sex offender laws of the 1950s. As constructed, sexual offenders constituted a person-type category of sexual deviants of varying degrees and kinds. The legal solutions focused on keeping them off the streets until they were "well," requiring their registration and expanding treatment programs for them.

While protecting children was the principal public concern with child molestation, in the psychiatric perspective, the child victim—in contrast with the offender—was an indeterminate person-type. By legal definition, children were the weaker party, unable to consent, and protected against the sexual advances of adults. Psychiatrically, however, they were indistinguishable as a collectivity. As I explained in the last chapter, researchers viewed many sexual offenses as nuisance experiences for the victim and without harmful consequences. And, even in more serious offenses, including incest, they did not find harm to be certain, uniform, or syndrome-like, or necessarily enduring. In other words, victims were not seen to share a common experience of harm from their sexual experience, either in the short term or the long term. Moreover, clinicians and researchers did not see all child victims, legally defined, as actually sharing victim status. Some children, they argued, were clearly victims, forced by an offender against their will and perhaps against their active resistance. Others, however, were found to consent at some level to the sexual contact and even in some instances to play a more provocative role. There was no single pattern and no clear definition of the victim person-category as always involving a psychological innocent.

Studies of social problems and the framing activities of social movements have demonstrated the importance of particular typifications of both the agent and, especially, the victim of harm for successful claims (e.g., Best 1990; Hunt and Benford 1994; Hunt, Benford, and Snow 1994; Loseke 1992; Lowney and Best 1995). Scholars have argued that a key component of the collective action frames of social movements is the identification of human actors (which can be groups as well as individuals) who are the agents of undeserved suffering and harm and to whom blame or causality can be attributed (Gamson 1992; Snow and Benford 1988, 1992). The most powerful frames identify concrete human actors who have motives and who can be presented as knowingly contributing to injustice (see also Holstein and Miller 1990). These agents of harm, or "victimizers," are constructed so as to arouse moral indignation; because they are immoral, they are "condemnation-worthy" (Loseke 1993).

In social problems theory, the "victim" label in its most pure form identifies the individual as "harmed by forces beyond his or her control, simultaneously establishing the 'fact' of injury and locating responsibility for the damage outside the 'victim'" (Holstein and Miller 1990: 106). A pure victim typification dramatizes the labeled person's essential innocence and thus status as a moral type of person. It establishes him or her as worthy of sympathy and assistance (Clark 1987; Holstein and Miller 1990; Loseke 1993).

In the 1970s, both the sexual offender and victim categories were recast in these morally pure and emotion-laden terms. Rather than mentally disordered, with its implication of less-than-full responsibility, the offender category was reconstructed in a moral framework as a type of person who chooses and intends harm.[4] The victim category was morally reconstructed in terms of innocence and purged of the psychiatric notions of participation/complicity and minimal injury. These redefinitions of the categories simultaneously redefined child molestation as a public problem and made the child victim a focus of professional concern and intervention. From the child victim the retypifications were subsequently extended to the adult victimized as a child, further mobilizing former victims and professionals concerned with their treatment.

Although I identify 1977 as the decisive year for the emergence of sexual abuse as a social problem, important changes in the characterization of child molestation had been building since the 1960s, when the term "sexual abuse" first began to appear in legal statutes and the writings of some professionals (e.g., De Francis 1969; Swanson 1968). These early efforts in the family therapy and child protection movements laid important groundwork for the sweeping transformations that would follow.

THE FAMILY THERAPY MOVEMENT

The field of family therapy began with 1950s research studies on schizophrenia and eventually became a movement that aimed to develop a new epistemology for clinical practice. In contrast with the then-dominant psychoanalytic approach, family therapists—principally psychologists and social workers—championed an ecological model of treatment that emphasized current interpersonal experience and the interrelatedness of individuals in their family system. As this perspective spread in the 1960s, a wide range of problems that had been the concern of traditional, individual psychiatry were reexamined and reinterpreted (Sturkie 1986). Incest, as I noted in the last chapter, was one of these problems. Beginning in the mid-1960s, a growing literature on incest treatment from a family-systems perspective began to appear.

Family therapy arose as a direct challenge to the psychoanalytic emphasis on the unconscious and the clinical methods derived from it (Haley 1971a). In the psychoanalytic model, intrapsychic processes are central. The analyst seeks change for patients by helping them to develop insight into the unconscious conflicts programmed by their past and to modify or eliminate the repressive forces that cause their incapacitation. Current interpersonal experience is considered secondary to internal conflicts, perceptions, attitudes, affect, and so on. Thus, while sexual traumas are of key theoretical significance in psychoanalysis, it is their role in the imagination (what Freud called fantasy) that is clinically most important. Against this perspective, family therapists reversed the order of emphasis, making current personal experience within the social environment—particularly the family—central to understanding emotional distress and impaired functioning. Rather than oedipal conflicts, family therapists were concerned only with cases involving actual seduction incidents; their treatment methods focused on preventing further incidents by addressing the family-system dynamics that contributed to their occurrence.

The family therapy movement's antagonism toward psychoanalytic doctrine and its clinical concern with actual molestation and the family system had several important consequences. First, they presaged a much more thoroughgoing attack on oedipal theory in the 1970s. In that decade, activists would charge Freud with a "cover-up" for interpreting certain of his patients' reports of incestuous experience as "reifying the remnants of an Oedipal fantasy" (Sturkie 1986: 129) rather than as actual life events. Second, family-system approaches led to an exploration of the "mutual needs" that incest satisfied within the family and, as I described in the last chapter, to the notions of the colluding wife and the complicit daughter. These ideas have had a lasting influence among family therapists, though many, particularly those aligned with child protective services, have taken pragmatic approaches in which the complicit daughter notion plays little if any role (see the discussion of the Child Sexual Abuse Treatment Program below). Notions of complicity, however, are also important here because they run counter to the frame of the innocent victim. When antirape activists, who adopted a conflict approach, launched their polemic against the existing literature on child molestation, this aspect of family-systems thinking was subject to the same moral critique leveled against various elements of psychoanalysis.

Third, and most significant, the theoretical emphases of family therapy led to the creation of treatment programs in which the child victim also received counseling, while in the psychiatric framework, treatment efforts were directed to the sexually deviant offender alone. For family therapists, however, the focus was on the family—and, in an important sense, the entire family, not simply the offender, was the source of the problem. This focus shifted concern from stranger perpetrators to the father or stepfather molester, a shift that was taking place in the child protection movement as well and that helped to shape the emerging definition of sexual abuse as a problem primarily of the family. The family focus also meant that in order to prevent recurrence, the entire family must be treated, including the child victim. Bringing the child under the care of psychologists and social workers contributed to the belief that children were almost always harmed by their sexual experience and to the emphasis in state "child sexual abuse" laws on the need for and funding of child victim treatments. While a number of developments were taking place simultaneously, a pioneering child sexual abuse treatment program in California was a crucial player in bringing about these changes.

The Santa Clara County Child Sexual Abuse Treatment Program

The earliest and most prominent treatment program based on a family-systems perspective was created in 1971 in Santa Clara County, California.[5] Dissatisfied with the way child molestation cases were being handled, officials in the Juvenile Probation Department asked a psychologist named Henry Giarretto to do part-time volunteer counseling of sexually molested children and their families. The pilot program, "Therapeutic Case Management of Sexually Abused Children and their Families," was initially limited to ten hours of counseling per week for ten weeks. The program, soon to be called the Child Sexual Abuse Treatment Program (CSATP), grew steadily and expanded its staff and services, securing regular funding from the county in 1973 and state funds in 1976. Giarretto, working through the probation department, became the full-time paid director in 1974. Referrals surged from 32 in 1973 to 135 in 1974, and were over 500 by 1977 (Kroth 1979: 14), continuing to increase thereafter. The bulk of these cases involved father offenders from middle-class backgrounds.

From the beginning, CSATP was based on a therapeutic admixture of humanistic psychology and conjoint family therapy (as developed by Virginia Satir).[6] Program professionals, working in cooperation with the criminal justice system, dealt with both familial and extrafamilial child molestation, though the majority of referrals were familial (father-daughter). The program objectives were to provide immediate counseling and practical assistance (especially to the child victim) to hasten the reuniting of the family and, if possible, the reconstitution of the marriage, and to foster the "self-managed growth" of the individuals involved. Treatment typically progressed from individual therapy with each party, including the child, to marriage therapy, to conjoint family therapy. The treatment approach stressed family-systems principles (e.g., incest is a symptom of a distorted "family homeostasis," especially of a troubled marital relationship) and the need to develop a "high self-concept" in the parents, for both a healthy marriage and a high self-concept in the children. Therapy sessions were designed to be warm and optimistic, with the therapist underscoring the sharing of positive traits, the identification of "weaknesses and maladaptive habits," and the probing of painful feelings. In father-daughter cases, the father was "induced to admit" that he was "totally responsible" for the sexual advances, the mother was encouraged to admit that her role in the problematic marital relationship contributed to the underlying cause of the abuse, and both parents were encouraged to relieve the daughter of self-blame and guilt by telling her that she was the "victim of poor parenting." If the father and/or his wife would not admit culpability, but blamed the child, they were dismissed from the program.

To complement the professional therapy, Giarretto early developed a self-help component for CSATP. Parents United was formed in 1972 in order to reinforce the therapeutic and family reconstitution goals of CSATP. Initially comprised of mothers, the first father began attending in late 1972 with the court's consent while still serving his sentence at a rehabilitation center. The group grew rapidly and also began assisting members with services and making public presentations before professional and lay audiences, an activity which led to the creation of a Speaker's Bureau. A self-help group for child victims, originally called Daughters United and subsequently expanded to Daughters and Sons United (DSU), was also formed by Giarretto in 1972. Like Parents United, DSU provided emotional and service support for members and advanced the broader therapeutic and resocialization goals of CSATP. Moreover, DSU members also engaged in public relations work of their own, giving talks at schools, appearing on radio and television, and so on.

As suggested by the public relations work, CSATP and its self-help groups were active in promoting their understanding of sexual abuse and its treatment to a wider audience. One of Giarretto's goals from the beginning was to provide a model that could be emulated or adopted by a wide variety of jurisdictions. The program developed informational and training materials that were distributed both locally and nationally "to abet the aim of having the CSATP serve as a model for other communities" (Giarretto 1976a: 156). Presentations and training seminars were conducted by CSATP staff and Parents United for professional groups, examples of model child sexual abuse legislation were widely circulated, and Giarretto wrote articles about the need to protect children from sexual abuse (e.g., Giarretto 1976a, 1976b). In 1975, program staff and Parents United members actively lobbied the California Assembly to pass legislation introduced by an assemblyman from Santa Clara County (Weisberg 1984: 33). Signed into law the same year, Assembly Bill No. 2288 included funding for the CSATP under the official name of Child Sexual Abuse Demonstration and Training Project. Funds were also earmarked for the development of programs for city and county personnel throughout the state relating to the prevention of child sexual abuse, and to assist professionals to participate in the training program (Kroth 1979: 13).[7]

Moreover, to take their message to a broader public, CSATP and Parents United solicited and received both local and national coverage in the media. Favorable stories appeared in the press, as well as in national magazines and television shows.[8] As a result of these efforts and the favorable legislation, the CSATP was replicated in many California counties and in several other states. The program was widely known among the burgeoning professional community concerned with child sexual abuse, and it functioned as an educational model for many of the other sexual victimization programs that had appeared by the late 1970s (Giarretto 1982; Kroth 1979: 173–86).[9]

The CSATP model represented a significant break with the psychiatric model. Giarretto and his colleagues subsumed all of their cases, including incest (broadly defined; this was seldom the legal charge), under the umbrella term *sexual abuse*.[10] For the CSATP, sexual abuse, unlike the psychiatric focus on sexual deviance and sexual perversion, involved a primary emphasis on a relatively, though not totally, powerless victim.[11] Because child victims were abused, and typically in the context of a dysfunctional family, the CSATP viewed them as virtually always psychologically harmed and requiring of professional help. In keeping with humanistic psychological principles, the harm to the child was conceptualized as an emotional trauma undermining her or his self-esteem, leading in turn to "self-sabotaging" behaviors, such as truancy, heavy drug use, and sexual promiscuity. This trauma, Giarretto argued in his polemic against the official status quo, was only aggravated by the typical response of the criminal justice system, a response which might equal or exceed the harm caused by the abusive incident itself. Without therapeutic intervention for the child and the family, the CSATP believed, victim feelings of guilt and self-blame and self-punishing behaviors would continue into adulthood, contributing to new dysfunctional families and perhaps sexual abuse of the next generation. Empowering child victims by raising their self-concept, therefore, was not only seen as a form of treatment but as a form of future abuse prevention. Parents with high self-concepts, in this view, create strong marriages and do not abuse their children.

Consistent with the belief that child victims require therapeutic help for successful adjustment, the CSATP included programs not only for children recently molested but also for adults molested as children. As the CSATP began to receive publicity, it became a rallying point for former victims, from whom the program received hundreds of letters. Individual and couple counseling for these clients was developed, and special self-help groups were convened within Parents United. For the victims in father-daughter cases, treatment centered on gaining self-knowledge and a sympathetic view of their mothers and father-offenders, and on learning to first confront and then reconnect emotionally with their parents. When ready, some of these former victims worked with young victims and served as group facilitators in sessions of DSU. In these forums, their personal stories of "lives devastated by parental rejection, promiscuity, drug addiction, inability to keep jobs, and broken marriages" (Giarretto 1981: 186) served to confirm the need for the CSATP by vividly illustrating the "long years of alienation and pain" that followed for victims untreated during childhood. A separate subgroup within Parents United, Women Molested as Children, was eventually formed (later, groups for men were added, and the name was changed to Adults Molested as Children United).

In the CSATP, the concept of the offender was also recast. From the beginning, Giarretto contrasted his emerging model with the approach taken in the criminal justice system, where felony sexual offenders were treated punitively as criminals or mentally disturbed. While the CSATP worked closely with the criminal justice system, it valued the system's coercive power for the immediate action and protection it could provide to families and for compelling offenders into treatment. Harsh punishment, however, was regarded by CSATP as reinforcing the offender's "self-hate/destructive energy syndrome" that contributed to the dysfunctional family and sexual abuse in the first place. The CSATP also did not view offenders as suffering from an "exotic mental disease"; such claims were regarded as deflections of the offender's responsibility. At least in Santa Clara County, due to the "growing acceptance of the CSATP by the psychiatrists and judges as an effective alternative," fewer and fewer felony sexual offenders were diagnosed as mentally disturbed and sent to the state psychiatric facility (Giarretto 1981: 192). Instead, they were sent to the CSATP, where they were regarded as fully capable of understanding and controlling their deviant impulses. Further, in the psychiatric definition, "a sex offense is a sexually motivated act indicative of some mental and/or emotional defect or maladjustment" (Gebhard et al. 1965: 5). In the CSATP understanding, by contrast, the victimizer is not primarily sexually motivated. His acts reconfirm and discharge his low self-worth, and are an expression of broader dysfunction in his family system, including his family of origin. The program, therefore, emphasized not sexual maladjustment but the offender's destructive guilt, chronic resentment, and marital/family problems. While emphasizing his responsibility for willful exploitation, it taught the "attitudes and skills for high self-esteem" and marital and family harmony.

The selling point for the CSATP's retypifications and corresponding treatments was that they got results. Family therapists had long insisted that while psychoanalysis could be effective for some individuals, it simply took too long and was too expensive (Haley 1971b; Satir 1964). Although Giarretto came to see his original ten-week program as too short and to believe that family therapy could be useful only after more individualized treatment, by the mid-1970s his small staff, complemented by volunteers and the self-help groups, was seeing hundreds of cases and claiming an extremely low recidivism rate among offenders. Rather than languishing in jails or mental hospitals at taxpayers' expense, most offenders were being rehabilitated and returned to the community as productive citizens, marriages were being saved, and the child victims were quickly being restored to their families. Giarretto argued that the mental health of all parties was improved, increasing numbers of cases were being reported, future violations were being prevented, and the deleterious effects of the abuse and of the criminal justice system on the child victim were being minimized. And all of this was being achieved in a short time and at minimal expense. Such claims to practical success proved to be a powerful argument, both for the CSATP and against the older psychiatric approach.

Giarretto's family therapy program represents an early and influential recasting of both victim and offender in a sexual abuse framework. It also contributed to the definition of sexual abuse as a serious social problem, principally of the family, including middle-class families. The category of sexual abuse, however, was not a family therapy idea. It originated in the child protection movement,[12] especially through the efforts of Vincent De Francis, a long-time activist with the American Humane Association, who influenced Giarretto (Giarretto 1976a). I turn now to the child protection movement, including the part played by De Francis, and its efforts to frame a social problem requiring government intervention under the category of child sexual abuse.

THE CHILD PROTECTION MOVEMENT

The widely agreed-upon watershed event for the emergence of child abuse as a social problem was the publication of Dr. C. Henry Kempe's 1962 report of a nationwide survey dealing with the symptoms of young children who had been repeatedly injured by their caregivers (e.g., Antler 1981; Best 1990; Hacking 1991; Nelson 1984; Parton 1985; Pfohl 1977). The article by Kempe and his colleagues, "The Battered-Child Syndrome" (Kempe et al. 1962), appeared in the prestigious *Journal of the American Medical Association* and was accompanied by an editorial urging doctors to report suspected abuse and suggesting that more children may die from battery at the hands of parents or guardians than die of leukemia, cystic fibrosis, or muscular dystrophy (*JAMA* 1962). Kempe had unveiled his findings at a meeting of the American Academy of Pediatrics (AAP) meeting in November 1961, but he and the notion of the battered-child syndrome first gained national attention in April 1962 in *Newsweek,* and then in other national magazines, such as *Time* and the *Saturday Evening Post,* following the *JAMA* article, which appeared in July.[13] The term *child abuse* and the idea that the physical battering of young children was a serious national problem of all social classes entered public consciousness, and a new social movement for child protection was born.[14]

Like all such shifts in awareness, the Kempe group's "discovery" of a new victim and thus a new form of deviance was preceded by several years of much more low-profile work by others. Pediatric radiologists began writing about the discovery (with x-ray technology) of unexplained bone fractures in infants in the 1940s, and the connection with parental behavior was made explicit beginning in the mid-1950s, first by radiologists, then by other medical professionals, and finally by social workers. Meanwhile, in 1954, the Children's Division of the American Humane Association (AHA), a private association of child protective agencies and a research group, hired a new director, Vincent De Francis, an attorney with graduate training in social work.[15] One of De Francis's first tasks at AHA was to launch a nationwide survey of the existence and extent of protective services for neglected, abused, and exploited children. His report, *Child Protective Services in the United States,* published in 1956, was widely distributed and, along with his organizational initiatives, helped to put child protection on the agenda of both private organizations concerned with child welfare and the U.S. Children's Bureau (Nelson 1984: 40–41). In the late 1950s, the Children's Bureau, a division of the Department of Health, Education, and Welfare staffed by social workers and public health physicians, began quietly funding a small group of child abuse researchers, including C. Henry Kempe. Over the next decade, such funding would play a major role in making child abuse a public issue.

Although child welfare workers like De Francis were important behind-the-scenes figures, physicians played the leading roles in the emerging public concern with physical child abuse. As others have argued, the original framing of child abuse in narrow medical terms as a "syndrome" affecting all social classes was crucial to its public and legislative acceptance (Antler 1981; Best 1990; Nelson 1984; Parton 1985). Kempe's research in the late 1950s, published under titles like "The Problem of Parental Criminal Neglect and Severe Abuse in Children," got little public attention. In 1961, however, on the recommendation of the program committee, Kempe organized his seminar at the AAP meetings under the name "Battered Child Syndrome" because it played down the legal and socially deviant aspects of the problem (Nelson 1984: 59). Under the medical label, the pathology seen to reside in the parents or other guardians was indirectly framed by describing a pattern of injuries to the child. The label and the focus on the very young child victim gave pediatricians a major and status-enhancing role to play in the diagnosis, treatment, and reporting of the new illness (Pfohl 1977). But the horrifying examples of brutalized infants and the high status of doctors also proved extremely useful in attracting the attention of the media and in diffusing political opposition to new reporting legislation.

The issue of child abuse was not long in coming to the attention of state legislatures. In early 1962, the Children's Bureau began drafting a model child abuse reporting law, which it subsequently disseminated widely. In that model statute, child abuse was defined as intentional and serious physical injury. Dissatisfied with features of the bureau version, others, including the American Humane Association, the American Medical Association, and the American Academy of Pediatrics soon followed with their own versions. With these models in hand, and with active lobbying from social workers, doctors, and various voluntary associations (Paulsen, Parker, and Adelman 1966), between 1963 and 1967 every state passed a law requiring the reporting of child abuse. In these laws, especially the earliest, child abuse was defined on the battered-child model and physicians were typically the professionals required to report it. However, many amendments were to come in the following years as lawmakers responded to the changing definition of child abuse and the changing "ownership" (Gusfield 1981) of this social problem.

Medical doctors like Kempe and his colleagues went on to have long careers in the child protection movement,[16] but the battered-child formulation of child abuse, despite its early media and legislative success, never fully replaced the older child welfare model. Championed particularly by social workers and the long-standing child protection organizations like the AHA and the Child Welfare League, the child welfare model set the physical abuse of children among a far larger set of moral concerns about the physical and mental health of the "neglected, abused, or exploited child." In contrast to the medical deviance model of battered children, child welfare advocates emphasized protective services, the role of the government and larger community in taking preemptive action, and the many social (not just individual) factors contributing to abuse and neglect.[17] In addition, a new subspecialty of family violence research was coming into being, and these scholars also took a broader social, rather than medical deviance, view of child abuse (e.g., Gil 1970).[18] As the sixties progressed, the battered-child construction of child abuse slowly lost its hold in state legislation, and the definition of abuse began to expand to include sexual abuse, emotional abuse, and neglect. "Ownership" of child abuse, or the ability to control its definition as a public problem, slowly shifted from the medical doctors to other experts, notably social workers, therapists, welfare workers, and other "human services providers."

Vincent De Francis and the Child Abuse Prevention and Treatment Act

Vincent De Francis was an energetic leader of the child welfare wing of the burgeoning protection movement and a key figure in expanding the domain of the child abuse problem. Although the AHA always had a child welfare emphasis, in the early 1960s it also emphasized physical injury. Its legislative guidelines, first circulated in 1963, differed from those of the Children's Bureau primarily in that they urged reporting to child welfare agencies instead of law enforcement agents, "based on the principle that the law should emphasize the service outcomes of reporting, not the punitive ones" (Nelson 1984: 78).[19] Moreover, in 1963 De Francis reported on an AHA study of child abuse cases reported in U.S. newspapers in 1962. The study documented 662 cases of physical abuse, including 178 that led to the death of the child (De Francis 1963a, 1963b). However, in 1965, with funding provided by the Children's Bureau, the AHA launched a three-year study in two New York counties that was to be instrumental in expanding the definition of child abuse and the conviction that public action was necessary. Rather than physical injury, the new study focused on child victims of sex offenders and on the response of parents and the criminal justice system to these children.

The AHA study resulted in two published reports.[20] The first "substudy," by Yvonne Tormes (1968), the study's on-site director, considered twenty incest cases. Tormes did not use the term *sexual abuse;* she defined incest as involving sexual intercourse, and in most respects she followed an interpretive approach similar to that of the family-systems theorists. Her report received modest attention, some of it negative (e.g., Rush 1974). The second report, by De Francis (1969), was the final report for the entire study. This report, compared with earlier studies, was both old and new. It was old in the sense that it was consistent with earlier approaches in making a distinction (albeit soft) between participating and accidental victims, in using a heavily lower-class sample, in finding high levels of family dysfunction and emotional disturbance in the child victim prior to the offense, and in finding the criminal justice process injurious to the child. In several important respects, though, the De Francis report was new and different. First, as noted in the last chapter, the AHA study was concerned to measure the effects of the criminal justice system on the child victim and so eliminated all cases that might not get prosecuted. The selection criteria yielded a much higher percentage of serious and violent cases (forcible rapes) than earlier studies, a much higher percentage of offenses committed by nonstrangers, and a higher level of reported victim harm. Second, De Francis used a broad definition of *incest* and subsumed all cases under the term *sexual abuse,* a type of the broader category of child abuse and neglect. Third, the study was new in that De Francis argued that child victims of sex offenders were also victims of the community that neglected their plight, and that not only they but their families needed professional help. Finally, De Francis, extrapolating from the number of cases seen in New York, suggested that the incidence of child sexual abuse may be "many times larger than the reported incidence of physical abuse" (De Francis 1969: 216).

Unlike the Torrance substudy, the final report by De Francis was widely influential. It influenced Henry Giarretto and the CSATP treatment model, feminists Florence Rush and Susan Brownmiller, and the feminist construction of sexual abuse to be discussed in the next chapter. Because it adopted a victim-centered approach (the hallmark of the child protection movement) and, in part, because it was the only data at hand, the De Francis report also became a standard reference for professionals involved with the treatment and prevention agencies that sprang up in the 1970s.[21] De Francis himself publicized its message. In an influential 1971 article, he summarized the report's findings while turning up the rhetorical heat. Freely generalizing, he argued that the study "shattered a commonly held opinion" that most offenders are stranger perverts; he went beyond his 1969 report in insisting that all involved children are victimized; and he emphasized the inadequacy of most parents to deal with the injurious consequences for the child. "Suffice it to say," he asserted with regard to incidence, "that the problem of sexual abuse is a very real one! It is a problem of immense proportions! It is pervasive!"

(De Francis 1971: 17). He called for a "coordinated attack on this national problem" (1971: 15). Among its own efforts, the AHA held two large national symposiums on the physical and sexual abuse of children in 1971 and 1972.

De Francis also took his message to the Senate hearings convened in 1973 to consider the first piece of federal legislation on child abuse, the Child Abuse Prevention Act.[22] Held over four days in March and April, these hearings focused, with one exception, on physical abuse and neglect. The one exception was the testimony of De Francis. In both his verbal remarks and submitted paper, De Francis returned to the argument first advanced in the 1969 study, namely, that sexually abused and what he called "psychologically abused" children represent a much larger problem than the battered child. And, he added, the "hazards and long-term damage" to these children are "grave and comparable to the damage inflicted in child battering." Therefore, he urged the committee to broaden legislative concern to the "entire problem" of the abused child.[23] Hearings in the House of Representatives followed six months later, held over four days in October and November 1973. De Francis did not testify at these hearings, but his view of the sexual abuse problem was cited by other witnesses who did.[24] Further, the House had three bills before it. The House version of the Senate bill (H.R. 6379) did not define child abuse, but the other two House bills (H.R. 10552 and H.R. 10968) included broad definitions of the kind used in child welfare. And the chairman of the House hearings, unlike the Senate chairman, who was content with the implicit focus on physical abuse in the Senate bill, was interested in defining child abuse: Each of the witnesses he asked provided broad definitions that included sexual abuse.[25] The version of the bill eventually voted on by the House altered the Senate version by adding a definition of "child abuse and neglect" inclusive of sexual abuse. This definition survived the reconciliation of the House and Senate versions, and the bill was sent to the president as the Child Abuse Prevention and Treatment Act (CAPTA). Signed into law by President Nixon in January 1974, CAPTA broadened the federal definition of child abuse from physical injury and neglect to include sexual abuse.[26] Because it required reporting to a much broader range of professionals than just doctors and granted child protection agencies new "gatekeeping" powers, it helped solidify ownership of child abuse with the child welfare wing of the protection movement.

The "Last Frontier in Child Abuse"

The broad definition of abuse in CAPTA and the emphasis of the bill on funding prevention and treatment "demonstration projects" helped put sexual abuse squarely on the agenda of the child protection movement. Even before the new federal money began to flow, however, the Office of Child Development in the Department of Health, Education, and Welfare (DHEW), including the Children's Bureau, had already begun in the early 1970s to fund "child abuse and neglect demonstration projects." Along with research grants, training sessions organized because of state reporting laws, and increased efforts by private child welfare organizations (such as establishing child abuse hotlines), these projects were drawing an increasing number of professionals into the child abuse and protection "industry." In the year or so after the signing of CAPTA, many of these professionals began to concentrate on sexual abuse. In 1975, for example, Suzanne Sgroi, incoming internist at one of the DHEW-funded demonstration projects, published an article in a special issue of *Children Today* devoted to child abuse. Widely read in professional circles (Vander Mey and Neff 1986: 8), the article was titled "Sexual Molestation of Children: The Last Frontier in Child Abuse." In Kempe-like style, she used typifying examples of assault victims under three years of age, and argued that "sexual abuse of children is the last remaining component of the maltreatment syndrome in children that has yet to be faced head-on" (Sgroi 1975: 19). She called on professionals working with children to admit that molestation happens and to overcome their reluctance to report suspected cases. Long-time activists like Kempe, associated as well with federally funded demonstration projects, also moved away from the prevailing battered-child model to a more inclusive definition of child abuse.[27] In 1977, for instance, Kempe gave a speech to pediatricians titled "Sexual Abuse, Another Hidden Pediatric Problem" (1978). He was also instrumental, along with other leaders of the child protection movement, in launching the journal *Child Abuse and Neglect* in 1976. This journal became an important outlet for articles reporting on sexual abuse research, which would soon attract an immense amount of interest.

Meanwhile, CAPTA, with an initial four-year appropriation of $85 million, swelled the ranks of the child protection industry even more dramatically. It created the National Center on Child Abuse and Neglect (NCCAN) within the Children's Bureau of DHEW. NCCAN was mandated to compile an annual report of current research and to conduct research into the causes, prevention, treatment, and national incidence of all forms of child maltreatment. Further, it was charged with funding treatment and prevention programs. Over the four years after its creation, virtually every state broadened its child abuse reporting laws to satisfy the funding eligibility requirements of NCCAN. In the process, the state laws that had not already been changed came to include sexual abuse in their child abuse and neglect definitions, and to focus, like CAPTA, on prevention and on treatment not just of the abusive parent but of the entire family unit (Weisberg 1984: 44). With its grant money, NCCAN initially funded four major treatment centers to develop incest programs, the best known of which was Giarretto's CSATP.[28] It also began disseminating research findings on sexual abuse and program material in 1976,[29] and in 1980 it began to fund demonstration projects in sexual abuse prevention for children. These projects, heavily feminist in orientation, were aimed at empowering children by teaching them prevention techniques. With the help of NCCAN funding, they spread rapidly across the United States in the early 1980s (Plummer 1986).[30]

The state and CAPTA reporting requirements, which made it a criminal offense for professionals working with children and public officials not to report suspected cases of child sexual abuse, led to a rapid increase in the number of reported cases (Berrick and Gilbert 1991). Due to the mandatory reporting legislation, noted Justice and Justice in 1979, "the size of the incest problem is slowly becoming better known" (15). In addition to estimates of the national incidence of sexual abuse based on official reports,[31] child advocates also drew estimates from extrapolations of local areas, such as the New York study by De Francis and the experience of Giarretto in Santa Clara County. However, advocates asserted that even the highest of these extrapolations, based on reported cases, could represent no more than the "tip of the iceberg." The expectation of a large hidden incidence of abuse was in part due to the belief that because of social stigma, most cases went unreported. In itself, of course, this belief was nothing new. But given the view of child advocates since De Francis that most sexual abuse was perpetrated by family members and acquaintances, and the view since Giarretto that it occurred as much in middle- and higher- as in lower-class families, nonreporting took on a heightened significance. Social scientists had long recognized that crimes that took place within the family, including incest, were much less likely to be reported than those committed by strangers. They also recognized that middle- and upper-class families were much better than lower-class families at shielding themselves from any kind of public scrutiny. If sexual abuse was concentrated in the family and was as prevalent in other classes as it was among the poor, then reported cases could be expected to be an especially poor indicator of the total incidence of the problem. The iceberg below the tip was significant indeed.

In fact, by the late 1970s, child protection advocates were coming to believe that sexual abuse, as De Francis had argued earlier, was "a problem of immense proportions." As noted earlier, the 1977 Ellen Weber article in *Ms.* magazine opened with the words, "One girl out of every four in the United States will be sexually abused in some way before she reaches the age of 18." Similarly, a 1978 book by a psychotherapist, which went through many printings, opened with the estimate that there were at least ten million incest victims in the United States (Forward and Buck 1978: 2). While movement professionals were not yet making such estimates (that would come in the 1980s), physical abuse—the issue that had galvanized the movement—was rapidly being displaced by the growing concern with sexual abuse. Since sexual abuse seldom involved any physical injury, the influence of medical doctors continued to erode. Amid the outpouring of commentary, Kempe's labeling of sexual abuse as a "pediatric problem" went virtually unnoticed.

Child Victim and Child Abuser

In the child protection movement, the new class of human behavior known as sexual abuse was constructed by extending the class of acts known as child abuse. The definitions of victim and offender fashioned for the physical abuse category therefore provided the models for the definitions of the sexual abuse victim and offender, and the treatment models for sexual abuse cases were modeled on those for physical abuse. Through this extension process, the movement reframed the categories of sexual molestation, victim, and offender in ways that sharply varied from the older psychiatric and legal approaches.

The article by Kempe and his colleagues (1962) on the battered-child syndrome set the basic framework for the new conceptualization of the child victim. The "battered child" was an unambiguously pure victim. Given the child victim's young age (under three), and serious (or fatal) and typically repeated physical injury, no question of legitimate punishment or parental authority clouded its status. The child was harmed by forces completely outside its control and was more sympathy-worthy for being injured by the very people responsible for its well-being. While Kempe and his colleagues noted that abuse can happen to children of any age, their focus on the beating and torturing of infants created an enduring archetype of the innocent and harmed victim. The connection between abuse and child innocence and harm was mutually reinforcing and mutually implicative. Nothing that an infant does deserves a severe physical beating, and so nothing that a child of any age does deserves any kind of "abuse." No sooner was the Kempe team bringing public attention to battered babies than the age of victims was rising, and the range and seriousness of physical harm broadening. The child welfare advocates soon added "neglect," their general and diffuse category of maltreatment, followed in the early 1970s with the specific categories of emotional abuse and sexual abuse. Each of these extensions was presented as a subclass of child abuse or child abuse and neglect, and raised almost no opposition.[32] Since all were kinds of the same thing, all children involved were innocent and sympathy-worthy victims and, in an important sense, equally so. Questions of the child's behavior, so irrelevant to the case of battered babies, were made irrelevant in all cases—including sexual abuse—grouped together under the same kind.[33]

Further, like baby battering, each type of behavior labeled child abuse came to share the implication of serious harm to the child, in both the near and longer term. Kempe and his colleagues not only identified immediate (and sometimes permanent) physical harm in battered children, but hypothesized long-term psychological harm as well. Battering, they argued, if somewhat indirectly, plants the seeds for aggressive and violent behavior in later years. Battered children, in short, very often grow up to be battering parents. As additional behaviors were added to the child abuse category, each was described following a similar pattern of immediate harm and long-term consequences. As this process took place, emotional and developmental harm came to overshadow physical harm as the principal cause of concern, even in physical abuse cases. When Helfer and Kempe dropped the term *battered child* in the mid-1970s, for example, they argued that they were doing so because the "most devastating" aspect of abuse, apart from permanent physical injury or fatality, was its "adverse effects on the developmental process and the child's emotional well-being" (Helfer and Kempe 1976: xix). All the behaviors grouped in the category of child abuse, then, implied harm to the child, a harm that was expected to grow more problematic over time if not identified and properly treated.[34] Sexual abuse was no exception.

In order to understand what is new here with regard to molestation victims, we need to recognize how the construction of the child abuse category radically extended the definition of incest. Although the domain of child abuse was expanded in the 1980s to include stranger perpetrators—abducting children (running kiddie porn rings, hiding razor blades in Halloween candy, and so on [see Best 1990; Nathan 1991]) and institutions outside the family (day care centers, foster homes, schools, and churches), in the 1960s and 1970s the emphasis was on the family.[35] Child abuse was a name for things that parents, grandparents, stepparents, parent surrogates, or relatives did to their own children, grandchildren, nieces, and so on. When sexual abuse was added, any kind of sexual touch or arousal (later, this would broaden still further) was defined as such a "thing," and these were now types of the same category of behavior. They were instances of sexual abuse, and since family members were involved, they came to be defined as instances of incest. As noted in the last chapter, the traditional definition of incest was sexual intercourse (or marriage) within forbidden degrees of kinship. With the creation of the category of child abuse and its subcategory of sexual abuse, incest was completely redefined. It became any sexual activity, touch or nontouch ("psychological incest"), between parents, parent surrogates, or older siblings and their children (or siblings). Incest was the subset of sexual abuse acts within the nuclear or extended family.

The redefinition of incest obviously had a powerful impact on the perception of its incidence, but my concern here is the impact the redefinition had on the question of victim harm. Extending the concept of incest meant that all manner of different acts now shared the horror of incest and its implication of serious harm to the child-participant. Child advocates drew from the older literature on incest (narrowly defined) to confirm the conviction that incest (broadly defined) was variously damaging to the child, both in the immediate and longer term. In addition, researchers interviewing various delinquent and deviant individuals, including prostitutes, runaways, drug addicts, and child abusers, reported that substantial percentages of these people had been victims of incest and other sexual abuse (see, for example, the review in MacFarlane 1978; Weber 1977). Such findings were not exactly new. A vice commission in Chicago reported as early as 1911, for example, that nearly half of the delinquent girls brought before the Juvenile Court were incest victims (see studies in Weinberg 1955: 147–48). But in the 1970s these correlations, interpreted as indicating that the delinquent or deviant behavior was the result of the sexual experience or, in the case of runaways, the result of fleeing from it, were fit into a larger picture. They added evidence to the growing belief that all of the many behaviors grouped together under the category of sexual abuse had deleterious consequences (not necessarily equally so) for the victims, including an increased susceptibility to being sexually exploited by others (e.g., Forward and Buck 1978; Giarretto 1976a; Weber 1977). Because a variety of different sexual experiences were reported, such correlations also added to the conviction that sexual abuse was a coherent—indeed, *scientific*—category.

The early physical abuse model shaped not only the definition of the sexual abuse victim but that of the sexual offender. Although their hospital survey did not deal with the parents, Kempe and his colleagues (Kempe et al. 1962) offered some observations on the abusers based on the scant literature that had already emerged. Child-beaters, they reported, displayed a variety of character defects, with some described as psychopathic or sociopathic personalities. Not all, however, had such serious problems, nor were all child abusers from the lower classes. Some had a good education and a stable financial and social background. Still, they noted, in these cases too, some "defect in character structure" would appear to be present "which allows aggressive impulses to be expressed too freely" (Kempe et al. 1962: 106). If there was a common factor among abusing parents, the literature suggested, it was that they had been subjected to similar abuse themselves in childhood. Psychologically, abusers were acting out of identification with a violent parent.

In its basic outlines, this profile proved to be remarkably stable. In the years following 1962, the knowledge about the category of persons lumped together as child abusers would remain fixed on psychological explanations for their behavior. Resisting the recurring suggestion that child abuse was a social-structural problem, most movement advocates argued that child abuse was not class-linked and that abusers were simply troubled people repeating the patterns they saw and experienced as children (see the review in Spinetta and Rigler 1972). Jolly K., for instance, the pseudonymous founder of Parents Anonymous (PA), a self-help group for abusive—including sexually abusive—parents, made this case forcefully at both the Senate and House CAPTA hearings. Claiming that PA had worked with "well over" four thousand parents, she told the Senate committee that the "average parent" in her group was middle class, and that 99 percent "have been abused themselves as children."[36] This typification came to be known as the "cycle of abuse" doctrine.

The psychological framing of physical child abusers had several important consequences for the characterization of sexual abusers. By specifying psychological root causes, it helped to establish the conviction that a child abuser was a particular kind of person who willfully inflicted harm on children—a conviction that carried over to sexual abusers, though different psychological causes were sometimes postulated. Because both physical and sexual abusers were of the same "child-harming species" (Hacking 1992: 198), all were equally worthy of condemnation. At the same time, the cycle of abuse doctrine reinforced the idea that child abusers—and this came to include sexual abusers—were suffering from a syndrome, further solidifying the individualization of the problem and the removal of social-structural issues, like the conditions of poverty, from causal considerations. Given that their behavior flowed from childhood deprivations (not, say, maliciousness), therapy rather than punishment was also indicated—a perspective, not coincidentally, that meshed nicely with the nonpunitive approach of child-welfare services. Moreover, after 1962, child advocates would typically argue that less than 10 percent of abusers were seriously mentally ill; thus, the prognosis for helping the rest and keeping families together was believed to be good (Kempe and Helfer 1972: xii).[37] This view carried over to sexual abusers.

The psychological conceptualization of the etiology of the battered child syndrome drew child advocates toward family-systems orientations and to Giarretto's CSATP. Somewhat inconsistently, the early hospital-based treatment centers, such as Kempe's in Denver, did emphasize securing social services for families needing help. At the same time, however, they also emphasized defects in the character or personality of the parents, perhaps exacerbated by added stress, the possibility of spousal collusion, and the need of the whole family for psychological help. The understanding of the consequences of abuse for the child shifted from an early focus on physical effects to a broader concern with emotional and developmental effects. So, likewise, did the cause of the harm shift from a focus on the parents' physical treatment of the child to a concern with broader dysfunctions in the family, of which the physical injury of the child was but one expression. Consequently, at the model Denver Center and in other programs, treatment for parents focused broadly on working through their own negative parenting experience, bolstering their self-esteem, dealing with marital conflicts, and teaching new skills and life-rearrangements to enhance their life experience, reduce stress reproducing situations, and improve their child care. Group therapy and the use of self-help groups such as Parents Anonymous were sometimes suggested as an additional modality of treatment, and some protective service departments began making referrals to PA.

Given the concern with the dysfunctional family, treatment for the child victim (and siblings) went beyond any needed medical intervention to a larger concern with developmental and psychological problems. These included problems with basic trust, social withdrawal or acting out, low self-esteem, and perhaps feelings of being exploited. Depending on the age and circumstances of children, a variety of treatment modalities were recommended, including traditional types of psychotherapy, special school-based programs, training for foster parents, and residential treatment programs. Further, in order to help the child as well as improve family relationships, family therapy was sometimes recommended.[38] What evolved, then, is a treatment model for physical abuse that shared many of the same psychological and treatment emphases of the CSATP model for sexual abuse.

In fact, as the child protection movement discovered the "last frontier," it discovered Giarretto (and vice versa) and began to promote the CSATP model. Giarretto's first major publication on the CSATP, for instance, was in a book by Helfer and Kempe (Giarretto 1976a), and was reprinted in *Child Abuse and Neglect* in 1977. Thereafter the CSATP was regularly featured in child protection publications and eventually began to receive NCCAN funding. A family-systems perspective on treatment became a major point of intersection between the CSATP, other programs modeled on it, and the child protection movement.

In terms of the framing of victim and abuser categories, the physical child abuse model also had another important influence on the way the child protection movement approached sexual abuse. From the beginning, physical child abuse was found to be practiced by both men and women, and perhaps somewhat more by women (e.g., Gil 1970), and on both boy and girl children (studies variously found more boys, more girls, and a rough gender equality among abused children—see the review in Parton 1985: 136). When sexual abuse was added to the child abuse category, movement advocates retained a theoretically gender-neutral approach. Like the CSATP, they saw sexual abuse as a product of dysfunctional family dynamics. However, De Francis had reported from the AHA study that men overwhelmingly outnumbered women as sexual offenders, and that girls heavily outnumbered boys as victims (1969). While the child protection movement did not emphasize this finding, another social movement, concerned in part with gender inequality, did (see, for example, NOW 1976; Rush 1974). In fact, the antirape movement took the male-female disparities between offenders and between victims as the starting point for its theorizing about rape and, by extension, sexual abuse. In the next chapter I continue tracing the emergence of the new collective story by turning to the antirape movement and its influence on the emerging definition of sexual abuse.

CHAPTER THREE

Constructing Sexual Abuse 2
The Antirape Movement and Victim Activists

At the conclusion of Florence Rush's presentation to the New York Radical Feminists' rape conference on April 17, 1971, which I briefly described in chapter 1, the assembled crowd erupted in a standing ovation. One of those clapping and cheering that day was Susan Brownmiller, an NYRF member and an organizer of the conference. She had come to the conference on crutches, having, ironically enough, sprained her ankle in the act of kicking a man who had goosed her while she was handing out flyers for the conference. After Rush's talk, she "was hopping around in high gear for the rest of the day" (Brownmiller 1999: 204). April 17 was a Saturday. By Monday morning, Brownmiller was in the office of a literary agent with a four-page proposal for a book on rape. Though originally she thought she could deliver the manuscript in a year, in fact it took four, and in October 1975 *Against Our Will: Men, Women, and Rape* was published. It was an instant bestseller.

The cofounder of New York Radical Feminists, Shulamith Firestone had, in her 1970 book *The Dialectic of Sex,* called on feminists to "include the oppression of children" in their revolutionary program. Then came Florence Rush, equipped with the De Francis findings and a radical feminist framework. As rape was a political act, she argued at the 1971 rape conference, so the sexual abuse of girls, by instilling fear, guilt, and shame, also socializes them to accept a subordinate role. Rush urged feminists to make the issue of child sexual abuse part of their analysis and to "think of children's liberation as being the same as women's liberation" (Rush 1974: 74). After the rape conference, Rush became friends with and passed along her research materials to Susan Brownmiller, who used them in *Against Our Will.* Brownmiller argued that the "unholy silence" that prevents the true incidence and meaning of the "interfamily sexual abuse of children" from being appraised is rooted in the "same patriarchal philosophy of sexual private property" that determined male attitudes toward rape of adult women (Brownmiller 1975: 281). She rejected the term *incest* because it "implies mutuality" and suggested instead "father-rape," a term that specified the preferred categorization. Although "father-rape" never caught on broadly (see below), the classifying of sexual offenses within the category of rape would have enduring consequences. As with adult rape, the attack on any notion of "mutuality" would be the driving force behind the moral critique of the old victim and offender constructions and the framing of new ones.

Scholars studying claims-making about new social problems have observed that once initial claims have been established on the social policy agenda, the boundaries of the problem often begin to extend to include new, more peripheral issues. Sociologist Joel Best calls this process "domain expansion" and notes that it takes the form of "[new problem] X is really a type of [established problem] Y" and therefore requires the responses and reactions already deemed appropriate for Y (1990: 66). He argues that domain expansion has important rhetorical benefits, allowing claims-makers to build new claims on an established foundation, delay controversy over peripheral issues, and keep a problem alive when media attention inevitably declines. Clearly, for the child protection movement, sexual abuse was an expansion of the domain of physical child abuse, and this categorization afforded claims-makers the benefits that Best identifies. More important for my purposes, the insertion of sexual offenses into the child abuse framework also had *consequences:* It patterned the way that the interconnected categories of sexual offender and victim were constructed and so warranted corresponding treatment approaches.

In just the same manner, when the antirape movement began to make claims about sexual abuse in the 1970s, it did so by expanding the domain of a more established social problem, with consequences for the characterization of offender and victim and for subsequent treatment models. Although antirape advocates took the concept of "sexual abuse" from the child protection movement, their early efforts were to set the problem in the framework of rape, not physical child abuse. In this framework, the offender was characterized very differently, affecting the way that victim harm was conceptualized and hence victim treatments as well. I begin, therefore, by considering the antirape movement and its definition of rape, and then discuss how this problem domain was extended to include sexual abuse.

THE ANTIRAPE MOVEMENT

As 1962 was for child abuse, 1971 was the watershed year for the emergence of rape as a social problem. Discussions of rape had been taking place quietly in feminist consciousness-raising groups earlier, but in 1971 these discussions went public. The first rape "speakout" at which women publicly shared their rape experiences was held by the New York Radical Feminists in January, and was followed by the rape conference in April (Connell and Wilson 1974).[1] In that year, feminist writer Germaine Greer interviewed a rape victim on ABC-TV, perhaps the first time rape had been covered in such a way by network television. A number of feminist antirape groups were also formed in the United States in 1971, such as Women Against Rape in Detroit, which, within just months of its founding, wrote, published, and widely distributed *Stop Rape*, one of the first advice handbooks. These groups soon attracted considerable media attention. In September 1971, *Ramparts* magazine published "Rape: The All-American Crime," by Susan Griffin, a founder of Bay Area Women Against Rape. Though earlier feminist writings made passing mention of rape, this widely read article was the precursor for the feminist analysis of forcible rape. Many other articles also appeared in general circulation magazines, the feminist press, law journals, and the research literature in 1971 (see reviews in Fogarty 1977; Mathews 1974). Additionally, Menachem Amir's *Patterns in Forcible Rape* was published in 1971. This sociological study, which moved away from the older focus on the pathology of rapists and stressed violence rather than passion as the dynamic of rape, heavily influenced the emerging feminist typifications of the rape offender (including Griffin's). Its findings were also widely used to create "fact and myth" sheets about rape and rapists that were distributed as part of antirape consciousness raising campaigns.

After 1971, the pace of antirape activism accelerated dramatically The first rape crisis centers were founded in Berkeley, California, and, shortly thereafter, in Washington, DC, in 1972 (Largen 1981; Wasserman 1973). Similar groups were formed about the same time in many other cities, including Boston, Detroit, New York, Los Angeles, Philadelphia, and Seattle (Csida and Csida 1974). The Washington, DC, crisis center, started by some ten women, most of them rape victims, began with an emergency telephone number for victims (333-RAPE) and gradually grew into a national information clearinghouse. Their forty-page booklet, "How to Start a Rape Crisis Center," published in 1972, was widely distributed, and the number of rape crisis centers mushroomed across the United States. In their simplest form, these centers provided an emergency phone line. In larger cities and university towns, they came to include self-defense courses, rape prevention seminars, the development and distribution of educational materials, and various post-rape services, such as escorting victims to the hospital or police, offering legal aid and medical information, and providing counseling services and support groups. By early 1973, the Washington crisis center was distributing a newsletter nationally. The newsletter was taken over by a related group, the Feminist Alliance Against Rape, formed in 1974, and became the sounding board for the burgeoning national movement. In 1974, the Law Enforcement Assistance Administration, a branch of the Justice Department, began offering grants for rape crisis services (Cimons 1974; Schechter 1982).[2] By late 1976, there were more than four hundred rape crisis centers throughout the nation (Largen 1981).

In addition to the crisis centers, many rape task forces were created in order to promote antirape activism and lobbying. The National Organization for Women (NOW), for instance, organized a national task-force on rape in 1973 as well as more than three hundred local rape task forces and state coalitions by 1976 (Largen 1981). By the height of the movement in 1976, according to Schechter, there were "approximately 1,500 separate projects—task forces, study groups, crisis centers, 'doing something about rape'" (1982: 39). Beyond victim services and consciousness-raising efforts, antirape groups pressured both police and hospitals to treat victims more sensitively.[3] Some early feminist groups, frustrated with the seeming ease with which rapists escaped prosecution, even experimented with group confrontational tactics against accused men as a way to exert community control over their behavior.[4] Antirape groups also won significant reforms of rape laws in many states, including modification or elimination of corroborating evidence requirements and restrictions on questions about the prosecuting woman's prior sex life (Rose 1977a).[5] Intensive lobbying from feminist groups, especially NOW, also led to the creation of the National Center for the Prevention and Control of Rape within the National Institute of Mental Health (NIMH) in 1975 (Largen 1976: 72). The center functioned as a clearinghouse and funding source for rape research, with an initial budget of $7 million for 1975 and $10 million for 1976 (Gager and Schurr 1976: 203). A stream of money began to flow into antirape projects,[6] and eventually into child sexual abuse research as well (e.g., Herman 1981; Russell 1986).

As already suggested, activists with a feminist orientation sponsored many of the new antirape and victim-support initiatives.[7] The Center for Rape Concern, founded in 1970 at the Philadelphia General Hospital, is one of the important exceptions.[8] The center was an outgrowth of a group psychotherapy program for probationed sex offenders begun at the hospital in 1955. In addition to providing medical and mental health services to rape victims, the Philadelphia center organized a rape victim study in 1972 with funding from NIMH to consider the social and psychological effects of rape and involvement with the criminal justice system on the victim. This multi-year study led to a variety of publications in the mid-1970s, including several articles on child victims by the center's director and founder, Joseph Peters (e.g., Peters 1973, 1974, 1976). One of these articles in particular, "Children Who Are Victims of Sexual Assault and the Psychology of Offenders," was especially influential in feminist circles, shaping their understanding of the victim and their critique of the older psychiatric approaches to rape.

Another important exception is the Victim Counseling Program at the Boston City Hospital, started in July 1972 by two Boston College professors: Ann Wolbert Burgess, a psychiatric nurse, and Lynda Lytle Holmstrom, a sociologist.[9] From the beginning, their objective was both to start a counseling program and to study the problems that rape victims experience. When a request for their services came from the hospital's pediatric walk-in clinic, the scope of the program and the study expanded to include child victims of rape, attempted rape, and sexual molestation. Beginning in 1973, with an article in the *American Journal of Nursing*, these two scholars produced a steady stream of publications that were influential for both the antirape and child protection movements' constructions of sexual abuse as a social problem. The most important of these was an often-reprinted article, "Rape Trauma Syndrome" (Burgess and Holmstrom 1974a). This trauma syndrome, as I explain in chapter 4, had a significant impact on the way that the harm of child sexual abuse came to be conceptualized.

While feminists were not the only voices raising concerns about forcible rape, they were the most active and vocal claims-makers. Groups and individuals adopting a feminist perspective framed the ideology of the movement (Rose 1977a). The main outlines of this ideology were already present in the 1971 article by Griffin, the papers presented at the NYRF rape conference, and the pamphlets distributed by various local antirape crisis centers and groups. But the major statement came in 1975, with the publication of Susan Brownmiller's *Against Our Will*. Reviewing this book alongside the earlier statements and the other major volumes that appeared in the mid-1970s, including Medea and Thompson (1974), Gager and Schurr (1976), and Russell (1975), reveals many differences. There are differences in how broadly rape is defined (though all go well beyond the legal definition of forcible penetration), for instance, and in interpretations of the nexus of rape and race. Yet, with regard to the framing of the victim and offender categories, there is an important sameness. In their general outlines, these constructions provided the model for the movement's emergent perspective on sexual abuse.

The antirape movement's ideology, formulated to change attitudes toward forcible rape and assumptions about the circumstances surrounding the offense, centered on exposing victim-blaming and countering it. Antirape activists argued that "blaming the victim," the phrase popularized and defined as an ideology by William Ryan (1971), involved blaming women for the offense, humiliating and "revictimizing" them when they sought help, and not believing or silencing them when they tried to speak out. To expose a pattern of cruelty and indifference to the rape victim, activists sought to document it historically, to identify it in social institutions and popular attitudes, and to encourage victims to "speak the unspoken" by giving testimony about their experience. They argued that victim-blaming was legitimated by often-conflicting characterizations of the victim that were in fact pernicious prejudices and "deadly male myths" (Brownmiller 1975: 312). Among the myths were the following: no woman could be raped against her will (forcible rape does not exist); women cause rape by the way they walk, talk, or dress; women fantasize about rape and want to be raped; a woman's "no" to sexual overtures often means "yes"; only "bad girls"—that is, the sexually promiscuous—get raped; and many women invent stories of rape out of regret or spite. Activists argued that these myths, constituting an "ideology of rape," were not only held by most men but internalized by many women as well, including rape victims, who often blamed themselves or even failed to recognize that they had been raped. Further, activists characterized the psychoanalytic literature and the sexual offender studies as based on the same myths, on the same underlying notion that if a woman is raped, it is because she "asked for it."[10]

In the effort to shift any hint of blame from victims of rape, activists defined rape as a violent crime, rather than a sexual one. They argued that the "true meaning" of rape is "male domination over women by force" (Brownmiller 1975: 209). The "myths" about the rapist paint him as a sexually frustrated male acting out of pent-up desires, or a lustful male reacting to a provocative woman, or a sexual psychopath acting out of perverted and unquenchable desires. But any focus on sexual motives, activists argued, implicitly shifts blame to the woman. If the rapist is acting out of sexual arousal toward the victim, then the victim must have done something, inadvertently or by choice, to stimulate this desire, and thus might be seen as bearing some responsibility for the rape and mitigating the offender's guilt. To affix blame solely on the male, therefore, activists argued that the great majority of rapists act not out of sexual desire but out of hostility and contempt for all women. Sex is merely the weapon by which they degrade. Any notion of "victim-precipitation" of rape, the criminological term used by Amir (1971) to define contributory behavior, is therefore just another instance of the doctrine that "women bring rape upon themselves" (Gager and Schurr 1976: 26).

Carrying the argument further, activists claimed that rape is not some special, isolated aberration, but rather the "end of a continuum of male-aggressive, female-passive patterns" in society (Medea and Thompson 1974: 11). Setting rape in this larger framework reinforced the conclusion that rape victims are attacked for no other reason than that they are vulnerable. Rape, activists argued, is an act by which a male demonstrates to a female that she is conquered by his superior strength and power (Brownmiller 1975: 49). As such, they continued, it is an expression of the broader pattern of male domination and in fact serves that domination by subjecting all women to an insidious fear and to constraints on their freedom. In this sense, for these activists, "rape victims are Everywoman" (Gager and Schurr 1976: 4), and rape is a "political act" of oppression and social control to keep women in their "place."[11] Not all men rape, yet rape occurs, they maintained, because of the social acceptance of degrading and depersonalizing attitudes toward women. These attitudes are socialized into women, who are taught that they are naturally passive and vulnerable, and into men, who are taught that they are naturally aggressive and their power over women is a natural right. Granted, activists argued, rape is an extreme act, but it is rooted in, and is an inevitable by-product of, deeply embedded cultural notions of masculinity and male prerogative. It is but the brutal end of a long continuum of male "power trips" taken at women's expense. Even the harsh penalties meted out to rape offenders, activists charged, reflect men's concern with the violation of their "property" rather than with justice for the victim. All such male protection, in their view, springs from the same antifemale attitude as rape.

In the antirape movement framing, rape involves a victim in the purest sense and a victimizer category that is nearly as absolute. In the power framework, all characteristics of the victim and the victim's circumstances, except vulnerability, are ruled irrelevant. And vulnerability is not the victim's fault: Virtually everything in society conditions her to that role. (Activists, incidentally, sought to make rape a gender-neutral crime, and with some success, thus avoiding the strict equation of vulnerability with women.) Further, because rape in this framework is an act of aggression that is fundamentally caused by social forces rather than individual perversion, the relevance of particular victim characteristics is even further removed. In no sense, then, in movement theory, are victims implicated in the production of their victimization. On the other hand, offenders cannot be construed as victims in any sense. Contrary to earlier characterizations of the sexual offender, activists emphasized the basic "normality" of the rapist—that he was neither sexually compulsive nor mentally impaired. They cited the Amir (1971) findings especially—that rapists were indistinguishable from other sorts of felons in psychological tests, or that most rapes were planned, not impulse crimes—in support of the characterization of the offender as knowingly and deliberately intending harm. Although in practice the movement focus on the broader constellation of power relations tended to shift concern away from the offender, the point of the power argument was not to reduce his responsibility but to relocate the source of his hostility toward women. Instead of his personality structure or dysfunctional family environment, including all notion of a rejecting or "castrating" mother or wife, activists identified the rapist's hatred as arising from patriarchal society and male socialization. They argued, therefore, that only an end to patriarchy and liberation from all sex roles would end rape. In the meantime, though, they also recommended vigorous criminal sanctions against the individual offender—including husband offenders, who were then exempt from rape laws—as a means of deterring future rapes and reinforcing public standards against rape. In some cases, they also called for the direct confrontation and public humiliation of rapists. Blame for rape, they argued, belonged *both* with the offender and with the society that created him.

Following from the definition of rape as an act of power, the experience of the victim was conceived as one of powerlessness, a denial of self-determination. In their grassroots efforts on behalf of rape victims—such as the rape crisis centers, which were originally organized outside the confines of the mental health system—activists, therefore, emphasized personal empowerment and the related strategy of "self-help." At a minimum, empowerment meant validating a rape victim's personal experience by listening to and believing her story, by affirming her inner strength and sanity, and by helping her to see that her experience was not self-caused, and thus the appropriate reaction was "healthy anger," not self-blame or self-doubt. Depending on the setting, empowerment could also mean teaching the victim to interpret her experience in terms of the movement's political framework (feminist consciousness-raising), providing her with opportunities to share her experience in support groups or in public and training her in self-defense. Similarly, self-help, according to the handbook *How to Start a Rape Crisis Center,* "returns to the woman power over her life—something she lost to some extent when she was raped" (quoted in Wasserman 1973: 21). Victim services were offered, for instance, but none were mandated. Instead, counselors encouraged victims to retain control over all decisions affecting their lives and to initiate their own adjustments. In this and other ways, victims were encouraged to see themselves as "experts about their own lives," to define their own experience, and to "learn to know their strength" for change and growth (Schechter 1982: 109).

In the context of the longer-term goal of sex-role liberation, the movement used the personal empowerment and self-help strategies as elements of a near-term effort to counter rape by changing the way women thought about themselves. Women must, activists argued, cease to "play the victim." That meant decreasing their vulnerability by resisting any sex-role socialization to be passive and submissive, by overcoming their fear of confrontation, by refusing to feel responsible for male problems or to hide them, by becoming prepared to defend themselves, and by learning to stand up for their rights. The incidence of rape could be decreased if women were stronger, physically and mentally, and more prepared to fight back. And, because women would be rejecting their sex roles, steps toward the larger liberationist goal would also be underway. The movement ideal for helping the rape victim adjust to her experience, then, was not an effort to return her to a personal *status quo ante;* it was to change her in light of other and larger goals of the movement. While changing individuals was not a sufficient condition for ending male domination, it was important and necessary. The strategies of empowerment and self-help were aimed to serve both purposes.

The early focus of the antirape movement was principally on the forcible rape of adult women. However, a concern with the sexual molestation of children emerged as early as 1971 and was given at least passing attention in much of the early antirape literature. A California chapter of NOW formed a Child Sexual Abuse Task Force in 1972 (NOW 1976). Rape crisis centers also dealt with child victims. About half of the rape victims encountered by the hospital-based program organized in Philadelphia by Women Organized Against Rape, for instance, were children (Gager and Schurr 1976: 46). As the movement theorized rape, then, the rape and sexual molestation of children were also in view. In time, many activists would come to prefer the more encompassing term "sexual assault" over rape, but whichever label was used, rape, as conceptualized in these early years, was the category in which sexual offenses, whether against young or old, were classified.

Sexual Abuse as Rape

As with rape, the feminist analysis of child sexual molestation advanced a new male-power interpretation by characterizing existing psychiatric interpretations as male-biased blame-shifting. Florence Rush had already initiated this strategy during her address at the 1971 NYRF rape conference, attacking both psychoanalytic and family-systems approaches to sexual molestation and incest for the way they characterized the victim and the non-perpetrator mother. While feminists would assail other social institutions—including the legal system, which they argued treated children, like women, as the property of men—the victim-blaming critique in subsequent years remained centered on psychiatry. This locus was consistent with the larger preoccupations of feminism from virtually its advent in the mid-1960s (Herman 1995: chap. 10). Feminists condemned psychology for the way it "constructs the female" (Naomi Weisstein's famous phrase) and characterized psychiatry as an institution heavily implicated in women's subordination (e.g., Chesler 1972). A concern with psychiatry also played a central role in previous feminist theorizing on rape and domestic battery. In the case of sexual abuse, psychiatry was not only indicted for blame-shifting but for precipitating a cover-up by knowingly suppressing evidence of male maltreatment of children.[12]

Ironically, feminist activists concerned with sexual molestation took part of their critique from family therapists and psychoanalysts, who were the first to raise questions about Freud's psychologization of some memories of sexual seductions as wish-fulfillment and defenses. As discussed in chapter 2, family therapists directly challenged the psychoanalytic emphasis on the unconscious and oedipal conflicts, and were important voices in drawing psychiatric concern to sexual molestations as actual life events. Indeed, psychoanalyst Joseph Peters was the most influential early critic of "Freud and his followers" for "oversubscrib[ing] to the theory of childhood fantasy" and overlooking actual sexual victimization incidents (1976: 401). This oversubscription, Peters argued, was rooted in "cultural and personal" rather than scientific factors, and resulted in analysts allowing patients with childhood sexual traumas to continue to "repress emotionally significant, pathogenic facts" (1976: 402). Feminist writers incorporated this critique into their more sweeping moral criticism of psychoanalysis as victim-blaming, and turned similar moral criticism back on family therapy as well.

Feminist activists accused psychoanalysts and family therapists of blaming the victims of all forms of child molestation in just the ways they had defined victim-blaming in the matter of rape. Child victims, too, they argued, were disbelieved and silenced, were blamed for the offense, and were revictimized when they sought help. All of these forms of hostility to the victim began, activists asserted, when Freud "discarded" (Rush 1980: 91) his seduction theory[13]—the theory, as we saw in the last chapter, that the etiology of the psychoneuroses was to be found in early childhood sexual experience. The key theorist here was again Florence Rush, who, in an influential 1977 article and even more influential 1980 book, extended the concerns raised by Peters into a more general charge of a "Freudian cover-up" (Armstrong 1978; Butler 1980; see also Herman and Hirschman 1977; Herman 1981; Rush 1977, 1980).[14] In its bare outlines, this account held that Freud originally listened to each of his female patients tell of their sexual molestation (often at the hands of their fathers) and so came to reluctantly recognize the traumatic significance of their experiences and to formulate his seduction theory. However, the male psychiatric establishment, which viewed hysteria as hereditary, ridiculed him, and he himself had trouble accepting the idea of the father as seducer—even altering the molester's identity in two of his original cases—and the notion that "perverted acts against children were so general" (Freud, quoted in Herman and Hirschman 1977: 737). Meanwhile, based on self-analysis of his inner struggles with a "death wish" toward his father, Freud began to suspect that the stories he had been told by his patients of fathers as seducers were in fact "defensive fictions" arising from unconscious processes in early childhood of love and erotic desire toward the opposite-sex parent and jealousy toward the same-sex parent. These unconscious processes he labeled the oedipal complex, and theorized that the origin of psychoneuroses was to be found in the repression of the conflicting desires and fears of this period. With the oedipal theory, activists charged, Freud eliminated the seduction theory, transforming his female patients' accounts into seduction wishes fulfilled through fantasy and fictitious stories. This move, they argued, served to deny the reality of child molestation within the family and thus abetted its perpetuation. It began what one prominent feminist critic would later dub the "age of denied abuse" (Armstrong 1982: 112).

Paradoxically, the feminist attack on Freud's rejection/revision of the seduction theory was not premised on the belief that the theory was true. Rush did not believe that *all* female neuroses were caused by childhood sexual seductions, nor did other feminists who accepted the cover-up thesis (e.g., Miller 1984: 41). They did believe that childhood sexual molestation could cause persisting psychological difficulties, but so did Freud *after* he had theorized the oedipal complex (Freud 1962b: 168). For Rush and other activists, the problem was not so much in the rejection of the seduction theory per se but in the effects they saw following from it. Besides denying the extent of child molestation, these effects were of two kinds. The oedipal theory, they argued, provided a long-standing rationale for later analysts to question and dismiss patients' memories of actual molestation incidents, thus revictimizing them by isolating them and suggesting they were deluded. With most therapists, they charged, women and children could not speak the truth about their experience and received not empathy or protection but speculative treatments. Secondly, these writers saw in the shift to the oedipal theory a crucial shifting of blame. Rush summarizes the point succinctly: "The seduction theory incriminated incestuous fathers, while the Oedipal theory insisted that seduction was a fantasy, an invention, not a fact—and it incriminated daughters" (Rush 1980: 95). The seduction theory, then, even if only partially accurate, was morally correct because it implicated the father. Oedipal theory, on the other hand, represented a victim-blaming stratagem that reversed the order of blame, vindicating the father and implicating the daughter—a stratagem warmly received by Freud's prominent disciples and effectively institutionalized thereafter.

Critics characterized oedipal theory, so understood, as initiating a broad legacy of antivictim approaches. Even if it was granted that a girl had actually been molested, activists argued, oedipal theory suggested the importance of her personality needs as inclining her toward being molested or even toward seducing—hence, the concepts of the participating or collaborative child and of the provocative and seducing child that were worked out by later theorists in the analytic tradition. Activists typified all such concepts as victim-blaming devices, further examples of the "she asked for it" myth. To illustrate, they routinely cited the same passages from the victim literature, especially Bender and Blau (1937) and Burton (1968), which questioned the psychological innocence of molested children. They added rhetorical force to their victim-blaming critique by connecting the attitudes they described in the analytic tradition with the contemporary molester-defending attitudes of pornographers and a so-called pro-incest lobby of sexual permissivists (DeMott 1980) and pedophiles (Bass and Thornton 1983; Herman 1981; Rush 1980). Some activists also saw the elevated role of desire and fantasy in oedipal theory as a device for devaluing the effects of actual seductions on the child victim, or at least on the girl victim; the few studies of boy victims tended to find serious effects (Rush 1980: 96). More generally, critics cited the victim studies (such as the Kinsey studies) that found minimal or no molestation aftereffects, suggesting that societal reaction may be more harmful than the molestation itself or suggesting that later victim psychological difficulties were probably unrelated, as instances of psychiatric downplaying of victim harm. This downplaying, they argued, was but another form of denial and mitigation of male responsibility. It betrayed a moral judgment against victims, an emotional distancing from them, and a failure to take their side.

To the critique of victim-blaming in psychoanalysis, some feminist theorists added an equally harsh condemnation of the family-systems approaches to incest (Armstrong 1978; Butler 1978, 1980; Chesler 1972; McIntyre 1981; Rush 1974, 1980). Although not accorded the same historical significance, family-systems approaches had been incorporated into psychiatric and social work textbooks (e.g., Henderson 1975) and the child protection movement when feminists began to take on child sexual abuse as an issue; they were, therefore, an important interpretive competitor.[15] Given the goal of locating ideas that might deflect offender responsibility, feminist criticism of family-systems thought centered on the thesis of the interconnectedness of members of the incestuous family. As discussed earlier, one aspect of this thesis, also found in some psychoanalytic reports, concerned the role of the mother. For feminist activists, suggestions of an implicated or colluding mother— effecting a role reversal with the daughter, being frigid or refusing sex with the father, offering the daughter to the father, failing to serve as a restraining agent on the father, denying or defending the spouse on discovery of the incest, having personality deficits, and so on—were expressions of psychiatry's misogynistic attitudes. Rather than recognize the personal difficulties and relative powerlessness these women face, feminists argued, theorists and therapists pathologized mothers for not performing their roles and reinforced the doctrines that women are responsible for the sexual conduct of men ("she drove him to it"), for the emotional climate in the home, and for the protection of children. All such premises in the matter of interfamily molestations and incest, whether wittingly or unwittingly, had powerful blame-shifting consequences. In this view, the offender's culpability was diminished if not effectively denied altogether.

A second aspect of the family interconnectedness thesis rejected by activists concerned the notion of the complicit daughter. As with typifications of the mother, a focus on the child's personality, her passivity, or her keeping of the "family secret" failed to take seriously the child's subordinate and highly controlled social position. They saw all such concerns as diminishing the father-offender's responsibility, another instance of displacing blame to the victim.

Finally, many activists attacked the emphasis in family-treatment models on the maintenance or reconstitution of the family. This emphasis, they argued, failed to put the safety of the child first. Indeed, exploitation was at the heart of the incestuous family, not connectedness, and "male supremacy," rather than the mother, was its cornerstone (McIntyre 1981: 466). Therefore, any effort to address "family pathology" and reunite families that did not address the true pathology (male domination) was bound to continue rather than end exploitation, even if the sexual abuse was discontinued.

Because of its adoption of family-treatment models, the child protection movement also came in for criticism by these feminist writers. Though notions of collusion and complicity played little role, activists challenged a perceived overemphasis in the protection movement on preserving the family. They also criticized the movement's lack of a gender analysis and nonpunitive approach to the offender. The movement's psychological explanations for the offender's behavior, feminists argued, failed to explain the virtual male franchise on the sexual abuse of children, and they allowed the offender himself to be characterized as a type of victim in need of therapy. (Indeed, for this reason, some in the child protection movement sought to avoid the term sexual *abuse*.) In the feminist critique, such a characterization, like similar typifications in the older literature, represented a mitigation of the offender's responsibility and a distraction from the true victim. Combined with the protection movement's optimistic prognosis of offender change, it allowed offenders to escape the consequences of their crimes by simply acquiescing to some therapy. Thus, while sometimes acknowledging a positive role for the child protection movement (especially in securing the inclusion of sexual abuse in the Child Abuse Prevention and Treatment Act) and of Giarretto's CSATP, feminists generally saw themselves as "discovering" sexual abuse and penetrating the "conspiracy of silence" (Butler 1978).Only *their* analysis went far enough in exposing blame-shifting.

As with rape, feminist activists morally reproached existing constructions of victim and offender as providing the conceptual justifications that perpetuated abuse and masked its true nature and incidence. Because sexual molestation was classed in the same category as rape, the activist effort to counter victim and offender definitions followed point-for-point the analysis worked out in the antirape movement. As with rape, theorizing power—not sex—as the crucial dynamic behind child molestations and incest established unequivocally victim innocence and offender intention of harm. The power disparity was most clearly illustrated in the case of a patriarchal father offender, married to a traditional and subservient housewife, victimizing his young daughter, and this incestuous family constellation became the theoretical paradigm. To affix sole blame, activists described the incestuous father not as a sexual or psychological deviant but as a basically normal male acting further along a continuum of socially condoned exploitation. This exploitative behavior, they argued, arises from objectifying and degrading views of women that give men—regardless of other social characteristics, such as economic class—license to treat daughters as their property and to demand their sexual "services" if, and when, they desire them. Like other rapes, the father's sexual actions are an abuse of his position of power, a position even greater than that of other rapists because of his authority over the child and hence his ability to engage in recurring episodes. Like other rapes, feminists argued, father-daughter incest is an inevitable outgrowth of patriarchal culture and hierarchical gender relations that will disappear "only when male supremacy is ended" (Herman and Hirschman 1977: 756). Still, incestuous fathers, like other rapists, were held individually responsible for their actions, and feminists stressed vigorous enforcement of incest and other sexual molestation laws.[16] In the feminist formulation, incestuous fathers and, by extension, other child molesters cannot be construed as victims. They intend harm, they cause harm, and they are to blame.

The father's dominance, combined with female socialization and perhaps her own childhood victimization, also explains failures on the part of a nonoffending mother to protect her daughter (activists noted that many mothers *do* act to protect when the incest becomes known). Such failures do not abate the father's guilt; much less are they the cause of his actions. Rather, they indicate the categorical nature of the father's rule and the physical, emotional, and financial dependence of the mother. Confined and controlled, and taught by society to view her subordination as natural, the mother in many incestuous families is ill-equipped to confront her husband or even side with her daughter. She is caught, in this view, in a double bind between caring for her children and safeguarding the very conditions of her existence.

The daughter, meanwhile, is truly a pure victim. Given the father's complete dominance, any question of "mutuality," as Brownmiller put it, any question of the child's initiation, cooperation, or consent is eliminated. By definition, like the adult rape victim, the child is always coerced; she is always abused. In the case of the incest victim, however, the coercion is more psychological and emotional than physical. The father's authoritarian position and the daughter's virtual entrapment mean that physical force is seldom necessary; typically it need only be threatened or used as a last resort to maintain the child's silence. Further, as with rape, the feminist characterization of incest as a pervasive social pattern rather than as an individual aberration effectively ruled out the relevance of the particular characteristics of the victim. All victims, in this view, are "accidental" victims, chosen not because of any "acting-out" on their part, or even because of their family constellation, but because of what patriarchy permits.

Beyond "pure" typifications of offender and victim, applying the feminist theory of rape to incest also had the effect of greatly expanding its definition. In the male power framework, as Ian Hacking observes, the "form of exploitation was relatively unimportant in defining the offense" (1992). Since all unwanted sexual touch was defined as an abuse of power, all were forms of the same thing: rape. When *incest* (or *incestuous assault*, with both terms being generally preferred to *father-rape*) was brought within the same definition, the term "came to mean any type of sexually oriented activity involving an adult and a child in the same family" (Hacking 1992: 203). In fact, the definition was broader still, since many included as incest offenders any adult (or significantly older) relative, "father figures" who were not actually related, and even any familiar adult whose sexual actions might cause a child to feel betrayed. By a route different from the child protection professionals, then, antirape activists arrived at much the same expansion of the concept of incest, with much the same consequences for the questions of prevalence and victim harm. The findings of older research studies, such as Kinsey's (1953), which did not specify incest cases, were now read as reporting a significant percentage (e.g., Herman and Hirschman 1977).[17] On the question of harm, older findings were similarly reread. Further, with regard to harm, the movement's use of incest as the paradigm of all sexual abuse meant that all forms of sexual contact came to share similar implications of potential victim harm.

In accordance with the classification of sexual abuse as rape, feminist theorists viewed victimization as an experience of exploitation having a high traumatic potential for the child. As with other forms of rape, sexual abuse was characterized as a profound violation of the self that could have many long-lasting deleterious effects. Drawing on the work of researchers who had worked with both child and adult rape victims, most especially Peters and Burgess and Holmstrom, some activists argued that the aftereffects of sexual abuse followed the same stress-reaction pattern as that seen in adult rape victims: an acute phase of psychological disorganization followed by a long-term reorganization process (e.g., NOW 1976). While some psychiatrists would, importantly, return to the idea of stress reactions later in the 1980s, feminist activists from the 1970s into the early 1980s emphasized a victim's experience of powerlessness and helplessness in the face of assault, and the persisting feelings of confusion, isolation, and degradation that it produced. In addition to assault, however, the focus on father-daughter incest and the patriarchal family led these activists also to frame sexual abuse as a betrayal of trust by the offender, perhaps by the mother, and by society. With this framing, some feminists began to move away from the classification of sexual abuse as rape because treating abuse as an assault but not also as a betrayal would be to minimize the harm to the child and fail to grasp the social and psychological dependence of the child on the offender (Armstrong 1978; Butler 1980; Herman and Hirschman 1977). Stranger rape, these feminists argued, was quick and brutal, and permitted an unalloyed emotional response of anger and hate from the victim. Interfamily sexual abuse, by contrast, involved an ongoing and complex relationship of trust and need, and these dynamics were believed to compound the potential traumatic impact for the victim and increase her risk of experiencing a variety of problems in later life (Herman and Hirschman [1977] combine some family-systems ideas with a feminist perspective to make this case most clearly). A deaf ear from the mother, a mental health professional, or other adult worsened matters even further.

On the issue of harm, then, feminist writers on sexual abuse began to challenge the typification of incest as rape. Other influential writers, such as David Finkelhor (1979), who emphasized that child sexual abuse was unlike rape because it seldom involved violence, would further this declassification. No doubt the progressive decline of the antirape movement and the concentration of feminist analysis on marriage and the family contributed as well. Nevertheless, the classification of sexual abuse as rape had enduring consequences, both theoretical and practical. On the theoretical level, the victim and offender typifications remained, as did the causal role of power and patriarchy. On a more practical level, the rape classification shaped the way that treatment providers responded to the problems created for children and women by their social location and personal experiences of victimization. The rape crisis centers, as noted above, were in contact with many child victims, as were programs for incestuous families that grew out of centers in private institutions.[18] However, as these centers professionalized (or disappeared) in the late 1970s, and the far more institutionally grounded child protection movement expanded, the role of the antirape movement in dealing with and counseling child victims shifted to child protective and welfare services and other institutionalized intervention. At the same time, however, feminist antirape groups began to develop sexual abuse prevention programs for children. The first Child Assault Prevention (CAP) program was launched in Columbus, Ohio, after the rape of an elementary school girl. School officials, seeking to respond, requested a prevention workshop from the local Women Against Rape collective, and, in response, the CAP program was developed (Plummer 1986). CAP and other similar programs spread across the country, fueled by NCCAN funding. By the late 1980s, an estimated 60 percent of school districts in the United States mandated classroom prevention instruction, and millions of children were being trained in prevention techniques (Berrick and Gilbert 1991). The feminist critique of rape and the antirape empowerment strategy, adapted to the situation of children in the original CAP program, remained at the heart of this broad prevention movement (Berrick and Gilbert 1991).

A second enduring, practical consequence of the rape classification, and one more directly relevant to present purposes, concerns not children but adult survivors. The antirape movement created forums in which women molested as children were encouraged, as rape victims were, to speak out and share their personal stories. As they did so—many for the first time— questions about enduring problems and the need for help in resolving past injury arose. Many former victims, for instance, began calling rape hotlines and visiting crisis centers to discuss their experiences, and self-help groups began to form. Meanwhile, in their emerging formulation of the victim category, feminist activists and mental health professionals were emphasizing that sexual abuse could have long-term consequences and arguing that the mental health profession had committed injustice by failing to listen to victims and recognize the traumatic impact of their molestations. These developments virtually demanded that some services be provided for adults victimized as children, including a therapy that corrected the errors identified in psychoanalysis and family approaches. As a result, despite hostility toward the traditional mental health system, feminist professionals began to formulate a therapeutic rationale to guide treatment of adults. Given the inclusion of child sexual abuse within the rape theoretical model, this rationale adopted the same antirape empowerment and self-help strategies. It too emphasized believing victims, affirming inner strength, rejecting guilt, expressing anger, claiming rights, and sometimes, like some of the antirape groups, publicly confronting victimizers. Like the abuse prevention programs for children, then, the conceptual link with rape had a far-reaching and enduring impact in the therapies that were developed for adult survivors.

THE COLLECTIVE STORY

I have argued until this point that a radical break in knowledge about child molestation occurred as two different social movements redefined its meaning and the kinds of persons signified as offender and victim. The meanings changed because professionals and activists associated with these new movements had theoretical orientations and professional and moral/ideological commitments, especially toward the victim, that differed from those of the psychiatrists and criminologists who came before them. These professionals and activists, with backing from some adult survivors (see below), successfully made a public issue of child molestation under the category of sexual abuse, building on a definitional foundation previously established for other social problems (physical child abuse and rape).[19] Along with the different professional and moral/ideological commitments, this domain expansion of preexisting categories also shaped the content of the new constructions and the ways in which they changed.

Each movement constructed sexual abuse differently in ways that justified and mandated their proposed remedies and responses to the condition. There were, however, important points of intersection. As noted, under-standings of sexual abuse in the child protection movement blended with the pragmatic family approaches espoused by programs such as the CSATP. More generally, by the early 1980s, with the partial exception of family approaches that emphasized a complicit daughter, we can speak of certain standardized and publicly shared ideas in the sexual abuse literature.[20] In the shared meanings, all forms of child molestation, including incest, were sub-sumed under the single and broad category of sexual abuse. In a way that the older categories of sexual offenses and incest were not, sexual abuse was a thoroughly moral and morally unambiguous category. *Abuse* was an evalua-tive term for certain behaviors, and it signified a status of ethical and partic-ipatory innocence for all victims, a status that only the "accidental victim" category had fully implied. Correspondingly, abuse signified moral blame of offenders, mostly males, who were not mentally ill but responsible for their actions (even where family dysfunction or past abuse was given causal sig-nificance in explaining their behavior). Their threats, bribes, and power posi-tion accounted for the passivity, silence, and even active participation of victims, behaviors that had earlier been seen to suggest potential problems in victims themselves. In the shared meanings, sexual abuse also indicated injury, very likely profound and long-lasting injury of many types, to the vic-tim. To have been sexually abused—including no-touch incidents and single, brief episodes of fondling—was to have been psychically, emotionally, and/or developmentally harmed to varying degrees by the offender and, typically, by the judicial or treatment system that responded to reported cases or by the social system that covered up abuse and prevented the victim from speaking out. Moreover, this double victimization caused forms of harm that often persisted into and were even magnified in adulthood.

In the shared meanings, sexual abuse was a very widespread but largely hidden social problem, even by victims themselves. It was especially concentrated in the family, but the families in which abuse (incest, as it was now understood) occurred were, at least externally, socially indistinguishable from other families. The "average" incestuous family was not marked by economic class or by racial, ethnic, or subcultural group. Nor was it obviously disorganized. Victims' injuries were seldom physical, and the lack of visible signs combined with criminal sanctions and a constellation of forces that worked to keep the victim silent meant that sexual abuse, despite new reporting laws, was unlikely to come to the attention of any child welfare organization or professional. Reported cases, as earlier, but now including figures published by the American Humane Association and by NCCAN for the late 1970s and early 1980s, were very poor measures of the "true scope" of the problem (see Peters, Wyatt, and Finkelhor 1986: 17–18). In the new understandings, the problem was far larger, though no consensus existed on exactly how much larger. Unlike the earlier categories of sexual offenses and incest, which encompassed legally defined acts, the category of sexual abuse was not limited to specific behaviors, specific ages (when did childhood end?), or specific types of relationships (who, for instance, was a peer?). Since there was disagreement over the evaluation of what constituted abuse, the category was left partly open, the definition depending on who was doing the evaluating: individuals considering their own experience, case workers investigating abuse allegations, survey researchers asking respondents, and so on. The ambiguous definition of abuse allowed movement activists, using broad definitions and specially trained interviewers, to generate very high prevalence figures, a strategic advantage for making claims about the urgency of the social problem and the need for public intervention (e.g., Russell 1983; Wyatt 1985). Higher numbers also served to affirm the rightness of activists' interpretations of causes. As Neil Gilbert reasons, "If 5 percent of females are sexually abused as children, the offenders are sick deviants; if 50 percent of females are sexually abused as children, the problem is 'normal' male socialization to take advantage of females" (1994: 30). Or the problem is massive numbers of highly dysfunctional families, a claim made by some. But the evaluative nature of what constituted abuse meant that the "true scope" of the problem remained elusive.[21] Still, researchers held to the view that sexual abuse was a scientific category that, with methodological refinements, could be counted accurately. Both researchers and activists agreed that there was a massive hidden incidence and that sexual abuse constituted a major threat to the well-being of children and demanded public action.

Moreover, in the shared meanings that emerged from movement activism, sexual abuse was a long-standing problem, an idea that had special relevance for the adult survivor category. While there was no consensus as to whether the incidence of sexual abuse had been increasing, it was agreed that abuse had been going on at high levels for a long time. At a minimum, the new prevalence studies found a considerable number of women molested as children among all adult age groups, and earlier surveys, such as those by Kinsey (1953) and Landis (1956), were cited to take the issue farther back in time. Moreover, many affected women, in both the old surveys and the new, reported that they had never told anyone before. In the present, when combined with the notion of long-term victim harm, this meant not only that there was a large number of undetected victims but that many were "walking wounded," still carrying their secret intact and suffering from their experience (even if they might not recognize it as such). The problem of child sexual abuse constituted a public health problem for adults previously victimized as well as for children. Assistance for victims young and old was indicated, and treatment programs for adults based on these new understandings began to spread.

ADULT SURVIVORS

In constructing sexual abuse as a social problem, the child protection and antirape movements recast the victim category in new moral, social, and psychological terms. The reframing was initially directed primarily to the child victim, but, as shown above, the category for adults victimized as children was reframed at the same time. This category displayed an elaborated narrative of experience for category members. This collective or formula story centered on themes of innocence, betrayal, silence, isolation, powerlessness, and emotional trauma, themes which applied as much to the adult survivor as to the child victim, and probably more so. Adults had been harmed as children not only by the offender's actions but perhaps also by the criminal justice system or by others who disbelieved them or blamed them. They were made to endure the fear, guilt, and shame of their experience alone; thus, rather than dissipating, the harmful effects of the abuse may have increased over time, opening them to "revictimizations" and to a variety of other distresses and dysfunctions in adult life. Perhaps even more than the child victim, they were in need of opportunities to vent their feelings and to receive, if necessary, peer or professional help in overcoming their experience. With children, the new definitions of the victim primarily shaped the ways in which adults related to them, whether in legal, social service, or therapeutic settings. But for adult survivors, who began to interact and share their stories, the collective story also provided the interpretive elements for a shared identity and the template for a new narrative emplotment of their experience.

The collective victim story provided a compelling warrant for individual account-giving. The strong possibility of long-term and insidious harm indicated that adults victimized in any way as children needed to seriously reexamine any current psychological and relational troubles in light of their likely causal connection to the childhood experiences. The enduring harm, combined with the common failure of victims to recognize their own victimization, indicated that any adult who suffered from what were regarded as the psychological aftereffects of victimization (therapists, self-help groups, and other victim advocates offered long symptom lists) should probe childhood recollections or attempt to recover lost memories in order to see if victimization might be at root. Together, the harm and lack of recognition also indicated the need for victims who understood their victimization to come forward and tell their stories in order to assist victims who did not yet see the truth and encourage them to get help. In more politically active forums, the call to end abuse by exposing it added still another reason for public storytelling. In all of this, the collective story thematized disclosure as essential to resolving past abuse and recovering psychological and emotional health.

The collective story also structured the way that audiences heard and responded to victim accounts. Stories are social practices that involve two parties, a teller (or narrator) and an interpretive audience (listeners/readers). The plot elements of harm, nonrecognition, and victim innocence all carried a powerful moral message to potential audiences: Recognize and honor victims. At the same time, the collective story of sexual abuse victimization also closed off alternative stories, including those from the earlier psychoanalytic and family-systems approaches. Here the resonance of this collective story with the broader social change in orientations and attitudes toward victims and victimization is particularly important. By the late 1970s, when adult survivors began to share their accounts with large audiences, segments of the public were already disposed to hear them in the desired way. Years of activist (civil rights, feminist, gay liberation, etc.) emphasis on the insensitivity and victim-blaming of dominant groups, professionals, and the courts, combined with the virtual absence of any formal resistance or counterattack by such parties, made the ground fertile for similar assertions about sexual abuse. In part, then, the new collective story trumped alternative stories about sexual molestation and incest because it conformed to a larger story about past attitudes and approaches that was already widely accepted.

Already in the early 1970s, former victims had begun to give personal accounts in terms that would shape the collective story, with important consequences. With some significant exceptions, such as Florence Rush, former victims did not play leading roles in defining the new knowledge about sexual abuse, which, as I have argued, was largely built on the extension of pre-existing categories. They did, however, begin to play early public roles by writing books, creating self-help groups and networks, and editing anthologies of victimization accounts and poetry.[22] Most fundamentally, they began telling their stories publicly and this practice played a crucial role in getting sexual abuse heard as a public problem. Survivors' disclosed accounts and active participation provided very strong backing for the new activism and resulted in both a changed public awareness of sexual abuse and support for the reformulated victim and offender categories that were emerging from the social movements.

Public Storytelling Forums

The several movements created new forums in which women molested as children could share their accounts with others. These forums had not existed previously. Of course, cases had been coming to the attention of psychiatrists and criminologists for a long time and had been reported in the clinical and research literature. In all likelihood, many other adults molested as children had also recounted their experiences in individual therapy. In 1971, for instance, a clinical psychologist, in a book-length discussion of a single incest case, reported on a survey of psychologists and psychiatrists he had done in 1969 through the facilities of the California Mental Health and Child Guidance Service. He does not provide the precise results of the survey, but argues that, on the basis of the survey, and taking into account factors leading to underreporting, the "incidence of incest" in the United States "implicates at least 5 percent of the population and perhaps up to 15 percent" (Woodbury and Schwartz 1971: vi). Such high numbers presumably reflect considerable experience with victims on the part of the nearly five hundred psychologists and psychiatrists who responded to the survey.[23] While clinical reports on adult survivors proliferated in the 1970s, what is truly different in this decade is the creation of forums outside of strictly professional contexts in which women molested as children could tell their stories. These women could share their experiences in their own words, rather than having them retold and interpreted, as in the clinical literature. As these alternative venues became available, survivors themselves began to have a public impact. The most prominent of the new forums were created by the CSATP in California, by the antirape movement, and by feminist activists more broadly.

The involvement of women molested as children (later men as well) in the Child Sexual Abuse Treatment Program was not intentional. The program was designed for children and their families. However, as the program began to attract public attention, it also attracted adults with abuse histories. The CSATP received thousands of inquiries from these adults from across the country (Giarretto 1982: 47) and incorporated many of them into Parents United and its subgroup, Women Molested as Children. These adults also shared their stories in sessions of Daughters and Sons United, in public awareness campaigns, in CSATP training materials, at Parents United conferences and in its newsletter (The PUN), and in the press coverage that these programs attracted. By the early 1980s, such public activity was national in scope, with Parents United chapters throughout California and in at least thirty other locations in more than twenty states (Giarretto 1982). Moreover, many other sexual abuse treatment programs were in operation nationwide by the early 1980s, and these too were in contact with adult survivors.

Among feminists, women first began to share molestation accounts in consciousness-raising groups. These groups encouraged women to come together and share feelings and experiences, and from these shared stories to find commonalities in the oppressive situation of women. The analysis of these commonalities as arising from male supremacy was, in turn, to lead to activism for social change. The *modus operandi* in these groups and in the movement more broadly was to privilege (to borrow a later term) the place of individual experience and to allow women to be heard in their own way. When feminists first attempted to make an issue of prostitution, this method defeated the effort. Prostitutes themselves, when asked to share their experience, did not accept the view that they were being exploited (Echols 1989). In the case of rape, however, it was just this process that led to the rape speakouts and the broader activism of the antirape movement. Participating in the same groups, women molested as children also began to "name" their experience as abuse and narrativize it.[24] Florence Rush went public with her personal story at the NYRF rape conference, and strongly encouraged the inclusion of childhood sexual experiences on the agenda of consciousness-raising groups, a recommendation repeated by others (e.g., Connell and Wilson 1974; NOW 1976). Given the model and expectation of moving from sharing to action, some of those who gave their accounts in these small groups began retelling them publicly at rape speak-outs and similar events.

A highly structured self-help program created in Minneapolis in the late 1970s provided another nonprofessional forum for women molested as children. Organized for the most part by former victims themselves, Christopher Street, as the program was called, was "fueled by a militant feminism" (Herman 1981: 198) and offered a two-stage group therapy process in which women (many of whom had also been raped) talked about their experiences and were directed in working through them. By the early 1980s, some 1,600 women (men were excluded) were reported to have been through the program (Tunley 1981: 138), and some were telling their stories publicly (e.g., McNaron and Morgan 1982). Additionally, feminist writers included such accounts in their books on rape and reported on those already in print (such as Maya Angelou's account of her childhood rape published in her 1969 memoir *I Know Why the Caged Bird Sings*). A "speak-out" exclusively for incest victims appeared in 1978 in the form of a book of recollections organized around feminist commentary. The book, *Kiss Daddy Goodnight*, was assembled by Louise Armstrong (1978), herself a survivor, from accounts solicited for the most part through press ads. An excerpt, including the author's description of her incest experience, was published in the wide-circulation *Cosmopolitan* a year later (Armstrong 1979). Other first-person accounts were included in feminist writings on sexual abuse (e.g., Butler 1978), in the feminist press (e.g., see references in Rush 1980: 11–12), and in feminist anthologies (e.g., Bass and Thornton 1983; McNaron and Morgan 1982), where the goal was to encourage yet other women to speak out.

Beyond the immediate influence of the CSATP, antirape movement, and feminist activism, new outlets for victim accounts also opened up as sexual abuse was increasingly recognized as a social problem. They included film documentaries, newspaper stories, talk shows, autobiographical books, and twelve-step recovery groups. The first film based on the testimonies of adult survivors appeared in 1976. Entitled "Incest: The Victim Nobody Believes," it was produced by J. Gary Mitchell, an independent filmmaker, and was intended to increase public awareness of the extent of incest and "the impact a childhood incestuous experience can have on a victim's entire life."[25] It won a New York Film Festival Award in 1976 for straight documentary (NOW 1976: sec. 3, p. 3) and presaged other documentaries that were to follow.[26] One of the three women who recounted her story in the Mitchell documentary was also featured in a widely reprinted article that appeared in *Ms.* magazine in 1977 alongside the influential Weber article noted earlier (Stucker 1977).[27]

The first autobiographical book by a past victim appeared in 1979 (Brady 1979). The author was subsequently interviewed on the *Phil Donahue Show,* as well as other talk shows, and her book became a national bestseller. Other such autobiographies followed (e.g., Allen 1980; Ricks 1981), and adults molested as children became a staple on the talk shows. Survivors launched at least two national networks of self-help meetings in the early 1980s. Incest Survivors Anonymous was founded in 1980, and Survivors of Incest Anonymous followed in 1982. The self-help groups in these networks were modeled on the twelve-step program of Alcoholics Anonymous, and typically excluded mental health professionals. Over the course of the next decade, these groups and others like them multiplied nationwide.

Ratifying the Collective Story

In general, the public accounts by adults molested as children ratified or were used by activists to ratify the categories of victim and offender as framed by the respective movements. In one common pattern, the account includes both a history (or some fragments) of the victimization experience, described in more or less detail and with more or less emotion, and, within or alongside it, an implicit if not explicit exposition of "lessons learned." The "lessons" component suggests a didactic purpose for making the story public, and in some accounts adult survivors expressly identify "helping other victims" as their motivation. Although not always indicated, most narratives of this kind suggest that the author had already had contact with therapy or feminist groups before giving her account publicly and had herself there learned the interpretive lessons she now offered to others. Mary C., for instance, whose story was told by Stucker in *Ms.* magazine, underwent two years of intensive therapy at a family-treatment center. Consistent with the offender characterizations of family approaches, she came to see incest as "a problem of the entire family" (Stucker 1977: 105). Louise Armstrong, by contrast, applying a feminist model to her own and other cases, came to no such conclusion (Armstrong 1978). Even in these early accounts, exposure to movement formulations appears to mediate survivor understandings and the accounts they give.

The most common of the interpretive "lessons" concern victims themselves. These lessons are variations on four propositions: that victims are not alone, that they are not to blame, that their victimization helps to explain other debilitating features of their lives in the intervening years, and that there is hope for overcoming it. Katherine Brady (a pseudonym), for example, who had been through therapy, lists all four propositions in her book-length personal account. She begins her book with the last two: "I've learned that my entire life was shaped by its [incest's] happening to me. And I've learned that by looking at it—releasing it from the prison of the past, letting it rise up into the present—I could at last leave it behind" (1979: viii). Her book ends with the first two: "If nothing else, I would wish them [incest victims] to hear in this tale the two things I needed most, but had to wait years to hear: You are not alone and you are not to blame" (1979: 216). While not the only victim lessons, one or more of these comes through in some form in each of the early survivor accounts of the history/lessons kind. And each reproduces the plot elements of the collective story: silence, innocence, harm, and positive prognosis.

The lessons communicated directly by survivors in their public accounts are one aspect of the reinforcement these accounts gave to the new collective story, and a powerful one. The personal immediacy and pain of the victim narratives infused them with a moral authority that professional and activist stories and arguments did not possess. A complaint of victim-blaming, for instance, or of no one to turn to, carried the weight and urgency of direct experience and genuine personal anguish. So too did a personal account of long-term and polymorphous forms of suffering, which, additionally, and unlike the writings of clinicians and nonvictims, seemed unmediated by any psychological theory. Given their commitment to the primacy of personal experience and the standing of individuals as "experts on their own lives," feminist activists were especially sensitive to and supportive of the moral authority of survivors. But, given the success of movement claims about sexual abuse as a social problem, recognition of victim claims and their moral status went much further, and so victimization accounts gave moral authority to their tellers in many settings and made compelling material for general media stories and documentary films. By making a public issue of sexual abuse in the ways that they did, the movements gave hitherto socially unrecognized victims a new moral authority. In making the collective story their own story and recounting it publicly, these survivors lent that authority back.

They did more than lend moral authority to movement claims, however. Holding out a promise of similar change, the lessons they conveyed in their stories also challenged other victims to pursue a similar course of action. In this sense, the public accounts and, typically, the volumes or documentaries they appeared in, represent a type of self-help medium. Of course, many former victims required no prompting to come forward or seek help. It is clear from the spontaneous contacts that women molested as children made with the CSATP, rape crisis centers, and other of the new forums, that they greatly desired the chance to talk about their experience. Many indicated that they had never told anyone and found the opportunity to reveal a long-held secret liberating and helpful in resolving their experiences. At the same time, in their public accounts, survivors were reaching out to others who had not talked with a message that stated or implied that telling was important and probably necessary for personal resolution. Feelings of isolation and guilt, they indicated, were common, but these unwarranted feelings could be overcome. They described other personal problems as the lasting effects of victimization, including, sometimes, harm which they had only recently come to perceive as such. These problems too, they testified, could be surmounted. But survivor accounts of this kind, written or spoken by women who had themselves received help as adults, carried the strong suggestion that resolution could not normally be achieved alone. Further, by describing the recent discovery of harm, and by describing enduring suffering from a wide range of sexual experiences, including nontouch, survivor accounts also implied that a previous sense of resolution might need to be reconsidered, even for events thought to be minor and inconsequential. Talking about the victimization in a sympathetic place and seeking help might be necessary. Thus, with their public stories, these early survivor-activists also validated the collective story by working to persuade other women of the personal benefits of mapping their experience in light of this general narrative framework and taking action accordingly.

A second form of survivor-account support for the collective story concerns not so much victims' intended messages as the instructional use to which their stories were put. In another pattern, survivor narratives consisting only of recollections of the victimization are presented in the context of movement writings or advocacy media stories. In these contexts, the story "lessons" are proffered not by the victim herself but by a third-party: author, editor, or narrator. Used in this way, survivor narratives serve the rhetorical purpose of a "typifying example" (Best 1990). This means that writers chose stories that most dramatically and unambiguously illustrated their understandings and evaluations of the nature of the problem and the moral status of the person-types involved. They did not necessarily claim explicitly that these stories were representative of all cases, but their presentation often implied it. Writers mentioned features believed to be atypical (for example, a mother-offender), for instance, leaving the impression that other features were in fact typical (for example, a white, affluent father-offender). And they did not specify selection criteria, leaving the reader/viewer to assume that the chosen narrative or narratives, though obviously not collected by a random sampling method, represented more or less prototypical cases. Treating them as representative, writers drew on the details of the selected stories to support specific typifications: of victim harm, of offender cruelty, of all children as vulnerable, and so on. Writers also drew on the selected stories to support the same lessons offered by victims themselves (not alone, not guilty, etc.). In these cases too, the messages directed to survivors strongly suggested that they needed help. Finally, writers also used survivor accounts to encourage other victims to speak out publicly about their experiences. A corollary to the cover-up doctrine was the belief that speaking out by victims, even if done anonymously, would help bring an end to abuse. This belief in effect created a moral responsibility for victims to come forward.

The lessons conveyed in and by survivor accounts ratified the collective story by also helping to create and reproduce the collective identity. As women who had been molested as children came forward in the new story-telling forums, they gave social expression to the adult survivor person-category. Narrated in terms of the themes of the collective story, their accounts made the basis for the common identity not simply past victimization but a present state of having moved beyond it. It was in this double sense that some women molested as children first began to call themselves "survivors" (Armstrong 1978), a label that would be widely adopted even as what it signified was being psychologically elaborated. By publicly labeling themselves survivors and ordering their heterogeneous experiences in light of this category, then, women molested as children began to reproduce the new victim category and narrativize the collective story that it displayed.

◦◌◦◦◌◦◦◌◦

I argued in chapter 1 that there were no public "adult survivor" stories before the 1970s because there was no single, unambiguous category of molestation/incest victim nor any collective story that provided a rationale for public disclosure and a framework by which a personal account could be formulated and publicly accepted. In tracing the developments that brought about a shift from public silence to profuse survivor storytelling, the reasons why the old formulations did not lead to public stories became even clearer. Only through the definitional work of the child protection and antirape movements did "adult survivor" become an integrated and meaningful category with deep psychiatric and social implications. Only then were adults molested as children established as victims of external forces, as sufferers of insidious and polymorphous forms of harm, as innocent of all blame or complicity, as deserving of sympathy and respect. Only then did a collective story exist that warranted, even dictated, individual public disclosure of abuse experiences and configured an account for tellers that both served personal identity functions and demanded of audiences a believing and sympathetic hearing. Only with the creation of the collective story did *adult survivor* become a social identity and speaking out become a social possibility.

The adult survivor category, shaped by a moral rejection of the old psychology of the sexual offense victim, configured a collective story organized around the plot themes of victim innocence, victim harm, and the hidden nature of victimization. These themes, worked out by social movements and drawn in part from theories of physical child abuse and rape, implied the general contours of a new psychology and the need for corresponding treatments. But while the old psychology had been rejected, a new psychology had not yet emerged. In the 1980s, movement activists and mental health professionals concentrated great energy on this challenge. As I argue in the following chapters, they worked through the implications of the collective story and produced a new psychology and a new treatment rationale that institutionalized and reproduced it. These interpretative structures, in turn, became the basis for identifying, labeling, and treating new survivor cases.

CHAPTER FOUR

Interpreting Abuse
From Collective Story to Psychological Trauma Model

To considerable celebration, Judith Lewis Herman, a Boston psychiatrist associated with the Harvard Medical School, published *Trauma and Recovery* in 1992. I have already had occasion to cite Herman's work on incest, which began in the late 1970s with "Father-Daughter Incest" (Herman and Hirschman 1977), a clinical study of fifteen adults molested as children. This paper was followed by a book-length study of the same name, which compared former incest victims with daughters of "seductive fathers" (Herman 1981). In these early works, Herman combined feminist and family-systems ideas. She set the experience of incest victims within the context of the patriarchal family, arguing in the 1977 study that "the severity of their complaints seemed to be related to the degree of family disorganization and deprivation in their histories rather than to the incest history per se" (1977: 742). In both studies, Herman reported an "almost uniform estrangement of the mother and daughter, an estrangement that preceded the occurrence of overt incest" (745). Although most of the study participants stated that they endured the sexual contact only because they felt helpless and powerless to stop it, they received special treatment from the father and a sense of power and gratification in displacing the mother. The feeling of specialness in the relationship with the father fed a continuing tendency to "overvalue and idealize men" (1981: 103) and a pattern of "conflictual and often intensely masochistic relationships" (1977: 752). The disturbed relationship with the mother and the sense of gratification in displacing her promoted a distrust and contempt for women as well as personal feelings of shame and worthlessness and a sense of responsibility for the incest. Yet other aspects of the incestuous family, such as negative sexual attitudes, similarly contributed to the enduring psychological legacy in the lives of these women.

A decade later, in *Trauma and Recovery,* Herman was working from a very different theory. The interpersonal family conflicts that she had described earlier and the role they played in her conceptualization of victim psychological harm are decidedly minimized. In their place is a post-traumatic stress model that locates psychological harm in the victim's effort to adapt to an overwhelming experience. Herman classifies incest (and sexual abuse) victims as "traumatized people" and describes their experience in a language that links it with victims of rape and domestic violence as well as combat veterans, members of religious cults, political prisoners, and concentration camp survivors. She argues that all such people, due to exposure to events that inspire helplessness and terror, suffer "predictable psychological harm" as the normally integrated system of human responses to danger—physiological arousal, fear, alterations in perception and attention—becomes overwhelmed, disorganized, and often fragmented. As a result, the traumatic reactions tend to "persist in an altered and exaggerated state long after the actual danger is over" and to be disconnected from each other (1992: 34). They also "have a tendency to become disconnected from their source and to take on a life of their own" (34). This disconnection or fragmentation, a "dissociation" or severing of traumatic memory and/or emotion from ordinary consciousness, is the central pathology for a "spectrum of traumatic disorders, ranging from the effects of a single overwhelming event to the more complicated effects of prolonged and repeated abuse" (3).

The shift in conceptualizations of psychological harm evident in Herman's influential work mirrors a broader shift that took place in the 1980s. Formulations like those in *Father-Daughter Incest* were prominent in the early 1980s, but by the time the first of the new textbooks on the treatment of adult survivors appeared in the late 1980s, a "psychogenic" or trauma model, a post-traumatic stress variant, had become established as a major approach within clinical practice. Why? Why did a trauma model emerge as the central interpretive paradigm for understanding the long-term effects of childhood sexual abuse? In *Trauma and Recovery,* Herman maintains that the psychological process of dissociation, along with the processes of denial and repression, are "phenomena of social as well as individual consciousness" (1992: 9). She makes this point in the context of arguing that understandings of psychological trauma, because they provoke intense controversy by challenging powerful elites, have been repeatedly repressed and pushed from social consciousness. Only in the 1980s, after the work of the Vietnam veterans in securing official diagnostic status for post-traumatic stress disorder and the work of feminists on rape, domestic violence, and child sexual abuse, could it be discovered that all were suffering from essentially the same syndrome.

Herman's is a broad argument, but, in part, my argument in this chapter with respect to a trauma model for child sexual abuse reverses the order of emphasis. Rather than working from psychological processes to social consciousness, I start with a social consciousness—the new collective story—and argue that the way psychological harm from sexual abuse was understood and clinically treated followed from and reproduced this consciousness. I begin by considering the development of post-traumatic stress disorder and its initial application to adults sexually victimized as children. The initial fit between diagnosis and victim experience was loose, but, given the advantages of this diagnosis in light of the new collective story, a concerted effort was made to tighten the fit. I then trace this effort and the resulting formulation of a dissociative-type post-traumatic stress disorder model (which I refer to simply as the "trauma model"). Having outlined the conceptual work that the diagnosis could do, I next consider the way in which it reflects the collective story and does so more consistently than earlier models, like the one involving conflictual relationships originally theorized by Herman. I then briefly examine the role of claims for mental health services and legal battles for compensation as structural factors that pushed the selection of this trauma model over other possibilities.

TRAUMA MODELS OF ENDURING HARM

As discussed in the last two chapters, professionals in the family therapy, child protection, and antirape movements simultaneously defined the victim category and specified the forms of harm, including long-term harm, that victims of sexual abuse might suffer. In new studies, and drawing on some of the older studies of incest, clinicians began to catalogue the symptoms and problems that were reported for children who had had sexual contact with an adult or older adolescent, and for adults who had had such contact in childhood. The lists could be extremely long. Patricia Mrazek and David Mrazek, for instance, drawing on nearly sixty older and newer studies, listed thirty-nine "possible short-term effects" and twenty-five "possible long-term effects" of sexual abuse (1981: 242–43).[1] As the authors recognized, these studies were methodologically distinct, observing very different kinds of behaviors, relationships, and populations, and using very different kinds of outcome criteria. Further, although associations were reported in the studies, it was not at all clear that disturbances, especially temporally distant disturbances, were causally related to the childhood sexual experience. In fact, as discussed in chapter 1, many of the authors of incest studies did not think that the effects they observed in the daughter (or son) could be differentiated from other dysfunctions in the family. However, given the definition of sexual abuse as a public health problem and the demand for new victim services, the matter could not be left at that.

The "catalogue" phase, as David Finkelhor called this period, therefore gave way to what he termed the "documentation" phase. In this phase, researchers used "recognized indices of psychopathology, comparison groups, and statistical procedures" to try to isolate the specific impact of sexual abuse (Finkelhor 1988: 61). Despite the scientific tools, however, the problem of defining sexual abuse did not go away, and reviewers of the literature continued to complain of difficulties in comparing studies as well as specific problems in sampling, design, and measurement. In the most widely cited review, Angela Browne and David Finkelhor (1986) noted that such problems could "invalidate" the findings of the studies (also see Kilpatrick 1987; Schetky 1990). Methodological problems notwithstanding, and despite considerable contradictory findings, they reported that the new research literature tended to confirm many of the long-term effects described in the clinical literature.[2] Again, these studies reported a wide variety of effects for some adults molested as children, including depression, anxiety, feelings of isolation and stigma, poor self-esteem, a "tendency toward revictimization," difficulty in trusting others, substance abuse, and various forms of sexual maladjustment. In considering just four recent studies that employed a multivariate analysis to control for background factors, Browne and Finkelhor reported that "the implication of these studies is that a history of childhood sexual abuse is associated with greater risk for mental health and adjustment problems in adulthood," although these studies were "not so informative" about the actual extent of impairment (1986: 72). Still, they remarked that in retrospective studies, disentangling the sources of effects "may be difficult or impossible" because key variables, such as information about the extent of family pathology before the sexual contact, social reactions to disclosure, and other problem-causing experiences, may be unavailable. Noting that documentation research was only in its infancy, they called for additional study.

More research was undertaken, but by the mid-1980s, and in part before the new documentation studies were even published, a new model was being introduced to explain how childhood sexual contact could cause enduring harm. This model located harm in the characteristics of the sexual experience itself and tied in the "prodigious array" (Herman's [1992] phrase) of symptoms and problems associated with adult survivors. It also introduced a new focus on amnesia, dissociation, and a "disguised presentation" that in effect broadened the types of symptoms and problems thus associated. As with the concept of sexual abuse, the new model of harm was constructed by extending a category already established for another purpose. In this case, the category was a classification of psychological disorder created in the wake of the Vietnam War and incorporated into the official *Diagnostic and Statistical Manual of Mental Disorders* (*DSM*) in its third edition (American Psychiatric Association 1980). Among its many consequences, linking child sexual abuse with post-traumatic stress disorder (PTSD) took the issue of documentation in a new direction: into the worlds of trauma and memory research.

Vietnam and Its Clinical Offspring: Post-Traumatic Stress Disorder
There is a generally accepted history of post-traumatic stress disorder (e.g., Gersons and Carlier 1992; Herman 1992; Trimble 1985). Researchers and clinicians who work on PTSD view it as a timeless disorder, and its history is one of intermittent discoveries punctuated by lengthy periods of inattention. Thus, several previously described syndromes relating to trauma and traumatic memory are believed to be describing PTSD under other labels. Different versions of the history include different syndromes.[3] Judith Herman (1992) begins with hysteria, a condition intensively studied around the turn of the twentieth century by psychologists Pierre Janet in France and by collaborators Sigmund Freud and Joseph Breuer in Vienna. All three came to the conclusion that hysteria was caused by memories of psychological trauma. These memories of unbearably distressing events produced an altered state of consciousness—a "dissociation," in Janet's term, of the traumatic memories from consciousness—which in turn generated hysterical symptoms.[4] Freud, as noted in chapter 1, initially theorized that a childhood sexual seduction was the trauma behind *every* case. He and Breuer, as well as Janet, believed that symptoms of hysteria could be reduced when the traumatic memories and the intense feelings that accompanied them were brought back into consciousness and put into words. Clinical techniques, including hypnosis, were directed to this end.

After hysteria, the PTSD history shifts to war-related conditions. During the First World War, *shell shock* was the term that British military psychologists and physicians used for mental breakdowns that were originally theorized to be the result of a physical lesion of the brain caused by the forces (shock waves, noxious gases, etc.) generated by exploding bombs. The term was then extended to emotional stress, since similar nervous symptoms were observed in soldiers who had not been subjected to any explosions. Other war disorders were also diagnosed, including hysteria. Following Janet's example, special treatment units used hypnosis to lead patients to relive painful and suppressed experiences and emotions. After the war, interest in shell shock and other conditions declined, only to be "rediscovered" during the Second World War with the condition popularly called "combat fatigue" or, clinically, "war neurosis." The leading theorist was Abram Kardiner, an American psychoanalyst, who outlined the criteria for a traumatic syndrome and also elaborated chronic and delayed forms. He and like-minded colleagues also emphasized the mediating role of altered states of consciousness and the importance of recovering and abreacting traumatic memories. He recommended the use of hypnosis to induce an altered state and so facilitate memory recovery, while others used sodium pentothal—"truth serum"—for the same purpose.[5]

These intermittent discoveries set the stage for the political struggles that finally gave the "syndrome of psychological trauma" its "formal recognition" in the *DSM-III* (Herman 1992: 28). These struggles began near the end of the Vietnam War.[6] In 1967, a small group of veterans, Vietnam Veterans against the War (VVAW), organized to oppose continuing U.S. involvement. In 1970 they invited two influential antiwar psychiatrists, Robert Jay Lifton and Chaim Shatan, to attend one of their "rap groups," informal self-help groups at which they discussed personal problems and raised concerns about the impact of war. Thus began a loose, ongoing association between VVAW and Lifton, Shatan, and other antiwar psychiatrists who had publicly begun to make the case for a "post-Vietnam syndrome," a syndrome which Shatan described in the pages of the *New York Times* as "delayed massive trauma" (quoted in Scott 1990: 301). In the following years, veterans continued to organize self-help groups nationwide, while the psychiatrists pressed their ideas within professional associations, including the American Psychiatric Association (APA). Learning of the APA's plan to revise the *DSM-II*, the psychiatrists, along with some veterans and other mental health professionals, formed a Vietnam Veterans Working Group and began collecting veterans' experiences for a new diagnostic category they called "post-combat disorder." However, contact with psychiatrists who had studied concentration camp survivors and noted similar readjustment problems in these survivors and in combat veterans soon shifted the focus to a more general diagnostic category, of which post-combat disorder was but one instance. Contacts with researchers working with victims of severe injuries and various types of catastrophes pushed this development further yet. Utilizing an official opportunity to influence the *DSM-III* task force, and outmaneuvering critics, who argued that PTSD's symptoms were stitched together by a dubious etiology, the Working Group developed an entry called "catastrophic stress disorder," and designated acute, chronic, and delayed manifestations. "They argued that the only significant predisposition for catastrophic stress disorders was the traumatic event itself, and stated that the symptoms, course, and treatment differed by the cause and onset of the disorder" (Scott 1990: 307). Changed only slightly and renamed as PTSD, the new diagnosis was approved by the task force and entered the *DSM-III* as one of the anxiety disorders.

Getting PTSD into the *DSM-III* was a political victory for the group of psychiatrists and veterans who worked to put it there. They succeeded, in Wilbur Scott's words, "because they were better organized, more politically active, and enjoyed more lucky breaks than their opposition" (Scott 1990: 308). They also succeeded, as Allan Young notes, in part because they were able to make a compelling *moral* argument for PTSD, albeit one initially resisted by the Veteran's Administration (VA) and the traditional veterans' organizations. In this argument, the "failure to make a place for PTSD would be equivalent to blaming the victim for his misfortunes—misfortunes inflicted on him by both his government and its enemies. ... Acknowledging PTSD would be a small step toward repaying a debt" (Young 1995: 114). And so it happened: in 1980, the VA accepted PTSD, delayed type, as a potentially compensable disorder (Atkinson et al. 1982: 1118).

The standard history of PTSD suggests that it is a timeless and unified category of disorder, observed over a long period of time in a variety of settings. These ideas were vigorously challenged by opponents of the new classification during the late 1970s and more recently and powerfully by Allan Young (1995) in his history of the idea of traumatic memory and ethnography of a VA psychiatric wing (also see Leys 2000). Whatever one makes of the question of the reality (universality, unity) of PTSD itself, its inclusion in the *DSM-III* institutionalized it as an officially recognized disorder and thus gave it a "reality" (status as objective knowledge) that none of its predecessors possessed. Facilitating compensation claims was one consequence of this recognition. There were, however, other consequences, including some that followed from the way that PTSD was formulated in the *DSM-III*. Some of these consequences were important for the application of PTSD to sexual abuse.

Applying PTSD to Sexual Abuse

Groundwork for the application of PTSD to sexual abuse had already been laid in the 1970s. I briefly noted in the last chapter the work of Ann Burgess and Lynda Holmstrom on rape and its influence on the antirape and child protection movements. In a 1974 article, they outlined the impact of forcible or attempted forcible rape on the victim as a "rape trauma syndrome" (Burgess and Holmstrom 1974a). Originally described for adults, this syndrome was subsequently described for child and adolescent victims as well (e.g., Burgess and Holmstrom 1974b: chap. 4). In their model, forcible rape was traumatic because it was experienced as life-threatening, and they described the pattern "of behavioral, somatic, and psychological reactions" as "an acute stress reaction" to this experience, involving both an "acute phase" and a "long-term reorganization process" (Burgess and Holmstrom 1974a: 982). Significantly, they also argued that the coping behavior of rape victims, which could include a "silent reaction," was similar to that of individuals involved in other life-threatening situations, and they cited the line of research, including the studies of war neuroses, that appears in the histories of PTSD. Their paper on adult rape victims was summarized in the influential 1976 book on the psychology of stress by Mardi Horowitz (1976: 53–54), who had become a member of the Vietnam Veterans Working Group (Scott 1990: 306). When the *DSM-III* appeared, rape was mentioned as a stressor that could produce PTSD (American Psychiatric Association 1980: 236).[7] Among clinicians and researchers writing about sexual abuse, the application of rape trauma syndrome to children had already been influential, at least as a model for cases of abrupt and forceful violation. They followed with interest the syndrome's trajectory into the PTSD category.

After 1980 a link between PTSD and sexual abuse was quickly forged. Although formulated with respect to adult traumas, PTSD, according to the *DSM-III*, "can occur at any age, including during childhood" (American Psychiatric Association 1980: 237). Following the publication of the *DSM-III*, mental health professionals began to apply the disorder to children who had experienced a variety of stressful events (see reviews in Benedek 1985; Eth and Pynoos 1985). These events included physical abuse (Green 1983, 1985) and then sexual abuse (Goodwin 1985). At the same time, some clinicians also began to forge a link between PTSD and adults sexually victimized as children (Blake-White and Kline 1985; Donaldson and Gardner 1985; Gelinas 1983; Lindberg and Distad 1985; Rieker and Carmen 1986).

The PTSD framework as a general model for sexual abuse was by no means obvious. In the *DSM-III*, PTSD's criterial features are the presence of a "recognizable stressor [psychologically traumatic event] that would evoke significant symptoms of distress in almost everyone," and three groups of "characteristic symptoms" to which the stressor gives rise (American Psychiatric Association 1980: 238, 236).[8] The first group comprises signs of a "reexperiencing" of the traumatic event, through intrusive recollections, recurrent nightmares, or feelings that the event will happen again. The second group comprises signs of a "numbing" of responsiveness or interest in one's environment, including "constricted affect" and feelings of detachment or estrangement from others. The third group includes miscellaneous symptoms, at least two of which must be present for the diagnosis: hyperalertness, sleep disturbance, survival guilt, memory impairment or trouble concentrating, avoidance of situations that bring the trauma to mind, and the intensification of symptoms after exposure to an event that brings the stressful event to mind.[9] Comparing these PTSD symptoms to the complaints recorded for sexual abuse victims, Finkelhor, whose work was influential in interpreting the documentation of those complaints, argued that the fit between them was "somewhat forced" (1988: 64). He believed that the PTSD framework only fit some cases (those most like stranger rape), and some of the complaints. His most salient objection was that "PTSD does not have a clearly formulated theory." "As a model," he continued, "it is mostly a syndrome defined by a group of symptoms, rather than an explanation of how these symptoms develop" (66). He then illustrated some of the several ways in which PTSD theorists had sought to explain the connection between event and symptoms. "Unfortunately," he argued, "no explanation fits the problem of sexual abuse very well" (66). Other researchers raised similar objections (e.g., Briere and Runtz 1988; Haugaard and Reppucci 1988: 94–95).

Given such prominent objections to PTSD as a general model, we might ask why clinicians would, even slightly, force a fit. Clearly, there were benefits to the PTSD framework, and Finkelhor himself argued that putting sexual abuse into this framework "has had a number of important salutary effects on the field" (1988: 63). Besides actually applying to some cases, these effects included increased interest in and salience of the problem of sexual abuse. They also included benefits that derived from the way that PTSD was formulated. To Finkelhor's observations, the broader sexual abuse literature added yet further potential benefits (e.g., Courtois 1988; Gelinas 1983; Herman 1992). What these benefits suggest is that clinicians and researchers found in PTSD an officially recognized category that uniquely reflected key requirements of the new typifications of sexual abuse and the adult survivor category, and that could be conceptualized to satisfy more.

A first suggestive feature of the PTSD formulation for sexual abuse was the unequaled etiological significance it placed on "outside" (i.e., external to the psyche) trauma. Here was a unified model that could be applied to sexual abuse to demonstrate how the experience itself caused enduring harm. And, crucially, it was a model that located the onus of pathology almost entirely outside of the individual, a placement that had important status-maintaining implications for the diagnosed. The PTSD construction, observed Berthold Gersons and Ingrid Carlier, "made it possible for victims of war and violence to be recognized as psychiatric patients, without the stigma of their being classified among the more serious psychiatric conditions" (1992: 742). Further, by defining PTSD as a reaction to a traumatic event that would distress "almost everyone," and by assuming a preexisting state of harmony before the event, it normalized conditions that had earlier been viewed as reflecting some personal weakness or pathology and so preserved the "goodness" of the diagnosed. With PTSD, even bizarre symptoms could be seen as a normal human reaction and an *adaptive* means of coping with disturbing memories of the traumatic event. Because the PTSD formulation made the traumatic event decisive but left open the question of what constitutes a psychologically traumatic event, it also eroded the grounds on which a link between stress-related complaints and malingering (a willful simulation of symptoms) might be made. This link had long been a source of dispute in contexts, such as warfare, where gain (escape from duty, financial compensation) could be had from feigning disturbance (Trimble 1985; Young 1995). With PTSD, the burden of proof for legitimate claims was effectively reduced. In the PTSD construction, then, we have a psychiatric category designed to foreclose status degradation, one of the elements of what advocates campaigning against sexual abuse (among others) called "victim-blaming."

A second suggestive feature of the causal role placed on outside trauma in PTSD was that it allowed for an indefinite "latency period." In the shared meanings of sexual abuse, it was almost always harmful. With the concept of the latency period, advocates could account for adults victimized as children who were asymptomatic and could explain studies that found sexual abuse not to have harmful effects on the victim. In the *DSM-III*, one of the two subtypes of PTSD was a "chronic or delayed" form. "Delayed" was specified as a period of at least six months between the trauma and the onset of symptoms, but no outer time limit was set. The explanation for the latency period is clarified in the *DSM-III-R*, where the second group of symptoms is reorganized around the idea of "persistent avoidance" (see note 9). The individual can appear asymptomatic as a result of efficient strategies to avoid reexperiencing the trauma. The traumatic event, therefore, might be far in the past, and yet the traumatized individual displays no direct signs of it (only the indirect and mostly unobservable "avoidance symptoms" and affect constrictions). Hence, the long latency could also be used, in the words of an influential clinician, "to explain some of the incest literature that contends that victims are not harmed by their experiences or that incest does not carry negative consequences" (Gelinas 1983: 318).

Yet another suggestive feature of the causal role of outside trauma in the PTSD formulation was the reciprocally determinative relationship it had with the symptoms associated with it. This feature also allowed for an enlarged understanding of the harm of sexual abuse. An outside trauma is PTSD's defining feature, for as Young observes, without it, "PTSD's symptoms [the other criterial features] are indistinguishable from syndromes that belong to various other classifications," and are traced to nontraumatic etiologies (1995: 7). What this means is that evidence of an outside trauma transforms nonspecific symptoms into signs of PTSD. This evidence, as in the concept of reexperience avoidance, can even signify the absence of symptoms. In the latent *DSM* theory of PTSD, causation, and thus time, starts with the traumatic event and leads to the symptoms. But while evidence of the event could be adduced from a client's active memory, Young argues (120), it could also be adduced from his or her embodied memory (traces of the event, mirrored in symptoms) or from collateral information that placed the client in traumatogenic circumstances. The disorder is thus predicated on a movement from the traumatic event to the symptoms but in practice leaves open the possibility of moving in the other direction, from the symptoms to the trauma (i.e., the clinician finds evidence of distress embodied in the client's current symptoms, such as "constricted affect," and then projects this distress back in time to establish a traumatic event). In the early 1980s, therapists began to argue that adults sexually victimized as children typically could not be recognized by the problems that brought them to therapy, and Denise Gelinas (1983) developed an "Incest Recognition Profile" as a therapeutic aid for seeing through the adult survivor's "disguised presentation." This idea was subsequently elaborated (partly *because of* the application of PTSD) as claims were made that a large class of adults molested as children were partially or completely amnesic with respect to their traumatic event(s). For these cases especially, the PTSD interpretive process permitted a reading of symptoms, including somatic symptoms, as embodied memory, which provided the evidence for the traumatic event that was lacking in actual memory.

A fourth suggestive feature of PTSD for sexual abuse was the framework it provided for a category encompassing a spectrum of "survivors"—a label, as I noted in the last chapter, that adults molested as children began to apply to themselves in the late 1970s. In the steps from "post-combat disorder" to "catastrophic stress disorder" to PTSD, the emergent diagnostic category picked up first survivors from Nazi persecution and then those who survived environmental disasters (for example, floods or earthquakes), as well as man-made disasters (hijackings, airplane crashes, bombings, rape, torture). The PTSD diagnosis, in other words, became an umbrella category under which many classes of "traumatized people" could be scientifically grouped. Each class shared trauma dynamics with the others; none was unique or isolated. Moreover, PTSD bridged the experiences of men and women. All were survivors, whether of combat or of rape, coping with a similar form of officially recognized human suffering.

A final feature of PTSD that is suggestive for its application to the case of sexual abuse was that it did not explain how the traumatic event causes the associated symptoms. Of course, such a lack might be read as countersuggestive of a sexual abuse application and, as noted above, this was one of Finkelhor's objections to the PTSD model. PTSD, however, was developed for the *DSM-III*. That edition, in contrast with prior editions, was explicitly designed to be "atheoretical" (American Psychiatric Association 1980: 7). Its goal was to create a standardized language for talking about mental disorders that was not particular to any theoretical orientation but was based on shared clinical features that any competent observer might identify (Kirk and Kutchins 1992; Young 1995: 94). Given the design of the *DSM-III*, it would seem to follow logically that PTSD is, as Finkelhor observed, "mostly a syndrome defined by a group of symptoms rather than an explanation of how these symptoms develop."[10] What the lack of causal theories in the *DSM* permits, however—and this is the suggestive feature of PTSD for sexual abuse—is the accommodation of various theories. Finkelhor argued that none of the existing explanations of PTSD fit the general case of sexual abuse very well. But if PTSD recommended itself, for the reasons suggested above, might not a theory of PTSD be developed that better fit the case of sexual abuse? The PTSD formulation in the *DSM-III* allowed for just such a development.

In fact, mental health professionals produced and refashioned explanations of PTSD to fit the sexual abuse and adult survivor categories. These explanations principally addressed three interconnected issues. One concerned sexual abuse as a psychologically traumatic event. Another concerned the associated symptoms and variation in symptoms. A third issue concerned the latency period, the so-called "denial/numbing phase," and how symptom expression could be so long delayed. While no consensus united the clinical literature on these issues, some broad points of agreement appear in much of the treatment literature, where the rationale is organized around a trauma/dissociation model encompassing an expanded PTSD formulation. The path to this agreement was complex, winding not only through the literature on PTSD and sexual abuse, but through other literatures as well, including discussions of alternative conceptual models for sexual abuse and research on another *DSM* disorder cluster, the dissociative disorders (especially multiple personality). In order to see how the PTSD model developed, therefore, we need to consider each of these literatures and their contribution to the model. There is no generally accepted history of this development. What follows is a general account of key conceptual steps and linkages.

Repression, Dissociation, and Multiple Personality

In the sexual abuse literature, adult-child sexual encounters constituted a psychological trauma for the child in nearly every case. But in what did the trauma consist, and what accounted for the wide variation in aftereffects? The PTSD model defined the trauma in terms of physical impact and affective overload (intense fear, terror, and helplessness), and it was in these terms that the model was first applied to sexual abuse.[11] While any single event might be overwhelming, the degree of trauma was generally believed to be a function of the abuse circumstances. The circumstances deemed relevant included, among others, the age of the child, her relationship to the abuser, the presence or absence of force and other manipulations, and the nature of the sexual activities. So, for instance, a child who had experienced multiple incidents of sexual intercourse with her father was more likely to be overwhelmed than one who had had a single incident, and both were more likely to be traumatized than a child who had been fondled once by a neighbor. Thus, a variety of descriptive features of the sexual contact were used to account for variation in the level of trauma, which, in turn, accounted for variations in the long-term disturbances that followed.

This was the approach criticized by David Finkelhor (1988), who insisted that the conceptualization of trauma in the PTSD model did not comport with the experience of sexual abuse victims. He argued that the circumstances of the prototypical abuse case (incest) differentiated it from the prototypical PTSD case—exposure to a discrete, overwhelming incident. He proffered his (and Browne's) "four traumagenic dynamics" model as more accurate and useful because of its greater focus on subtle contextual factors and the cognitive—not just affective—impact of victimization, as well as its conceptualization of abuse as a situation or unfolding process rather than an event or sequence of events.[12] This model, first proposed in a 1985 paper concerned with immediate victimization effects on children (Finkelhor and

Browne 1985), identified four trauma-causing factors ("traumagenic dynamics") as the core of the psychological injury inflicted by sexual abuse. Finkelhor argued in the 1988 paper that the degree of presence or absence of these dynamics—traumatic sexualization, betrayal, powerlessness, and stigmatization—also explains the four clusters of long-term outcomes associated with each dynamic. Although offered as an alternative to PTSD, the traumagenic dynamics model shared key features with it. Like the PTSD framework, trauma was assigned direct pathogenic power, and the characteristics of the original sexual experience (more or less sexualization, more or less betrayal, etc.) were used to explain the variance in long-term adverse effects. The dynamics model, however, lacked a causal theory to explain how the adverse effects actually, and often in a much-delayed way, developed. Thus, despite its designed intention, the model appeared in the clinical literature not as an alternative but as a supplement to the PTSD framework. Some used the four "dynamics" to broaden the conception of trauma from simply an anxiety-producing event to an ongoing and complex interpersonal experience, while others went further and drew a more broadly framed traumatogenic event directly into a revised PTSD model (e.g., Davies and Frawley 1994; Herman 1992, who emphasized betrayal, helplessness, and captivity). What began as an argument against the application of PTSD to sexual abuse, then, actually contributed to that application by suggesting how the etiological trauma might be reconceptualized to better account for sexual abuse and the extensive catalog of long-term disturbances described by adult survivors. However, the problem of explaining the connection between the trauma, more broadly defined, and the later disturbances remained. In the concepts of coping and dissociation, researchers found the keys they needed.

Already in the early 1980s the idea of coping was beginning to be emphasized to account for the wide range of reported sexual abuse effects and their delayed expression. In order to cope psychologically with the abuse trauma, researchers and clinicians argued, victim defense mechanisms were engaged which, while crucial to psychic survival, were also potentially pathogenic in later life. Initially at least, researchers and clinicians postulated three somewhat different defense mechanisms as common forms of coping with sexual abuse: dissociation, denial, and repression.[13] All three shared some common features. Each mechanism was believed to vary along a continuum of traumatic memory avoidance, ranging from partial to complete, and along a continuum of time, with each mechanism capable of warding off intrusions for days or decades. The elements of the traumatic memories that were avoided or "forgotten" could also vary, including behaviors, cognitive knowledge, and emotions, either singly or in combinations. Moreover, all the mechanisms were seen to have a voluntary component, and at least in the case of repression and dissociation, an involuntary component as well. Each of these psychological defense mechanisms played a role in the PTSD model as it evolved to cover adult-child sexual contacts. The most significant of these was dissociation, which emerged as the dominant explanation for the containment of symptoms during the latency period, shaping treatment strategies and linking PTSD to other disorders—which were also postulated to be induced by childhood trauma—and to a far wider symptom range.

Distinguishing dissociation from the other two defense mechanisms is difficult because different writers used the terms differently, and sometimes interchangeably. In its simplest form, *denial,* for instance, meant that a victim refused to acknowledge to herself the fact of the sexual contact or some aspect of it, such as her genuine emotional response (which could lead to a numbing or detachment from these feelings). Many writers also included a refusal to acknowledge the *importance* of the trauma as a type of denial (e.g., Gelinas 1983; Rieker and Carmen 1986; Goodwin 1985). Gelinas illustrated this type of denial by a former victim as follows: "I never think of it, so it's behind me and I want to leave it there" (1983: 316). (Clearly, as explained in subsequent chapters, such meanings of denial could have important ramifications in the treatment setting.) Sometimes, too, as in the phrase "denial/numbing phase," denial was also employed as the name for the category of avoidance strategies, and thus subsumed both repression and dissociation. Especially in the sexual abuse literature of the 1980s, repression was another fluid concept, sometimes used as the name for the avoidance category, sometimes used interchangeably with dissociation or as a subtype of dissociation, and sometimes used as a discrete mechanism distinct from either. And even when used in the latter sense, repression could signify different things.

As a psychoanalytic term, *repression* dates to the studies of hysteria at the end of the nineteenth century. It emerged at the same time as *dissociation,* and the two were originally models in conflict. Both were theorized as defense mechanisms, as psychological processes that provide protection against painful memories and unacceptable wishes (not against experiences per se). But they embodied different conceptions of memory. Repression was Freud's concept, and he came to it indirectly. As has been widely discussed (e.g., Erdelyi 1990; Haaken 1994; Spiegel 1990; Young 1995), Freud (and Breuer) originally held that traumatic experiences are always charged with intense emotions. Normally, reactions to these experiences (for example, crying, acts of revenge) discharge these emotions, but such discharge is not always possible. Under these circumstances, the memories of the trauma remain painful and unmanageable, and the conscious personality suppresses them in self-defense. They enter a "second consciousness," not unlike a hypnotic state, where they are isolated in a separate and autonomous operation within the ego. Having entered the second consciousness, the memories are gradually lost to access by the conscious personality. However, the pathogenic power of the memories, now secret, produces symptoms of distress. The distress, Freud believed, could be relieved if the memories of the event that provoked it, still largely intact, could be brought back to consciousness (through hypnosis, persuasion, etc.) and accompanying emotional reactions aroused, and if both event and emotions could be put into words, thus finally discharging the emotion (abreaction). In his early "double consciousness" model, then, Freud posited a "vertical" split in consciousness, with the memories of the original trauma preserved, more or less whole, in an alter ego state.

Still very early in his career, Freud came to reject the idea that traumatic memories were preserved in a second consciousness, and he theorized the mechanism of repression as an alternative model. Rather than a vertical split in consciousness, with its implication of a kind of coherent and parallel state of awareness, he argued instead for "horizontal" splits dividing levels of consciousness (see Hilgard 1977). This shift coincided with his increasing emphasis on the role of fantasy and unconscious conflicts in mental life and the view that memory is revisionistic, containing defensive elaborations of events. In the repression model, painful memories, whether of external events or of internal conflicts engendered by oedipal fears and wishes, are defensively driven into the unconscious, with some level of consequent amnesia. This process, however, is not a passive preservation of these memories in some unaltered form, but an active symbolic transformation of them, involving, in Janice Haaken's words, "reversals, substitutions, and transpositions of images and ideas" (1994: 133). Memory and meaning, in Freud's revised perspective, were *mediated* by developmental capacities, the imagination, and psychic defenses, both in the original encoding of trauma memories and in their subsequent recall. Thus, the clinical task was no longer conceived as activating some alternative state of awareness and linking it with the conscious personality, but as an exploration of the latent symbolic content of memory. Freud abandoned techniques like abreaction in favor of free association and the interpretation of resistances that emerge in the clinical encounter. While this process (psychoanalysis) was believed to draw out unconscious conflicts, it could not unambiguously identify some original traumatic experience.[14]

By contrast, the defensive process of dissociation, as conceptualized by the French theorist Pierre Janet, was very similar to Freud's original double consciousness model. Janet, like Freud, was interested in the psychological origins of hysteria and, like Freud, believed the disorder was produced by a reaction to trauma memories, though for Janet the traumas were not sexual or even acts of human agency (Hacking 1995: 191). He too argued that trauma-induced altered states of consciousness were very similar to hypnotic states and that hypnosis could be used to access the altered states. Janet's dissociation model, like double consciousness, was a vertical-split model: a single individual could simultaneously have more than one stream of consciousness and store of memory. Janet believed that when the meaning of traumatic memories could not be assimilated into the life history, despite repeated attempts by the individual, they did not enter normal memory but rather were "dissociated," or split off, from normal consciousness as "subconscious fixed ideas." These fixed ideas, because preserved and isolated in an alter ego state or states, yet still dynamic, could produce various "psychological automatisms" (for example, alternating [multiple] personality, fugue, a spectrum of bodily symptoms) over which the conscious personality had no control. As with Freud's early approach, the goal of therapy for Janet was, in Allan Young's summary, "to help the patient discover his fixed idea and bring it into consciousness [hypnosis was the cardinal tool for this recovery]. Then he must recite it and re-recite it, until the recital and its memory are independent of the event and the emotions that they memorialize" (1995: 35). At this stage, with further therapy, the memory can be integrated into the patient's life history (see also Ellenberger 1970).[15]

In the conflict between the two models, repression won out, at least until recently.[16] In fact, Janet himself quickly dropped the word *dissociation* and, like Freud, he moved away from his early model as hysteria ceased to be a recognized condition in France. In the United States, the concept was briefly kept alive in the early years of the century by Morton Prince and his Boston School, who advocated the multiple personality diagnosis, but they were eventually overtaken by the predominance of psychoanalysis. Dissociation made an appearance in the periodic writings about the war neuroses, and the techniques of hypnosis and abreaction were used during the world wars because of their seemingly quick results. But not until the 1970s, with the decline of psychoanalysis and a renewed interest in multiple personality and hypnosis (Putnam 1989), does the concept reemerge with new force and begin to gradually swamp repression in explanations of trauma-induced psychopathology. Although researchers and clinicians continued to use the word *repression* in the sexual abuse literature alongside the term *dissociation,* it was a vertical, not horizontal, split in consciousness that provided the central explanatory mechanism not only for coping with trauma and the latency period but also for a wide range of symptoms.[17] And with the ascendancy of dissociation, both hypnosis and abreaction reemerged as important treatment techniques.

The new incarnation of dissociation was principally the work of clinicians and researchers interested in "multiple personality"—elevated to a major diagnostic category in the *DSM-III*—and the larger *DSM-III* category of "dissociative disorders," of which it was a part. Multiple personality, first described in the late nineteenth century (and typically connected to hysteria, as for Janet), was considered extremely rare until the 1970s.[18] In that decade, a small number of mental health professionals began to revive interest in it. The leading figures included Cornelia Wilbur, the psychiatrist who treated "Sybil," the case made famous by the 1973 book (Schreiber 1973) and subsequent film, and Ralph Allison, who in the late 1970s was giving workshops on multiplicity at the annual meetings of the American Psychiatric Association. The status of multiple personality in the *DSM-III* was a significant coup for this small group, and since 1980, the diagnosis of multiple personality (now called "dissociative identity disorder")[19] has risen dramatically in the United States (Acocella 1998; McHugh 1992; Putnam 1989), along with a considerable professional apparatus, including a professional society, annual and regional conferences, and an academic journal.[20] Others have detailed the history of multiple personality and its rediscovery (Hacking 1995; Putnam 1989; Ross 1989). I need not retell this history, but I must briefly summarize two points: the reconceptualization of dissociation and the link it provided between multiple personality and child abuse. I then turn to the effect that both of these developments had on understanding the role of sexual abuse in the etiology of PTSD.

In the descriptive language of the *DSM,* the dissociative disorders are characterized by an alteration in consciousness affecting memory, identity, and ongoing awareness. The various disorders listed include psychogenic amnesia (sudden inability to recall important personal information, like one's name), psychogenic fugue (sudden and unexpected urge to travel, with identity change and inability to recall the past), depersonalization disorder (an experience of self-estrangement, with the usual sense of one's reality temporarily lost or changed), a residual category of "atypical dissociative disorder" (some dissociative symptoms are present but not enough to meet all the criteria of a specific disorder), and—the most chronic condition—multiple personality (two or more distinct personalities within the same person that operate independently of one another and alternately take control of the individual's behavior).[21] By the mid-1980s, professionals studying these disorders believed that the vast majority were traumatically induced (Putnam 1985). However, it was multiple personality, which could encompass the symptoms of all the others, that had become explicitly linked to a childhood history of severe sexual, physical, and/or emotional abuse (e.g., papers in Kluft 1985), a linkage that would turn a whole new set of professionals into claims-makers about sexual abuse as a social problem (a similar process took place with many PTSD researchers).[22] But, as Hacking (1995: chap. 6) points out, multiple personality, as described in the mid-1980s, was a disorder of adults, not children. Although a search did begin for child multiples, the idea that childhood abuse was the cause of multiple personality was forged by a new conceptualization of dissociation as a childhood coping mechanism.

Mental health professionals studying multiple personality described dissociation as a normal process of everyday life (for example, brief "spacing out," daydreaming, creating imaginary playmates) that could become pathological under certain conditions. Further, they believed the predisposition to and capacity for dissociation to be innate and to vary by individual, and the use of dissociation as a response to stress to be more common in childhood than in adulthood. Healthy dissociation was brief, with control by ordinary awareness being quickly reestablished. However, in the face of overwhelming experiences, the defensive functions of dissociation could lead to a range of more severe disengagements that persisted long after the trauma had passed. For Janet, dissociation was a defense against painful memories and thus arose some time after a traumatic event as a result of weakness and suggestibility. The new professionals, by contrast, conceptualized it as a defensive response to a trauma *as it was experienced* and as an ability, a kind of creativity, rather than a weakness. In order to cope with the intolerable (a single event or repeated events),[23] they theorized, a child escapes by disengaging feelings, thoughts, behaviors, or sensations. This process was, in a sense, almost deliberate; the child cultivated a dissociative state during abusive incidents that subsequently became a generalized response. Some theorized that it might even be encouraged by the adult abuser to ensure his victim's passivity. In either case, they held that the dissociated elements were deflected to a separate consciousness, where they were recorded and encoded. At the same time, the dissociation created a more or less firm amnesia barrier between the split-off elements and normal consciousness that prevented the subsequent free interchange of memories and awareness, and blocked the development of a single sense of self across behavioral states. In the extreme form of multiple personality, alternative personalities or identities ("alters") were formed and isolated, "each," in the words of the *DSM-III* and *DSM-IV*, "with its own relatively enduring pattern of perceiving, relating to, and thinking about the environment and self."

While emphasizing its highly adaptive value for coping with childhood traumas, professionals believed that dissociation could be maladaptive later, "in an adult world that stresses continuity of memory, behavior, and sense of self" (Putnam 1989: 54). Whether more or less severe, professionals did not believe that dissociation was sufficient to fully protect the individual from the traumatic experiences, as dissociated material could be reactivated and leak back into normal consciousness, generating periodic and fragmentary reexperience of the trauma. And coping mechanisms that were functional for surviving trauma, still habitual in the adult, could be highly dysfunctional. In adults diagnosed as multiples, professionals noted a wide variety of symptoms. These included dissociative symptoms, which covered a broad spectrum of phenomena, such as memory impairment of varying degrees (from total amnesia to detached or shadowy recall) and types (periods of time, specific information, etc.), depersonalization (an experience of estrangement from self), "out-of-body experiences" (awareness is perceived as being outside or separated from the physical body), derealization (a feeling of unreality or detachment from the environment), fugue episodes, sleepwalking, and trancelike states. Among other identified symptoms were depression, anxiety and phobias, substance abuse, auditory hallucinations, and self-destructive behaviors. Multiples were also believed to be at increased risk for adult revictimization experiences. Because of the sheer profusion of symptoms, professionals believed that most multiples were repeatedly misdiagnosed. Once recognized, they required intensive therapy to identify and reintegrate the various personalities or identity states (some therapists claimed to have found one hundred or more alters in a single individual) and replace dissociative reactions. Recovery and reworking of the early traumatic event(s) was a central task, with the techniques of hypnosis and abreaction playing major roles.

Dissociation, PTSD, and Sexual Abuse

The incorporation of dissociation into a PTSD model for sexual abuse was an incremental development. In the Browne and Finkelhor (1986) review of studies mentioned above, dissociative experiences were not even mentioned as a problem correlated with childhood sexual experiences. Yet an emphasis on dissociation and dissociative experiences was already emerging in the clinical literature, which cited the literature on dissociative disorders.

An early model by Roland Summit (1983) played an influential role in this development. In "The Child Sexual Abuse Accommodation Syndrome," Summit described what he believed to be the reasons why children often make delayed and unconvincing abuse disclosures, and sometimes recant them. The "syndrome" (it was not a psychiatric syndrome) of victim behaviors had five components. The first two dealt with children's circumstances—secrecy, helplessness—and the last three with disclosure—entrapment and accommodation; delayed, conflicted, and unconvincing disclosure; and retraction. Summit's formulation, which he devised to "challenge entrenched myths and prejudice" and provide "credibility and advocacy for the child" (177), and Summit himself, a child protection movement advocate, had quite a career in the battles over child sexual abuse accusations in the 1980s, including in the courts (Hechler 1988: 157–61). But the significance of his formulation for the PTSD model was in its central concept of accommodation. Summit argued that negative outcomes for the child followed from normal and necessary *coping* responses to the abuse and the "parental environment" in which it took place. He identified a whole range of adult disturbances as the "habitual vestiges of painfully learned childhood survival skills" (1983: 184). Further, negative outcomes for the child might not be actively expressed.[24] According to Summit, accommodations to helplessness and rage could also involve the creation of a "psychic economy," such as the development of multiple personalities or the discovery of "altered states of consciousness to shut off pain or to dissociate from her body" (185). By means of such psychic accommodations, the child or adolescent could appear to be "perfectly well-adjusted." Finally, following on the belief that minors almost never fabricate sexual abuse stories, even retractions were identified as a form of accommodation.[25]

Others took the concept of coping and interpretively linked it to delayed PTSD. Gelinas (1983), for instance, argued that incest victims use a variety of self-protective defenses, including denial (of the event[s] or of its importance), repression, emotional numbing, and the induction of dissociation. In those who use dissociation, she argued, "the tendency toward dissociation under stress continues after cessation of incest, often showing up in the presenting picture as 'confusion,' or as dissociative behavior erroneously interpreted as psychotic" (316). On the last point, she raised the possibility of a link with multiple personality. In general, Gelinas argued that the operation of the defenses tended to alternate with intrusive reexperiences of the trauma (for example, nightmares, panic attacks, sexual promiscuity). She also maintained, however, that the untreated trauma below this classic post-trauma sequence of denials and intrusions could generate over time various psychiatric symptoms not specific to PTSD, such as chronic depression, poor self-esteem, and "learned helplessness," among others. She called these non-specific problems "secondary elaborations," and argued that they often constituted part of the presenting problems that brought adults victimized as children to therapy. The therapist's challenge was to see through this "disguised presentation" to the underlying trauma below.

The work of Patricia Rieker and Elaine Carmen (1986) provides another influential example of expanding the symptoms linked to delayed PTSD by broadening the interpretation of coping responses. They argued, on the basis of earlier findings from a study of psychiatric inpatients, that victims' sense of self was damaged by their sexual trauma, and they formulated a "schema" that explained this damage as arising from the context in which the stress reaction took place. Focusing on exploitative and disordered family systems, they theorized that in order to cope with the incest in this relational environment, the child was forced to alter the reality of the victimization by the use of one or more of three defensive strategies. One, similar to Gelinas's conceptualization, was not to acknowledge the sexual contact, whether "through repression, dissociation, denial, or some other process" (364–65), both initially and continuing into adulthood. A second was to alter the affective response. Unable to express the "true feelings arising from abuse" and dependent on the abuser(s), the child delusionally registers the abuser(s) as good and represses her rage or turns it inward in a process of "self-scapegoating." This distorted and displaced anger later manifests itself in repetitive reenactments involving anger and aggression directed toward the self and others. A third defensive strategy was for the child to let go of her own perception of the abuse and accept and internalize the meaning given to it by the abuser (for example, her fault, not abusive, in her best interests). But since the child experiences pain in the very acts that the abuser finds pleasurable, she is left in a state of "extraordinary confusion about the meaning of the abuse." This state may later be reflected in adult relationships "in which love, pleasure, and pain become inextricably linked" (367). For Rieker and Carmen, the most enduring legacy of these three trauma-coping strategies is a "disordered and fragmented identity" that expresses itself in many disturbances of the self and relationships.

Still other formulations emerging in the mid-1980s emphasized dissociative behavior as an aftereffect of child sexual victimization and dissociation as a key defense mechanism. In a series of papers, for instance, John Briere and Marsha Runtz (1988), argued that they found dissociation to be "relatively common" among adult survivors and hypothesized that it "may initially function as a coping technique, later becoming a semiautonomous symptom" (89). In their "post sexual abuse trauma" model (a PTSD variant), they argued that all of the long-term psychological disturbances arising from severe childhood sexual victimization were "initially adaptive responses, accurate perceptions, or conditioned reactions to abuse during childhood. Elaborated and generalized over time, however, they became 'symptoms' and/or contextually inappropriate components of the victim's adult personality" (92–93). Jill Blake-White and Christine Kline argued that in their experience, "most victims of sexual abuse have very few memories of the actual incest" (1985: 396; see also Herman and Schatzow 1987). They explained this partial or complete amnesia as following from the victim's use of dissociation to adapt to the trauma while it was occurring. They then briefly outlined a group treatment model for PTSD, "with dissociative processes," that began with "recollecting the memories" (using various therapeutic techniques, including hypnosis) that were the source of a wide variety of ongoing problems.

Several other clinicians and researchers also advanced the idea of a dissociative form of PTSD with significant amnesia.[26] David Spiegel (e.g., 1984, 1988), for instance, an influential theorizer of the new dissociation model, argued in a number of papers that dissociation was a key adaptation to trauma and that most of the PTSD symptoms listed in the *DSM-III-R* had a "dissociative flavor" (1990: 250; see also Ross 1989). These included "the re-experiencing of a traumatic event through intrusive recollections, nightmares, or flashbacks; emotional numbing with feelings of detachment or isolation; stimulus sensitivity (including the avoidance of environmental cues that are associated with recollections of the traumatic events); survivor guilt; and difficulty concentrating" (Spiegel 1990: 250). Given the central role of dissociation he assigned to both disorders, he held that multiple personality was a form of chronic PTSD. For much the same reasons, Bennett Braun, a major figure in the multiple personality movement, argued that PTSD could be considered a dissociative disorder, with multiple personality as a special case of chronic PTSD (1986: 21). Bessel van der Kolk, a prominent researcher of PTSD, and one among several who saw a link between childhood trauma and yet another disorder, borderline personality, argued (with Kadish) that "except when related to brain injury, dissociation always seems to be a response to traumatic life events. Memories and feelings connected with the trauma are forgotten and return as intrusive recollections, feeling states (such as overwhelming anxiety and panic unwarranted by current experience), fugues, delusions, states of depersonalization, and finally in behavioral reenactments" (1987: 185). Dissociation in this PTSD formulation accounts for the denial/numbing phase, the periodic reexperiences, amnesia, and a variety of other symptoms.

By the late 1980s, the link between child sexual abuse and just such a delayed, dissociative-type PTSD was becoming cemented in the clinical studies and in the rapidly growing treatment literature. In these writings, an expanding number of disturbances were conceptualized as arising from childhood coping responses to sexual victimization experiences. These coping responses, while necessary for psychic survival, could subsequently become dysfunctional or pathological in themselves and throw off additional "secondary elaborations." Among the postulated coping mechanisms, dissociation represented the most efficient "survival skill," and the most potentially pathogenic over time. It was theorized to serve many protective purposes. In the summary of one clinician,

> It provides a way out of the intolerable and psychologically incongruous situation (double bind), it erects memory barriers (amnesia) to keep painful events and memories out of awareness, it functions as an analgesic to prevent feeling pain, it allows escape from experiencing the event and from responsibility/guilt, and it may serve as a hypnotic negation of the sense of self. (Courtois 1988: 155)

As this list suggests, the experience that is coped with need not be overwhelming in the sense of an affective overload arising from experiences of danger, threat, or violence, as in the original, adult-onset formulation of PTSD. The adaptation, clinicians argued, could be to sharp psychological incongruities brought on by trying to adjust to contradictory messages communicated by the parents; or by struggling to maintain a good image of the abusive parent despite feelings of betrayal or exploitation; or, at the most general level, by facing the sexual experiences themselves by reason of their being "developmentally inappropriate" (an idea included in the *DSM-IV*).[27] While protective, dissociation, especially as a repeated defense, was also theorized to lead to different forms and levels of self-fragmentation and amnesia, including multiple personality at the end of the continuum. The model encompassed the classic PTSD symptoms—denial/numbing, reexperiencing, anxiety, and so on—as well as disturbances in personality development and functioning.[28]

The spectrum of defensive purposes and effects/symptoms assigned to dissociation provided the conceptual link that more completely fit PTSD to sexual abuse, especially the paradigm case of incest. In the early 1990s, some clinicians made further efforts to formalize and institutionalize a dissociative-type, or complex, form of PTSD. Herman, in her *Trauma and Recovery*, argued that responses to trauma represent a spectrum of conditions that range from "a brief stress reaction" to "classic or simple" PTSD to "complex post-traumatic stress disorder" (1992: 119). *Complex PTSD* was the name she proposed for a new diagnosis for those subjected to prolonged, repeated trauma, including incest. It largely subsumed the categories of multiple personality, borderline personality disorder, and somatization disorder (physical complaints without medical explanation), the last being another disorder that some argued was caused by childhood trauma, especially sexual abuse (e.g., Locwenstein 1990).[29] Complex PTSD covered the *DSM-III-R* symptoms of PTSD as well as developmental and personality dimensions not found there but found in the other disorders.

The working group for the *DSM-IV* considered a form of complex PTSD under the name "disorders of extreme stress, not otherwise specified." While it was not included, the conceptualization of "classic" PTSD was expanded. The *DSM-IV* dropped the definition of the traumatic event as "outside the range of usual human experience." Advocates in the sexual abuse literature had argued that sexual abuse was not "outside the range of usual human experience," but was etiological of PTSD nonetheless. The *DSM-IV* eliminated this dissonance between definition and clinical practice. Further, as Young notes, the changes in the *DSM-IV* enlarged "the variety of experiences and memories that can be used to diagnose PTSD" (1995: 289). The criteria are more subjective, he observed, and the diagnosis can include "cases in which individuals discover their distressful feelings (intense fear, etc.) long after the fact [of the trauma]" (289). Further, the list of associated features is much longer, including numerous symptoms associated with an "interpersonal stressor" such as "childhood sexual or physical abuse" (American Psychiatric Association 1994: 425). Young argues that the revised PTSD entry in the *DSM-IV* signaled the diminishing focus on the experiences of war veterans, "the repatriation of the traumatic memory, the act of bringing it back home from the jungles and highlands of Vietnam" (1995: 290). It also signaled the institutionalization of a connection between PTSD and child sexual abuse, between adults molested as children and the person-category of "traumatized people."

The formulation of a delayed, dissociative-type trauma model had a defining influence on the psychotherapy of adult survivors: It formed the organizing principle for a new therapeutic rationale. Before discussing that, however, and having sketched the development of the trauma model, I first return to the implications of the movement-generated collective story. Earlier I discussed some ways in which the PTSD model, in light of these implications, recommended itself as a model for sexual abuse. Now I want to explore further how the emergent model covered the psychological implications of the collective story and consider why a reformulated PTSD and not another model was mobilized for treatment purposes.

THE COLLECTIVE STORY AND THE SELECTION
OF THE TRAUMA MODEL

In constructing the trauma model, clinicians and researchers sought to reconcile a psychiatric science and corresponding clinical practice with the collective story of the blameless and harmed victim. As formulated, the trauma model supported the coherence of the condition-category of sexual abuse and the innocence of victims by locating harm in the conditions of the sexual experience itself. It supported the unequivocal moral blame of the offender, including his responsibility for the child's passivity and silence, by locating the cause of pathology in his complete domination. It explained enduring victim harm by providing a causal model, with an associated biology, that encompassed a very wide range of distresses, disabilities, somatic symptoms, and life problems as trauma aftereffects. It helped to depathologize and destigmatize the adult survivor's symptoms and experiences by explaining them as necessary coping responses. Guilt, too, was defined as a coping measure, thus reducing its power to signify any culpability. Finally, it supported the victim's innocence by shifting the focus from the victim's own emotional reactions or interpretations of the sexual contact to the contact itself. In the trauma model, no aspect of the harm could be construed as self-inflicted.

The concept of dissociation played a decisive role in the reconciliation. It accounted for delayed symptom expression, but it did so in a way that reflected more positively on the victim than did repression. As conceptualized, dissociation is more of a credit to the client. The emphasis in dissociation is on coping, a kind of active and creative ability, and less on the defensive warding off of the intolerable or unacceptable. Dissociation, more than repression, supported an unambiguously positive representation of the victim. As Janice Haaken writes, "The good self of the patient is preserved within a field of dissociated trauma memories" (1994: 123). In this "field," fantasy in the Freudian sense—the mind as active and imaginative—is not in operation. Thus, dissociation, more than repression, supported an uncompromising stance of belief toward all accounts of past abuse. Dissociation is a response to actual trauma, whereas memories that are repressed include unconscious wishes and fears. Moreover, the dissociated memories are relatively intact and recoverable, not mediated in the unconscious as with repression. Colin Ross, a prominent theorizer of multiple personality, argued that with dissociation, as opposed to repression, "[t]here is nothing deep or hidden" (1989: 70). Consequently, there is "no need for obscure theory and jargon" (70), and the client can rely less on the therapist to decode the meaning of the pathogenic secret and its resulting disturbances. Dissociation, then, much more than repression, was compatible with the already established and favored strategies of empowerment and self-help, with allowing adult survivors to see themselves as "experts about their own lives."

In yet a broader way, the trauma model also expressed the collective story in the individual-level interpretations. The concept of a society-wide silence and denial, for example, had its analogue in the amnesia and defenses of the victim. As public recognition and "speaking out" were emphasized for their remedial effect, so forgetting was conceptualized as pathological. The inherent coercion attributed to sexual abuse was mirrored in the personal resistance (coping, defenses) and the unexpressed negative emotions attributed to the victim. Such mirroring of the social in the individual was not by design but rather suggests the workings of a basic social process. I have argued at length that disorder was conceptualized to reflect the collective story already worked out by movement activists. This story followed from the social experience of the defining movements. In this sense, the conceptualization of disorder expresses a particular social experience and reproduces it. Such reproduction is a basic function of symbolic systems of all kinds (e.g., see M. Douglas 1970).

Perhaps I have already said enough to make it clear why the trauma model was selected over alternatives. It did, in short, moral and explanatory work that others did not. The new trauma model preserved and encoded victim innocence. Unlike family pathology models, Herman's (1981) early emphasis on mother-daughter conflict, or repression, it placed the burden of pathology on the abuser alone. While most clinicians did not believe it could explain every disturbance correlated with adult survivors, it covered a wide range. Unlike Herman's early model, it could also readily accommodate the disturbances correlated with male survivors. In the late 1980s, these victims, hitherto the subject of only passing attention, began to receive increasing research and clinical concern as they joined support groups, published personal accounts, wrote self-help books, and otherwise spoke out. Unlike Finkelhor's model, the new trauma model could explain delayed onset of symptoms, memory loss, and somatic experiences, and it specified mechanisms rather than vague "dynamics." Finally, the new trauma model linked sexual abuse with officially recognized *DSM* diagnostic categories, including PTSD and multiple personality. In addition to the advantages noted earlier, this linkage also facilitated claims for services within the mental heath industry and compensation claims through legal proceedings.

THE TRAUMA MODEL, RESOURCES, AND THE COURTS

The selection and elaboration of a dissociative-type trauma model for adult survivors was driven by the effort to reproduce the victim person-type and the identity attributions, especially innocence, associated with this category. However, the selection of the new trauma model was also pushed by the adjudication of claims for services and compensation. Within the mental health industry in the 1980s, diagnoses like PTSD and multiple personality, based on clearly defined psychic trauma, achieved a favored status (Haaken 1996). Despite the general decline of services for the severely mentally ill during the decade, for instance, many hospitals created special inpatient units just for multiple personality cases. This new legitimacy received major support from the social and psychiatric movements that aggressively campaigned for it. Locating the long-term harm of child sexual abuse in the trauma framework supported this legitimacy and, in the competition for mental health resources, provided an advantage that other models lacked.

Perhaps more important, the 1980s saw the rise of lawsuits brought by adult survivors against their alleged abusers. Activists recommended such suits as early as 1983 for children and adult survivors (Allen 1983), but for the latter, the statute of limitations for bringing such an action often prevented it. In most states, at that time, the statute of limitations for injury suffered as a minor began to run at the age of majority (age eighteen) and expired two or three years later, at age twenty or twenty-one. Since many victims did not begin attending therapy until later, they were barred from bringing suit when they began to connect adult problems with childhood sexual contact or recover memories of such contact. Some early plaintiffs, however, filed suit on the grounds of a "delayed discovery" of sexual abuse—due to memory repression or failure to connect injury with past abuse—in order to take advantage of a legal remedy that allowed for a delay in the running of the statute of limitations when the cause of injury could not be known during the statutory period. These early legal cases met with mixed success, and so activists turned their attention to state legislatures.

In the 1986 *Tyson v. Tyson* case (107 Wn.2d 72 [Wash. 1986]), the Washington Supreme Court refused to allow for a delayed discovery in a suit brought by a woman against her father after the statute of limitations had expired. Nancy Tyson, twenty-six at the time of her suit in 1983, alleged that she had been sexually abused between the ages of three and eleven, but that she had repressed all memory of the abuse until therapy brought it to consciousness and helped her to see how it caused her adult emotional problems. The court argued that, unlike other delayed discovery cases, "in the present case, no empirical, verifiable evidence exists of the occurrences and resulting harm which plaintiff alleges" (77). Her claim was seen to be subjective, and the testimony of psychologists or psychiatrists "would not reduce, much less eliminate," this subjectivity (78). Although this decision was later overruled by legislative action, it continued to play an important role in subsequent cases.[30]

In *Raymond v. Ingram* (737 P.2d 314 [Wash. Ct. App. 1987]), the Court of Appeals of Washington summarily rejected the claim of Pamela Jo Raymond against her paternal grandparents: the grandfather for sexually abusing her between the ages of four and seventeen, and the grandmother for negligently allowing it to occur. Unlike Tyson, Raymond argued that she remembered some past acts of sexual abuse and had experienced mental anguish associated with the abuse as a child. It was not until she entered therapy in 1982, however, that she came to recognize that her current physical problems, including insomnia and stomach ailments, were related to the abuse. The court ruled that because she knew of the abuse and some injuries associated with it earlier, the statute of limitations applied. As in *Tyson,* fact patterns similar to those in *Raymond* led to similar rulings in cases in other states.[31]

In *Johnson v. Johnson* (701 F. Supp. 1363 [N.D. Ill. 1988]), in which Deborah Johnson brought suit against her father for sexually abusing her from ages three to twelve or thirteen, and against her mother for failure to protect her, the court distinguished between the two types of cases represented by *Raymond* and *Tyson:* (1) those in which the plaintiff claimed knowledge of the sexual abuse while still a minor but only later connected her adult problems with the prior abuse; and (2) those in which the plaintiff claimed no recollection or knowledge of the abuse until adulthood. In the *Johnson* case, the Court ruled that the statute of limitations could be extended because the plaintiff claimed, with support from her therapist, who diagnosed her as suffering from multiple personality, that she had no prior knowledge of the abuse until shortly before she filed suit. The running of the statute of limitations could thus be delayed in type 2 cases, though not in type 1. With the exception of a few cases in which the statute of limitations was allowed to be delayed for both type 1 and type 2 cases (e.g., *Hammer v. Hammer*, 142 Wis. 2d 257 [Wis. Ct. App. 1987]; *Osland v. Osland*, 442 N.W.2d 907 [N.D. 1989]), courts allowing delayed discovery tended to follow the broad approach of the *Johnson* court in these years.[32]

Meanwhile, dissatisfied with court decisions, some adult survivors and plaintiffs' civil attorneys began lobbying for legislative enactments that would codify the delayed discovery doctrine into statutes of limitations for child sexual abuse civil cases.[33] A key figure in this effort was Patti Barton, who, when blocked from suing her alleged abuser by the *Tyson* decision in Washington state, successfully lobbied to get a 1989 legislative enactment that tolled (delayed the running of) the statute of limitations in sexual abuse cases. Subsequently, she and her husband pursued similar legislation across the nation. Their efforts were credited for the legislative changes in many other states (Ernsdorff and Loftus 1993: 145). Another such activist was Los Angeles attorney Shari Karney, also a survivor, who played a key role in changing California's statute of limitations (Mithers 1990). Following the lead of Washington, much of the legislation so enacted tolled the statute of limitations in both type 1 *and* type 2 cases.

Many court rulings and considerable legislative change, then, facilitated the filing of civil lawsuits in adult survivor cases.[34] In the courts and legislatures, testimony by mental health professionals played a defining role, providing credibility to claims of recovered memories or delayed discovery of a causal connection between childhood sexual contact and later psychological difficulties. Especially in the empirically oriented setting of the courts, these experts needed scientific evidence that would allow them to defend survivors' memories of childhood events as literal accounts and to explain delayed symptom formation and defenses that blocked discovery. Posttraumatic stress disorder and multiple personality—established categories and even court-tested[35]—but especially the concept of dissociation (or repression understood as dissociation) met this need in a way that no other available theories did. All were used successfully in court and in facilitating claims for victim compensation in several states that had established funds for this purpose.[36]

◦◗◦◦◗◦◡◗◦

In this chapter I traced key conceptual developments that emerged from the work of clinicians and researchers who were cataloging, documenting, and modeling the psychological harm correlated with adults victimized as children. In significant part, these developments arose in conjunction with actual treatment practices, and authors typically accompanied their findings and theoretical observations with the implied treatment recommendations. As the new trauma model took shape, so too did a therapeutic rationale for diagnosing and treating adult survivors. The rationale, the subject of the next chapter, both followed from that model and contributed to its conceptualization.

PART TWO

Defining Client Experience

CHAPTER FIVE

Therapeutic Rationale and Therapeutic Persuasion

It came to be known as the Bible of the incest survivor movement. It was widely hailed as "ground-breaking" and an inspirational "lifesaver." "This book," wrote Judith Lewis Herman for the back cover of the second edition, "advances the empowerment of survivors another major step—from breaking the silence to sharing recovery." Extremely popular, it reportedly sold 750,000 copies in its first four years and was a favorite of therapists as well. In a survey of five hundred clinical and counseling psychologists surveyed for *The Authoritative Guide to Self-Help Books* (Santrock, Minnett, and Campbell 1994), it was rated number one among self-help titles. "This book" is *The Courage to Heal: A Guide for Women Survivors of Child Sexual Abuse* by Ellen Bass and Laura Davis. First published in 1988, *The Courage to Heal* is a hefty five hundred pages of psychological advice, survivor testimonials, and detailed steps for the "healing journey." It was, in turn, the basis for a small industry of related titles by the same authors, singly or in combination, including *Beginning to Heal, Allies in Healing,* and *The Courage to Heal Workbook,* which was also a bestseller (350,000 copies in print by 1994). Although not the first self-help book for adult survivors, *The Courage to Heal* has been by far the most celebrated, the most discussed, and the most controversial.[1]

Neither coauthor brought any formal psychological training to the project. Davis, who would subsequently author the *Workbook,* had recovered memories of sexual abuse by her grandfather just months before entering into the collaboration with Bass, and elements of her story appear in the book. Bass, the senior author and the coeditor of an earlier anthology of survivor accounts, had been offering workshops for survivors and training seminars for professionals in the years leading up to the writing. She had also had, in her words, "the opportunity to train with a number of excellent therapists" (1988: 14). Still, she insisted, speaking for both authors, that "none of what is presented here is based on psychological theories. The process described, the suggestions, the exercises, the analysis, the conclusions, all come from the experiences of survivors" (14).

The notion of experience being unmediated by psychological theories is common in self-help books. The wider feminist commitment to the primacy of experiential knowledge is also evident here. Disavowing psychological theories lends the book a populist authority and, combined with the weaving of a wide range of women's grievances into the language of sexual abuse, surely helps to explain the appeal of the book as inspirational. The claim that psychological theory plays no role, however, should not be taken at face value. By the time *The Courage to Heal* appeared in the late 1980s, new psychological approaches to sexual abuse had been circulating among movement activists, mental health professionals, and survivors for a decade. This new knowledge was informing the way that survivors themselves were coming to interpret and describe their experience, and it informs the basic framework of the book.

Already in the late 1970s, a separate rationale for therapy with adults molested as children began to emerge. In part this was due to the hostility toward psychoanalysis and family therapy—the alternative rationales in which treatment recommendations were then typically framed—and the feminist rejection of rape as an encompassing model for sexual abuse. Eclecticism as a theoretical approach was also spreading rapidly (Garfield and Bergin 1986) among practicing therapists, furthering the emergence of separate rationales for particular conditions and populations. Treatment for adults molested as children was beginning to be conceptualized in its own terms, as a kind of therapy in itself, with its own logic and methods. The development of the new trauma model in the 1980s worked in tandem with this process, providing a model of disorder that unified many therapeutic approaches. As the trauma diagnosis emerged, so too did a corresponding therapeutic rationale.

Therapeutic rationales are conceptual systems that explain disorder and health, deviancy and normality. They include propositions about the cause and signs of distress or disability, about the nature and signs of health, and about healing procedures necessary to move from one state (disorder) to the other (health). They range from whole cosmologies and religions to very specific healing systems, such as psychoanalysis, and discrete rationales for treating specific disorders (diseases or syndromes). Therapeutic rationales are governed according to interpretive codes, the rationale's "truth rules" (Rice 1996), that specify which interpretations are valid and which are not and order the relationship between valid interpretations. In order to be changed, a client's experience must first be rendered meaningful. Otherwise, it remains an unintelligible and thus unalterable mixture of complaints and life problems. The therapeutic rationale provides the interpretive key that transforms what is "meaningless" and inextricable in the client's story into meaningful, interconnected patterns. It explains symptoms according to theories of their causes and provides an idiom or discourse in which those symptoms can be expressed, thereby allowing for their clarification and for their exploitation (Staiano 1986: 17). In its redefined form, the client's experience draws forth the rationale's therapy. Moreover, in its altered form, the client's experience demands the expertise of the therapist, who, understanding the discourse, can decode it.

The therapeutic rationale for adult survivors that emerged in the 1980s shaped a wide range of treatment approaches with adult survivors (though by no means all).[2] In this chapter, I review the key elements of the rationale and briefly discuss its initial influence in two treatment modalities: self-help books and self-help groups. I then briefly explore the role of persuasion in psychotherapy as a prolegomena to the more detailed discussion of the application of the survivor rationale in individual therapy in subsequent chapters.

THE ADULT SURVIVOR THERAPEUTIC RATIONALE

In the adult survivor rationale, the "healing" or "recovery" process is conceptualized as an identity change, a transition from being a victim to being a survivor and then beyond.[3] As previously noted, some adults molested as children began to call themselves "survivors" in the late 1970s, rejecting the label "victim" which they saw to have negative connotations. In the survivor rationale, however, not all victims are survivors. The term *survivor* has a more specific meaning. It connotes a present state of being and of understanding. To be an "adult survivor" is to be a victim but one who has come to understand her childhood experience as sexual abuse, who recognizes its effects on her life, and who is working to overcome the powerlessness of "being a victim" by making particular personal changes. The survivor rationale provides the interpretive framework of new understandings and accompanying emotion norms that define this identity change and its requirements.

The survivor rationale is underwritten by the trauma model, which is the basic framework in the treatment literature for ordering and explaining the long-term psychological harm correlated with childhood sexual abuse. This harm is organized into four general categories. Childhood sexual abuse, therapists argue, can undermine the victim's self-esteem, inhibit her from establishing clear personal boundaries, cause her to have a fragmented identity, and prevent her from developing appropriate social skills. Over time, such disabilities are incorporated into the victim's identity and shape how she interacts with others. They are expressed in and account for a wide range of symptoms—troublesome thoughts, emotions, behaviors, and relational dynamics—that therapists encounter when adults molested as children finally come for help. Therapists do not necessarily view *every* distress or disability observed in adult survivors as arising from an accommodation to childhood sexual contact. In her early formulation, Gelinas (1983), for instance, argued that victims also show the effects of "relational imbalances" that exist within incestuous families, and these effects are in part distinct from and even prior to the effects of the incest. Similarly, other writers have argued that some disturbances and assumptions deemed problematic (for example, about the role of women in the family) are not the result of sexual contact but of other factors, including the family system in which the victim was raised (e.g., Courtois 1988; Meiselman 1990).[4] Following the trauma model, however, all agree that the long-term effects of childhood sexual contact are serious and manifold, and the principal textbooks include symptom lists that cover a wide range of problems. Given the pathogenic power of the sexual experience, therapists argue that it must be made the "central core" around which treatment is organized.

In the survivor rationale, child sexual abuse is an act of domination that deprives the victim of agency in broad areas of her personal life. The paradigm case is repeated sexual acts between a father and young daughter, but sexual abuse refers to sexual or sexualized activity of any kind between a minor (up to age eighteen) and anyone possessing greater power.[5] Those with greater power include adults, but also include children who are older, physically stronger, or otherwise can dominate another child. Given a power differential, sexual or sexualized activity is by definition coercive and harmful. All experiences take their pathogenic implications from the father-daughter paradigm, but in the survivor rationale, the types and intensity of victim distresses or disabilities need have no correlation with the circumstances or intrusiveness of the sexual experiences.[6] Even multiple personality, the limit case, could theoretically arise from a single incident. Discovering if any sexual abuse occurred, therefore, is essential. It is not the therapist's task, however, to judge whether childhood incidents constitute abuse or trauma if the client believes they do. As one therapist writes: "The adult survivor's perception of the experience as traumatic and a determination of the impact it has had on his or her life are of greatest interest to counselors in defining an abusive childhood sexual experience" (Draucker 1992: 3).

In the survivor rationale, however, victims' perception of their experience is neither necessarily given nor fixed. Experiences or key aspects of the trauma may not be remembered. According to the trauma model, victim efforts to cope with the trauma may mean that they are consciously unaware that it happened. "At more extreme levels of preservation," according to one textbook, "the sexual abuse remains dissociated from the everyday consciousness of the patient, thus constituting a secret even from the victim herself" (Davies and Frawley 1994: 86). If the experience itself is a secret, then the meaning must be as well. Even if aware of other aspects of the abuse, victims, through defenses of denial, repression, or dissociation, may partially or wholly block off their emotional responses. "Without the consensual validation she needs to honor and accept her real feelings, the survivor is forced to choose another route. She betrays her authentic self and becomes false" (Kirschner, Kirschner, and Rappaport 1993: 55). The victim, in other words, has given her experience meaning, but it is false, shaped by a "desperate attempt to maintain internal stability" rather than her true feelings. Further, on exposure to new meanings, adult survivors may decide that their previous perceptions were inaccurate. "It must be noted that a client's perception of the intrusiveness of any specific sexual activity is subjective. His perceptions may change as he redefines his childhood experience through his adult understanding" (Crowder 1993: 10). In the survivor rationale, victim interpretations of and labels for experience can change; indeed they almost always need to change. Healing requires true meanings, the meanings that the rationale provides. Memory deficits and resistance to new meanings in the form of defenses or old coping strategies must be overcome. Buried feelings must be drawn out and expressed.

In the survivor rationale, the correct assignment of blame is pivotal. Because sexual abuse is always an act of domination, nothing the child victim did or did not do, before, during, or after sexual contact, has any bearing on the question of responsibility. While victims, therapists argue, often interpret their experience as involving some responsibility and experience guilt accordingly, self-blame in any manner is always wrong. It is an impediment to the understandings and accompanying emotions that are central to healing. The moral meanings that underlie self-blame must be reframed. People besides the abuser are not to blame either. To be sure, therapists note, other "nonprotecting" adults, such as the mother, who deny the abuse may fail child victims. Their denial can take the form of not doing anything to stop the sexual activity once they know about it. In cases where the child attempts to disclose the abuse, it can take the form of refusing to discuss it or accusing her of making it up. To blame others for the abuse, however, even if they failed to help, would, according to the rationale, be to misdirect responsibility. They did not sexually abuse the child: the abuser did. Besides, therapists argue, people who could potentially protect child victims are frequently powerless, economically and emotionally bound to abusers, and often victims themselves. The abuser alone bears complete moral blame. Healing, in the survivor rationale, requires that this attribution not be watered down or deflected to the self or others.[7]

In the survivor rationale, the matter of responsibility extends from the sexual contact itself to its effects on the victim. Given the efficient domination that abuse represents, victim defenses and coping are necessary for psychic survival. Without such internal operations, the victim's self would be overwhelmed. With them, she is able to achieve a measure, perhaps a large measure, of psychological balance and personal success. In this sense, the victim's responses are a personal strength, even if they might lead to various dysfunctions later in life. In the survivor rationale, abuse causes enduring psychological harm, but it does not cause survival. Survival is an accomplishment of the victim and signifies an internal strength that is the basis for further empowerment. At the same time, defenses and coping mechanisms arise in response to an imposed condition. Hence, the victim is not responsible for the long-term psychological problems that these defenses and mechanisms can eventually create. In the survivor rationale, healing requires recognition of both "survivor strength" and non-responsibility for the effects that abuse has wrought.

In indicating symptoms of disorder and the change that healing requires, the adult survivor therapeutic rationale also indicates a model of health. This model has two aspects. One aspect, implicit in the trauma model, is the mirroring of the collective story in the definition of individual health. Individual health, as with social health, means no denial or forgetting; it means disclosing rather than remaining silent; it means believing and affirming rather than doubting or blaming the victim; it means empowerment rather than dependency; and it means wholeness not fragmentation. A second aspect of the health model is a deeper level of implicit assumptions about the self, about society, and about the proper ordering of the relationship between the two. Such assumptions necessarily formed the foundation on which the new definitions of victim psychological harm were formulated, since disorder is, by definition, a deviation from a conceptually prior standard of health. In the trauma model, and therefore in the survivor rationale, the standard of health is drawn from a therapeutic ethic of personal liberation. In much of the clinical and research literature, the assumptions that inform this standard are so taken-for-granted that they go virtually unexpressed.

FROM CULTURAL MEANINGS TO EMBODIED EXPERIENCE

In the introduction, I briefly outlined the consensus model of symbolic healing developed by the psychiatrist and anthropologist Arthur Kleinman (1988). In that model, the process of symbolic healing is conceptualized as a kind of downward movement of cultural or subcultural understandings to the lived experience of the "patient." The articulation of the adult survivor rationale in effect completed an "upward movement" of new understandings of sexual offenses and their personal consequences into an authorized system of cultural meanings. This process began with social movements forging new definitions of sexual abuse and the abuse victim rooted in an unequivocal moral claim to victim innocence and a sharp rejection of then-dominant psychological and legal formulations. It continued with mental health professionals developing a trauma model of victim harm that incorporated these definitions and the collective story they created. Woven together into a therapeutic rationale, these new understandings constituted a conceptual system that could be used to organize and account for individual experience. Having traced that history, my next task is to consider the "downward" movement, the process by which therapists use the new rationale in therapy to redefine client experience and persuade clients of its validity.

Before turning to a consideration of individual therapy, I consider two other modes of therapy, "bibliotherapy" (self-help books) and self-help groups, which are also informed by the survivor rationale. Each of these modes of therapy is, in a sense, complete by itself. Yet in practice they overlap a great deal and seldom seem to be practiced in total isolation from the others. Approaches in one mode typically included strong recommendations for participation in other modes. The self-help books, for instance, typically recommend that readers find a survivor group and often include "resource guides" and other information for how to do so. While tending to express disapproval of the mental health establishment, the books are not averse to professional therapy (though they emphasize that a therapist must be chosen carefully) and often take it for granted that such help will be sought. Some of the self-help groups are also hostile to professional therapy, yet others recommend it, and self-help books are widely encouraged. Professional therapists often recommend books or participation in self-help groups to their clients. In fact, for adult survivors, the therapeutic modes are so interconnected that many insiders refer to an "incest survivor's movement" (e.g., Bass and Davis 1993) or "sexual abuse recovery movement" to name a kind of populist alliance of professionals and survivors that practice and participate in them.

Self-Help Books

As the survivor therapeutic rationale took form, it shaped an emerging self-help literature. The earliest self-help materials for adult survivors may have been the literature distributed by the CSATP in response "to the thousands of inquires received from women molested as children" (Giarretto 1982: 47). These materials included a short list of "ventilation exercises" for "purging" strong feelings toward the father and perhaps the mother (but not to them). They also included a number of "assimilation exercises" for imaginary letter-writing and role-playing in which the adult sought to identify her own feelings and to imagine empathetically what the father offender (and perhaps mother) might be feeling. A few self-help books also appeared in the early 1980s based on adaptations of earlier models (e.g., Daugherty 1984). However, by the late 1980s, a steady stream of new titles was coming off the presses, and these books followed the basic outline of the survivor rationale (e.g., Bass and Davis 1988; Bear and Dimock 1988; Lew 1990).[8]

Self-help books are not a description of how to do therapy; they are a form of therapy in themselves.[9] Unlike the professional textbooks—which outline a treatment process to guide therapists and form the basis for the analysis of therapy in the following chapters—the self-help books administer this treatment in steps that readers can take, partially or completely, by themselves. Because they are addressed to different audiences, the material in the two kinds of books is presented very differently. The professional textbooks, for instance, recommend various techniques to "normalize" and "depathologize" clients' problems, and often use case histories to illustrate these techniques. The self-help books, on the other hand, apply these techniques. Heavily punctuated with the autobiographical accounts of adult survivors, these books encourage readers to identify with the accounts and so recognize that no problem they have experienced is really unique or unnatural. For my purposes, most of the differences between the two types of books are not particularly important. The key point is that both are informed by the survivor rationale. There is one difference, however, that bears special mention because of its potential unintended consequences. In the self-help literature, unlike the professional texts for therapists, a central goal is to help the reader self-diagnose as a survivor.

The self-help books begin with the stated conviction that child sexual abuse (defined very broadly) is extremely widespread in American society and that a large percentage of affected adults do not recall their abuse due to some form of repression or dissociation. According to one popular volume written by a therapist, "Incest is easily the greatest single underlying reason why women seek therapy or other treatment" (Blume 1990: xiii). However, most adults victimized as children do not self-diagnose: "Indeed, so few incest survivors in my experience have identified themselves as abused in the beginning of therapy that I have concluded that perhaps half of all incest survivors do not remember that the abuse occurred" (81). The popular recovery movement writer John Bradshaw put the figure at 60 percent (Bradshaw 1992). Others, like survivor therapist Renee Fredrickson, made the claim that "millions of people have blocked out frightening episodes of abuse" (1992: 15).

Given the perceived prevalence of abuse and widespread loss of memory, the focus of the literature is on helping readers first to determine if they might be victims and then to provide therapeutic guidance. For the purposes of determination, long checklists of general symptoms are supplied.[10] These lists vary widely, always including sexual difficulties and common habitual problems (particularly eating disorders), but then extending in many directions. Some of these symptoms can be very innocuous—for example: "You are mildly ill all the time," "You have never to your knowledge had sex with anyone" (Bradshaw 1992); "You have trouble feeling motivated," "You feel you have to be perfect" (Bass and Davis 1988); "Inability to complete tasks," "Difficulty receiving from others" (Engel 1989); "Basements terrify me," "I startle easily" (Fredrickson 1992). Regardless of whether childhood sexual contacts are actually remembered, authors encourage readers to consider a self-diagnosis as a survivor if they have some stipulated minimum number of such symptoms. The books urge readers not to doubt their memories of abuse and, if they have certain symptoms, to suspect abuse even if no memories are forthcoming. A famous passage from *The Courage to Heal* states, "So far, no one we've talked to thought she might have been abused, and then later discovered that she hadn't been. The progression always goes the other way, from suspicion to confirmation. If you think you were abused and your life shows the symptoms, then you were" (1988: 22).[11] The books also encourage readers to work at recovering memories, and they provide strategies and techniques for doing so. Readers are counseled not to be discouraged if memories are not forthcoming, to believe memories that do come, even if they seem incredible, and to be prepared to face ridicule and misunderstanding from family and friends, especially if they engage in a confrontation.

Although there is no empirical data, what evidence that is available suggests that the main self-help books, including *The Right to Innocence* by Beverly Engel, *Repressed Memories* by Renee Fredrickson, *Secret Survivors* by E. Sue Blume, and *The Courage to Heal,* have all been popular with adult survivors, with the latter book, as noted, becoming a major bestseller. Surveys of therapists have also found that considerable percentages recommended these and other survivor self-help books to their clients (e.g., Polusny and Follette 1996; Poole et al. 1995). In surveys conducted by the False Memory Syndrome Foundation, a very high percentage of accused parents reported that their daughter had been strongly influenced by one of these books, most especially *The Courage to Heal.* While there were many possible paths to being labeled an adult survivor over the past two decades, the self-help books were clearly an important one.

Self-Help Groups

By the late 1970s, the claims-making about sexual abuse as a harmful condition was already beginning to take social structural form in the emergence of story-sharing groups and networks of communication outside the confines of the mental health professions. Both groups and networks proliferated widely in the 1980s. Most commonly, survivors themselves organized these initiatives, sometimes in the form of treatment programs (for example, Christopher Street) but more often as personal support or self-help groups. In such groups, participants are encouraged to self-label as adult survivors and to forge a common identity rooted in a shared language, shared elements of a common past, and a shared effort to overcome the effects of victimization. In an environment of mutual support and empathy, participants tell and retell their personal accounts with the aim of "working through" past hurts, overcoming isolation and low self-esteem, and gaining greater control over their lives for the future. The survivor rationale informs this change process.

Depending on the survivor self-help group, different treatment models shape the intergroup storytelling process. One common approach is based on an adaptation of the twelve-step recovery program that was originally formulated by Alcoholics Anonymous (AA), the organization for problem drinkers that emphasizes the importance of small-group involvement for overcoming alcoholism. Especially since the late 1970s, with the formation of Adult Children of Alcoholics, a burgeoning "recovery" movement has emerged that focuses on many other forms of "addiction" and caregiving roles defined as pathological that are believed to arise in conjunction with living in dysfunctional and abusive families.[12] In the movement, growing up for most people—96 percent of Americans in one famous estimate (Bradshaw 1988)—is characterized by pain, abuse, and conflict, and leads to a troubled adulthood consumed with keeping family secrets. To initiate and sustain recovery from the adult disturbances brought on by family experiences, the movement typically urges "adult children" to get in touch with their good "inner child," to break free of the pathological "family rules" that continue to victimize them, to recognize their past powerlessness, to assert the primacy of the self over social conventions, to embrace an unconditional self-regard, and to build new models of relationship in the context of the small support group. Thousands of groups have appeared throughout the United States based on some form of this model, including groups for "co-dependents," debtors, gamblers, overeaters, self-abusers, compulsive shoppers, shoplifters, sex addicts, drug abusers, former fundamentalists, and hundreds more (see Moskowitz 2001).

Both of the initial self-help group networks for adult survivors of childhood sexual abuse were based on twelve-step models. Founded in Long Beach, California, in July 1980 by survivor Erin May, Incest Survivors Anonymous (ISA) sponsors self-help meetings for survivors and "prosurvivors"—a sympathetic family member, spouse, or friend. Mental health professionals are not allowed (they may attend if survivors themselves), nor are "incest initiators (perpetrators/Satanists)." The goal of ISA meetings is to

> share our experience, strength, and hope, so we may recover from our incest experiences and gain new tools to live by so as not to be revictimized by our past. As survivors, we strive to recognize the negative behavior patterns, brainwashing, and programming initiated on us as children, in the midst of torture. We break free to a new understanding, a new peace of mind, and a new way of life. . . . (ISA letter, personal communication, 1994)

Using a very broad definition of "incest" (synonymous with sexual abuse), the "only requirement for ISA membership is a desire to stop being an incest victim and become an incest survivor" (ISA website).[13]

Survivors of Incest Anonymous (SIA), started in 1982, is an "international network of autonomous, self-help meetings" (SIA brochure, n.d.).

Like ISA, the groups can include prosurvivors. SIA also uses a very broad definition of incest and holds that victims "were affected by the abuse whether it occurred once or many times since the damage was incurred immediately" (SIA website).[14] Like ISA, SIA initially adopted the twelve steps of AA with only minor modifications. Later, however, this network made further adaptations. Step 6, for instance, originally read, We: "Were entirely ready to have God remove these [i.e., our] defects of character." As revised, it reads, "Were entirely ready to have a loving Higher Power help us remove all the debilitating consequences of the abuse and became willing to treat ourselves with respect, compassion and acceptance." Step 7, which originally read, "Humbly asked Her/Him [God] to remove our shortcomings," was revised to read, "Humbly and honestly asked a loving Higher Power to remove the unhealthy and self-defeating consequences stemming from the abuse."[15] SIA also publishes several dozen pamphlets. One, entitled "Remembering," takes it for granted that at least some important aspects of past abuse have been forgotten. Another brochure, similar to one published by ISA and to information given in the self-help books, includes a twenty-point questionnaire of symptoms designed to allow the reader to self-label. They suggest that if you marked "yes" for three or more of the symptom questions, then SIA could help.

Like self-help books, these groups represent another important pathway to the survivor identity. As I note in chapter 7, professional therapists often recommend such groups to their clients to assist with both labeling and treatment processes.

PSYCHOTHERAPY AND PERSUASION

Therapeutic rationales are tools used by therapists to help people explore and change the meaning of their experience. This interaction is necessarily collaborative. The therapist redefines the client's experience in terms of the therapeutic rationale and its interpretive codes. Along with acts and rituals, he "cures by talking and listening," dealing not with the physical body, as the conventional physician does, but with "ideas, memories of experiences, painful and untoward emotions" (London 1964: 3). The client's understanding of her experience and of herself is at issue, which means that change cannot be forced or imposed. She must accept the efficacy of the therapeutic rationale and anticipate beneficial change. Consider an extreme case: "A psychoanalyst trying to cure a client who does not believe in oedipal conflicts and a witchdoctor trying to cure a client who does not believe in spirit possession will be equally ineffective" (Torrey 1986: 25). Clearly, as this case suggests, some degree of initial cultural similarity between therapist and client is essential to therapeutic effectiveness (Berger and Luckmann 1966; Horwitz 1982; Kleinman 1988). Rationales do not possess an intrinsic plausibility; they gain it from resonance with cultural beliefs, and unless at least some of these beliefs are shared, a rationale will not be plausible to a client. Even assuming some cultural similarity, the therapist must still convince the client of the validity of his rationale and of its power to bring about desired change.

Gaining client trust is where therapeutic persuasion begins. Such trust is in part a function of educational credentials, office (for example, clergy), and/or reputation of the therapist. Therapists with medical training use medical terms such as *patient, symptoms,* and *diagnosis,* which suggest that they, like conventional doctors, cure people who need skilled help for some illness or incapacity. In these cases, the social legitimacy of therapy comes from its direct association with medicine.[16] Other therapists, however, disavow a medical approach. Emphasizing a link with other service professionals, such as attorneys, and avoiding the terminology of medicine, they refer to those who come for help as "clients." These therapists do not regard their clients as sick or in need of a cure (Efran, Lukens, and Lukens 1990; Engler and Goleman 1992) and may even regard such a framework as inimical to gaining client trust and cooperation. They describe psychotherapy as a contractual relationship, with specific terms agreed to in advance by both parties (Efran, Lukens, and Lukens 1990; Zeig and Munion 1990). These therapists emphasize the role that clients play in helping themselves. Engler and Goleman, for instance, like many current writers on psychotherapy, argue that "[t]herapy is a *collaborative* process ... designed, not to change you, but to help you change yourself" (1992: 20; emphasis in original).

Yet in important respects medicine and science remain crucial to the social legitimation of contemporary psychotherapeutic practice. Therapeutic rationales and healing procedures are linked to dominant cultural beliefs, and as Frank and Frank note, in the United States, "faith in science still seems to provide the predominant source of symbolic healing power" (1991: 42). Clients may not be sick in some physiological sense, or sick in the sense of severely mentally ill, but problematic areas of their lives, whatever the cause, are typically interpreted or diagnosed in a quasi-medical framework. Health is a broad interpretative schema for understanding and classifying personal problems, whose use has expanded rapidly as more and more types of undesirable attitudes and behavior have been "medicalized" or "scientized," with a consequent expansion of categories of illness, including mental disturbances (Conrad and Schneider 1992; Fox 1977; Gergen 1994). Undesirable ideas, attitudes, practices, even relationships are "not healthy" and require, even mandate, intervention. Therapists lay claim to making an intervention based on a kind of scientific expertise rooted in a trained capacity to distinguish between healthy and unhealthy with regard to matters of the mental and emotional life, and professional competence with techniques that can help the client change. While science is clearly not as powerful an explanation as it once was, it remains a principal authorization that inspires client trust.

In addition to issues of reputation and expertise, gaining client trust is also a function of the therapist's ability to build rapport. He must demonstrate to the client that he wants to help her, that he is genuinely concerned about her well-being. The therapist's relationship to the client is not spontaneous or casual; rather it is structured, normally involving scheduled appointments, clear rules, a prescribed setting, and the payment of fees. Yet, at the same time, if it is successful, it is a relationship that is strongly affective and personally supportive of the client (Pande 1968; Schofield 1964; Thoits 1985). Its formality and structure also allow for intense emotion and intimacy, and its quality for the client either strengthens or diminishes her trust in the powers of the therapist, her willingness to collaborate, and her expectation of beneficial change. The relationship is the context for a very personal form of persuasion and a laboratory and vehicle for making change, and its success hangs on the therapist's personal engagement of the client. One part of this effort centers on establishing a therapeutic setting that simultaneously exudes an aura of professionalism and healing and creates a sense of comfort and protection wherein the client feels free to engage in the experimentation that the therapy prescribes (Frank and Frank 1991). The other part of building a warm and supportive therapeutic ethos centers on the therapist's personality and self-presentation. Therapists in some therapeutic schools have attempted to hide their personalities under general techniques. Freud, for instance, thought that by controlling his speech and sitting behind the patient, the therapist could prevent his personality from intruding into the encounter. While attempts at affective neutrality continue to characterize some therapists, many if not most contemporary therapists make no effort to exclude personality factors. On the contrary, they actively cultivate personality qualities (including empathy, warmth, tolerance, and sincerity) and self-presentations of confidence and energy so as to increase the client's commitment to the change process and her trust in their abilities and intentions[17]

As therapists apply their interpretive codes to the client's experience in order to redefine it, they also use techniques to persuade clients that the redefinition is making sense out of their experience and will have healing consequences. The healing techniques are those words, acts, and rituals, along with any auxiliary practices, that the therapist uses to particularize his rationale in the experience of the client and to mediate change. The techniques a therapist uses, of course, vary with the way a disorder is conceived. In the rationale of some cognitive therapies, for instance, symptoms are believed to result from distorted perceptions of reality based on erroneous assumptions that the individual has internalized. Given this rationale, a cognitive therapist focuses on unearthing "automatic thoughts" and correcting the distortions with new cognitions. To this end, he uses various techniques to disrupt and expose habitual ways of thinking and teach new understandings. The specific techniques vary with the particular client and with the therapist's own experience and conviction about what techniques work. Even within the same rationale, no two healing trajectories are exactly the same. Healing techniques differ with rationales, but they are also determined in the context of specific therapist-client dyads.

Within a rationale, therapeutic techniques may be bundled into packages— treatment models—that specify in general terms the sequencing of techniques for addressing distress or dysfunction. The models divide the total therapy process, which might be quite lengthy, into discrete, interconnected steps or stages, each consisting of particular tasks, rituals, and reinterpretations. Typically, therapists explain each therapeutic step in terms of the transformative goals that it serves, highlight progress toward the goals, and attribute to the client's own efforts each achievement of new insights or behaviors. Completing these smaller, more manageable changes signifies the client's therapeutic progress. The signs of progress are in turn used to build the client's motivation for taking the next steps in the process and to underwrite their logic and necessity. The signs of progress are also used to challenge any subsequent action or resistance by the client by interpreting it as a deviation from progress previously marked. By taking one step at a time, the client is drawn to reinterpret her experience progressively in light of the therapist's rationale and to participate in learning experiences that mediate change. Moreover, these techniques virtually create success experiences that not only persuade the client that she is changing but may, by themselves, build morale and an increased sense of mastery and control that are common measures of successful therapy (Liberman 1978).

While particular treatment models differ, they are designed to transform the meaning of client experience by achieving a number of key purposes.

These purposes include teaching clients, overcoming their resistance, arousing their emotions, and fostering their internalization and consolidation of new learning.

Teaching. Therapists teach clients new interpretations of their problems and communicate new beliefs and attitudes.[18] They socialize clients into the therapeutic relationship, teaching them how to take the client role. As they explore the client's narrative, therapists identify discrepancies in the client's interpretations of herself and her experience, and teach her alternative interpretations based in the therapeutic rationale. In light of the rationale, and their assumptions about self and society, therapists teach clients what it means to be healthy and what steps they must take to achieve health. They teach clients new "technologies of the self," as Foucault (1988) called them: various techniques that individuals use to modify their own thoughts and actions—for instance, how to be more personally assertive, how to manage and express emotion, how to handle problematical relationships, or how to be more sexually responsive. In all such ways, therapists act as teachers to promote new learning.

Therapists' teaching operates on several levels. At one level, therapists directly communicate new cognitive understandings. They provide practical instruction, they explain, they illustrate, they promote new ideas and challenge the adequacy of old ways of thinking. At another level, therapists provide clients with experiential learning opportunities. They create opportunities for clients to experience for themselves the rightness of new interpretations or the wrongness of their current assumptions. They might coach clients, for instance, as in behavioral therapies, to safely face frightening situations and so convince them that their fears are unfounded. Finally, at a third level, therapists use more subtle and indirect means of teaching. They might, for instance, conduct themselves in the therapeutic relationship so as to model to the client new attitudes, alternative relationship strategies, and ways of behaving. They might offer incentives, use subtle punishments, provide cues, selectively validate, and in a host of other ways steer clients toward new understandings. While therapists differ in rationale and style, psychotherapeutic teaching takes place at all three of these levels.

Overcoming resistance. As they attempt to teach clients, therapists must simultaneously overcome their resistance to change. The principal obstacles are personal defenses or problematic adaptations to life experiences. Therapists conceive of defenses as conscious and unconscious processes that include blocking off emotion or awareness, inhibiting action or expression, and self-protective patterns and ideas, such as denial or other acts of concealment and avoidance. In order for new interpretations to be accepted and activated, old understandings and coping patterns must be dislodged and deconstructed. The therapist therefore uses techniques to discern the client's defenses and interpretations in order to overcome them.

Every element of therapy can be an occasion for client blockage and resistance. The therapist's effort to win the client's trust and his creation of a therapeutic ethos that is nonjudgmental, safe, and emotionally supportive are important conditions, as discussed above, for successful therapy. Open, sincere communication reduces the client's tendency to protect the stability of her assumptions. In addition, therapists use techniques to focus the conversation, reduce blockages of emotion and awareness, and surmount rejection of key interpretations. In order to overcome resistance to self-disclosure, for example, insight-oriented therapists (for example, psychoanalysts) carefully direct the conversation, focusing the client on material they view as significant and working to keep her from changing the subject. Without getting heavy-handed, therapists tease out information that the client is reluctant to divulge. They might request clarifications, interrupt the client, use praise and other forms of social reinforcement to express approval ("validation") for desired disclosures, or use special methods (for example, hypnosis) to facilitate recall and reduce psychological blocks. Or, if the client seems disinclined, they may drop the matter temporarily only to bring it up again, perhaps repeatedly, later. They might disclose some personal information in order to support discussion of a sensitive topic and to model to the client the type of talk that is being invited. Such methods, along with many others, open the client to cooperation and change.

Emotional arousal. Arousing emotional responses is essential to therapeutic change (Frank and Frank 1991: 46), both for reducing resistance and for promoting new learning. Changing personal behavior and beliefs is seldom an easy process. Timely emotional arousal can overcome inertia and resistance, and motivate the client to want to change and to stick with the therapeutic process. Intense emotional experience can facilitate attitudinal change, and, especially if it disrupts habitual responses, can heighten client suggestibility, promote bonding with and dependence on the therapist, and work to break up old patterns of self-integration (Frank and Frank 1991). Moreover, arousing emotions gives the therapist opportunities to address the client's emotional states and emotional displays, and to teach her new norms of emotion and expression.[19]

Therapists arouse emotions in any number of ways, primarily by providing new interpretations for the client's experience. Emotions are evoked not by experience directly but by judgments concerning experience. As one therapist notes with regard to anger: "[I]t is the perception or appraisal of ... events as provocative, rather than the events themselves, that evoke anger" (Jehu 1988: 120). Changing the appraisal of an experience, then, can change the emotions that are aroused by it, especially when therapists couple new interpretations with instruction about what sorts of feelings the client can expect to have and validate some emotions but not others. Therapists use these changed emotions to underwrite the validity of the new interpretations and promote additional ones. On the other hand, new feelings may lead to new interpretations. Therapists may also use specific techniques in order to directly arouse particular emotions. The most intense of these techniques include exposing clients to situations they fear, as in behavioral therapies, and having them re-evoke past traumatic experiences, as in abreactive therapies. Particular emotions support particular interpretations. Anger, for instance, or indignation supports an interpretation of an experience as an injustice. Evoking the emotion, then, encourages the client to reconsider the experience to which the emotion is believed to be a response. In this way, the emotion (anger) precedes a new interpretation (injustice).

Consolidation of change. As therapists lead clients to new interpretations of their experience, teaching and modeling new beliefs and behaviors, they provide them with opportunities for practice as well as incentives to internalize and maintain therapeutic gains (Frank and Frank 1991: 50). To have staying power, new learning must be reinforced, and it must be transferred from therapy into daily living. In order to promote internalization and transfer, therapists have clients practice and test what they are learning, both within and outside the therapeutic relationship. Indeed, much of the therapy session may consist of evaluating practice opportunities since the last session. Further, therapists build in incentives aimed to consolidate gains and make it difficult for clients to deviate from them. Giving an account of practice experiences can itself have this effect, as can success experiences, noted earlier, and the emotionally intense therapeutic relationship. Not wanting to disrupt or jeopardize an intimate relationship by disappointing the therapist can be a strong incentive to stay on course. Therapists use this dynamic for just this purpose.

Methods of practice and consolidation of change come in many forms. During sessions, therapists have clients essentially try on and rehearse new interpretations, new emotional responses, and new behaviors. They might, for instance, have clients practice new responses to stressful situations by role-playing, creating hypothetical situations in which they act out different ways of conducing themselves and managing their emotions. Or they might have clients practice being assertive, or write out an account of their experience in light of new interpretations and feelings. Outside of therapy sessions, therapists might have clients do "homework," such as reading books or practicing with new technologies of the self. A particularly powerful tool for consolidating therapeutic change, and an important one in adult survivor therapies, is to restructure the client's support system. An important feature of healing rituals in non-Western societies (Kleinman 1988: 135), restructuring social relationships in the contemporary Western context can take at least two forms. Therapists might encourage clients to participate in a therapeutic self-help group or in group therapy, where they can forge new relationships supportive of their change, and practice new understandings and behavior. Therapists might also recommend that clients change their personal relationships, distancing themselves from relationships that are seen to be inhibiting or enervating and forming new ones, organized in light of clients' changed assumptions about themselves and their social world. Whatever its other effects, restructuring relationships can consolidate therapeutic change by building external support for it, providing performance opportunities, and creating new expectations of clients, as well as an incentive for them to live up to these expectations.

The Goals and Consequences of Psychotherapy

Psychotherapy is a very specific effort at social influence. Through techniques of persuasion aimed to teach, overcome resistance, arouse emotions, and consolidate new learning, therapists draw clients to collaborate in a renegotiation of the meaning of, and their assumptions about, their experience. Some individual therapies focus on changing meaning fairly directly (more insight-oriented therapies), while others do so more indirectly (more directive therapies that focus on changing cognitions, emotions, behaviors, or relationships in order to produce changed meaning and thus enduring symptom improvement).[20] In either case, as clients are persuaded, their experience comes to resonate with and be conditioned by new meanings that follow from the interpretative codes of the therapist's rationale superimposed on their behaviors, beliefs, past history, relational functioning, and so on (Frank and Frank 1991; Kleinman 1988). The new meanings transform clients' emotional reactions and their views of themselves and their relationships with others. The life problems that constituted the original presenting symptoms may or may not be directly affected, but the perception of them is, and changed perceptions can change the quality of the client's experience

(Kleinman 1988: 134)—creating new hope, reducing fear, alleviating tension, and so on. Therapists heal by redefining the meanings of clients' experiences to what they regard as more favorable ones.[21] Therapy is considered successful if clients are persuaded and at some level feel and function better than they did before.[22]

Redefining the meaning of experience may be a more or less profound process. Therapists address many types of client distress or disability with short-term, focused therapies. Mild depression, grief, phobias, awkward social behavior, and the like may be relieved to the satisfaction of all with only minor adjustments to the way clients understand their experience. The assumptions connected to the troublesome thoughts, feelings, or behaviors are circumscribed in scope and not deeply held. They are "weak" assumptions that are not central to the individual's identity and not especially resistant to change. In many other cases, however, the therapist's diagnosis of clients' illness episodes and his rationale indicate a program of more fundamental change. In longer-term treatment models, as with adult survivor therapies, techniques are aimed at progressive change in clients' understanding of their experience and a significant alteration in their assumptions about self and relating to others. Therapists target more enduring, deeply held, and less conscious assumptions—"strong" assumptions that by definition are more resistant to change.

In working to change client assumptions, especially deeply held ones, therapists work to effect a more or less significant transformation in clients' identities, their self-narratives. The identity, as a number of scholars have conceived it, is the self as understood by the individual in terms of his or her ongoing story (e.g., Bruner 1987; Gergen 1994; Giddens 1991; Kerby 1991; MacIntyre 1984; Taylor 1989). It is an understanding of who one is and what one's life means that is built up and maintained self-consciously, though always, at some level, in interaction with other people. Socialization experiences in the family and in institutional settings, with friends and other reference groups, shape one's identity. Our responses to our social environment and our choices do so as well, but even these responses and choices are not free of social influence. In order to interact with those around us, we are constrained, whatever our private fantasies, to describe ourselves in ways that others will recognize and understand.

Our identity includes those assumptions we use to make sense of our experience and to guide and justify action. It includes values, expectations, and images of self, others, and the larger environment. It also includes moral evaluations. As the philosopher Charles Taylor (1989) has shown, we define our identity in reference to a moral horizon or framework. "To know who you are," he argues, "is to be oriented in moral space" (28). Moral space is a realm of questions about what is good, what is worthwhile, and what has meaning. In this view, our identity cannot be detached from our beliefs about what things have significance, from our fundamental evaluations with regard to questions of the good in life.

Identity, conceived as a narrative, shares the characteristics of stories.[23] Stories have a particular structure. First, they place events within a framework that reaches toward a valued endpoint(s). Narratives are goal-directed: They are told to explain, to exhort, to teach, to indicate what is of value and why. Self-narratives plot the type of moral agent the individual is and his or her purposes and intentions. Second, narratives selectively recruit past events that are relevant to and anticipate the story's valued endpoint. Self-narratives reveal the value directions in the narrator's life "by selectively plotting only those actions relevant or tributary to certain central purposes" (Kerby 1991: 56). The past is interpreted in light of an anticipated future (more or less distant), the possible self that one might be or become. Recollection, therefore, is directly tied to story emplotment, an understanding that suggests why memory is so typically emphasized in therapy as founding the experience of selfhood. Third, a narrative is ordered as a sequence of events or episodes that unfold in a way that portrays a meaningful sequence of events—a plot. Events are related in an interdependent, causally linked fashion to indicate and demonstrate a unity of purpose. Finally, the characters (or objects) in narratives exhibit a stability of identity throughout the story—they behave characteristically. Of course, characters in many stories do undergo a transformation, but when this happens, the story itself is typically told to explain the transformation and in terms that maintain the character's consistency. Fragmentation or multiplicity of identity implies incoherence and instability. As these characteristics suggest, a well-formed narrative is shaped by value determinations and distinctions, the fundamental evaluations emphasized by Taylor (1989). It is a reconfiguration of experience, with events selected and emplotted within a framing context or history that infuses them with significance and allows them to be exploited for valued ends.

Conceiving of identity as possessing, or needing to possess, the characteristics of a well-formed narrative permits a specification of key goals and outcomes of therapeutic identity change. The depth of identity change, desired or effected, varies, as does the specific content of the new stories that clients come to tell. Therapists, using different therapeutic rationales, with their different interpretive codes and different assumptions about human nature and the moral order, interpret client experience differently and thus influence the self-narrative of the client differently. But in each case, in redefining the meaning of client experience, therapists address, explicitly or implicitly, the fundamental evaluations, moral or otherwise, that characterize and give direction to the client's self-narrative. While a client may maintain a moral autonomy (Kelly and Strupp 1992), the therapist's redefining of the client's experience in terms of his rationale typically draws the client toward new distinctions and understandings. Kenneth Calestro (1972) calls this confluence the power of "therapeutic suggestion" (see also Cushman 1993; Pande 1968). Changing assumptions about the self and its status is the most obvious outcome of redefinitions, but the influence also extends to a broader set of evaluations. In analyzing a number of therapy studies, L. E. Beutler and colleagues found that "there is apparently a decided tendency for successful therapy dyads to be associated with the patients' acquiring therapists' belief systems, both about religious and moral attitudes and about more general concepts as well" (1986: 275). Changed meanings for experience evoke changed evaluations and a reworking of the endpoints of the self-narrative. Changed endpoints, in turn, prefigure a changed way of living and a changed future.

°☙° °☙° °☙°

Therapy addresses client distress and disability by translating cultural meanings into embodied experience. The goal is an identity change, and the various elements of therapy—relationship, persuasion, decoding of symptoms, redefinition of experience, and so on—are organized to promote this goal. With the articulation of the adult survivor rationale, the emergent cultural meanings of sexual abuse and its personal consequences were codified for therapeutic application to individual cases. I have already briefly touched on how the rationale informed new survivor self-help books and self-help groups. I turn in the next two chapters to a far more detailed examination of individual psychotherapy with adult survivors. In survivor therapy, therapists redefine client experience, past and present, and teach new normative reorientations to the self and others. Constructing a victim account is where the process begins.

CHAPTER SIX

The Victimization Account

Accounts, to return to a concept introduced at the outset, are a type of personal narrative that people tell to explain and attribute causality to stressful, traumatic, or socially disruptive experiences and life events. Scholars studying accounts argue that people are constrained to describe and order their stories through the sense making procedures and possibilities that are socially available in their context of action. Thus, a person could not, in this interpretive sense, be an "adult survivor" before the 1970s because the description of experience that it entails simply was not yet a social possibility. However, from the themes of the collective story and its psychological elaboration in the trauma model emerged the prototype of a new account, a narrative that explains how a disempowered adult with a false and frag mented sense of self can result from sexual contact as a child. A new "way of being" was, in effect, created that people could appropriate as a socially rec ognized and intelligible account of their experience. Survivor therapy begins with the therapist helping the client to make this appropriation.

In this chapter and the next, I analyze the stages of survivor therapy. This analysis is based on the various treatment models—as articulated in the professional textbooks—that practitioners use to influence client change. Most of these models are theoretically eclectic (see the methodological appendix). Consistent with their eclectic orientation, they present techniques from a variety of therapeutic schools to address specific problems. Psychodynamic techniques, for example, are often recommended for unearthing memories and working through them; cognitive techniques are recommended for handling "faulty thinking"; and behavioral techniques are recommended for desensitizing emotional responses to traumatic memories. While there is a great deal of overlap, these models do not share all the same assumptions and do not recommend all the same approaches or the same stages. For purposes of analysis, however, I have created a composite picture of the process and refer to it in the singular as "survivor therapy." Obviously, with a composite, some specificity, nuance, and variability in clinical practice are lost. Yet, the structure that I present here, with varying modifications, is common to the different models. It is the common narrative prototype for developing a victimization account and survivor identity according to the survivor therapeutic rationale.

To provide a sense of the therapeutic landscape and how I will analyze it, I begin with a survey of the stages of survivor therapy and how they cohere in the larger "mediating narrative" that guides client change. In the balance of this chapter and the next, I describe in greater detail the diagnosis, the structuring of the therapeutic relationship, how the stages of the healing process unfold, what techniques therapists employ in each stage and why, how the stages build on one another, and what goals the whole process is designed to serve.

Two quite different descriptions of the self operate throughout the stages of the therapy process. One is a language of external determination (often referred to in terms of the "false self"); the other is a language of agency and self-direction (the language of the "true self"). Therapists use the latter language to characterize the self-understandings toward which the therapy aims, while they use the first to characterize the self-understandings that the client is encouraged to reject. The juxtaposition of these two contrasting languages of determination and agency, I argue, is part of a discursive strategy to bring about a change in client identity and moral orientations. Therapists use the language of external determination, already central to the trauma model and the collective story it psychologized, to guide the client in constructing an account of innocence. In this account, client assumptions about the self and about others deemed problematic are defined as outcomes of inflicted trauma. At the same time, therapists proffer new assumptions, contrasted with the old, and for these they employ the language of self-determination. To the client, the new assumptions are pictured as arising from within, from an originary, or "true," self, as it were. This is not a coercive process, but neither is it, I intend to show, the mere emancipation and recognition of a hitherto silenced voice.

THE THERAPEUTIC PROCESS: OVERVIEW

The construction of a new account and identity in survivor therapy is a negotiated accomplishment. To foster personal healing, therapists employ what I will call a "mediating narrative" to authorize and structure the client's rejection of old self-understandings and the appropriation of new ones. The mediating narrative is the symbolic vehicle, the sequence of words, acts, and rituals that therapists use to convey a message of personal transformation through a reordered self, and that mediates the transformation by providing an account template for achieving it. Survivor therapists describe the treatment process as a sequence of stages, which some label "victim," "survivor," and "thriver," a usage I follow. These stages constitute a narrative structure of "stories"—about the past, present, and future—which, taken together, represent an unfolding plot directed toward the new understandings of the self and others that constitute the endpoint attitudinal ideals of health and wholeness. To reach the endpoint, the therapist organizes each element of therapy, especially the therapeutic relationship, to foster a "narrative fit" (Goodman 1978), helping the client to reflect upon and evaluate her experience and repeatedly renarrate it until it is internally consistent with the narrative model.

In the initial stage of therapy, the therapist leads the client, whatever her current understanding of her experience, to recast her life story in terms of being an abuse victim. He works to loosen her attachment to her interpretations of the past, while directing her in building an account of abuse. Interpreting her symptoms as aftereffects of abuse, he links her presenting problems—anxiety, depression, flashbacks, an eating disorder, sleep disturbances, and so on—with the long-term consequences of being a victim. Once the client can give an account of her past in terms of being abused, she is ready to work on telling a story about the present in terms of being a survivor. In the second stage, the therapist emphasizes the client's strength and potential, not her vulnerability and powerlessness. Applying the survivor rationale to the way she views herself and others, he leads her to a more pervasive sense of the effects of abuse on her life. These effects fall into the categories of low self-esteem, uncertain personal boundaries, identity fragmentation, and social dysfunction. At the same time, the therapist uses the therapy sessions as a workshop for overcoming these effects by teaching the client new orientations to the self and new techniques for relating to others. He advocates her innocence and basic goodness to promote greater self-esteem. He teaches norms of boundary management and self-care to promote autonomy, and he provides the mediating narrative and the normative framework it embodies to promote identity cohesion and more consistent living.

In the third stage, the client's two stories, victim and survivor, are transcended by a third. In the third story, a story about the future, the client is no longer primarily victim or survivor. She is beyond these categories; she is a "thriver." Encouraging her to no longer see herself as conditioned by abuse or defined by her resistance to it, the therapist now leads her to describe herself as an individual who is capable of directing her destiny. By overcoming the effects of the past, he teaches her, she is empowered to tell a story of agency. This is an open story about the future in which she increasingly makes satisfactory life choices and becomes the person she wants to be. Therapy ends when the therapist is satisfied that the thriver story and the lessons of the mediating narrative are increasingly defining the client's identity.

To accomplish its work, the mediating narrative requires each of the three component stories. Since clients begin with different experiences, have different understandings of their experiences, and need varying lengths of time in therapy, "Therapists should expect each survivor's path to recovery to be somewhat different" (Bolton, Morris, and MacEachron 1989: 101). In actual practice, therapists note, the process of therapy is seldom a neat and orderly progression. Nonetheless, each stage is important. For all clients, the victim account is important because it identifies the source of the client's suffering, increases her motivation to change, provides justification for the change, and serves as the benchmark against which the therapist defines progress toward healing. For therapists, until the client has emplotted her experience in and presented a victim account, she is not ready to move forward. The survivor story is important for all because it increases the client's expectation of change; it mandates change by associating old perspectives and behaviors with abuse, and it indicates the changes to be made and the experimentation and practice required to make them. In telling the survivor story, the client progressively internalizes the attitudes and principles of the identity that the therapist is persuading her to adopt. The final thriving story is important because it provides a positive story, uncoupled from abuse, for going forward, and its telling motivates the client to continue to live according to the principles she has been taught. Only with the thriver story is the journey to healing, for which the therapist is guide, complete. It alone represents the identity that the whole process is designed to persuade the client to embrace.

Because all the stages of therapy are important and form a single, coherent process, therapists insist that if the client cuts therapy short, she will leave important issues unresolved and undermine her healing and her ability to maintain the gains that have already been made. A hasty "fleeing into health" by announcing a quick resolution of abuse-related problems is, in this view, a fleeing from health back to the false psychological safety of denial and old coping strategies. Healing requires more than symptom improvement; it requires the client to construct a new account and a new identity. A new identity does not come quickly or easily. Therapists agree that survivor therapy is "generally a demanding process" (Dolan 1991: xiii). Therapists motivate clients throughout the therapy process by emphasizing the new life the client can gain, rather than a speedy recovery. If she perseveres with the slow and painful process of therapy, if she learns to pattern her story after the mediating narrative, then her "true self" will finally find expression.

THE THERAPEUTIC PROCESS AS ACHIEVING NARRATIVE FIT

In this analysis, I describe survivor therapy in terms of a narrative reconstruction of a client's life story. However, none of the treatment models are organized on an explicitly "constructivist" or "narrativist" basis. Constructivist therapists describe their goal as an imaginative reconstruction of life stories and identities that are believed to be constraining or incoherent. When old identities have become problematic, often due to painful interpersonal experience, or are simply felt to be unsatisfactory in some way, the constructivist method is to help individuals build new self-narratives. These new narratives build on an understanding of what the client's old stories have done for them but at the same time reorient them, opening new courses of action and offering new potential for positive feelings and accomplishments (e.g., Gergen 1994; Howard 1990; Neimeyer 1995; Neimeyer and Mahoney 1995). Although survivor therapy is not theoretically constructivist or narrativist,[1] I frame it in narrative terms because in coding the treatment literature, story editing, building, and replacing emerged as the decisive features. Survivor therapy is an iterative process, emphasizing the development of narrative facility as the client tells and retells (and perhaps also writes out, even experimenting with different voices and literary styles) a developing account of her life and its significance. As one guidebook for therapists notes, "[T]he words chosen must be the patient's own—carefully selected, always subject to change and reformulation. The therapeutic process, like a piece of sculpture, brings the patient ever closer to a final construction with which she can feel satisfied; but the work remains 'in progress' for some time" (Davies and Frawley 1994: 212).[2]

Not every element of therapy involves storytelling as such. Many therapeutic techniques require the client to perform rather than narrate new understandings, such as expressing emotion, role-playing with assertiveness, engaging in "body work," and confronting the alleged abuser. Yet each non-storytelling element serves as a precondition of constructing a narrative or makes its conveyance in a narrative possible. The client can tell a story about self-assertiveness once assertiveness is expressed, for instance; or anger, once discharged, can be added to the story that brought it about. Survivor therapy, then, is a fundamentally narrative process. In each stage of therapy, therapists bring clients to terms with their tarnished identities and direct them in a process, beginning with a new self-history, of "narrative repair" (Nelson 2001).

In analyzing and describing the structure of survivor therapy, my concern is with the therapist's recommended strategies and goals. I discuss the model client's responses only insofar as they are described in the treatment literature. Of course, in actual therapy, the client is never simply passive: she is responding, resisting, even initiating. The mediating narrative and each of its component stories will have more or less resonance with each client's interpretations of her experience. Her collaboration may come more or less readily. She may have various reasons for adopting a new self-narrative and see the narrative as serving any number of different personal goals. Her goals and intents may mesh with the therapist's, and they may not. However, the concern here is not with the client's actions and intents, but with the treatment model, the strategies and goals recommended by the survivor therapist. What the treatment literature describes is where the client needs to be and how the therapist can help get her there. The relationship is clearly give-and-take, but structured and directed toward defined ends. For the therapist, the client's resistance to those ends is something to be overcome, and her pursuit of them must be motivated. Achieving a fit for the mediating narrative is an accomplishment, and the therapist's persuasion techniques are designed to realize it. In the presentation that follows, then, my goal is to explain not the client's reasons or responses, but the therapist's techniques, the rationale for them, and the ends they serve.

"DISCOVERING" ABUSE

When they come to therapy, clients typically do not see their adult problems as caused by childhood sexual episodes. Clients have not linked the depression, anxiety, over- or undereating, marital conflicts, mood swings, or other problems that brought them to therapy with abuse. According to one therapist, "Occasionally a client immediately expresses a desire to 'work on incest,' but this is rather rare in therapeutic practice" (Meiselman 1990: 98–99). More commonly, "a survivor who enters therapy is driven to seek help by problems that she does not associate with her childhood abuse, even when the memory of incest is accessible" (99). According to another therapist, however, "More women than ever before are seeking professional help to cope with past incest"

(Courtois 1988: 129), and the incidence rose steadily in the 1990s.[3] Still, many survivors do not associate the abuse with the distress or disability for which they seek help, and many do not disclose abuse during intake or early in therapy.

Survivor therapists offer three types of reasons why clients typically fail to connect their adult problems with childhood sexual contact. First, a client may not have interpreted an experience as abuse. In survivor therapy, abuse is defined to cover a wide range of experience, from sexual intercourse all the way to incidents perceived as sexual but involving no touch. The client, on the other hand, may define abuse differently or even view her experience more neutrally. She might not, therefore, see any of her childhood experiences, even if sexual in some way, as constituting abuse. Second, a client's failure to make sense of her problems as outcomes of sexual abuse may follow from the explanations she has been offered in previous therapy experiences. As the authors of one treatment book argue, "It is not uncommon for adult survivors to present with a laundry list of prior diagnoses that are wide-ranging, contradictory, and confusing to those not familiar with this population" (Davies and Frawley 1994: 49). In other words, other therapists often do not make the connection between the client's problems and sexual abuse either. Their diagnoses suggest to the client ways to interpret her problems without reference to abuse. Third, adult survivor therapists argue that clients fail to connect their problems with sexual abuse because when they enter therapy their trauma defense mechanisms are still fully functioning. These mechanisms account for clients' efforts to minimize the significance of abuse, to deny that they were abused, or, because they have no memories, to fail entirely to recognize abuse. In the latter cases, informed by the trauma model, therapists argue that a mental process—repression or dissociation—has buried or split off the client's memories from normal consciousness. So while the memories remain " 'in storage' in relatively unaltered form" (Briere 1989: 108), they are not available until the client recovers them, either on her own or with the therapist's active assistance.

For survivor therapists, knowing if a client was abused as a child is essential to understanding her distress or disability and helping her to change. However, since they believe that a client's own understandings of her past and of the origins of her problems may be partially or completely unreliable, they cannot always rely on her disclosures to determine if she was a victim. Rather, they treat abuse as something they have a responsibility to discover. To make the discovery—the "diagnosis"—therapists consider a number of external signs or symptoms.[4] In the initial therapy sessions, the client describes the problems for which she is seeking help. The survivor therapist probes with questions, which might include inquiries about childhood sexual experience, and observations aimed to ascertain the presence or absence of "avoidance" or other symptoms seen to be caused by abuse. If the results of this initial evaluation raise suspicions, but the client does not report abuse, therapists believe they should initiate discussion of the issue. As one therapist argues, "If the counselor strongly suspects a history of childhood sexual abuse, based on presenting symptomatology, and the client does not disclose this experience upon inquiry, the counselor may 'gently confront' the client by suggesting that his or her symptoms are frequently experienced by someone that has been abused at some point in childhood" (Draucker 1992: 30–31). Some therapists consider it their duty always to raise the possibility of abuse. If he does not pursue the matter, even in the absence of any abuse memories, the therapist "runs the risk of retraumatizing the client with a form of denial or 'not hearing' " (Kirschner, Kirschner, and Rappaport 1993: 114).

For survivor therapists, many problems and emotional states are possible indicators of an abuse history. The professional treatment books, like the self-help books, present long and wide-ranging lists of symptoms. Drawn in part from the same research and clinical literature, most of these lists share the many disturbances correlated with adult survivors. These include depression, self-destructive behaviors, sexual problems, eating disorders, somatic complaints, and certain other problems associated with the personality disorders (mood swings, unstable relationships, impulsive behavior), the dissociative disorders (identity-fragmentation, amnesia, dissociative reactions), and PTSD (flashbacks, nightmares, "avoidance" behaviors). The presence of relevant symptoms may be ascertained from the client's disclosures. The therapist may also find the in-therapy behavior of the client symptomatic. For example, dissociative behaviors (such as "spacing out"), memory lapses, sudden shifts in voice and behavior, and blatant attempts to sexualize the therapeutic relationship are all regarded as symptoms. For some therapists, suspicion of childhood abuse may be aroused by characteristic responses to psychological tests (for example, dissociation questionnaires). The fact that a client has been through multiple therapy experiences may even be suggestive. Some therapists imply that a sexual abuse diagnosis should be explored for any client unable to find help in other diagnoses.

THE THERAPIST–CLIENT RELATIONSHIP

Diagnosing a client as an adult survivor of childhood sexual abuse may happen at the beginning of therapy, or it may take some time. Once the diagnosis is made, however, the therapist works to create a relationship that is the foundation and an important vehicle for his efforts.[5] In and through the relationship, he aims to lower the client's defenses and reduce her mistrust. He aims to increase the client's willingness to take new psychological risks and to reconsider her past as well as her future from a new perspective. He aims to motivate her to experiment with new thoughts and feelings, with a new outlook and attitude toward herself and others. He aims to build in her an expectation that she can become someone new. To meet these goals, the therapist not only works to build a cordial, relaxed, and freely interactive ethos, but he structures the relationship to embody and promote each of the key changes he believes the client needs to make. Strategic structuring is apparent in each of the major relationship elements that therapists emphasize.

A Safe, Well-Boundaried, and Trusting Relationship

Therapists structure and conduct the relationship with the client so as to build trust and rapport, and to overcome resistance and suspicion.[6] "At the beginning of any therapeutic relationship with an incest survivor, trust is of crucial importance" (Hall and Lloyd 1989: 122). Therapists, however, describe clients as typically very reluctant to trust and resistant to their feedback, which they interpret as part of the legacy of abuse. Victims expect to be mistreated by authority figures, as they were by their abusers. Since he is an authority figure, the therapist regards the client's resistance to him as expressing a victim's instinctive tendency to project onto others generalized expectations of being violated or let down. He may even see the client as prone to cast him in an abusive or nonprotecting role,[7] especially since he will insist that the client recall and narrate the details of childhood sexual abuse and evoke emotions attached to it. Survivor therapists regard such projections as understandable, even normal, and they structure the relationship in order to change the client's perception.

To head off any assumption or conclusion by the client that therapy itself shares features with abuse, therapists closely manage their own emotional reactions to the client. They identify several types of problems that can arise. Many adult survivor therapists, for example, are themselves survivors, and some have even reported recovering memories of abuse in the process of helping a client do so.[8] While therapists generally regard speaking from experience as potentially increasing effectiveness, those who are victims themselves may have strong feelings about abuse that can affect how they relate to their clients. Other therapists too, though not victims, might have a difficult time controlling their feelings. Both, for instance, may be so outraged by what they hear that they encourage the client to express rage before she is ready. As in abuse, therapists argue, the client may feel pressured and misunderstood. Or therapists may become so engaged with a client that they allow therapeutic boundaries and even professional standards, such as those regarding sexual contact, to be violated. The client in this case, as with abuse, will fail to witness a well-boundaried relationship and may, in the case of sexual contact, actually be victimized by the therapist. Alternatively—and gender differences between therapist and client are believed to be important here[9]—therapists may find it personally difficult to express the desired level of empathy and unconditional positive regard. In this case, the client, as with abuse, may not feel safe or may feel she is being judged. To shape the right environment and ethos, then, therapists emphasize their own need for caution and care in directing the process.[10] Their therapy is not supposed to be an experience of domination, and safety and trust cannot develop or endure if the client gets the impression that it is.

In order to make the right impression, build trust, and promote open communication, the therapist aims to create a relational environment and setting that is "safe," that is, one in which the client can feel relaxed in the knowledge that she will not be hurt, her needs will be respected, and she will be protected from external contingencies. Early on, the therapist lays out the general conditions for the therapeutic relationship. These conditions are designed to order the therapy sessions and to delimit the boundaries of both parties. The therapist invites the client to enter into a (revisable) therapeutic contract that clearly outlines their joint expectations and goals. This process provides practice in defining boundaries and needs: "For many survivors, developing a therapeutic contract is an opportunity to practice negotiating their needs" (Crowder 1993: 46). The therapist also sets out other ground rules—such as time limitations, payment arrangements, agreements about support the client can expect outside scheduled sessions—so that as little as possible is left to chance. To emphasize his respect for her boundaries, he gives the client control over any touch: "It is imperative for clients to control when and how they are touched during therapy" (47).

To foster a sense of safety, the therapist adopts a stance of empathy and acceptance toward the client, controlling his body language and listening to her disclosures without making judgmental comments.[11] Throughout therapy, he continually reinforces the idea that he believes her and he believes in her. "It is crucial that the counselor validate and affirm the survivor by believing her. This means not only believing her abuse experiences, memories and pain, but also believing in her as an individual who has the capacity to heal"

(Sanderson 1990: 106).[12] Because survivor therapy is often a painful process, he gives her charge over the pace at which it proceeds. "Certainly, the analyst must learn extreme patience, allowing the patient to control the timing and progression of reconstructive work, as she struggles to keep anxiety and panic within tolerable limits" (Davies and Frawley 1994: 204). While "opening the door for information about the abuse to surface" is important (Crowder 1993: 49), he avoids asking her intrusive questions that might be seen as a boundary violation and voyeuristic. He reassures the client that he will hold her disclosures in strictest confidence. Finally, in the ideal case, the therapist promises to be available even after treatment formally ends, assuring the client that she will always have a safe place to which she can return should future needs require it.

An Alliance Relationship

Survivor therapy, like all psychotherapy, is a collaborative process. Often in survivor therapy, however, clients do not readily take the client role, making the "development of a therapeutic alliance a slow and often tedious task" (Courtois 1988: 215). Therapists explain a client's reluctance to fully engage her role in terms of the dynamics of abuse. Abuse disempowers the victim. Having been abused, victims no longer feel that they can affect the world, that they have strength, or that they can control their destiny. The survivor therapist works, therefore, to motivate the client by structuring the relationship to downplay his authority status and emphasize an alliance. He positions himself as her ally. During therapy, the client's dependence on the therapist will grow as she comes to rely upon him to control feelings that are being evoked and to guide the decoding process. However, therapists understand this dependency as a temporary, "healthy dependency." Healthy dependency is "dependency that takes place in the context of a reparative relationship where the intent of the therapist is to have the client grow to the point of individuation; that is, dependency in the service of independent growth" (Kirschner, Kirschner, and Rappaport 1993: 89). Healthy dependency, then, does not justify passivity and, therapists argue, serves growth rather than delaying or limiting it.

To build an alliance and gain the cooperation that it demands, the therapist structures the relationship so that the client feels that she is in charge of her healing. The therapist defines the roles in the relationship so that she understands that she is responsible for changing her own behavior. He encourages her to see herself as "the expert on her own experience" (Courtois 1988: 169). He, on the other hand, presents himself "as a supportive person who helps her to explore that experience" (170). He defines his role as one of support and assistance, so that in the client's understanding, "'cure by the therapist' is replaced with 'recovery by the survivor' with assistance from the therapist" (Briere 1989: 60). As therapy proceeds, he suggests interpretations of the client's experiences and symptoms and points out alternate courses of action, but he emphasizes her freedom to choose. If need be, he reminds her that she "has the freedom to accept or reject interpretations without incurring punishment, such as being labeled 'resistant' " (Meiselman 1990: 97). The client is thus encouraged to relax and called on to cooperate. She can relax because she is reassured that the therapist's interpretations will be offered rather than imposed. She must cooperate because for therapy to be successful she needs to understand the process; she needs to make the new interpretations her own; she needs to renarrate her life story.

A Model Relationship

The therapeutic relationship is designed to be a safe, well-boundaried, trusting alliance. But more than that, it is designed to serve as a model for all personal relationships, including the client's relationship to herself. Once established, "[t]he therapeutic relationship becomes the vehicle, the laboratory, and the metaphor for teaching the client about healthy, appropriate, well-boundaried, and caring relationships" (Roth 1993: 13). The therapist teaches the client that, like therapeutic relationships, all healthy relationships have clear and self-consciously maintained boundaries. In healthy relationships, the parties assert their limits and avoid becoming enmeshed in each other's lives. As with the trust and safety of therapy, so in healthy relationships the parties' needs are respected, and neither is pressured or related to as a dependent. Both have freedom to choose, and each serves the growth of the other. As with the therapist's accepting attitude in therapy, so in healthy relationships the parties are empathetic and nonjudgmental, believing in and validating each other. So too the client should relate to herself with these attitudes. As the therapist relates to her, so should she relate to herself: not doubting, not blaming, affirming her strength, and confirming her capacity to grow and develop.

As a strategy for persuading the client to see the therapeutic relationship as a model of healthy relationships and attitudes, the therapist builds into the relationship an implicit, and at times explicit, contrast between his own attitudes and actions and those of a sexual abuser. In contrast with a sexual abuser, for instance, who disregards the boundaries of a victim, the therapist respects the boundaries of a client. Not to respect personal boundaries in the way he does is to imitate an abuser. Similarly, in therapy, the therapist does not express any doubts about the client's account of her pain: not to believe her imitates an abuser. In each such contrast, the therapist defines his own attitudes and actions as the antithesis of an abuser's and thereby enhances his own standing as a model of genuine care. Moreover, juxtaposing the two relationships implicitly aligns any attitudes or actions contradictory to the therapist's, including those of the client herself, with those of an abuser. All disbelief, for instance, whether in the form of self-doubt on the part of the client or disbelief by her significant others or society at large, is associated with abuse. Belief, as modeled by the therapist, is the only right response. With the contrast, then, the therapist's actions and attitudes gain status as models of what is appropriate and healthy. For clients and their supporters, an imitation of his actions and attitudes is thus indicated, while resistance and contradictory views are stigmatized.

Relationships Outside of Therapy

Therapists argue that for survivor therapy to be successful, the client must typically change her relationships with others outside of therapy. The client will make drastic changes in the course of therapy that people in her life may not like. These people may challenge her trust in the therapist and his ability, working against the relationship that he is building and the new account she is constructing. On the other hand, family members and friends who support the changes introduced in therapy enhance the efforts of the therapist and the process of change. Thus, early on, the therapist may advise the client to seek out the company of those who support the changes she is making, while minimizing or avoiding conversation about therapy with those who might resist them. The therapist may also recommend participation in a therapy or survivor (self-help) group as a way to bolster her experience with peer "allies" who are sympathetic.

Therapists see group involvement as having drawbacks as well as advantages for meeting therapeutic goals. The main problem with groups, either therapeutic or survivor, is that they can become overwhelming. The pace and sequence of survivor therapy is very important. To reach the goal of healing, therapists lead clients through the victim-survivor-thriver stages. Each stage is crucial to the larger process, and the client is not considered ready to move to the next stage until she has adequately mastered the tasks of the last. Because clients are different and have different experiences, therapists note, they necessarily move at different paces through the stages. In individual therapy, pace can be controlled, but in group therapy it is much more difficult to maintain a pace that is comfortable for all. Similarly, in a survivor group, the various members may be at different stages in their journey. Exposed to ideas and emotions for which she is not yet prepared, a client can easily get overwhelmed. The goals of therapy are thus set back.

When the group is right and the client feels safe, however, therapists believe that adjunct group involvement can greatly advance therapeutic goals. Groups can provide peer affirmation and support for every step that the therapist is leading the client to take, as well as ready models for emulation or identification. A group, for instance, can reduce the client's resistance, trigger memory recovery, arouse strong emotions, and validate her emerging account, reassuring her that the story is believable and her feelings real. "It is one thing to tell one therapist about the incest privately and quite another to tell a dozen people who nod knowingly, which is energizing and empowering" (Roth 1993: 105). A group can encourage the client not to feel isolated, stigmatized, ashamed, or crazy but to see her story as normal, something she shares and can share with other victims. "There is nothing more normalizing than participating in a group subculture where the 'unknowable' is known, the 'unspeakable' is spoken, and the 'secret craziness' is shared by others" (Kirschner, Kirschner, and Rappaport 1993: 104). A group can motivate the client to endure therapy, foster her expectation of a positive outcome, affirm and model therapeutic norms of right relationships, be a source of new friendships, support her in a confrontation of the alleged abuser, and in other ways advance therapeutic goals. Therapists support group involvement, then, because it enlists committed and like-minded people to foster and socially endorse the client's emerging account and behavioral changes, and to provide models she can emulate. A group can mobilize momentum for change, authorize the rightness of the change, and create an incentive—continuing membership, others' expectations—not to deviate from it.

For purposes similar to those served by group involvement, therapists also recommend that clients read the autobiographical accounts of other survivors. A large number of survivor accounts have been published in a wide range of formats, including book-length autobiographies, anthologies, self-help books, newsletters, and Internet postings. Such accounts of personal change and healing are powerful tools for elevating the legitimacy of the trauma model and survivor therapy. They provide an immediate, deeply personal, unquestionably sincere, and often highly charged testimony to the profound, long-term consequences of abuse and the possibility of their successful resolution. Clients may also use survivor accounts for the purpose of comparing and locating their own experience in these stories, and this is one of the principal reasons for their public telling. They can also trigger client memories of abuse, can elicit appropriate emotions, can help clients see their own distress and disability as the result of victimization, can reduce a sense of being unique or different, and can inspire hope in therapy and hope in a changed future. Like group involvement, they can supplement the therapeutic relationship with an external, culturally authorized, and congruent witness to the change that the therapist is persuading the client to make. Therapists recommend survivor accounts to clients for all of these reasons.

STAGE ONE: THE VICTIM ACCOUNT

As in all psychotherapy, a successful relationship between therapist and client is crucial to therapeutic success. As it begins to take shape in survivor therapy, as trust and cooperation form, the client is prepared to begin the journey to self discovery. In the initial stage, the therapist helps the client, whatever her current understandings, to construct a victim account about her experience. To do so, the therapist takes the client through a series of reinterpretations in which she slowly detaches herself from and deconstructs her previous account and identity. Therapists understand and explain these reinterpretations as a dismantling of the defenses and coping mechanisms that the client erected as a child to deal with the trauma of abuse and that now express themselves in her conscious and unconscious resistance to see her victimization and to change. The process begins with the therapist helping the client to remember childhood sexual episodes.

Memory Retrieval

In helping a client to build an account of victimization, the therapist begins by leading her in a process of remembering childhood sexual episodes and discussing them in detail. Most clients, whatever their initial level of recall, are expected to access additional or more detailed memories. In an especially strong statement, one therapist argues that "[n]o matter how much a client has consciously remembered about her abuse there will inevitably be new memories" (Roth 1993: 57). New memories are inevitable in this view because as the therapist helps the client to lower her defenses, memories that she would not let herself have can finally return. Clients, therapists argue, dissociate or simply repress memories of abuse to varying degrees. Many have fairly complete recall (though they may dismiss these memories as not important or meaningful to their lives), some have only vague or shadowy memories, and some have no memories whatsoever. Therapists can begin treatment, however, whatever the level of recall. Any memory of a sexual episode is significant, but for some therapists memories are not absolutely required; symptoms that suggest an abuse history, or the client's perception that she might have been abused, are enough to start. In general, these therapists expect at least some specific memories of the abuse to return, though they allow that memories are not absolutely necessary during treatment either. The client's current symptoms, understood to signal an original trauma, may be witness enough.

The therapist helps the client to recall and discuss memories in several ways. He gives her what therapists call "permission to remember," which authorizes her to begin thinking about and discussing memories with the therapist's assurance that he will support her and make sure she is not overwhelmed by what emerges. It also includes the therapist's assurance that he will greet the disclosure of any memories with a sympathetic, nonjudgmental response. Perhaps unlike others earlier, he will believe what the client says happened to her. He can be trusted with her secrets. The relationship is safe.

Having given permission, the therapist actively encourages the client to seek out memories and bring them to mind. Her resistance makes this challenging work. The therapist may use "memory-enhancement" techniques, such as hypnosis, age regression, and guided imagery to help with the recovery process. When the client is in an altered state of consciousness, some therapists believe they can get beyond the operation of her trauma defenses and avoidance strategies to the buried or incomplete memories.[13] The therapist carefully directs the conversation to probe the client's childhood, helping her to identify relevant memories and interpret them. He also encourages her to work on remembering outside of therapy sessions. Therapists recount that numerous experiences and stimuli can trigger memories. For example: "Clients report that some of the most powerful triggers—for memory or for hope—have been television documentaries or dramas" (Jones 1991: 12). Therapists note the particular importance of therapy or survivor group involvement for stimulating memories: "The stimulation of hearing the abuse experiences of other survivors in a group situation is extremely effective in precipitating memory retrieval for survivors with partial repression of abuse experiences as well as for those who have complete amnesia" (Draucker 1992: 46). According to the textbooks, survivors also report that abuse memories have been triggered by reading newspaper and magazine stories, by reading the autobiographical accounts of other survivors, and by a wide range of experiences entirely outside of a therapy or adult survivor context (for example, during medical examinations, during sex).

Therapists identify a number of different things as constituting abuse memories. Simple recall of childhood events is the most common, though these range on a continuum from quite detailed to extremely vague. Over the course of therapy, clients typically move along this continuum. Memories may be initially vague—someone did something frightening—but then become more and more detailed as the past is explored and repeatedly described. Nightmares, brief flashbacks, or other frightening disturbances can also represent abuse memories. These are commonly interpreted as "an unconscious response to a stimulus relating directly or indirectly to the original abuse trauma" (Dolan 1991: 13). Some therapists also argue that the body itself can signal abuse memories: "When a person experiences a traumatic event, the memory of that event is stored both physically and emotionally in the body. Any association to the original trauma can trigger the memory emerging either as a bodily reaction (body memory) or an emotional reaction" (Weiner and Kurplus 1995: 136). Therapists help clients recover memories based on such "wordless" experiences by interpreting them. Physical symptoms may be interpreted as psychosomatic indicators of abuse experiences—as "somatic experiences that symbolically represent some aspect of the original traumas" (Davies and Frawley 1994: 99). In each case, the therapist treats somatic experiences as an "unfamiliar language" that, together with the client, he must listen to and interpret (211).

A third way in which therapists foster memory recovery and exploration is by validating the client's memories as they surface by believing them. "At this [early] stage [in memory recall] the therapist will need to facilitate further recall by believing and validating the client" (Sanderson 1990: 99). If memories are not forthcoming but the client believes that she was abused, the therapist nonetheless validates her perceptions. "When counselling a survivor who has considerable memory deficits relating to childhood but who feels that she was sexually abused, it is essential to ratify the survivor's feelings even in the absence of concrete memories" (135). By validating and believing her memories or perceptions, the therapist lets the client know that her childhood sexual abuse was real, and thus encourages continued memory exploration and reconstruction.

Despite their validation and belief, therapists concede that doubts are common and persistent. The client's doubts about the truth of her memories are interpreted in terms of her defenses. The defenses, maintained over a long period of time, protected the victim. Accepting now the fact and significance of abuse does not come easily, and so doubts and resistance to belief do not easily disappear. Throughout the early part of therapy (and often well beyond), therefore, the client is expected to waver often between belief and doubt: "[I]t is also universal in work with survivors of childhood abuse that at many points along the way, patients will question the veracity of their statements, the reality of their memories" (Davies and Frawley 1994: 224). At virtually any point, the client is viewed as vulnerable to using psychological defenses to deny the memories. "She [the client] can be vividly remembering the event and feeling very strongly that it is true and that it is the key that makes sense of many events in her life and simultaneously be thinking, 'It can't be so! You're making it all up!' " (Meiselman 1990: 148). Therapists view such episodes, which set therapy back, as attesting to the strength of the defenses and coping mechanisms. The therapist counters doubt by validating the memories and frequently reminding the client that doubts are common and to be expected. At the same time, he is careful to "tread softly" and not attempt to "convince her of something that she 'knows' is false" (Briere 1989: 121). If he forces the memory work to proceed at too rapid a pace for the client, she might lose faith in her memories or show a significant increase in negative affect. Her doubts are expected to grow less intense as her trust in the therapist increases, as her memories become more detailed and she becomes more desensitized to them, and as she gains confidence in the explanatory power of victimization for making sense of her problems.

By talking through the past and through experiences like nightmares and somatization, and—perhaps for the first time—by remembering abuse or interpreting an experience as abuse, the client is beginning to construct a personal victim account. To assist this process, many therapists encourage clients to write regularly about their past in a journal. They might also assist the process by providing a language the client can use to begin to put the abuse experience into words. Or they might offer interpretations of, for instance, the alleged abuser's or nonprotecting mother's behavior that help the client to construct her account. "When the client is struggling to find meaning in abuse, the therapist can actively generate interpretations of parental behavior for the client to 'try on.' It is the client's right to decide what explanations really fit the family she remembers, but her reconstruction of events will be facilitated by the therapist's knowledge of the motivations that are often involved in incest" (Meiselman 1990: 163). If the therapist's efforts are successful, over the course of time, the client's story will begin to take on a reality for her that, even for those with clear memories, it did not have before. Despite her continued resistance or doubts, the coherence of her previous interpretations is being eroded. A first goal of therapy is being realized.

Reenacting Emotions

In constructing a victim account, and to promote further memory recovery, the therapist also directs the client to reenact (abreact) and describe emotions associated with abuse. Therapists believe that defensive coping mechanisms have protected the client from explosive emotions that accompany sexual abuse. She may have repressed or denied her emotions, or experienced a dissociative "detachment (also referred to as 'numbing') [which] serves as a primitive protection from old pain (i.e., the trauma of child abuse)" (Briere 1989: 113). Male clients, especially, "often report explicit details of their abuse without any emotionality, as if they were talking about events that had happened to someone else" (Crowder 1993: 25). Therapists argue that these bottled-up or split-off feelings are still very much alive within the client and prevent insight, including the recognition of her cognitive distortions and that the abuser no longer threatens her. To overcome emotional inhibition and avoidance, and to encourage a mood in which memories can more easily be recalled, therapists believe abuse feelings must be identified and expressed.

In order to abreact her abuse trauma, the therapist encourages the client to release appropriate emotion and may use relaxation techniques, cues, and selective validation as he directs the process. Therapists encourage clients by indicating "that all emotions are good" (Briere 1989: 86) and that expressing them has a therapeutic effect. They may use hypnosis and bodywork techniques to release buried tensions. They expect that many emotions, some positive and many negative, such as rage, sadness, depression, a sense of abandonment, betrayal, grief, loss, shame, and guilt, will flood over the client during this remembering phase. Therapists may help the client sort out and explore her emotions by providing a language to describe them: "Many clients need support in developing a vocabulary for identifying their different emotions" (Crowder 1993: 65). On the other hand, the client's expression of emotions may emerge only very slowly and tentatively, and this delay is understood in terms of the strength of the defenses erected to avoid them. To move the process along, therapists sometimes suggest emotions by "making statements such as 'I'm making an assumption that you are feeling some sadness (or anger, or whatever) about what you're telling me' " (65). As the client describes her feelings, the therapist helps to label them, and validates them as real and genuine "so that survivors can learn to trust and accept these feeling states" (Draucker 1992: 48). The client, for instance, "must be allowed to see that her angry feelings are valid emotions, and they are often entirely justified, especially when dealing with her childhood experiences" (Hall and

Lloyd 1989: 185). Not all emotions, however, are validated. For example, the "client may have mixed feelings about the perpetrator, and she is encouraged to express these feelings in her therapy. This statement implies that even though the therapist will not *endorse* expressions of guilt about incest, the survivor can explore and analyze her guilt feelings" (Meiselman 1990: 72; emphasis in original). Moreover, since the therapist believes clients are prone to deny the importance of some emotions, he may assert their true importance himself. For this reason, it is "crucial" to "encourage the expression of anger and negativity toward family members in addition to the positive feelings with which the clients are more comfortable" (Kirschner, Kirschner, and Rappaport 1993: 110–11). These techniques augment victim "feeling states" that can be conveyed and triggered by the emerging victimization account.[14]

Experiencing the emotions of abuse often brings a crisis point in therapy that therapists anticipate and use techniques to address. On the one hand, intense emotion creates confusion, which might increase the client's suggestibility and dependence on the therapist for support, clarification, and relief. The memory and abreaction work are in part designed to have this effect. On the other hand, clients may feel that the initial effects of therapy are harmful because of the increase in painful emotions. To avoid this painful experience, a client may seek to claim a quick recovery or for other reasons terminate treatment. Therapists, therefore, warn clients in advance what to expect. "The therapist must ... explain that it will get worse before it gets better, and that there is a normal process of healing in which the memories come up at a pace that is tolerable, and along with them will come self-hate, shame, and guilt and depression and rage" (Kirschner, Kirschner, and Rappaport 1993: 114). Therapists also work to quell anxiety while promoting emotional expression by helping the client to maintain a sense of emotional control. She is told that she can feel bad yet maintain control—many other survivors with whom he has worked have done so—and that she will not be revictimized by the therapist. Even strange and potentially frightening experiences need not lead to or represent a loss of control. During the therapy session, for instance, a client may suddenly adopt the voice and behavior of a child. The therapist calms the client by explaining that such a shift is acceptable and manageable, and because it can allow her to get in touch with the abused child still locked inside, even helpful. By correctly predicting intense emotions, and by carefully initiating and terminating the abreaction work, then, the therapist addresses the client's heightened uncertainty and reassures her that he can control the process. With his help, her resolution will be promoted by experiencing the emotions of sexual abuse and by mastering them.

By taking the client through the emotions of sexual abuse, the therapist solidifies her sense of past victimization. New memories are brought forth, and doubts about her memories are further eroded by a sense of reexperiencing the abuse through emotional reenactment. These intense emotions about her past are real *now*; they help solidify her belief that something real happened *then* as well. She did not make this all up; she would not feel this way if she did. Reenactment and the increased certainty it brings also heighten the emotional energy and motivation available for taking the next steps in the construction of her victim account. Able to describe past experiences and feelings, she is now ready to make a new connection between the past and the present.

Recognizing Victimization

By themselves, the memories and feelings of abuse tell only part of the victim story; the other part concerns the consequences. The client's victimization account does not end in childhood. It is not even primarily about childhood. It is about explaining how her life has come to be what it is. In order to tell this part, the client needs to recognize that what happened to her, whatever its specific details, was serious victimization. She also needs to recognize that her victimization has had serious long-term consequences and caused many, though not necessarily all, of her adult problems. Therapists work to promote this recognition.

Despite the memory and emotion work up to this point in therapy, the client may still resist the conclusion that she was a victim of abuse or that it is important. The client may not yet be "ready to identify his experience as 'abuse' or himself as a 'victim'" (Crowder 1995: 87). According to therapists, men have an especially hard time seeing themselves as victims. "They [male clients] may acknowledge that a sexual event occurred but are reluctant to actually accept the experience as abusive" (Bolton, Morris, and MacEachron 1989: 103). Therapists explain the particular reluctance of men to see themselves as victims in terms of male socialization and as a method they use to protect themselves from having to deal with strong feelings. However, female clients may also minimize the importance of the sexual contact, contending, as male clients do, that it was not as bad as the therapist seems to think. The "predominant fantasy presented by our patients is that the sexual abuse was not really as bad as it sounds or that the abuser, often a parent or other trusted relative, was not as self-serving as the memories suggest" (Davies and Frawley 1994: 14). Among other things, therapists argue, the tendency to disavow the "full extent of exploitation and betrayal" (Briere 1989: 115) reflects the continuing hold of false ideas implanted by the abuser.

In order to persuade the client to understand herself as a victim, thera-pists explain to her that her adult problems (again, not necessarily *all* of them) were caused by abuse and coping with it. For reasons attributed to their defenses or a failure of psychological insight—some clients are simply "unable to see any connection between their symptoms and their abuse" (Sanderson 1990: 92)—clients do not readily make the connection on their own. "Many women do not attribute their current problems to their past, but they can be helped to do so" (Hall and Lloyd 1989: 67). Therapists note that explaining post-traumatic stress disorder is an especially useful tool for helping clients link their adult problems to abuse and express the connec-tion. Such a diagnosis "often gives the survivor her first inkling of the fact that *abuse,* as opposed to something intrinsic in her, produced a number of the problems in her current life" (Briere 1989: 83; emphasis in original). Therapists also commonly encourage clients to read the autobiographical accounts of survivors and (or) attend a survivor group to promote her recognition of victimization. "It is only when they have adequate opportu-nity to compare their experiences with those of others that they begin to suspect or comprehend that they have been deprived and abused" (Nichols 1992: 42).

Explaining the client's current problems as aftereffects of trauma allows the therapist to "normalize" or "depathologize" her problems. To support the trauma explanation, the therapist often describes how widespread childhood sexual abuse is in society and situates the client's problems in a broader framework of experience common to many women and children. Explaining the client's problems as trauma aftereffects offers her assurance that she is not crazy. As one therapist writes, "The PTSD diagnosis in and of itself can be quite therapeutic in reconceptualizing the incest and its effects. This diagno-sis directly communicates to the client that her symptoms do not mean that she is crazy; rather, they result from traumatic circumstances in her life and efforts to cope with them" (Courtois 1988: 150). Likewise, by normalizing, the therapist provides an account that destigmatizes her problems. "When symp-toms of childhood sexual abuse are explained as initially reasonable and, in many cases, valuable efforts to survive extreme psychological stress, they become less stigmatizing in clients' eyes" (Dolan 1991: 5). Rather than seeing her behavior as weird, idiosyncratic, flawed, or shameful, the client is encour-aged to recognize it as entirely normal. Moreover, by normalizing her prob-lems, the therapist works to overcome any sense of isolation by assuring the client that she is not alone—others have also been victimized and have reacted in similar ways—and that she is not to blame. "Seeing themselves in the same group as victims of natural disasters, airplane and car accidents, and random criminal assaults can be helpful in overcoming a tendency to blame themselves rather than the perpetrator" (5).

By normalizing her problems as trauma aftereffects, the therapist uses these problems as additional evidence to draw the client toward a conclusion that was not self-evident: She is a victim, and victimization has shaped many areas of her adult life. Exploited by the abuser, she has had to pay the consequences, and her life is not what it might have been. Therapists expect the client's recognition of victimization to arouse strong emotions, including anger and even rage. Expressions of strong anger can be dangerous and may require the therapist's help to control. But, because anger promotes the goals of survivor therapy, therapists regard it as beneficial and to be encouraged. The expression of anger by clients signals a "transition from coconspirator or deserver of pain to injured (and angry) party," and this transition "is a healthy one" (Briere 1989: 90). Anger means that the client is plotting her experience in the victim account, accepting that she was violated and her sense of self damaged. It means that the client is beginning "to recognize that *he* was not responsible for the lost childhood but someone else actually *stole* his childhood from him" (Bolton, Morris, and MacEachron 1989: 108; emphasis in original). Validating anger and encouraging its expression in turn mobilizes this emotion in support of a deepening of victim recognition and a determination to change.

The client's recognition of victimization and its causal relationship to her adult problems represent a milestone in treatment. Victimization and its aftereffects are the interpretative key offered to help clients make sense of their painful and otherwise disconnected experiences, to help them see a general pattern to their lives, and to locate responsibility for negative outcomes. Therapy encourages the client to use this interpretative key to change features of her life. As clients make the victim story their account, they are prepared to move forward. "When they [clients] develop an understanding that all their behavior makes sense, they begin to decode their experience rather than disowning or judging it" (Crowder 1993: 37). The client decodes her experience by interpreting it in light of victimization and the survivor rationale, a process the therapist helps her accomplish. In accepting the need to decode, the client demonstrates to the therapist that her defenses and old explanations are being dismantled. By linking her all-too-real current problems and emotions to abuse, the therapist is overcoming her resistance to and doubts about victimization. She is prepared to go forward.

Disclosure and Changing Relationships

At this point in therapy, the essential elements of the victimization account—memories, emotions, connection between past and present—are coming into place. Through a slow, halting process of being told and retold, the client's self-narrative is taking the shape of the mediating narrative. The client has narrated conditioning and disempowerment through victimization into a new account of her experience. She is now ready, if she was not earlier, to "break silence" and disclose to carefully selected others her victim story. By retelling her story in the presence of sympathetic listeners and by avoiding those who are unsympathetic, she further crystallizes her story. The reality of her account is enhanced by social acceptance; it gains external coherence with the accounts that others give of her, and thus social obstacles are created that impede any tendency to recant her testimony.

While still taking shape, the client's emerging victim account is extremely fragile, and so therapists believe it must be protected. The client's own doubts and denial are still strong, and others have not yet come to understand her as an abuse victim. Perhaps only the therapist firmly attests to the reality of her victim story. Further, because a personal abuse allegation is involved, some who hear her account are expected to react with disbelief and hostility. Thus, when the time comes to widen the circle of those who hear the story, therapists insist that care must be exercised. They strongly recommend that the "survivor should, if possible, make her initial revelations to those individuals who have the best potential for offering a supportive response" (Courtois 1988: 329). That is, the client's disclosure should first be made to people— family members, friends, a survivor group—who will most likely relate to her in terms of the new identity she is adopting in therapy. A sympathetic audience is advantageous, even necessary, therapists argue, because the client is not ready to have her account seriously challenged, and the act of disclosure itself can be very difficult and frightening. For example, the client's loyalty to the person or persons she accuses of abuse and a fear of betraying her family may cause her to resist disclosure, as may her fear of others' reactions, including disbelief, hostility, or accusations of insanity. Telling others, especially if they express disbelief, may resurrect strong doubts that the abuse ever occurred. Furthermore, according to therapists, disclosure can bring back to the client's consciousness whatever threats or promises the abuser once used to obtain silence.

As a client begins to disclose her story, she identifies those who fully accept it and those who do not. The therapist advises the client to make this distinction the basis for "realigning" her significant relationships, including some and excluding others depending on how they respond. Those socially included are the "prosurvivors." These are the people who will patiently listen to and "honor" her victim account as she tells and retells it, working it out. Because these individuals can decisively aid the therapeutic process, the therapist may ask to train key prosurvivors, especially a spouse. "Once the partner agrees to help, the therapist needs to contract to teach him the necessary therapeutic skills. These include listening, empathy, and nonjudgmental validation. The spouse must also be taught to take the survivor's 'side' and not to defend other members of the family" (Kirschner, Kirschner, and Rappaport 1993: 119). After disclosure, and for at least the time she is in therapy, the therapist recommends that the client's primary relationships be with her prosurvivors. Those excluded after disclosure are the family members and friends of the client who do not accept her account or who defend the alleged abuser. Since the alleged abuser himself is expected to deny the abuse allegation, he is virtually by definition a part of this group (see the discussion of the confrontation in the next chapter). "Nonprotecting others"—a mother, older sibling, or other person that the client alleges could have protected her but did not—may also be in this group. The therapist advises the client to seriously reconsider her relationship with these people, including family members, but leaves it to her to decide what manner of contact, if any, she will continue to have. However, if their denial or lack of sympathetic acceptance is affecting the client or her therapy, he may recommend termination of contact.

Realigning relationships according to the response people make to the client's disclosure promotes the therapist's goals in several ways. First, it reduces the number of challenges to the client's claim to have been abused. If the client's own resistance to accepting victimization is isolated and denied reinforcement by others, it will be weakened. Second, changing some relationships at this stage frees the client to make her own growth and recovery the first priority of her life. Third, prosurvivors reinforce the therapist's message that the client's memories are genuine and thus support the reality of her emerging account and the deconstruction of her old interpretations. Moreover, by believing and validating her claims of abuse, they make it harder for her to retract those claims and change explanations. Finally, by believing and validating her victim account, prosurvivors, implicitly if not explicitly, encourage her to trust the therapist who is directing the process and to persevere in the struggle toward a successful conclusion.[15]

In carefully disclosing her account to others, the client gains the recognition of others and thereby deepens her own recognition of victimization. Because secrecy and nonrecognition are believed to have contributed to a false and distorted mode of being for the client, therapists view disclosure in itself as a healing act. Reducing her resistance by dismantling her defenses has made this step possible. Her recognition, enhanced by that of others, prepares the client to move to stage two, the survivor story.

Letting Go

The transition to the survivor story involves a ritual of grieving and symbolically letting go of the past. The victim account is not the last word; it is only the beginning. To encourage the client to make the transition to a new story, the therapist centers her attention on what she has lost and on what she stands to gain by moving beyond the victim story. If she is to become a new person, the survivor "must psychologically separate from the past in order to develop her unique self" (Courtois 1988: xvi). She must not stop with the recognition of victimization but be prepared to use this recognition as a tool for transformation in the next stage.

The transition to the next stage of therapy begins as the therapist encourages the client to recognize and mourn for "losses" associated with childhood abuse. In addition to promoting the expression of anger at victimization, therapists encourage clients to express feelings of loss and sorrow. Profound personal losses are defined as central to abuse: "Any woman who has been sexually abused as a child has suffered many losses" (Hall and Lloyd 1989: 197). However, as in the other steps of survivor therapy, the client may not see her own experience in these terms. "She may," according to survivor therapists, "be unaware of her losses, or of her need to grieve for them" (197). The therapist, therefore, may need to help the client identify what she has lost. The most significant losses mentioned include a normal childhood, protective parents (especially but not exclusively in cases of incest), a sense of safety, innocence, trust, agency, her self before victimization, certain life assumptions, a "sense of possibilities," or "identity (i.e., I am not the person I might have been)" (Courtois 1988: 126, 226). By helping to identify such losses, the therapist again reinforces the message of victimization and powerlessness, and promotes the client's experience and expression of grief and sorrow.

Identifying losses and expressing grief are part of the therapist's effort to convince the client that in order to make a fresh start in her life, she must let go of the past. What has happened, the therapist argues, has happened, and the client is encouraged "to recognize that he cannot return to childhood and recover that which was lost" (Bolton, Morris, and MacEachron 1989: 107). There is no going back, but the client can move toward a new future and a new life. "As these multiple losses are processed," one therapist notes, "the survivor will begin to acknowledge that she cannot change her past but she can influence and control her future" (Sanderson 1990: 114). In order to take control of her future, the client is told not to cling to the idea that she was a victim. "Seeing herself as victim inhibits the survivor from acknowledging her true strength and courage" (115). The therapist also tells her that letting go and taking control may require additional and permanent changes in her personal relationships: "Letting go of the past may mean letting go of past relationships, or of the hope of reparation" (Jones 1991: 66). By letting go of such relationships, therapists argue, "[e]motional energy is withdrawn from past relationships and reinvested in the self and in the development of new relationships" (Courtois 1988: 127). In taking the client through a process of mourning and "letting go," then, the therapist prepares her to make a fresh start by encouraging her to see herself in control of an open future. If "less encumbered by the past," then "she is more free to reclaim those lost or undeveloped parts of herself" (192). The victim account explains the past, while letting go prepares the client to tell another story about her present and future.

◦◷◦ ◦◷◦ ◦◷◦

If stage one of survivor therapy has been successful, the therapist has led the client past doubt and resistance to narrate a story of her past and of her problems in terms of a victim account that is broadly consistent with the pattern of the adult survivor mediating narrative. Constructing a victim account is important in survivor therapy because it locates the injustice that explains the client's personal experience, providing her with a way to make sense of her problems and recast them from a new, normalizing perspective that establishes her innocence and basic goodness. By this account, a "false self" is narrated that will serve as the epistemological "other" against which a "true self" will be subsequently defined and warranted. A human actor(s) who is the knowing agent of her undeserved suffering and harm is also identified. The identification of this actor and his actions together with the client's conformity to the expression and emotion norms of stage one promote the arousal of her moral indignation and her motivation to act. She cannot prevent the injustice; that is a matter of the past. But she can, the therapist assures her, change the effects of injustice on her future. However, more than moral indignation at past injustice is required to convince the client that she can and should make radical personal changes. She must also believe that she has the power to effect the change. Building this sense of personal power is where the next stage of survivor therapy begins.

CHAPTER SEVEN

From Victim to Survivor and Beyond

Through the first stage in therapy, the therapist has led the client to narrate her past anew in terms of the victim account. Told rightly, the victim account is the essential beginning for the larger mediating narrative of survivor therapy. Getting the beginning right is crucial because "the beginning [of a story] is not merely the first of a series of events; it is the event that originates those that follow" (Trilling 1980: 125). Stories configure selected past "events" (meaning both human actions and experiences) into a plot, which portrays them as a meaningful sequence unfolding from the beginning event toward the valued endpoint or "moral" the story anticipates. In this way, stories endow the past with meaning and continuity, and so also project a sense of what will or should happen in the future. The mediating narrative follows this basic discursive pattern. Abuse is the defining event that explains how the client came to be who she is. It is the foundation for the larger lesson of *who the client can become* that the whole narrative anticipates and is designed to communicate.

Beginning the client's life story with abuse teaches her about herself. The victim account teaches the client that the trauma model has explanatory power for her life situation; it is a key to decoding her experience. It teaches her that her life and how she copes with it is, perhaps in large measure, abuse-determined rather than self-determined. It teaches her that she is disempowered: "By the midphase of treatment, survivors have begun to experience an entitlement to their feelings, and they recognize their unhappiness about the lack of fulfillment, power, or generativity in their lives" (Kirschner, Kirschner, and Rappaport 1993: 143). The victim account also teaches her that identifying and overcoming the effects of abuse in her life and relationships is the path to future happiness and life satisfaction. It mandates and authorizes a new beginning.

The lessons of the victim account—the false self—are the normative and explanatory foundation on which the next stage of therapy, the survivor story, is built. In this chapter, I continue analyzing the process of survivor therapy by first considering the themes of the survivor story, the middle part of the mediating narrative, and the techniques therapists use to help clients tell and, in part, act out this story. The survivor story is, in turn, the foundation for the thriver story, the goal of the mediating narrative, and the transition point at which therapy ends. With this story, according to therapists, the client is finally realizing her "true self" as she appropriates and acts from new assumptions about the self and others. I conclude the chapter with a discussion of these assumptions—the therapeutic lessons—and how they come to "fit."

STAGE TWO: THE SURVIVOR STORY

In the first stage of therapy, the therapist led the client to give an account that emphasized vulnerability, powerlessness, a false identity, and psychological defenses and coping mechanisms that have blocked genuine self-awareness. In this account, the client is victim. In the second stage, the therapist again leads the client to tell a story about herself, but now the time frame shifts. Therapy is moving away from a concern with the past to a concern with changing the way the client presently views herself and lives her life. To build a sense of agency and spur the client's motivation for the next steps, the therapist emphasizes her strength rather than her past powerlessness. She suffered trauma, he tells her, and lived to tell about it. She is, therefore, a "survivor," possessor of the inner resources that enable victims to persevere. To persevere, therapists argue, is to resist the complete obliteration of the "true self," the originary self that is strong and healthy: "Even though a client may describe that 'true self' as bad, stupid, ugly, or weak, the therapist knows that at the very core of this adult rests a beautiful and powerful child who is a pivotal resource for healing" (Roth 1993: 88).[1] In the words of another therapist, "[T]he very term 'abuse survivor' emphasizes the fact that the victim persevered despite her or his psychic injuries; . . . this resilience and willingness to struggle should be reinforced and relied upon by the therapist, whose task is lessened by the existence of the 'strong, healthy part' in most survivors" (Briere 1989: 60–61). In emphasizing a "strong, healthy part," the therapist communicates to the client a central therapeutic idea: The story of her life is really two stories. One story, victimization, signifies the part of herself conditioned by abuse and expressed in her symptoms and other problems identified during therapy. The other story, survival, signifies the part of herself that has remained true and that is expressed in her inner strength, resilience, and willingness to struggle. The telling of the survivor story begins with the therapist leading the client to affirm that she possesses the survivor qualities, and because she has them, she has the power and can expect to heal.

Beyond building a sense of agency and expectation of positive change, the therapist uses the idea of a strong, healthy part as a symbolic resource for the reinterpretations that constitute the survivor story. In stage two, the therapist takes the client through a process of reframing her view of herself and others in light of the survivor rationale. The therapist has already led the client to link her adult problems with childhood abuse and to commit herself to reject all that being an abuse victim entails. Now he works to identify a broader pattern of deviations from therapeutic norms in matters of the client's sense of self-worth, the way she manages her personal boundaries, the coherence of her identity, and her social skills and relationships. In the process of decoding her life according to the survivor rationale, the therapist persuades her to see problems with the way she is living that go well beyond the issues that brought her to therapy. He creates for her a fuller picture of the "false self" that, he argues, has informed and divided her identity. The false self is the benchmark against which the therapist contrasts the true self. By describing this true self as embodied in a strong, healthy part within her, the therapist positions his teaching as the natural drawing out of a story and a reality that were always present but heretofore unrecognized and unexpressed. The idea of a strong, healthy part suggests that by collaborating with the therapist, the client is authoring an undistorted account of her unique self. Because of the strong part, not only the victim story but also the survivor story has narrative fit for her life.

The survivor story is a story of personal change, a story about overcoming the conditioned responses of the false self. Building on the idea of her "survivor strength," the therapist emphasizes risk-taking, experimentation, efficacious action, personal development, and new possibilities for relationships. As in the victim account, where the therapist has the client act out key elements of the drama—for example, remembering, expressing anger, disclosing, grieving—so in the survivor story, he will lead the client to act out a new way of knowing and possessing the self. These actions are the preconditions for telling the story and create experiences that can then be conveyed in it. A new reflexive relationship to the self, including skill with the authorized "technologies of the self"—techniques for managing emotions, interpersonal relationships, the body, and so on—for living this reflexivity, is the key sign of healing. A new sense of her self-worth is where the next story begins.

Self-Esteem

In the first step, the therapist reiterates to the client that her sense of self-worth has been shaped by childhood abuse.[2] Drawing on the trauma model, he explains feelings, such as guilt, shame, depression, and anxiety (some of which, due to reinterpretation and new memories, she may have come to experience for the first time in therapy), as well as problems like eating disorders, promiscuity, patterns of self-abuse, and neglect of her physical appearance, as abuse effects on her self-esteem and self-image. Measuring the client's experience and feelings against his norms for healthy self-esteem, the therapist considers if her self-esteem has been impaired and identifies how these impairments are expressed.

The therapist has already worked to lay the foundation for addressing the client's sense of self-worth by leading her through the major themes of the victim account. Connecting her adult problems with abuse has transformed them from inexplicable events, personal failures, or signs of mental illness into understandable, destigmatized, and normalized by-products of trauma. The therapist has treated her with positive regard, has believed and supported the story he has helped her to tell, and has encouraged her to disclose her story to others who will respond in a manner similar to his own. He has assured her that she is not alone and may have encouraged her to join a survivor group to experience the support of others. Group involvement, therapists argue, provides an opportunity for the client to help others and not just be helped—"a process that supports self-esteem and lessens the sense of being a deviant, passive recipient of treatment" (Briere 1989: 143). He has encouraged her to believe in and "trust herself and her perceptions and not be fearful of taking risks in expressing and exploring her new self" (Sanderson 1990: 241). He has refused to validate any feelings of guilt or complicity the client may have. The plot line of the victim account has already emphasized her innocence.

In preparing the client to tell the survivor story, the therapist further draws out the theme of her innocence. Adding to the victimization account, he leads her to explicitly assign responsibility for abuse and its outcomes in her life to the alleged abuser(s). According to therapists, "[c]orrectly assigning the responsibility for the abuse to the abuser is a crucial step in the recovery process" (Bolton, Morris, and MacEachron 1989: 104). The therapist's guiding principle is that "the *perpetrator* bears the moral responsibility for the predatory act, no matter how many preventive strategies can be perceived after the fact" (Meiselman 1990: 135; emphasis in original). This principle structures the way the therapist discusses the meaning of abuse with his client, and he is careful not to redirect responsibility back to her. In exploring the question of why abuse happened, for instance, the therapist might discuss the widespread nature of sexual abuse, or power and family dynamics, in order to help "provide an explanation that allows survivors to place their abuse in a meaningful context" (Draucker 1992: 113). What he does not do is promote understanding of the alleged abuser, attempt to exonerate him in any way, or precipitate forgiveness of him. The therapist does not attenuate the alleged abuser's responsibility, in other words, and does not allow the client to do so. Exploring the meaning of abuse, then, becomes a means to foster the client's attribution of full responsibility to the alleged abuser.

To convince the client that she can bear no guilt for her situation, and to circumvent any tendency to resist assigning responsibility, the therapist also talks through and, if necessary, reframes every way in which the client might remember or believe that she had some role in the sexual contact. For instance, if the client remembers that she experienced sexual pleasure, the therapist reframes this experience as a natural physiological reaction to sexual stimulation. It does not indicate that sex was sought or enjoyed, and, lest the client interpret her experience as idiosyncratic, the therapist emphasizes that many abuse victims experience some sexual pleasure. Likewise, the therapist reframes any positive feelings toward her alleged abuser the client may remember as common, spontaneous childhood responses that in no way mean the sexual activity was consensual. Reframing is aimed to help the client "resolve her feelings of guilt for aspects of the sexual abuse" (Hall and Lloyd 1989: 114) by teaching her that no such feelings have any warrant. By changing the client's perceptions and feeling through reinterpretation, the therapist seeks to remove any obstacles that still inhibit the client from recognizing her innocence and the alleged abuser's culpability for the abuse and its outcomes in her life.

Assigning responsibility to the abuser is a way in which therapists "externalize" (Briere 1989) self-blame. When the client comes to see her problems as the result of something that was done to her, not something she deserved, caused, or could have prevented, then, therapists argue, she is able to embrace innocence and overcome guilt. According to therapists, her self-acceptance is thereby enhanced and, by more completely rejecting any sense of complicity, her discharge of anger and other strong emotions will be less restrained.

In leading the client to narrate innocence into her victimization account, the therapist also addresses the issue of shame. In therapy, the client's identity has been treated as imprisoned by a terrible secret, distorted, both by others and by herself, by the nonrecognition of her victimization and of her innocence. The client's recognition of victimization, combined with her disclosure to prosurvivors, has exposed the secret, and, according to therapists, shame "dissipates through the process of exposure and acceptance" (Kirschner, Kirschner, and Rappaport 1993: 116). The therapist further addresses shame—"the myth of personal 'bad'ness" (Briere 1989: 119)—by teaching the client that her innocence is more than blamelessness for particular actions or deficiencies: It is a truth about herself. Bringing her to recognize an essential, childlike innocence is the foundation therapists offer for self-acceptance and a key to the untangling of the true self from the distorted identity.

Along with innocence, the therapist provides "new cognitions" about the self to help the client tell a new story about herself. As with innocence, the therapist uses these new cognitions to enhance the client's self-esteem by identifying negative self-perceptions and replacing them with positive ones. He identifies and helps her to express personal strengths and weaknesses, for instance, and to adjust expectations that he views as inappropriate because they are either too high or too low. He encourages her to take a positive, compassionate, and tolerant attitude toward herself. He teaches her not to let her sense of self-worth depend on others' evaluations and, emphasizing her survivor strength, assures her that deep down she is alive, energetic, and creative. He uses the therapeutic relationship to model the new attitude and counters self-critical and self-abusive tendencies with positive evaluation. He teaches her to relate to herself in kind and supportive ways, and proffers new ideas about what is healthy and normal with respect to body image and self-care. Some survivor therapists view this teaching as a kind of skills training for self-parenting, a training that offers the client "the opportunity to learn to parent herself in a positive and nurturing way" (Sanderson 1990: 133). Along with new cognitions, he also encourages her to experiment with and cultivate habits of comforting and nurturing herself.

Therapists argue that in teaching new cognitions about the self and new behaviors, the client's inner " 'cruel parent' is being gradually restructured into an inner parent that she can live with" (Meiselman 1990: 132). They promote a new level of self-esteem by teaching assumptions that restructure the client's dialogue with herself about herself. In the survivor story, the client overcomes low self-worth by recognizing her fundamental goodness and innocence.

Personal Boundaries

By helping to plot the client's experience within the victim account, the therapist teaches her that abuse may have made it difficult for her to define her personal boundaries, act autonomously, assert her rights, and "own" her body. Applying the trauma model and measuring her behavior against normative standards of personal autonomy, the therapist seeks "to increase the woman's [client's] awareness of her 'victim behavior' and to gently challenge her assertions that she has no needs, rights, or choices in her life" (Hall and Lloyd 1989: 133). Due to abuse, her life is likely to be characterized in part by fear, by a learned powerlessness, by an inability to make demands in her relationships, and by being out of touch with her emotions. Whether she previously understood it or not, the therapist argues, her autonomy and self-possession may be impaired.

In leading the client to give the victim account, the therapist has already begun to teach her new norms of autonomy and boundary construction. By normalizing her defenses and coping strategies as survival mechanisms rather than personal flaws, he affirms that she is not inherently powerless. By leading her through a process of emotional expression, he has sought to teach her that her emotions are good. Through disclosure, he has worked to put her in a position to "begin to discover [her] own needs, wants, beliefs, and goals" (Kirschner, Kirschner, and Rappaport 1993: 19). In letting go of the past, he has encouraged her to acknowledge her "true strength and courage," to reject behavior linked with being a powerless victim, such as being taken advantage of by others, and to take control of her life and life circumstances.

To help the client tell the survivor story about autonomy, the therapist actively models and teaches her how to "identify and manage" her personal boundaries (Crowder 1993: 72). The therapeutic relationship itself, as noted earlier, is designed and conducted so as to model boundary management. Therapists stress "that the client is trying to develop a more separate self, to become the kind of person whom she likes and respects" (Kirschner, Kirschner, and Rappaport 1993: 165). To foster separation and the definition of a distinct identity, the therapist uses the therapeutic sessions to help the client try on empowering thoughts, practice contract-making and personal choice, express her feelings and needs, and learn to monitor the self. He teaches her, for instance, her rights and how to assert them. He teaches her to set her own priorities and define her own needs and interests, encouraging her to see choices in matters that seemed to her closed, such as in sex roles, and to make demands where she had not before. He encourages her to take responsibility for her actions, while "letting go of things that she has no control over and taking on things that can be controlled" (Sanderson 1990: 167). He tells her not to set her boundaries too rigidly. Taking advantage of opportunities for self-development means remaining open to taking "the psychological risks that are always necessary when a person is growing" (Meiselman 1990: 103). The goal is to possess the self in an open and even fluid fashion, not in a rigid or static way.

In addition to a new definition of her psychological boundaries, a changed perspective on her body is also a crucial element of the autonomy theme. The therapist teaches the client to "reclaim" her body. Reclaiming involves a new and positive image of and possession of the body, as well as a new approach to establishing and maintaining physical boundaries. Among other things, the therapist may utilize "body focused" techniques that are designed to help the client negotiate "safe touch"—touch that the client controls—and gain a reflexive awareness of her body and how to manage it. He explores issues of sexual functioning and satisfaction, and may recommend refraining from sexual activity while he teaches her to set and assert her boundaries. He may teach her different cognitions about sexuality and techniques for how to say no to, relax in, and control sexual expression.

For therapists, teaching the client to take particular attitudes toward herself and others is to teach her to identify "victim behavior," to reverse it, and to live by a new, more reflexive pattern that extends to the body. This is the route to empowerment and personal autonomy. In the survivor story, the client overcomes disempowerment by learning her rights and how to manage her boundaries.

The Confrontation

As the therapist led the client to attribute responsibility for the abuse, he also promoted a change in her attitude toward the alleged abuser.[3] As he leads her to reject victim behavior, demand her rights, and become more self-assertive, he readies her to confront him, and perhaps others as well. "Once survivors begin to discharge anger and reattribute responsibility for the abuse to the abuser, they feel a need to break their enforced silence by confronting the abuser, and/or other family members" (Sanderson 1990: 203). They might, however, also express a desire to forgive the alleged abuser. While the therapist does not prohibit forgiveness, he treats the desire to forgive with great reservation. Therapists argue that "forgiveness may represent survivors' attempts to close the healing process prematurely by denying repressed anger, hurt, or betrayal toward the offender and may be a form of self-blame or minimization" (Draucker 1992: 108). For therapists, forgiveness is not necessary for healing and may even be an obstacle. He wants the client to deal with the alleged abuser, but confrontation—face-to-face or symbolic—rather than forgiveness is the form that he endorses.

The therapist advocates confrontation because, when handled properly, it expresses the themes of innocence and empowerment and reinforces them. The confrontation of the alleged abuser is a kind of personal (witnesses may or may not be present) "degradation ceremony" (Garfinkel 1956), in which the client expresses her moral indignation by denouncing the alleged abuser as a child molester and degrading his total identity. She forcefully asserts her victimization, the harm it has caused her, and his complete responsibility for moral injustice. She asserts her innocence, her moral status as aggrieved party, and her right to shame and degrade him. For therapists, whatever its public consequences, the confrontation reinforces the survivor story by providing the client with an emotionally charged context in which to demonstrate to herself that she is no longer a victim and no longer silent, and to "showcase" her new "emotional strength, power, and control" (Bolton, Morris, and MacEachron 1989: 117). It may also force a further and desired realigning of relationships, both with the alleged abuser, no matter what his response to the confrontation, and with others who take sides. Depending on response, a confrontation with an alleged nonprotecting other could potentially do likewise.

While therapists emphasize the important role that confrontations can play in the client's telling of the survivor story, they also argue that confrontations involve serious risks. The therapist has structured therapy to be safe (contractual, low-risk, client in control, warm and supportive) and has advised careful and selective disclosure of the client's victim account. The confrontation, however, exposes the client to a possibly harsh and unbelieving reaction that may do her more harm than good. Therapists observe that even at this stage doubts remain, and that the client's emerging identity may still be quite fragile. Rather than reinforcing her survivor story, the confrontation might unsettle it. The therapist, therefore, does not advocate a confrontation until he has brought the client to the point of readiness. As one therapist argues,

> The survivor should confront only when she can view it as an act of personal mastery that is symbolic of relinquishing the role of victim. When she can honestly tell herself that her self-esteem will be strengthened by the very act of confrontation, *regardless of the other person's reaction,* then she has reached a state of readiness and can begin to plan and rehearse the confronting statements. (Meiselman 1990: 169; emphasis in original)

To be therapeutically successful, the confrontation must be "orchestrated carefully" (Briere 1989: 141). The therapist guides the client's preparation, insisting that she control the conditions of the encounter. He encourages her to be very cautious about confronting alone and, at a minimum, always to have some prosurvivors nearby. If she or the therapist feels the need, he might suggest that he, her survivor group, or other prosurvivors be present for the confrontation. He helps her to shape an agenda, select the setting, and, most important, establish realistic expectations of what will and will not happen. The possible reactions of the alleged abuser—fierce denial, refusal to talk about it, blaming the victim, asking for forgiveness, and so on—are anticipated and prepared for so that the accused is given no opportunity to weaken the client's story. To be considered ready, the client must not need or expect an apology. The therapist tells her that the possibility of gaining an admission of guilt and genuine remorse from the alleged abuser is extremely remote, and that such an outcome is not the goal. Rather, the confrontation is orchestrated to serve therapeutic purposes *for the client.* The goal is for her to further relinquish victim behavior and to exercise her survivor self-esteem and assertiveness. The alleged abuser's response need only be taken into account in determining whether she has advanced sufficiently in therapy to face a direct challenge to her victim and survivor stories.[4]

If the therapist does not feel the client can handle a face-to-face confrontation, or if she does not want to do so, he may recommend that she confront her alleged abuser symbolically. He might arrange role-playing sessions, having the client imagine that the alleged abuser is sitting in an empty chair and then go through her rehearsed confrontation. Or he might have her write one or more letters of confrontation, knowing that she will not actually send them. In some instances, such as when the alleged abuser is dead or otherwise unavailable, the client has no choice but to use symbolic gestures. For example, if the alleged abuser is dead, the therapist might suggest that the client hold a symbolic confrontation at his graveside.

Therapists also encourage clients to work through and express their feelings about any alleged nonprotecting other(s). During the building of her victim account, the client may have expressed or come to experience intense anger not only toward the alleged abuser but toward another person(s) she believes knew of the abuse and either did nothing or refused to believe her. To consolidate the survivor story, the therapist may recommend a confrontation with this person(s) as well. Therapists emphasize, however, that a client's confrontation of an alleged nonprotecting other should not replace the confrontation of the abuser. Because nonprotecting others are often easier to face, they argue, responsibility assignment and anger appropriate to the alleged abuser can get misdirected. If misdirected, the therapeutic purposes of the confrontation—expressing victimization, innocence, and assertiveness—may fail to be fully experienced, with negative consequences for the client's conviction about her survivor story.

Identity and Development

Using the victim story and the trauma model, the therapist also indicates to the client that in some measure her identity has been fragmented and her development interrupted. By leading her to retrieve hidden memories and by interpreting nightmares, "flashbacks," and bodily pain as reexperiencing abuse, the therapist shows the client that there is a determinative part of herself of which she is not fully aware. In taking her through the experiencing and expressing of abuse emotions, he leads her to release feelings that seemed to have been lying dormant within. He interprets any reluctance to trust, rigid thinking, emotional suppression, elaborate safety needs, and other ways of thinking and acting as reflecting the continued use of childhood coping strategies and defenses. He argues that unpredictable, erratic, or radically disjointed behavior shows that her experience of herself lacks coherence and unity. Contrasting a victim self with a survivor self, he suggests that the client has a child within whose self-development has been stunted. He works with the client to identify patterns of thought, feeling, and action that, he argues, reflect the damaged "inner child."

In leading the client to construct her victim account, the therapist has modeled and taught new norms of development and self-awareness. He has indicated that she needs an explicit narrative, authored by herself, to gain closure and an integrated sense of self. He has repeatedly taught her that expressing and articulating her emotions is essential "for increased self-understanding and self-determination" (Courtois 1988: 179). He has taught her that thoughts, feelings, and behavior can be entirely determined by external contingencies and that, as in therapy, a vigilant self-monitoring is required for consistent, self-determined action. He has taught her to make her self-development a self-conscious project, letting go of whatever encumbrances stand in the way. He has used the process of building a victim account to dramatically illustrate how important the self-development project is for a better future.

To foster identity integration, the therapist uses the trauma model to tie together her fragmented experiences with a single, coherent explanation that is thematically harmonious and scientifically plausible. His explanation makes intelligible what was earlier mystifying and "split off" in the client's experience. He provides a framework that allows her to recognize and understand inconsistent, unacceptable, and "intrusive" thoughts and feelings. The possession of this framework, because it is understood to be rooted in a true self-knowledge, is believed to reduce the actual experience of erratic and inconsistent behavior.

The therapist also promotes a "reintegration of her self" (Meiselman 1990: 102) by connecting the client's past, as expressed in the victim account, with an anticipated future. The account already defines the effects of abuse in terms of the changes in identity that therapy advocates. As the therapist leads the client to make the advocated changes, he presents them as an overcoming of abuse conditioning and a completion of unfinished development. In this way, he links the victim account with the new approaches to life that he is teaching in the survivor story. The past and the future are therefore not disjointed but part of a single narrative that establishes a continuity of meaning in the client's biography. Both past and future fit together in the new story of her life.

Teaching the client a different normative framework for living is another way in which therapists promote identity integration. Patterns of thought and action reframed as expressions of impaired development are addressed with new normative orientations to the self and others, presented as the orientations the client would have had if her development had been normal. These norms, based in a particular orientation to the self, are principles for handling the multiple expectations, moral demands, role conflicts, and tensions of life. As she internalizes these principles—"becoming her own therapist"—the client's development evens out. She will be able to pursue her newly discovered interests and goals in a consistent and unified way as the old story of fragmentation is replaced.

As part of the client's development, the therapist encourages her to replace old coping strategies and defenses with strategies believed to be more "appropriate to the client's present life circumstances" (Crowder 1993: 55). As with other elements offered in therapy, the therapist encourages the client to experiment with new patterns: "The counsellor's role is to encourage the survivor to explore alternative coping strategies and to support her in her experimentation and validate her in her final decisions" (Sanderson 1990: 216). He recommends strategies that are "self-determined and healthy" (Courtois 1988: 10) for handling personal anxiety and stressful, conflictive situations. Rather than denying her anger, for example, the client is taught to recognize it and manage it, not letting it overwhelm her but expressing it in a way that channels "its energy into the responses that will be most likely to preserve [her] rights and relationships" (Meiselman 1990: 110). With these strategies, therapists aim to teach the client a reflexive awareness of her coping patterns and psychological defenses, and to view them in light of the risks and opportunities of self-development.

For therapists, the client's "reintegration" means "moving from an identity based on being unaware of and constantly defending against the eruption of unacceptable thoughts and feelings to one that encompasses all aspects of her past experience" (Meiselman 1990: 102). In the survivor story, the client overcomes fragmentation with a newly organized life history and gains a normative framework and techniques for living in accordance with it.

Relationships

In leading the client to construct a victim account, the therapist has taught her that her personal relationships need to be renegotiated on different terms. Through disclosure, and the realigning of relationships based on the responses it elicits, he shows her that not all of her relationships are supportive. In the letting go process, he emphasizes that old relationships can be a serious obstacle to her new life. Applying the trauma model, he teaches her that difficult or encumbering relationships in her life have been formed around an inner, abuse-determined tendency to be revictimized. These relationships, he argues, must be changed as the client begins "to break the habits that have kept her enmeshed in abusive relationships" (Jones 1991: 59). He considers whether she relates to others from low self-worth and whether her social skills, including perhaps her parenting skills, have been impaired. She probably does not know how to trust or be properly nurtured or intimate, and so experiences isolation, loneliness, sexual problems, and troubled personal relations.

In helping the client emplot her experience in the victim account, the therapist has authorized the change of any relationships that the client regards, or comes to regard, as nonsupporting, revictimizing, or encumbering in some way. Through his teaching and the modeling in the therapeutic relationship, he has begun to teach her norms of "mutually satisfying relationships" (Courtois 1988: 226). He has encouraged her to identify those who really care about her by their support for and encouragement of her emerging account. A survivor group may also be providing a "social milieu where respect for personal boundaries is paramount and [the client] can practice new skills for relating to the self and others" (Crowder 1993: 77).

In the themes of the survivor story already discussed, the therapist has promoted new ideas about the way the client should select, build, and manage her personal relationships. He has taught her to take a positive attitude toward herself and not to measure her sense of worth in terms of others' evaluations. He has stressed the need to set new ground rules in relationships that reflect her needs and boundaries, to set her own priorities, to assert her rights, and to take calculated risks. He has taught her new ideas about sexual expression, negotiating touch, and relating to her physical boundaries. He has proffered and encouraged her to experiment with new strategies for coping with anxiety and situations of stress and conflict, and advised that "current relationships based upon old survival strategies may no longer be viable once different and more adaptable skills are learned" (Bolton, Morris, and MacEachron 1989: 112). He has led her to assign responsibility for the abuse and its continuing effects to the alleged abuser(s) and has prepared her for the confrontation(s). Her relationship to the alleged abuser(s) and, perhaps, nonprotecting others, has changed as a result.

In the survivor stage, the therapist adds another principle: He encourages the client to change or restructure her relationships on the basis of how much personal satisfaction they provide. Encumbering or revictimizing relationships, he argues, must be renegotiated or replaced with supportive ones that reflect the client's new story about herself. "This is not to say that all survivors will rid themselves of significant interpersonal relationships as they improve. It does mean that they now have the option of selecting relationships based upon something other than the results of being abused as children" (Bolton, Morris, and MacEachron 1989: 112). In order to build relationships on this changed basis, the therapist tells the client that each of her relationships, including those with a spouse and children, will have to be renegotiated and restructured. To further the process, he "may assist survivors in evaluating their current relationships by exploring how these relationships meet the survivors' needs for independence, as well as for intimacy, and how the relationships enhance or detract from the survivors' growth and healing" (Draucker 1992: 96). Some relationships when evaluated in this light will simply be ended. While therapists argue that the client need not drop all problematical relationships—it may be acceptable, for instance, for the client to learn to live with a "degree of ambiguity" (Jones 1991: 52) toward an alleged nonprotecting mother—she must restructure these relationships based on her new identity. Clients "need to approach family contact based on the changes they have made in the healing process, rather than interacting with their [families] based on old roles and patterns" (Draucker 1992: 111). He also encourages the forming of new friendships. If he has not already done so, he may recommend a survivor group for this purpose.

To further the survivor story of changed relationships, the therapist teaches the client additional strategies for relating to others. For instance, he uses the therapeutic relationship as a model for teaching her new norms about establishing safety and about how to judge the trustworthiness of other people. He assists the client "in judging the trustworthiness of others by teaching [her] to objectively evaluate the other's behavior in different situations and at different times" (Draucker 1992: 98). He works with the client to inculcate new social skills—such as how to be more sensitive and caring, how to "nurture and be nurtured" (Bolton, Morris, and MacEachron 1989: 108), and how to resolve conflicts—and, if necessary, extends his advice to how to care for children. In his teaching, he emphasizes self-expression and talking things over as keys to right relationships.

Letting Go

The therapeutic work on the victim account and survivor story involves a detachment. The therapist forms a special relationship with the client, who in turn takes the dependent client role and makes personal change the focus of her life for a period of time. The rhythm of ordinary life is, in an important sense, suspended during the transition time. During the course of therapy, the therapist also leads the client to detach herself from a previous identity, from old relationships, and from the view of herself as a victim. As the client tells the survivor story, the period of detaching is coming to an end. To ready her for reincorporation, for the termination of therapy and a "getting on with her life," however, the therapist leads her to let go of yet one more thing. In the next and last stage of therapy, the telling of the thriver story, the therapist now leads the client to let go of the view of herself as survivor.

STAGE THREE: THE THRIVER STORY

The survivor story is a story about reversing the present effects of the past. For therapists, the client can tell the story when she has internalized the therapeutic norms and techniques and is acting on them—when, in other words, she can describe the effects of the past and how she is overcoming them. When she can tell the survivor story, healing has been largely realized and its signs can be observed: "Healing occurs when the client has achieved a reasonable level of resolution around the abusive events, has unraveled the resultant distortions of self and reality and replaced them with healthier views, has learned new skills that were not taught in childhood, has the ability to establish and maintain positive relationships, and has an experience of herself as efficacious in her world" (Roth 1993: 24). The steps of the survivor story, including the confrontation, have been addressed to achieving these goals. With the telling and retelling of the survivor story, therapy nears its end.

Although principally framed as a story about growth and healing, the survivor story is built directly on the victim story about abuse. Survivor strength is defined in terms of resistance to abuse, and personal change in terms of overcoming a self conditioned by abuse. As therapy moves toward its denouement, therapists encourage clients to move beyond the view of themselves as survivors. Abuse remains a part of their story, but because they have made and are making desired changes in their identity and consequent behavior, clients "no longer need to define themselves in terms of their experience of childhood sexual abuse" (Draucker 1992: 116). Thus, "Counselors, in the later stages of treatment, might well discuss with the client the process of giving up the survivor identity" (116). At this advanced point in therapy, the transitional stories of victim and survivor have accomplished their purpose. The therapist now readies the client to end therapy and reincorporate into normal life with a positive, thriver story, which moves abuse and overcoming abuse to the background. He does not ask the client to let go of the thriver story but to embrace it as the ongoing story of her life. When therapy ends, the thriver story is just beginning.

The thriver story is the end of the mediating narrative and its climax. It is the conclusion that is anticipated throughout the process of constructing the narrative, guiding the building of the therapeutic relationship, the selective recruitment of past events (whether real or imagined), and the interpretation of present life circumstances. It is the goal, the lesson toward which the whole narrative builds and takes its meaning. It is the promise used to motivate the client and justify her efforts to part with old understandings and patterns and learn new ones.

The thriver story is a story of liberation. According to the plot of the mediating narrative as it has unfolded in the victim account and survivor story, the pathological secret has been identified, and its effects progressively overcome. The hold of the past on the client has been broken; she has been freed from who she was, freed from the wrong story, freed from encumbering relationships, and has the power to become someone new. In the thriver story, she is free to let her true self flourish fully for the first time. She "is ready to infuse her life with new hope and new choices" (Roth 1993: 65). She can live with new vitality and satisfaction, express her creativity, enjoy intimacy, and define her goals and strive to reach them. She can become who she wants to be and do what she wants to do. In the thriver story, the future is unscripted, open and full of possibilities.

The therapist emphasizes themes aimed to confirm her transformation and motivate her to continue to act according to the new norms and relationship strategies she has learned. By linking her old ideas and behavior with abuse, and by framing his teaching in terms of health and normal development in the survivor stage, he has already made a forceful case for not returning to old or other patterns. Moreover, because the survivor story represents a commitment to a continued course of action, ordering her self and renegotiating her relationships through that story constrains the client to continue to act in a manner consistent with the commitment. In the thriver story, the therapist connects future growth and vitality with a steady living of the new story and emphasizes themes of self-determination and responsibility to reinforce it.

In leading the client to tell the thriver story, the therapist contrasts two journeys, one now nearly complete and another about to begin. In the first journey toward healing, the client has moved, via the mediating narrative, from a life that was abuse-determined to a life capable of being self-determined, from a life shaped by domination to a life empowered with agency. In the second journey, she will move into the future choosing her own path. For the second journey, as thriver, she no longer needs to depend on the guidance of the therapist. She is ready, he argues, for "healthy separation" (Courtois 1988: 10). Although "it is all right for the client to have needs again" (Roth 1993: 70) that might warrant a return to the therapist, any such return in the next journey would be qualitatively different and temporary. She is now, the therapist tells her, able to reflexively direct her own journey. He has taught the normative orientations and a technology of the self that equip clients to become their own therapists. The therapist's message is that if the client follows these new principles, she can do for herself in the second journey what he did for her in the first.

Because she is believed to be self-determined, the client is also now responsible to herself for her life and her choices. While the past may have been outside her control, and thus she is blameless with regard to it, in the journey that begins with the thriver story, things are different. In the new journey, she has "total responsibility for [her] own destiny" (Draucker 1992: 108). She is becoming an individual, free of false consciousness, and therefore able to shoulder the burden of responsibility for all aspects of her life. The victim account was an "excuse," an "appeal to defeasibility" (Scott and Lyman 1968) of responsibility for the problems the client has experienced, because her will was not free. To tell the thriver story, she cannot make any further excuses. If she continues to live her new identity, therapists imply, she will never need to.

The Lessons of the Mediating Narrative

In leading the client to tell the thriver story, the therapist has been concerned with far more than simply addressing the problems that brought her to him in the first place. He has sought a significant transformation of her identity rather than simply giving advice or aiming to reduce or eliminate specific symptoms. Symptom reduction is important. Therapists expect that as the client moves through the stages of the mediating narrative her symptoms, especially signs of distress but also signs of impaired functioning, will improve. In the survivor stage, for instance, they expect that the client will experience a reduction in dissociative behavior and that anxiety, outbursts of rage, emotional inhibition, loss of sexual interest, nightmares, flashbacks, physical pain, or adjustment problems they associate with abuse will begin to go away. They use any such success in symptom reduction to underwrite the narrative's rightness. But healing, as most of the treatment books explicitly make clear, is defined much more broadly than symptom reduction. Indeed, due to the therapist's view about the underlying cause of symptoms, improvement by itself may not even be viewed favorably. Survivor therapists argue that denial of the underlying cause—abuse—may bring some symptom control. Thus, when the work begins in the first stage of therapy, symptoms frequently get worse. Effective denial, rather than true healing, could yield symptom improvement. Thus, not symptom improvement per se, but resolution of the underlying cause is what therapists consider essential. Resolution means telling all of the stories of the mediating narrative, and only when the client can tell the thriver story is she considered ready to end therapy. The signs of health are fundamentally matters of a changed identity; the distress or disability that brought the client to therapy may improve or disappear, yet it might not. What is considered essential is a resolution that equips the client to live in a new way.

The new identity is a reconstitution of the past as the client masters each of the stories of the mediating narrative. Therapists believe that in the process the right story is replacing a wrong story and that this replacement is essential to healing. Thriver living requires the right story. Therapists also believe that a new ordering of the self is essential to healing. In the mediating narrative, they convey assumptions about the self and the moral order that inform their norms of health and normality and shape the technologies of the self they teach. In order to make explicit key lessons of the mediating narrative, I have distilled a number of these assumptions about the self and its interactions with others. The exposition necessarily relies on inferences, since the assumptions tend to remain latent in the texts, taken for granted rather than delineated. On what set of assumptions, I asked, must the therapeutic process be based if its guidance is logical and internally consistent? I make no claim that all survivor therapists explicitly hold these assumptions. The analysis presented in the past two chapters, however, supports the idea that they constitute an implicit therapeutic message about the self and society whose adoption by the client signifies her recovery.

In survivor therapy, therapists teach clients that the self is innocent and good: not only innocent of complicity in childhood sexual experience, but innocent also in a more fundamental sense. The true self is presented as childlike in its purity and innocence, and genuine self-worth originates in an affirmation that the self is good. Therapists teach clients that the self is multidimensional and has the potential to grow in many possible and simultaneous directions. Tapping this potential is the greatest source of empowerment, richness, and meaning in life. Therapists teach clients that the self is properly unencumbered. The self can be who it wants to be, and *should* be. There are no binding obligations or social roles that take precedence over personal autonomy. True personal relationships do not bind, but are "pure relationships," as sociologist Anthony Giddens calls them, existing "solely for whatever rewards ... [the] relationship as such can deliver" (1991: 6). Such relationships engender and maintain trust by balancing the demands of autonomy and mutual self-disclosure. There is vulnerability but not dependency. Each party supports the self-defined development of the other. Each party's ultimate responsibility is to him or herself. Finally, therapists teach clients that the self is known through and strengthened by the emotions. Knowing one's emotions, managing them, and openly expressing them avoids great personal strain, fosters self-knowledge and growth, and is a requirement of honesty in true personal relationships.

Survivor therapists also teach clients that the self is deeply vulnerable to wounds inflicted from outside it and therefore great vigilance must be exercised in self-protection. While the self is presented as being innocent and good, capable of unfolding in unique and creative ways, people are also presented as bad and dominating, out for themselves at the expense of others.[5] Parents and other adult authority figures are presented as a particular source of danger to the self-development of children, both during early socialization and beyond. For the true self to find expression as an adult, right beliefs and attitudes about the self and how to relate to others must be taught during a carefree and playful childhood. A 47-year-old survivor expresses the belief succinctly: "If I had a comfortable childhood, I could be anything today" (quoted in Bass and Davis 1988: 33). Adults, however, through their actions and speech, frequently teach children false beliefs and attitudes about themselves, which, because they are internalized, constitute a persistent danger to the self. For therapists, self-development gone awry requires the therapeutic reconstruction of childhood so that the false lessons can be "unlearned." For clients to maintain self-development and nurture it, therapists also emphasize their ongoing need to protect their autonomy—in marriage, family, friendships, institutions—against all forms of "enmeshment," dependence, or being taken advantage of. The precise nature of these external dangers is not always clear, but therapists emphasize that the self has rights and teach clients a contractual mode of relating in order to assert and protect them. The rights of the self preeminently include the rights to self-determination, autonomy, and growth. Therapists teach clients that they have the rights, among others, to state and pursue their own priorities, to freely express their feelings, to own their bodies, to expect from others a return in proportion to what they give, to live up to their self-defined potential, and to have their identity respected.

While certainly not exhaustive, these ways of conceiving of the self and its orientation to others are central lessons of the mediating narrative. By moving through each of the stories, the client comes to the end of therapy prepared to know and possess her self in a new way.

NARRATIVE FIT

In the last two chapters I have described survivor therapy as a progressive dismantling of a client's old understandings and orientations through the narrative construction—via an iterative process of successive "tellings"—of a new account and identity. In each stage of the mediating narrative, the therapist works to convince the client that the new story she is telling about herself is finally right, and that with the right story she can become someone new; she *is* someone new. In order to persuade the client of the "rightness" of the new version, including the moral and normative lessons it teaches, he works to make each story, and thus the whole mediating narrative, "fit," or cohere with the client's lived experience.[6] While therapists treat the fit of the mediating narrative as arising from the client's progressive discovery of her true history and self, I have argued that this fit is an achievement of therapy. Far from a discovery, narrative fit is the outcome of a specific therapeutic approach. While the treatment manuals describe therapy as an alliance in which the client is in charge of her healing, they also instruct therapists to direct every element of the process according to norms for healthy attitudes, beliefs, emotions, and behaviors. In each stage, therapists work to overcome the client's resistance, arouse appropriate emotions, reassign moral responsibility, teach and model correct ideas about the self, and consolidate the changes made. Therapists guide the process, in short, by assumptions about what does and does not constitute a truth about the client's self—as victim, as survivor, and as thriver.

In building the client's sense of fit with the mediating narrative, the therapist uses the therapeutic relationship and specific techniques to persuade her that her old identity fails key criteria, while the new identity meets them.[7] First, he argues that her old identity lacks internal coherence because it does not adequately or accurately take account of her painful experience. Important constituent elements of her identity are contradictory or mystifying, and her version fails to reconcile or resolve them. At the same time, he provides an internal coherence to the new identity by ordering the client's painful experiences as symptoms of trauma and by using the trauma model to identify other deviations from his standards of health. He provides continuity by coupling the overcoming of the past with the new norms he is teaching her for living in the future. He builds a sense of unity by identifying the client's approved change as arising from her inner survivor strength. The therapist also argues that whatever external coherence the old identity had was rooted in the denial of abuse, both by the client herself and by the larger society. He provides an external coherence for the new identity by drawing on the cultural approval of the survivor collective story in explaining the trauma model and in recommending the published accounts of other survivors. He uses the disclosure process to surround the client with those who will support and affirm her new account, and to weed out those who will not. He may also recommend a survivor group for the external affirmation it provides. He uses his authority as a mental health professional to affirm a connection between the lessons of the mediating narrative and her psychological health and well-being.

Second, the therapist uses the client's painful experiences and her need for help as evidence that her old identity is inappropriate. Because the trauma is unresolved, her identity fails to provide a basis for a satisfactory experience of self and relationships, and stifles and distorts her natural creativity and self-development. By contrast, he affirms that the new identity is appropriate by teaching the client a new reflexive relationship to herself and new techniques for living the lessons of the mediating narrative. He uses the therapy sessions for experimentation and practice, and does not declare the client ready to end therapy until she can demonstrate competence with the new approaches. He also ties the claims of a new, empowered life to her consistent adherence, post-therapy, to these approaches. Any improvement in her sense of well-being proves the value of her new identity.

Third, he argues that the client's old identity is empirically inadequate (perhaps along with diagnoses offered by other therapists) because it either leaves out altogether or marginalizes the traumatic experience. It is a form of false consciousness, rooted in an evasion of the event that determined her past and who she has become. In persuading the client to adopt the new identity, he gives the mediating narrative a sense of empirical adequacy by interpreting certain experiences as external indicators of its validity. Any number of experiences—from anxiety to physical pain, from self-abuse to resistance toward the therapist—are interpreted as evidence of an unresolved abuse history. Old memories and new—however triggered or elicited, however vague or detailed—signify the occurrence of trauma; emotional re-enactment signifies the return of repressed or dissociated abuse emotions; and symptom improvement signifies a resolving of abuse effects. By having the client act out key elements of the mediating narrative, the therapist also gives her empirical experience on which to ground her emerging account. Mourning dramatizes a break with the past, disclosure brings a predicted change of relationships, and the confrontation demonstrates her empowerment. In working to establish empirical adequacy, therapists counter the client's doubts. The stories of the mediating narrative are not invented; he has given her an experience of their reality.

In addition to relationship and techniques, therapists also promote narrative fit at a more subtle level by juxtaposing two seemingly contradictory descriptions of the self. The first is used throughout therapy to characterize the self-understandings and orientations that the client is encouraged to reject. This is the "false self," and it is pictured as determined and fixed through unconscious processes arising directly from traumatic formative experiences. The second description is used to characterize the self-understandings and orientations that the client is encouraged to adopt. This is the "true" or "authentic self," and it is pictured as determining itself, drawing its purposes and life-plans from within. The "thriver" client is ready for termination because she is finally realizing her true and unique self and is able to direct her own affairs. The use of these two descriptions, while paradoxical, is not contradictory. Survivor therapy, like all psychotherapies, is designed to alter clients' self-understandings by altering their suppositions about what it is good to do and good to be. Together, the two descriptions of the self serve the transformations that constitute the mediating process. In the victim and survivor stages, memories and emotions are emplotted according to a sweeping theory of victimization's enduring personal consequences. Giving an account of the way their identity was externally determined prevents clients from taking a contingent or morally uncertain view of their past, and it links particular views of the self and of other people with pathology (as outcomes of abuse).[8] At the same time, it provides the "other" against which the self-determining view and its moral orientations are narrated and their adoption warranted. Narrating the false self dictates a change in moral orientations, conceived in precisely the terms in which the true self is depicted. Thus, the first description of external determination is internally related to and sets up the use of the second. In the thriver stage, the description of self-determination more directly expresses the already implied ideal self and its orientations toward what is good, what is worthwhile, and what has meaning.

I have sought to show in the past two chapters how, according to the textbooks, the collective story is instantiated in the lives of individuals and the category of adult survivor is reproduced in survivor therapy. This is, to come back to Arthur Kleinman's image, the downward movement of an authorized meaning system, a movement that completes the circle first begun with Florence Rush and the social movements with which she was associated. The moral logic of innocence that informed the historical creation of the adult survivor category and the collective story it displayed become, in the life of the client, an account of innocence by which she can organize her experience and make it intelligible. It provides her with a new "voice," a form of recognition, and the promise of a new beginning. In every sort of public venue, from conferences and books to television talk shows, websites, films, and courts of law, adult survivors have given their accounts in these basic terms.

In the course of the analysis of the mediating narrative of survivor therapy, we saw two descriptions of the self in operation. In part 3 of this study, I want to consider further implications of these descriptions and their interrelationship. I begin, in the next chapter, with the description of external determination, embedded in the trauma model. One of the consequences of its application is to destabilize a client's understanding of her own past. In survivor therapy, "memory work" is crucial, because only in recovering the early traumatic events can they be properly narrated. Given the understanding of the defenses marshaled to combat trauma, however, the client's own recall may be doubted, either by the therapist or by the client herself. Through about the mid-1990s, as noted in chapter 5, therapists and self-help writers argued that a substantial number of sexual abuse survivors had no continuous memory of their traumatic experience. E. Sue Blume, for instance, in her popular 1990 book, *Secret Survivors,* concluded "that perhaps half of all incest survivors do not remember that the abuse occurred" (1990: 81). That sort of sweeping claim is seldom heard today, partly because of the intense opposition that it aroused. Beginning in the early 1990s, a growing chorus of critics, including but not limited to the False Memory Syndrome Foundation, arose to challenge the idea that traumatic memories are routinely lost to consciousness. With respect to those "survivors" who claimed to have dissociated abuse memories and only later exhumed them, these critics argued that the "memories" were in fact bogus, a product of social influence. In the next chapter I describe the "memory wars" and explore implications of this study for the conflict over recovered memories.

PART THREE

Victimization and the Self

CHAPTER EIGHT

Memory Wars

In the early 1990s, Beth Rutherford began therapy with a church counselor for help with work-related stress. Over time, they formed a close, emotionally intense relationship. In addition to ongoing therapy sessions each week, Beth would also regularly call her therapist, sometimes four or more times in a single day. Based on Beth's presenting problems, the therapist early inquired if Beth had been sexually abused. At first, Beth insisted "No, never," but as therapy proceeded and she talked through her experiences growing up, she began to reconsider and to increasingly suspect that her memories of childhood were "incorrect." Her therapist assured her that if there were repressed memories, they needed to be recovered and dealt with if she was to "become a truly whole person." Beth's memory work included analysis of her dreams, which had grown more intense and sexual, and hypnotic age regression. During her trances, according to her therapist, who took notes, Beth would reveal events of sexual abuse. She also began to have "body memories." "When coming out of a trance," Beth recounted later, "I could actually feel the pain of being penetrated." Together, she and her therapist discussed what a "victim 'feels' like and focused on the emotions of a victim: feelings of helplessness, loss of control, anger, hatred of your mother for not protecting you from your father, feeling dirty and afraid." Further, she was sent for evaluation to a psychiatrist and a psychologist, who concluded from their tests and questions that indeed she had been "severely traumatized as a child." Beth began to realize that what she had thought was a "good and happy childhood" was actually a "cruel joke."

In fostering her personal healing, the next step was to break off contact with her parents. Beth also staged a confrontation with them. Her parents denied the abuse, but, "I told them," she recounted, "that just because they wouldn't admit what they had done to me didn't mean I would back down from my belief that they did it." And what they had done, she now recalled in exact detail, was indeed horrendous. Among his abuses, her father had twice impregnated her—followed each time by a coat-hanger abortion—and had inserted various sharp instruments into her. Her mother had, on occasion, also participated by restraining her so that her father "could carry out his sadistic acts." To get away, Beth moved to another state with the help of her sister, who believed her account, and ended all communication with her parents.

Beth's victimization account might have ended there. But subsequent events changed matters fundamentally. Her second thoughts about her childhood were soon to be trumped by another reconsideration. In fact, the details described above are not part of a survivor account at all. They were told as part of a "retractor" account, a story of being a victim of "false memory syndrome." In the larger story, Beth argues that she did not truly recover abuse memories; they were implanted in her mind by her therapist. According to Beth, only after her relocation, and a consequent decline in the direct influence of her therapist, did she begin again to "think on [her] own." Despite two and a half years of therapy, she did not thrive. Rather, her problems only increased. She had deteriorated mentally and physically, weighed 87 pounds, was on medication, and "hated life." She felt isolated and lonely. Tentatively, she began to reestablish contact with her mother and then her father. Their concern and generous behavior toward her did not "line up" with her image of them as "monsters," and she began to entertain serious doubts about the veracity of her abuse memories. During one marathon talk with her parents about the accusations, Beth recounts, "I first heard the words 'false memories.' " The key to her reunion with her parents was their unconditional acceptance and nonthreatening response to her. "They accepted me," she writes, "just as I was, pieces and all." She retracted her abuse accusations and asked for her parents' forgiveness, which they "willingly and quickly gave." Her story closes with a testimony to their new closeness and collective gratitude in surviving "this almost fatal nightmare."

I first heard Beth Rutherford give her retractor account at the 1997 annual meeting of the False Memory Syndrome Foundation, the coalition of parents and professionals briefly described in the introduction.[1] She has subsequently told it many times, including on *60 Minutes* and in a video distributed by the FMS Foundation, and published a lengthy version in two installments in the foundation's newsletter (*FMSF Newsletter,* January/February and April 1998). She is not alone. There are now several hundred retractors. Like Beth, many of these people have made their stories public. Retractors recount deeply troubling clinical experiences, during which, they allege, they came under the control of a therapist, were pressured to manufacture "repressed memories" of child sexual abuse, and then encouraged to level false accusations, typically against one or both parents. Only when they were finally able to get away could they see how they had been manipulated and deceived, retract the false accusations, and be reunited with their parents (see Davis 2000). Like Beth, some retractors have received considerable media attention, including newspaper and magazine coverage, television appearances on talk and investigative shows, and features in documentaries. Many have filed and won, or settled out of court, lawsuits against their therapists, with judgments reaching into the millions of dollars (there have also been some successful third-party lawsuits in which parents sued their daughter's or son's therapist).

Retractor accounts, told in terms of false memory syndrome, have played a major role in the countermovement—spearheaded by the FMS Foundation—that emerged in the 1990s to discredit the theory and practices of the "recovered memory movement." Retractor storytelling is a regular feature at the local meetings and national conferences of the foundation and the foundation newsletter regularly prints retractor narratives. Such stories are also a staple in the many books written by professionals associated with the foundation (e.g., Goldstein and Farmer 1993; Loftus and Ketcham 1994; Pendergrast 1996).[2] These accounts powerfully ratify and reproduce the victim and offender categories defined by the countermovement and reinforce its demands to hold therapists accountable and increase professional oversight. Indeed, by the mid-1990s, the success of retractor lawsuits in the courts had already made them the countermovement's most potent weapon. In a period of just a few years, licenses to practice were revoked, hospital dissociative disorder units were closed, punitive damages were assessed, and the potential for retractor lawsuits began to change the way therapists (even those not directly involved) conducted their practice (Alpert 1995).

As noted earlier, the efforts of the child protection and antirape movements to define sexual abuse sparked little serious public resistance. The 1980s efforts to create a trauma psychology of sexual abuse also generated little public controversy. But by the time the first retractors began to tell their stories of false memory syndrome in 1992 and 1993, organized opposition had mobilized. In this chapter, I begin by assaying this opposition and its central arguments, using data drawn from the literature distributed by the FMS Foundation (including its newsletter, regularly published since 1992), books and articles written by the professionals on its advisory board, media reports of their opinions and activities, the accounts of retractors, and the writings of a wider circle of critics. I make no effort to evaluate specific arguments or the counterclaims made by therapists and other researchers in defense of their positions. There are important issues at stake in these memory wars, especially with respect to the very nature of memory, but these issues have been exhaustively discussed elsewhere and are not reviewed again here. Rather, my aim is to consider how the moral logic that infused the definition of the sexual abuse victim and the psychology of victim trauma has had unintended and unfortunate consequences. Some of these consequences bear on the specific issue of "false memories." Others, discussed in the next chapter, touch on the medicalization of sexual abuse and on survivor therapy and the trauma model used there.

CRITICS AND COUNTERMOVEMENTS

The prehistory of the memory wars begins in the 1980s, a decade when activism on sexual abuse issues expanded dramatically. The compulsory reporting by professionals mandated by the Child Abuse Prevention and Treatment Act of 1974 and its legal successors spurred continuously rising numbers of child abuse reports (and the perception that abuse was on the rise) and greatly increased investigative activity by child protective services, newly empowered with tough laws and augmented authority. Beginning in 1983, a series of high-profile criminal cases was initiated against day care providers and preschools in many localities for the alleged sexual exploitation of children. The most prominent of these, the sensational McMartin preschool case in Manhattan Beach, California, involved allegations that several teachers had abused hundreds of toddlers in a ritualistic context. Though less intensely, media attention also focused on allegations of sexual and ritual abuse in foster homes, schools, and churches. Activists in the missing child movement of the 1980s alleged that as many as 1.8 million children went missing each year (mostly runaways), and that 50,000 of them were abducted by strangers. The movement partly framed the menace in terms of sexual abuse: runaways were fleeing incest; children were being abducted for exploitation in child pornography and prostitution (Best 1990). As noted in chapter 4, it was in the early 1980s that psychologists linked multiple personality disorder (MPD) to a childhood history of sexual, physical, and/or emotional abuse. Within a short span of time, this hitherto obscure disorder was diagnosed in tens of thousands of patients, with many of the cases involving sexual abuse memories recovered while in treatment. MPD patients also accounted for an important percentage of the burgeoning number of claims to have remembered experiences of abuse in the context of rituals, typically performed by satanic cults (Nathan and Snedeker 1995). These "ritual abuse" cases were in turn part of a still larger set of claims of therapeutically exhumed memories of trauma, including the sudden remembering of past witnessing of crimes and brutality (Terr 1994), past life experiences (Woolger 1987), and encounters with aliens from outer space (Mack 1994).

This expanded activism ran into serious credibility problems and sparked sharp reactions. In 1985, the *Denver Post* won a Pulitzer Prize for showing that the estimates of missing children were vastly exaggerated and that a serious "numbers gap" existed between the claim of 50,000 stranger abductions and the 70 or so child kidnappings investigated each year by the FBI (Best 2001: 128). The McMartin case and most other day care and preschool prosecutions resulted in either acquittals or convictions on counts that involved neither ritualistic nor satanic elements, and even some of those convictions were later overturned (Jenkins 1998). Substantial police and court efforts failed to produce anything like credible evidence for the alleged activities of "pedophile rings" and intergenerational satanic cults as described by the preschoolers or in the wider MPD and testimonial literature (Lanning 1992). Criticism was also directed at the techniques used by therapists and social workers to elicit testimony from children, as well as mass abuse charges more generally. Detractors argued that repeated and leading questioning, subtle rewards and punishments, the use of "anatomically correct" dolls, and other techniques used with children were creating false memories and coaxing children into making false accusations (Nathan and Snedeker 1995).

Opposition to abuse claims came from a number of sources, including journalists, social scientists, and lawyers. Those who themselves had been accused of abusing or neglecting a child, however, spearheaded the most organized and sustained reaction. In 1984, following one of the first day care center trials in Jordan, Minnesota, a small group of accused parents and providers created Victims of Child Abuse Laws, or VOCAL. Growing rapidly, by the early 1990s, the organization had more than 150 local chapters, claimed a membership of some ten thousand (Fine 1995), and continued to expand steadily after that (Costin, Karger, and Stoesz 1996). VOCAL identified its members as victims of overzealous social workers, therapists, and prosecutors intent on finding abuse no matter how slight the suspicion or dubious the accusation (child custody cases were especially contentious sites). Raising the specter of a "witch hunt," and framing claims of a social problem as a "false accusation syndrome" (Armstrong 1994), VOCAL criticized these people for unethical investigative techniques, presuming the accused to be guilty, denial of due process, and the misapplication of vague child abuse laws.

By such practices, VOCAL claimed, the state was harming children, unjustly revoking parental rights, and ruining the reputations of innocent people (Hechler 1988).

By the early 1990s, VOCAL and other claims-makers were already leveling charges of a "hysterical epidemic" of false child abuse accusations. They were attacking therapist methods and impugning the motives of the "child-abuse industry." More broadly, the debunking of ritual abuse charges at day care centers was beginning to feed a growing skepticism regarding adults' recovered memories of such abuse as well. With the emergence of another parent-led group, the False Memory Syndrome Foundation, which sparked a larger debate within the mental health professions, skepticism about recovered memories and attacks on certain survivor therapy practices grew and deepened.

The False Memory Syndrome Foundation

In early November of 1991, four families met in New York to discuss a common problem. An adult daughter from each family had suddenly accused one of the parents of sexually abusing her as a child. In each case the accuser had had no knowledge of the incest until memories of it were unearthed in psychotherapy sessions. The parents responded to the accusations with shock, with incredulity, and with a categorical denial: no abuse ever took place. What had happened in therapy? How was it possible that their daughter could believe such a thing? Was there some common thread that tied their children's varied and seemingly unique cases together? Previous contact with a few additional families and several mental health professionals, including those at the Institute for Psychological Therapies in Minnesota, had convinced these parents that their stories were not unique. They initiated efforts to contact other parents who had been similarly accused. They established a toll-free number at the Institute and placed, wherever they could, the following notice: "Has your grown child falsely accused you as a consequence of repressed 'memories?' You are not alone. Please help us document the scope of this problem" (*FMSF Newsletter,* March 15, 1992). Well-publicized, the notice brought an immediate response from around the country. Many affected families called or wrote.

In February of 1992, the parents and professionals organized the False Memory Syndrome Foundation, a not-for-profit educational organization based in Philadelphia.[3] The Foundation published its first newsletter in March 1992, and in its second issue, Pamela Freyd, the parent chosen as director of the Foundation, wrote as follows: "In just a few months most of us have moved from a situation in which we were enduring heartbreaking pain in isolation to being part of a group of more than 260 families who recognize that what we are experiencing is a phenomenon of our times. It still hurts, but it helps explain a little what is happening" (*FMSF Newsletter,* April 1, 1992). By May, according to the foundation, the number of contacts had risen to 400, and would grow steadily after that, reaching 10,000 within two years.[4] According to Freyd, the family "stories we hear are amazingly similar" (for an early anthology of 20 families' stories, see Goldstein 1992). To wit, an adult daughter, with a previously "satisfactory if not excellent" relationship with her parents, suddenly recovers memories of abuse during some sort of therapy, confronts the parents, and cuts off contact. Further, the treating therapist, when approached by the parents, refuses to discuss their daughter's case or listen to their challenge of the accusations (*FMSF Newsletter,* May 21, 1992). While the founders of the foundation did not investigate each other's stories or those they heard, the consistency of the stories led them to conclude that false accusations based on recovered memories constituted a serious social problem. They set about documenting its scope and vigorously making their case with the media. They wrote letters challenging stories about recovered memories of child sexual abuse that they perceived as one-sided and looked for reporters who might listen to their side of the story. Favorable press coverage was not long in coming (e.g., Goleman 1992; Sifford 1991, 1992; B. Taylor 1992), and grew steadily in the following years.

The scope of the problem, described by Freyd as "mind-boggling" (Morris 1992), was, as suggested in the quotation above, comforting for the parents. They were not alone. They could see their experience as part of a larger "phenomenon of our times," which in itself suggested that the accusations were more than a private family trouble. Something bigger was afoot. Every professional consulted, the foundation reported, indicated that it was unlikely that the daughters were lying.[5] Rather, they had "somehow become convinced of the truth of the horrible things that they say" (*FMSF Newsletter,* May 1, 1992). They were not, the professionals averred, acting from their own volition. The problem was not with the daughters but with their therapists. These therapists, the foundation claimed, were obsessed with the etiological power of sexual abuse. It was they who had led the daughters to adopt the identity of an incest survivor, to attribute the cause of contemporary personal problems to childhood incest, to vent indignation at the parents, and to change family relationships. The daughters claimed to be "healing" or "in recovery," but to the parents drawn together in the FMS Foundation, they were ensnared in a bizarre therapeutic relationship that was responsible for both harming them and "tearing apart" their innocent family.

According to the foundation, the social problem engulfing both accused and accusers was an induced condition they named *false memory syndrome.* As formulated, the syndrome encapsulated the parents' central claim that their daughter's recovered memories were both an artifact of therapy and sincerely believed to be true. Defined descriptively, it is

> a condition in which a person's identity and interpersonal relationships are cen-
> tered around a memory of traumatic experience which is objectively false but in
> which the person strongly believes. Note that the syndrome is not characterized
> by false memories as such. We all have memories that are inaccurate. Rather, the
> syndrome may be diagnosed when the memory is so deeply ingrained that it ori-
> ents the individual's entire personality and lifestyle, in turn disrupting all sorts of
> other adaptive behaviors. (FMSF brochure, n.d.)

Appearances to the contrary, the syndrome was not, according to John Kihlstrom, the psychologist who wrote the definition, proposed as a psychiatric disorder.[6] It does refer to an identifiable pattern of beliefs and behaviors (a "syndrome") that are theorized to develop in therapy, but the affected client is a victim not a sufferer of the syndrome. More precisely, in the foundation's typifications, the client is the "primary victim." On her, the "deeply ingrained" false memory has "a devastating effect," and the syndrome "typically produces a continuing dependency on the very program" that created it (FMSF brochure, n.d.). In turn, the syndrome also creates secondary victims, "other members of the primary victim's family," whose "psychological well-being" is destroyed through the disgrace and distress of "false accusations of incest and sexual abuse" (FMSF brochure, n.d.). The abuse accusations against the parents, then, are conceptualized as one of the "symptoms" of the condition, and both the daughter and the parents are defined as victims.

In the foundation's formulation, the cause of false memory syndrome is a "disastrous 'therapeutic' program" referred to as "recovered (or repressed) memory therapy." Although the foundation's publications are confusing on this point, recovered memory therapy is not a name for a specific therapy. None of the different therapies for adult survivors of childhood sexual abuse, for example, go by that name. Rather, it is a designation that the foundation, its advisors, and a wider circle of critics use for techniques and practices employed in a variety of different therapies to assist clients in exhuming memories that are believed to have been repressed or dissociated from everyday consciousness. In terms of adult survivor therapies, only when the therapy involves these techniques and practices, and, apparently, a client with no continuous memory of being abused, is it considered an instance of recovered memory therapy. According to these critics, "genuine survivors" seldom if ever lose all memory of their abuse (e.g., Loftus and Ketcham 1994; McHugh 1992), and so their treatment is not properly called recovered memory therapy. Other types of treatment designated recovered memory therapy include any which facilitate client "recall" of such previously unknown occurrences of trauma as "near-natal" abuse, satanic cult involvement, encounters with space aliens, and past-life experiences. The foundation regards all such "rememberings" as false and believes their "recovery" in therapy to involve the same iatrogenic (induced in the therapist-client interaction) program.

According to the foundation and other like-minded critics, those who advocate and practice recovered memory therapy are culpable for the havoc it wreaks. Most responsible, in their view, are the trauma and victimization researchers, designers of treatment programs, and therapist-authors who have articulated and popularized a completely unfounded theory that memories of traumatic events are routinely repressed or dissociated, even for decades, but can, given the right conditions, be recovered more or less intact. The foundation and other critics dispute the claim of these proponents that cognitive and neurophysiological research supports the idea that traumatic memories have special properties or greater accuracy than ordinary memories or can be dissociated and return as symptoms (Shobe and Kihlstrom 1997). They reject on methodological grounds proponents' research studies—such as the widely cited papers by Briere and Conte (1993), Herman and Schatzow (1987) and Williams (1994)— claiming to verify cases in which abuse memory has been lost until adulthood (Ofshe and Watters 1994; Pope 1995; Kihlstrom 1996). The long and vague lists of symptoms based on the trauma model and used by survivor therapists, recovery groups, and self-help books, they argue, are completely unreliable for identifying an abuse history. The memory enhancement and retrieval techniques therapists use—including hypnosis, dream analysis, guided imagery, "body memories," and drug-mediated interviews—heighten the risk of suggestion and increase the likelihood that clients will confuse images that are stimulated by the technique with historical facts (Loftus and Ketcham 1994). The routine procedures therapists use to diagnose multiple personality disorder (now called dissociative identity disorder) can elicit artificial symptoms and induce alternative personalities (Merskey 1992; Piper 1997). Without seeking to relativize the truth of all remembering, the critics argue that memory is an interpretation of the past, not some static "thing" waiting to be excavated. They not only claim that "memories" can be implanted, but have conducted studies to show how this can take place (Loftus and Ketchum 1994).

Moreover, drawing in part on the early retractors' accounts, the foundation and other critics argue that recovered memory therapists—intentionally or unwittingly—engage in other violations of sound therapeutic practice that contribute to false memory production and client deterioration. According to the foundation, given the belief in the prevalence of amnesiac survivors, therapists typically focus "exclusively on a search for memory of childhood trauma" (FMSF FAQ brochure, n.d.), leaving unaddressed the common emotional and psychological problems that brought the client to therapy in the first place. Therapists disregard clients' accounts of their own histories and quickly conclude that incest and abuse are at the root of their problems, relentlessly insisting that memories must be remembered in order to heal. Communicated to the client, the inference of an abuse trauma can instigate a self-referential cycle of interpretations in which images and feelings are taken as "memories" that "confirm" that abuse in fact occurred. Rather than respect and maintain proper boundaries, the foundation contends, therapists foster an inappropriate personal dependency, even creating a "cult-like" clinical environment (e.g., *FMSF Newsletter*, October 1, 1993). In many cases, therapists advocate adjunct group therapy or self-help groups, which inappropriately conceive of themselves as a kind of alternative family for members. These therapists often counsel clients, in the absence of any objective corroboration of abuse memories, to confront the alleged abuser and to break off relations with any family member or friend "who does not agree with this newly adopted history" (FMSF FAQ brochure, n.d.). The client, in this view, is thus progressively cut off from outside viewpoints, and her life becomes increasingly organized around a false incest survivor identity.

The FMS Foundation's constructions of the victim (primary and secondary) and the "offender" (therapist) categories formulate a collective story about these characters and a clear plot that ties them together. The story unfolds to "explain" how and why individuals come to a false identity as an incest survivor and make false accusations based on it. The story specifies the central characters and assigns motives, moral characteristics, and responsibility for outcomes to each.[7] It requests from its implicit audience appropriate moral and emotional responses, including sympathy toward the victims and condemnation of the therapists. And, in reconfiguring what took place in the past and endowing it with meaning and direction, the story also projects a sense of what should happen in the future: recovered memory therapy should be stopped, and its promoters and practitioners sanctioned; false memories should be abandoned, and the accusations retracted; the family estrangement should be ended without recriminations toward the accuser.

The foundation's collective story has received a wide hearing and had a significant influence. At the same national conference in 1997 where Beth Rutherford shared her retractor story, Pamela Freyd titled her opening address "Making a Difference." In her talk, Freyd argued that the "results of our work are everywhere," and, although more work was needed, many of the foundation's initial goals had been reached. Change was creeping into the mental health profession, she said; the discourse on memory was changing, and some feminists were beginning to break ranks. Moreover, many affected individuals had retracted their false memories and some had successfully sued their therapists. Although Freyd was wary about reading too much into the change, the FMS Foundation had also seen a great decline in new contacts by accused parents. Two foundation staff members reported that new legal cases involving adults claiming memory loss for childhood sexual abuse had dropped off in recent years, while retractor lawsuits had sharply increased. Several retractors, including Rutherford, shared stories about their successful lawsuits and family reunifications, further supporting the view that the foundation's goals of healing affected families and undoing the damage of false memory syndrome were being realized.

The pressure from the foundation and the wider countermovement of which it is a part has had an undeniable effect on professional discourse and practice. The notion of false memory syndrome has become commonplace. According to the FMS Foundation, it has been a topic of "lawsuits, documentaries, television news reports, talk shows, soap operas, books, continuing education seminars, professional conferences, general psychology textbooks, and almanacs. ... Hundreds of scholarly articles and many professional journals have been devoted to the topic" (FMSF FAQ brochure, n.d.). Foundation advisory board members, such as the distinguished psychologist Elizabeth Loftus, have also been extremely vocal on the subject of recovered memories, and accused parents as well as retractors have received a great deal of media coverage. These efforts have brought attention to the foundation and carried its construction of the false memory problem out into the wider culture. As noted, the initiation of lawsuits against alleged offenders based on recovered memories began to fall off dramatically after 1994 (the FMS Foundation has filed friend-of-the-court briefs in such cases), as did the legislative movement to adjust statutes of limitations in such cases. Several key associations, including the American Medical Association, the American Psychiatric Association, the Canadian Psychiatric Association, and the Royal College of Psychiatrists, issued reports in the 1990s that criticized the use of memory-enhancement techniques and warned against the acceptance of recovered memories without corroborating evidence. There is now a vast literature available about memory, about false accusations, and about how memory can be manipulated.[8] A concern with the iatrogenic creation and confabulation of abuse memories is now a regularly expressed concern in the therapeutic literature, as well as at seminars and conferences for therapists on treating adult survivors. The collaborative role of the client and her ownership of memories, personal history, and narrative are doubly emphasized. Therapists are encouraged to study the workings of memory; to exercise caution and get proper training in the use of hypnosis, abreaction, and related practices; and to avoid diagnosing abuse on the basis of symptoms alone. The literature also notes that some therapists, in the face of public skepticism, malpractice suits, and regulatory challenge, are practicing a more defensive "lawsuit therapy." Judging from the fall-off of new parental complaints to the FMS Foundation, these adjustments have had an impact.

Though many issues remain unresolved, the foundation and other critics believe that the "hysterical epidemic" of false memory claims and the "recovered memory fad" are now in decline. They are less optimistic about family reunification. Although many accusers have since retracted, and an even larger number have "returned" (reestablished family contact but not retracted), the majority of families involved with the foundation remain divided (*FMSF Newsletter*, January/February 2002). In recent years, the foundation's energies have increasingly been focused on this goal.

Wider Concerns and Response

The FMS Foundation and other critics are quick to point out that they too see childhood sexual abuse as a serious national problem, abhor the behavior of genuine child molesters, and recognize the potentially deleterious psychological effects of abuse. Most (though by no means all) have refrained from direct challenges of survivor therapy in those cases in which the client's abuse was never forgotten. Elizabeth Loftus, for instance, believes the therapeutic advice in *The Courage to Heal* "is likely a great comfort to thousands of genuine survivors" (Loftus 1993b: C2). Nonetheless, the countermovement critique has implications beyond what they define as recovered memory therapy.

The FMS Foundation and other critics have largely framed the memory wars as a battle between empirical science and therapeutic romanticism. Their debunking effort has played itself out along familiar lines, with the axis of tension being defined by different conceptions of what constitutes valid psychological findings. A long-standing polarization within the mental health professions pits psychiatrists and academic psychologists, who define their discipline in terms of rigorous scientific observation and methodology, against therapeutic practitioners who rely heavily on insights gleaned from the treatment of individual cases (Grob 1994; Szasz 1970). The scientifically oriented have long accused therapists of fad treatments and of relying on inspiration and myth. Claims of recovered abuse memories, where the effects of therapy cannot be considered purely personal or socially benign, and where therapists make expert status claims, proved to be a lightening rod for a replay of this internal professional debate.[9]

The countermovement couches its critique of recovered memory therapy in a larger message of caution about the very practice of psychotherapy (e.g., Crews 1995; McHugh 1994; Ofshe and Watters 1994; Pendergrast 1996; Wakefield and Underwager 1994). The use of metaphor and narrative in psychotherapy, they argue, now as in the past, leaves it without a firm foundation in reality. Recovered memory therapy, including its concern with multiple personalities, satanic cults, and past-life experiences, is but the most recent and deleterious illustration of therapy's persistent tendency to get engulfed by mass hysterias and moral panics. To remedy what they see as therapy's reliance on pseudoscience and "inspiration," countermovement professionals argue not only for better training and scientific education, but also for "evidence-based therapies" that draw on methodical study of patients and for more behavioral and cognitive approaches that self-consciously limit the goal of therapy to matters of better functioning in daily life. These arguments implicitly extend to the psychodynamic approach of most survivor therapies, as does the countermovement's larger rejection of the trauma model and of the mental mechanisms of repression and dissociation.

At the same time, the FMS Foundation and other critics have held that more than fundamental transgressions of proper therapeutic practice are at issue. They argue that a social movement is at work here, which they call the "recovered memory movement."[10] According to Pamela Freyd, for instance,

> Repressed memory therapy is not about patients. It is about a sociopolitical movement. For example, Judith Herman, M.D., writes that the advance of her

work would never have been possible "without the context of a political move-ment." She writes that her book, *Trauma and Recovery*, "[O]wes its existence to the women's liberation movement." Laura Brown, Ph.D., another recovered memory proponent and a recent candidate for president of the American Psychological Association, writes that she sees "psychology as a path for social change rather than as a medical intervention." She has argued "that the initial and ultimate 'client' of feminist therapy is the culture, with the first responsibility always to be the project of ending oppression that is at the core of feminism." (*FMSF Newsletter*, April 1998; references deleted)

For the countermovement, the recovered memory movement is a coalition of feminists, survivor therapists, self-help book authors, and trauma researchers who, it argues, are using the trauma model and psychotherapy to reinterpret personal misfortune and anxieties so as to manufacture victim claims for recognition and redress.[11] The movement's notion of recovered memories opens the door to unbridled parent blaming and a seemingly limitless num-ber of victimization claims. It taps therapy's power of personal persuasion, in this view, for ideological—especially feminist and antifamily—purposes. Using their quasi-scientific credentials as healers, therapists draw unsuspect-ing clients into an alliance to directly challenge authority, and particularly the father's authority. According to critics, the recovered memory movement not only manufactures deviants but also refashions psychotherapy in service of political ends. The countermovement emphasis on empiricism and training, from this angle, is also aimed at delegitimating this use of therapy, which critics argue is underwritten by research that is "distorted by the predilection to find data that confirm the assumptions of the movement" (Ofshe and Watters 1994: 11).

While making some adjustments and granting that some inept survivor therapists may use improper persuasion and may elicit distorted accounts (e.g., Alpert, Brown, and Courtois 1998; Berliner and Williams 1994; Calof 1993; Gross 1994), survivor therapists hotly contest the countermovement's claims. They emphasize that clinical issues belong in the hands of clinicians, who, contrary to the charges of the countermovement, do have specialized training and expertise. Survivor therapists argue that the assertions of the countermovement are profoundly overstated and indiscriminate. They strongly affirm the empirical foundations of the trauma model and reject, on empirical grounds, the countermovement's characterization of therapists as routinely implanting memories and post-traumatic reactions (Brown, Scheflin, and Hammond 1998; McFarlane and van der Kolk 1996). There is no scientific evidence, they argue, for the existence of a false memory "syndrome." Further, they argue that the whole emphasis on false memories by therapy clients is extremely one-sided. It is abusers who are most likely to have "false memories" about the occurrence of real abuse (especially in the face of lawsuits). And it is abusers who have "a propensity to attack those who challenge their prerogatives and the secrecy surrounding their behavior" (Courtois 1995: xiii). Many survivor therapists and activists have denounced the False Memory Syndrome Foundation, arguing that it is an agent of a "backlash" against adult survivors and against women, and accusing it of harboring perpetrators of abuse (e.g., Bass and Davis 1994; Blume 1993; Herman 1994, 1997).

Meanwhile, research on trauma, post-traumatic stress reactions, and dissociation continues. Most recently, the focus of research has moved from the mind to the body. We encountered "body memories" in the discussion of survivor therapy. Moving further in this direction, leading theorists, such as Bessel van der Kolk and his associates, have increasingly sought to explain traumatic memory in the language and with the findings of neurobiology (see the discussion in Leys 2000). This new science is being incorporated into the treatment literature. Babette Rothschild's *The Body Remembers* (2000), for example, seeks to consolidate "current knowledge about the psychobiology of the stress response" and to bridge "the gap between talk therapy and body therapy." In the words of the book's dust jacket: "This gives clinicians from all disciplines a foundation for speculating about the origins of their clients' symptoms and incorporating regard for the body into their practice." In the specific areas of dissociation and the dissociative disorders, including dissociative identity disorder (DID, multiple personality), new research has also been drawing on neurobiology and giving new emphasis to "somatoform dissociation" (failure to adequately process somatic experiences). A recent issue of the *Journal of Trauma and Dissociation,* the publication of the International Society for the Study of Dissociation, for example, was given to this topic. Some of the hospital-based dissociative-disorder units have closed, and the use of the DID diagnosis appears to be decreasing (Acocella 1998).[12] Still, diagnosis and treatment continue, and new popular titles and textbooks, such as *The Stranger in the Mirror: Dissociation: The Hidden Epidemic* (Steinberg and Schnall 2001) and *The Myth of Sanity: Divided Consciousness and the Promise of Awareness* (Stout 2001), roll off the presses. When it comes to the rival science, though victory has been declared in some circles, the memory wars have not finally settled the issues.

As the number of new parental complaints has plunged, much of the energy driving the memory wars has subsided. But deep divisions remain, and the debates over memory, over trauma and its consequences, and over therapeutic practice will no doubt continue. Many significant interests are at stake. However, precisely because of those interests, the conflicts have consistently been waged over narrow questions of the historical past and scientific claims about memory. These issues are unquestionably important, and I do not mean to minimize them. The academic and clinical literatures, the published accounts by persons affected, as well as the small number of interviews I conducted and conversations I had with survivor therapists, therapy clients, retractors, and accused parents, all testify to the profound human consequences involved and the struggle to make sense of them. It is not hard to see why the questions of what actually happened in the past and who is responsible and who is not are so urgent. At the same time, the very narrowness of the debate also obscures the moral and social context. I have tried in preceding chapters to draw out the fundamental moral claims that movement activists and mental health professionals used to construct a new victim psychology and subjectivity. These foundational claims are marginalized in debates over the science of memory and trauma, legitimate therapy techniques, and professional authority. Further, arguments about hysterical epidemics, fads, witch hunts, and so on suggest an irrational process, and contested outcomes, such as false allegations or ritual abuse memories, are explained with little or no direct reference to underlying person categories, their logic, or the ways they "story" the victim self. A concern with moral meanings and the discursive construction of selves does not resolve the narrow empirical questions that have dominated the memory wars. But it does provide some analytical purchase on the issues and outcomes that have led to controversy.

UNINTENDED CONSEQUENCES

A distinction between intended and unintended consequences seems appropriate here. At least since *The Protestant Ethic and the Spirit of Capitalism,* in which Max Weber (1958) explored the possibility of religious ideas having unintended consequences for economic change, sociologists have explored the ways in which meaning systems can lead to outcomes that their creators did not anticipate. In the case of sexual abuse, as described throughout this book, movement claims-makers and mental health professionals pursued purposes that were moral and progressive. First, they sought to nominate a new social problem, the sexual victimization of children, with attendant and far-reaching changes in institutional practices (legal, social service, medical) and social attitudes. Second, they sought to understand the personal effects of victimization for both children and adults molested as children, to give them a "voice," and to gain some measure of recognition for their psychic suffering. Third, they sought to help the victimized to overcome their experience, to gain confidence as survivors, and get on with their lives. Together, these efforts constituted a collective moral project. They increased public awareness, protections, and avenues for legal redress; they sensitized professionals and caregivers; they opened up spaces for personal sharing; they institutionalized understandings that helped to shift the burden from victims to perpetrators; and so on. These were the intended consequences.

The definitions of victim and victim trauma and the practices of survivor therapy that ensued, however, have also had unintended consequences. One of these is the problem of "deceptive-memories" (Hacking 1995: 259) and false accusations. While concerns with deceptive-memories and false accusations are important, these concerns should not be overemphasized. The number of "genuine survivors" is large, and most survivor therapy involves such clients and is thus not "recovered memory therapy" as understood by the countermovement. The debate over memory in psychology has consumed a vast quantity of ink, but this attention, I would argue, reflects the substantive issues involved, not necessarily the number of people adversely affected. The countermovement makes large estimates of the false memory problem by extrapolating from surveys of therapists who use memory-enhancement techniques (e.g., Pendergrast 1996: 504). While the surveys certainly indicate that many therapists in the mid-1990s were using such techniques to help clients recover suspected abuse memories, we need to remember, as we saw in the analysis of survivor therapy, that "memory work" is recommended for clients without complete amnesia and whose experience of abuse is not in doubt. The countermovement claims about authoritarian or overly directive therapists are based primarily on the stories of retractors, of which there are only a few hundred. In what follows, therefore, I devote only limited attention to the issues of false memory and false accusations.

Memories and Metaphors

Conflicts over recovered memories involve three general positions. For the false memory countermovement (including the public retractors), abuse memories recovered in therapy are, in virtually all cases, artifacts of the therapist's persuasion. They are the type of deceptive-memory that Hacking terms "contrary-memory." The supposed memories are not only false; they are contrary to reality. Those accused not only did not commit the alleged acts of abuse, they were loving parents. For many survivor therapists, recovered memories of abuse are an undistorted record of childhood experience. They insist that therapists have neither an incentive nor the power to implant false memories and that only in rare cases do clients make up or embellish an abuse history. Both sides, for normative reasons, avoid talk of metaphorical possibilities that might be operating in abuse accounts. For the countermovement, allowing that memories of abuse, even if empirically false, might signify other family problems does not rule out "parent-blaming." For survivor therapists, abuse-as-metaphor is the essence of the Freudian error, and results in "victim-blaming." Both view the past, in Hacking's words, as "determinate," that is, as unmediated. In this perspective, "A true memory recalls those events as experienced, while a false one involves things that never happened. The objects to be remembered are definite and determinate, a reality prior to memory" (1995: 246; see also Prager 1998: 92).

A third view, rooted in a more intersubjective or interpretively mediated view of memory, pays serious attention to metaphor, suggestion, and the role of present-day motivations and desires in representations of the past.[13] Feminist critic Elaine Showalter (1997), for instance, describes recovered memories as a form of "hysteria." Hysteria, for Showalter, is not meant as a term of derision, a weakness or irresponsibility (as it is for many memory-war participants). Rather, it describes a "cultural symptom of anxiety and stress" (9), a kind of prepolitical language of the body by which (especially) women express their social circumstances. Showalter asks what needs women are attempting to meet through their recovered memories and how these memories might be seen as expressions of compensation for a lack of challenge or as efforts to deal with "real sorrows, dissatisfactions, and disappointments" (205).

My analysis of survivor therapy suggests the distinct possibility of metaphorical appropriation. Bear in mind, however, that since sexual abuse, trauma, and recovered memories have been so extensively covered in the mass media, including newspaper and magazine stories, films, novels, talk shows, and soap operas, we should not assume that therapists necessarily play the leading role in stimulating memory retrieval. The idea is "out there" in the wider society and can be adopted without any therapist intervention. Further, self-help books, like *The Courage to Heal,* with their long symptom lists and assurances that intuitions and feelings represent confirmation, virtually invite turning sexual abuse into a metaphor. Indeed, as noted below, the senior author herself does just that.

In the analysis, we saw that the trauma model and its formulation of coping responses deeply problematizes survivors' understanding of their own historical experience. Trauma is understood to create a disorder of memory. The mind, unable to register the wound in normal consciousness, resorts to dissociation in a "desperate attempt to maintain internal stability." What survivors know and represent about their past, therefore, may be quite wrong. In the model this is not a problem. The truth of what happened is imprinted in the dissociated memories; it can be glimpsed in phenomena such as flashbacks or dreams and will emerge once client defenses are relaxed. In practice, though, the fact that a trauma occurred and what the specific trauma was may require an inference. Recall, as discussed in chapter 4, that the PTSD formulation leaves open the possibility of moving backward in time, establishing a traumatic event from current symptoms (embodied memory). Different traumas are also understood to lead to similar and protean stress reactions—"predictable psychological harm," in Judith Herman's phrase. Given a suspicion based on symptoms, which trauma is the root cause? Among the possible candidates, sexual abuse stands out as a category for self-understanding. Sexual abuse is a widespread, socially recognized, and "normalized" form of suffering, with a therapy and a network of social support. In the next chapter, I discuss the personal functions of an adult survivor account. Suffice it to say here that the account has great explanatory potential: It economically orders a wide range of confusing and troublesome experience, settles the question of self-blame, and is set within a discourse of hope for the future.

Further, psychotherapies are not only a window on individual distress, but also a window on a culture's sources of distress (cf. Kleinman 1988). Survivor therapy, with its themes of self-fragmentation and multiple identities, forbidden sexuality, female violation, the vulnerability of children, guilt and innocence, the oppressiveness of the past, the authority of the "father" (real and symbolic) and so on, resonates with deep anxieties and stresses in contemporary culture. Ellen Bass, for example, coauthor of *The Courage to Heal*, argues in her introduction to *I Never Told Anyone*, an anthology of survivor accounts, that sexual abuse is a symbol of the contaminated relationship between the sexes. She writes, "I was not sexually abused. Yet I was sexually abused. We were all sexually abused. The images and attitudes, the reality we breathe in like air, it reaches us all." She continues, "We are all wounded. We all need healing" (1983: 53). The sheer reverberation with so many features of social experience gives the trauma model and the mediating narrative an almost unique explanatory power. In light of its social legitimation and personal functions, it is not hard to see how sexual abuse might serve, however unwittingly, as a kind of container for other experiences, grievances, or anxieties that do not have such legitimacy or account-making power.

The literature suggests various possibilities. Like Showalter, the feminist and psychologist Janice Haaken focuses on the issue of gender. The survivor narrative, as we saw, provides a means by which relationships with parents, and the obligations that accompany them, can be changed. These obligations, including the care of aging parents, fall largely on daughters. Given an historical tendency of parents to put more constraints on female rebellion and strivings for individuation, and the continuing role of women as primary caretakers within the family, Haaken argues that "incest allegations may metaphorically express other female boundary violations within the family, including but not limited to sexual abuse, and provide a socially sanctioned means of breaking free from familial entrapments. Because child sexual abuse mobilizes public horror and outrage, as well as denial, incest allegations may provide a morally decisive bridge out of the world of the father" (1996: 1072). In such a case, the countermovement argument has it exactly backwards.[14] It would not be therapists who were luring clients, but clients engaging therapists as allies in a struggle against the parents. Recall how the therapeutic emphasis on "hearing" the client and not revictimizing her creates an almost ethical obligation to believe the story she tells. The survivor narrative, in turn, justifies any break with the parents that may be desired.

Some of the survivor accounts hint at the use of the term *incest* as a metaphor for possessiveness by a parent. Toni McNaron, for instance, the coeditor of *Voices in the Night,* an early anthology of survivor accounts and poetry, who went through the incest treatment program at Christopher Street, writes:

> For me, Toni, the process of naming myself an incest victim has been very gradual. My issues are with my mother. ... For years, I acknowledged that my mother had been possessive and that her way of loving me had felt suffocating at times. ... Finally, I remembered enough dreams and did enough therapy to begin to understand the sexual aspect of my relationship with my mother. For me, she was my first lesbian lover: if I doubt this, I need only to look at the Valentine's and Mother's Day cards I wrote her. The language is excessive and based on a romantic world view. (McNaron and Morgan 1982: 13)

In a letter to the FMS Foundation, to give another example, a mother reported that her daughter had changed her sexual abuse accusation to a charge of negligence (*FMSF Newsletter*, August/September 1993). Neglect was one of the forms of child abuse included in the Child Abuse Prevention and Treatment Act, and has been of continuing concern to the child protection movement. However, as a public issue, it has, so to speak, been neglected relative to the initial concern with physical abuse and the later concern with sexual abuse. Compared with these other types of abuse, neglect is a more diffuse idea, signifying an absence rather than a discrete trauma. While neglect is certainly regarded as harmful, and in an enduring way in forms like emotional neglect, there is no person-type of the "adult survivor of neglect," to my knowledge. Since it lacks comparable social recognition, a grievance like neglect might get transposed from a harmful absence to a harmful presence, like sexual abuse.

"Psychological abuse" may be another such issue. Jennifer Freyd, a psychology professor and the daughter of Pamela Freyd, who alleged incest by her father after recovering memories, suggests this possibility:

> In individual cases of reported trauma, we should never forget to ask about the *meaning* of that report to the person experiencing the memory, whether we do or do not have documentation of the trauma. Even if an adult claiming a particular type of abuse is proved to be in error about the historical facts, the emotional reactions may well be a sane reaction to a horrifying and confusing external world. An example of this would be a painful memory of being forced to eat one's own baby when in fact there was no external infant, but instead the psychological destruction of the survivor's own childhood through more mundane but extremely damaging psychological abuse. In essence, she may have consumed parts of her very own soul in order to survive her ordeal through a process of dissociation. Her pain may be well captured by the metaphor of eating her infant, and it would seem overly simplistic and downright inhumane for the world to judge her memories as simply false. (Quoted in Wakefield and Underwager 1994: 287–88; emphasis in original)

Of course, accusing someone of having forced her to eat her infant would be a false accusation. So too would an accusation of sexual abuse when nothing sexual actually took place. However, as Freyd and Showalter and others suggest, the use of metaphor does not necessarily mean that the deceptive memories have no referent in painful experience. Even if the past is wrongly described, the metaphor may symbolize experiences or feelings that have a basis in reality.

These few points certainly do not exhaust the possibilities. Yet other scholars inquire about the ways in which sexual invasion, family trauma, ritual abuse, and multiple personalities might represent metaphors for cultural and political anxieties, and the fragmenting and disempowering experiences of everyday life (e.g., Farrell 1998; Haaken 1994; Mulhern 1991; Nathan and Snedeker 1995; Tavris 1992). As we saw in the discussion of survivor therapy, the trauma model provides powerful explanations for relationship conflicts, emotional constriction, a sense of identity fragmentation, and feelings of low self-worth and a lack of generativity. Many explanations based on the realities of contemporary life might account for these experiences, but few are likely to be as immediately personal and dramatic as childhood abuse. These observations are necessarily speculative; they cannot be proven in any unequivocal way. But they do take seriously the symbolic power that the category of survivor has come to possess, the pathogenic power attributed to trauma, the explanatory power of a sexual abuse account, and the cultural success of these ideas.

Trauma and Client Rememberings

The trauma model itself can also have consequences that bear on the question of client "rememberings." The model defines the therapeutic task as one of facilitating rather then interpreting. In the model, there is "nothing deep or hidden" about trauma memories. Once a sense of safety is achieved and the defenses are relaxed, the "relatively intact" memories can be recovered. No interpretation, no "obscure theory" seems to be required. Memory and emotion work bring only greater clarity about what happened and how the client reacted to it. In this conception, memory is isolated, to use Jeffrey Prager's words, "from the social world in which remembering is embedded" (1998: 15). The past, virtually thing-like, is simply there to be known. The seeming transparency this view of memory gives to the past permits advocates of the model to downplay if not ignore questions of social influence and of the social context in which memories and emotions are retrieved, described, and narrated. At least until the heat of the countermovement began to be felt, there were few cautions in the treatment literature, for instance, about activities that help "trigger" memories or comprehension of victimization, such as exposure to media stories about sexual abuse and reading survivor accounts and self-help books. Pressures to conform, the dynamics of suggestion, and even a voyeurism that might obtain in self-help groups were seldom addressed. Neither was there much discussion of the implicit personal expectations, loyalty issues, and other influence dynamics that arise with the use of a relational model in therapy. By the logic of the trauma model, dismantling defenses, memory retrieval, and the arousal of strong emotions facilitate a return of the dissociated and its transformation into narrative, and nothing else.

In the trauma model, the traumatic impact of an experience is typically correlated with the coping responses marshaled to deal with it. The more traumatic the abuse, the more likely that powerful coping mechanisms will be required to protect the victim's self. Thus, "lost" memories may signify greater trauma than clearly remembered experiences, and whatever memories are recovered will virtually by definition be profoundly traumatic (a point relevant to the inflation of trauma claims as with satanic and ritual abuse recovered memories). By the same logic, more substantial adult problems may signify more extensive coping. If a survivor experiences considerable psychological and somatic problems, then she has very likely dissociated or denied her abuse or key aspects of it. The fact that she might vividly remember sexual victimization would not therefore preclude a search for other memories, especially if the remembered experiences do not seem severe enough to explain her symptoms. Because they drew a strong coping response, the other memories become the decisive ones for explanatory and therapeutic purposes. Some of the retractors describe such a trajectory (de Rivera 2000). In the public account of Lynn Price Gondolf, for example, one of the earliest retractors, she indicates that in fact she was sexually molested as a child by her uncle and had never forgotten it. Her therapist, however, believed that her symptoms—a long-standing eating disorder—indicated that more abuse took place. What she eventually retracted was not the original memories of being molested, but a different story based on incest "memories" that were recovered with therapeutic intervention.[15]

Finally, I want to consider one other implication of the trauma model: unintended consequences for the symbolization of the offender. In the early feminist literature, the victimizer is a male who, socialized to dominate by patriarchal culture, uses his power position to abuse children for his own satisfaction. This power arises from male privileges within a social system of hierarchical gender relations and an economic system stratified to give men unequal access to and control over resources. However, the development of the trauma model, and the categorization of adult survivors as "traumatized people," brings a conceptual shift. This is most clearly seen in Judith Herman's *Trauma and Recovery*, where a kind of moral equivalence is established between the various person-categories of trauma perpetrators, including child abusers, slaveholders, Nazis, totalitarian government authorities, cult leaders, and so on. In this categorization, the power of the child abuser, rather than rooted in material differences, becomes, in Janice Haaken's words, "a primary drive to dominate or a spiritual impulse toward evil" (1996: 1080).

As the shift in conceptualizations of power suggests, framing the victim person-category in terms of innocence does not of itself require that the offender category be framed in terms of evil. While the offender is characterized as fully responsible for causing harm, the real "evil," so to speak, may be located, as in the early feminist model, in social patterns rather than in the person of the offender. The child protection movement's definition of the child abuser, to give another example, was of a parent repeating an abusive pattern learned from being abused. And the mainstream view of sexual offenders in the 1990s, in fact, saw them as suffering from a compulsive psychological disorder. These typifications locate a more fundamental problem or pathology behind the actions of offenders. However, characterizing the offender as acting from a will to dominate or as evil, while reinforcing victim innocence, the externalization of self-blame, and the mobilization of anger, also implies sharper symbolic boundaries with the "other." Consistent with a characterization as evil, the offender (real or imagined) has been symbolized in some therapy contexts as an agent of the devil. As briefly noted above, beginning in the 1980s, an increasing number of people, some religious, some not, began reporting that they were sexually abused at the hands of satanic cultists, often including one or more parents, in the context of secret rituals.[16] In addition to the physical and sexual abuse of children, accounts of these rituals describe them as involving the sacrifice of infants, the eating of human flesh, and other horrors (e.g., Rose 1993; Smith and Pazder 1980; Spencer 1989). Most such accounts appear to follow memory recovery in survivor therapy, especially by those diagnosed with multiple personality disorder. Some therapists were even using exorcism as a treatment approach. The abuser has also been symbolized in terms of various "social devils." According to Debbie Nathan and Michael Snedeker, many therapists and clients are "replacing the term *satanic* with *sadistic* and lengthening the list of possible conspirators to include more traditional social devils, such as the KKK, the neo-Nazis, the survivalists, marginal religious cults, and the brainwashing enthusiasts of the CIA" (1995: 281; emphasis in original). Given the lack of any empirical support for these conspiracy theories, it seems very likely in these cases that the symbolization of the sexual abuser as evil has led to personifications of alleged perpetrators through devil and devil-like images.

°☞° °☞° °☞°

Representations of the past are contested ground. This is most clearly seen in the efforts of political, ethnic, and "identity" groups to rewrite history and collective memory, and the opposition these efforts engender. But, as in the case of claims about forgotten traumas, whether in war or family life, battles can also be joined at the level of individuals and individual memory. In the latter type of conflict, rival sciences of memory have historically played a central role. As the discussion in chapter 4 concerning PTSD and the discussion of the memory wars above suggest, this role has serious limitations. Behind the science lie deeper concerns. In the case of PTSD, these concerns include malingering, compensation, the consequences of war and genocide, and a moral debt to the veterans; in the case of sexual abuse, they include a conspiracy of silence, the innocence of victims, the status of women, and the integrity of the family. These concerns are not about science and should not finally be settled by science. Scientific reductionism obscures larger issues

In political struggles over psychological knowledge, it is precisely moral concerns and moral claims that fuel the mobilization of movements and collective actors to work for change. But at precisely the moment these claims are gaining a public hearing, as was so clear in the case of sexual abuse, the ground shifts. Professional groups enter the picture, embracing the moral claims—as I have tried to show—but remolding them within a seemingly value-neutral scientistic or medical framework. So obvious a moral category as sexual abuse is reframed as a medical/scientific category with a corresponding causal theory and imagery. Now we hear of "recognized indices of psychopathology, comparison groups, and statistical procedures," "established diagnostic concepts," a "spectrum of traumatic disorders," and the like. Whatever the scientific status of this psychological knowledge, it becomes real as it shapes professional and lay opinion and is confirmed—through psychotherapy or otherwise—as having a place in people's lives. It mediates the way that distresses and disabilities are interpreted, the way that individuals understand and feel about themselves. The new knowledge has, in short, and despite the obfuscating language, moral and political consequences. Not all of these were necessarily intended; certainly not all are to be celebrated.

CHAPTER NINE

Accounts of Innocence

In 1979, Louise Armstrong published *Kiss Daddy Goodnight: A Speak-Out on Incest.* The book, as noted in chapter 3, is a collection of conversations and letters from incest victims interwoven with Armstrong's own victimization story and her feminist commentary. Being the first book of its kind, it received considerable attention and was widely read and discussed. According to Armstrong (1994), her subsequent engagement with the media made her something of an icon, the "World's First Walking, Talking Incest Victim." Fifteen years later, Armstrong returned to the topic of incest with an "informal biography" on the issue entitled *Rocking the Cradle of Sexual Politics.*[1] There she decries much of what had transpired in the intervening period as the issue of sexual abuse was continuously engulfed in public controversies (the McMartin preschool case, ritual abuse, false memories) and was also progressively medicalized. Feminist speakouts and consciousness-raising, she argues, were political actions. They often involved the sharing of painful experience—about rape, sexual abuse, battering—but they were conceived as antithetical to therapy. "Exploring inner reality," she writes, "was a pathway to identifying external realities, toward advocating for change" (1994: 12). By the early 1990s, however, when Armstrong was writing *Rocking the Cradle,* speaking out had been "transformed into confession, survivors were perceived exclusively in terms of their wounds," and many survivors also saw "themselves that way." In the "name of empowerment," they were now immersed in therapy, following the "therapeutic ideology along diagnostic trails" of dissociation and MPD, of PTSD and trauma disorders, and absorbed in "journeys of healing and recovery" (211).

Armstrong does not question the fact of victim harm or even the need to seek emotional help. She affirms unequivocally that incest can be a devastating experience, though she questions the view that it is "necessarily permanently deforming." "Women," she argues, "who don't see themselves foremost as victims ... are not inclined to embrace the claim that they are 'scarred

forever' " (1994: 30–31). But her principal criticism of the therapeutic ideology is that it individualizes and depoliticizes the social problem, making
sexual abuse an issue of problem management. Once medicalized, sexual
abuse/incest is removed from the "political sphere to that of individual
pathology" (183). The inner pain of survivors takes public center stage, driving all concern with the social causes of abuse, with offenders, and with social
change deep into the shadows. Meanwhile, victims' private struggles, end-
lessly broadcast, convey a message of neediness, of diminished capacity, of
fragility, of identities defined by woundedness. Amidst the "garish display
of pathologies" and the "florid rhetoric of recovery" (258), survivors are once
again being silenced.

Armstrong's criticisms, echoed by other critiques that appeared in the
1990s, express considerable discontent with the psychological turn as it has
played out for adult survivors. In chapter 8 I considered some unintended
consequences of this turn with respect to the issue of false memories. In this
chapter, I explore additional consequences of medicalization, especially with
respect to the trauma model and the mechanistic psychology it embodies.
Moving beyond the case study, I end by returning to the larger question of
why, in our time, we place such causal and explanatory significance on
victimization in people's lives.

MEDICALIZATION

Louise Armstrong and other critics make important points about the psychological turn. Although the key professionals who took up documenting
and theorizing the long-term effects of sexual abuse did not see themselves
as undermining social movement claims with respect to the abuse victim,
medicalization unquestionably introduced a consequential reorientation. As
we saw in the analysis of survivor therapy, the focus is on the individual, and
the past is explored and retroactively redescribed in light of new understandings. A victim account is constructed, but at the same time abuse is
symbolized to serve a self-transformation. Even confrontations of the abuser,
realignments of relationships, and lawsuits, while clearly having social control implications, are conceived as therapeutic gestures, aimed to consolidate
therapeutic gains. A language of social protest, then, is admixed with and
transformed into a language of individual change and reflexive identity
construction.

Armstrong is also correct in arguing that movement claims-makers did
not intend by their emphasis on innocence and injury to pathologize the

victim of sexual abuse: quite the reverse. Yet as mental health professionals entered the picture, they argued that adult survivors, if untreated as children, needed expert help, and a corresponding emphasis on the damage to victims pervades the clinical literature. According to psychologists Lindberg and Distad, for instance, "Incest is a traumatic event that leaves its victims scarred into adulthood" (1985: 334). Many clinicians would want to add qualifiers, but statements like this are not uncommon in the literature. While intended to draw attention to the very real problems that victims can face, they make sexual abuse, independent of individual personality differences and circumstances, a signifier of psychological problems. Adult survivors are, virtually by definition, troubled people; they are expected to display many abuse symptoms, and their healing is expected to be a long and painful process. Survivors' own convictions that they have dealt satisfactorily with past abuse can be interpreted as minimization, a form of denial arising from the abuse. The logic of the model can create a vicious circle.

Moreover, in the conceptualizations of victim harm, sexual abuse becomes almost uniquely pathogenic, capable of causing every sort of adult problem. The clinical literature is filled with case vignettes making interpretive connections between contemporaneous client experience and childhood victimization. In her early paper on the negative effects of incest, for example, Denise Gelinas gives this explanation:

> For instance, several women, ranging in age from 29 to 54, have required first psychiatric hospitalizations for depressions when the *only* recognizable precipitant was a job promotion. During treatment, histories of incest were uncovered. Each of these patients noted that the promotion was well deserved and that she was able to perform well in the new job. The problem lay in their felt inadequacies, and in discrepancies between their self-esteem and the prestige implications of the promotions. They also felt guilty about receiving promotions when other people had not, and feared resentment of their "favored" position. This repeats a common dynamic in incestuous families when the siblings do not know about the sexual abuse but do notice that the father gives the victim more attention. The victim is too isolated from her siblings to disclose the price for the attention, and they resent her because of the perceived favoritism. (1983: 318; emphasis in original)

Judging from just the facts presented in the example, Gelinas appears to convert an analogy into a causal explanation, moving from a comparison of the reaction to the job promotion and favoritism by an incestuous father to the conclusion that the incest experience caused the depression. Whatever else one might say about this case, it illustrates the common clinical approach of always giving etiological priority to childhood incest over more mundane and social-contextual explanations for adult difficulties. If a connection can be forged to abuse, it is.

The trauma model elevates the pathogenic power of sexual abuse even more. To deflect emphasis from the particularities of individual victims and to establish victim innocence, characteristics of the sexual contact itself were defined as inherently traumatic, and a wide array of adult psychological and somatic problems were causally and mechanistically linked to it as coping responses. In this formulation, virtually every problem or issue that might arise can be interpreted as a symptom of abuse, with the corresponding implication that all are externally caused. The adult survivor becomes psychologically defined by her victimization, and her account of her experience becomes a story of how she was determined by formative events.

The individualizing and depoliticizing of the issue of sexual abuse, the dominance of experts and the forms of help they prescribe, and the pathologizing of victims are real consequences of medicalization. Other studies of other instances of medicalization observe the same sorts of problems (e.g., see Conrad 1992; Conrad and Schneider 1992: 248–52; Riessman 1983). This is the "darker side" (Conrad and Schneider 1992: 248) of medicalization that critics like Louise Armstrong and medical sociologists generally tend to emphasize. But that is by no means the whole story. The psychological knowledge produced about sexual abuse victims was driven by the same moral and progressive impulses that motivated the social movements. In light of the older clinical and research orientations, there were compelling reasons for creating new therapeutic rationales and treatment approaches. As I aimed to show, preserving victim innocence, a core movement theme, was central to these efforts. Clinicians were not deaf to a social analysis. They too were interested in reducing the stigma attached to victimization, in countering the self-blame that victims engaged in, in believing and not minimizing survivor accounts, and in encouraging victims to disclose their experience. Who can deny that the treatment programs for adult survivors have not contributed importantly to achieving these valued goals, even in the much-maligned contexts of recovery movement groups? Care must also be taken not to indiscriminately associate every negative outcome with medicalization. Granted, as Armstrong and other critics argue, by the early 1990s an almost carnival atmosphere had come to surround the public discourse on sexual abuse. We had "celebrity incest" (Roseanne, LeToya Jackson, a former

Miss America), ever more lurid talk-show topics and soap opera plots, images of women clutching teddy bears, people with as many as 350 alters, and the rest. But medicalization cannot be blamed for much of this spectacle; other forces—cultural, commercial, and media-driven—were at work.

Medicalization, in fact, would seem to have been both important and necessary. Given that the social movement emphasis from the beginning was that sexual abuse psychologically harmed victims—indeed that a major problem with the existing clinical literature was that it denied and minimized this harm—it is difficult to imagine how medicalization could have been avoided. The very success of the grassroots efforts to get public and especially governmental attention was guaranteed to shift problem ownership away from social movements to mental health professionals. Who but professionals could set up the demonstration projects, collect the data, coordinate funding, and handle all the other requirements of the bureaucratic state? Who but professionals could institutionalize mental health services and treat the psychological harm of abuse? Access to individual care necessitated medicalization. Further, victims of abuse desired and sought professional help. Many victims saw their experience as having continuing negative effects in their lives. Their own sense of personal isolation, "craziness," frustration with existing attitudes, and lack of recognition were real, and they turned to professionals for understanding and assistance. Feminist critics like Armstrong write as though adult survivors in the 1970s possessed some prior and uncontaminated interpretations and dispositions that were later trumped by psychiatric discourse. This view embodies the sort of naive assumption found in the self-help books that understandings of psychological distress can be unmediated by psychological theories, and it denies the active circulation of emerging psychological knowledge that victims were in fact drawing upon to interpret their experience. Certainly mental health practitioners had material and professional interests in adult survivors as clients/patients, but it was felt needs and lay pressure, not just some psychiatric "imperialism," that brought about medicalization.

Assessing the pros and cons of medicalization can easily give the impression that medicalization is a single thing. It is not. Medicalization studies (see Conrad 1992) emphasize that it can vary by degree (some conditions are more fully medicalized than others) and by the relative elasticity of the medical category (some are narrow, others are more expansible), as well as by the comparative involvement of medical professionals. Studies also show that in the process of medicalization, competing medical definitions and categories may be in play. Although one model normally gains ascendancy, the selection is not inevitable. Any given problem could be defined in more than one type of medical framework. As discussed in chapter 4, the adoption of the trauma model to order and explain victim harm was by no means the only possibility. It emerged as the leading theory because of specific historical, cultural, and institutional circumstances that conspired to select a highly mechanistic psychology over possible alternatives and lines of inquiry.

Medicalization per se, then, only gets at part of what is important here. We also need to consider the specific psychological knowledge that informed how adult survivorship has come to be understood. Because it addresses the nature of health and normalcy, such knowledge necessarily includes guiding normative and moral assumptions about the human person and the social world, however enshrouded in a medical/scientific vocabulary (Cushman 1993; London 1964; Mahoney 1995). Throughout these pages, this issue has never been far from the surface. I turn now to the following question: What are the implicit assumptions about human subjectivity in the trauma model, and what are their implications for therapy and the stories that survivors construct there?

TRAUMA: MECHANISTIC PSYCHOLOGY

The trauma model that has come to dominate thinking about the long-term effects of child sexual abuse is conceptualized in terms of mechanism and causation. Abuse is defined as a traumatic event that overwhelms the psyche, causing it to dissociate as necessary in self-protection, walling off the traumatic experience from ordinary consciousness, and generating any number of later disturbances. In the model, trauma imprints itself on the mind. It is the mind that objectively and automatically responds to trauma, not the individual subject who experiences and attaches significance to it. Judith Herman, for instance, argues, "The most powerful determinant of psychological harm is the character of the traumatic event itself. Individual personality characteristics count for little in the face of overwhelming events" (Herman 1992: 57). In the regions of the brain where trauma is etched, the mind is not active and imaginative. Dissociated memories are theorized to be "undistorted or uncontaminated," to quote from Ruth Leys' powerful genealogy of thinking about trauma, "by subjective meaning, personal cognitive schemes, psychosocial factors, or unconscious symbolic elaboration" (2000: 7). The external event of trauma determines the internal response of the trauma victim. Personal characteristics and symbolization/meaning are effectively eliminated.

In this mechanistic psychology, the distinction between memory and history is collapsed. The past is neither uncertain nor contingent, but has one unmediated meaning. In the therapeutic encounter, therefore, the task of decoding "disguised presentations" of symptoms, "unfamiliar languages" of the body, client defenses, emotional reenactments, and so on, is straightforward. The linking of past to present is not produced; it is seen not as a subjective process of meaning-making that involves the therapist and others, but as a reclaiming of historical truth. The significance of the past and the importance of traumatic events for self-understanding are there to be discovered. The therapist merely helps the client transform them into narrative. Narrating the victim account, as we saw in the analysis of survivor therapy, is, to borrow Jeffrey Prager's words, a "form of externalization" (1998: 134) in which the client, as subject, remains "outside the story" (135). Her narrative, indexed to reality, is a recounting of the external formative events that have caused her pain and her unhappiness. Needless to say, authorizing only one form of understanding and representing the past sharply constricts the stories that clients can tell. The qualities of individual character and the variability of possible responses to harmful pasts are unexplained and unacknowledged. Understanding persons causally, seeing the mind as a passive holder of past experience, diminishes the space for agency—will, choice, intention—and for creativity, freedom, and responsibility (see Elliott 1994). It diminishes the generative capacity to break free of the oppressiveness of the past, to find meaning and personal growth in dealing with pain and suffering.

The assault on the complexity of the human person represented by the trauma model has not gone unnoticed. Even survivor therapists themselves seem to recoil from the full implications of this mechanistic view and the fatalistic attitude to which it might give rise. Along with the victim account, as we saw, they also weave a counterpart survivor story about inner resources undetermined by trauma. Critics, such as Jeffrey Prager, a sociologist trained as a psychoanalyst, see the development of trauma psychology as a "powerful tendency within psychiatry to offer an external theory of psychic pain," a tendency "characterized by an effort to replace an elaborated conception of individual psychology with an objectivist, biological, and antivolitional model of the human being" (1998: 15). For Prager, what is being replaced is the "richer subjectivity originally offered by Freud" (174), and Freudian theory, he argues, has come to have a "special iconic status" (150) in a wider cultural movement "to replace a focus on the interpretative, meaning-making, symbolizing self with a focus on history and its determinative impact upon individuals" (132; see also Lasch 1984). In a similar vein, Jonathan Lear argues that Freud has become a "stalking horse" for a deeper debate "over our culture's image of the human soul." Are we, he asks, "to see humans as having depth" (1995: 24), as psychologically complex, as "inherently makers and interpreters of meaning" (22)?

The iconic status of Freud is nowhere clearer than in the memory wars themselves. Participants on both sides have been unsparing in their criticisms of Freud. For activists and clinicians on one side, we have the "Freudian cover-up" charge. Freud, by this account, made a genuine discovery about the etiology of hysteria: it was caused by external trauma, episodes of sexual abuse in childhood. But, this often-repeated critique continues, Freud, for purely personal reasons—unwillingness to accept the fact that sexual molestations might be common within the family and concern to advance his career—promptly abandoned his seduction theory, replaced it with oedipal theory, and so initiated a long legacy of denying abuse and blaming the victim. Freud's error, in effect, was to posit an autonomous psychic reality, to distinguish memory from history, to emphasize symbolic transformations and unconscious motivation.

Paradoxically, the vitriol directed at Freud has been no less intense from the false memory countermovement, and for some of the same reasons. At least a few of these critics also espouse the Freudian-cover-up thesis (for example, Ofshe and Watters 1994: 293; Pendergrast 1996: 423). More centrally, critics view Freud, in the words of Richard Ofshe and Ethan Watters, as the "father of the recovered memory fad" (1994: 294; see also Crews 1995; Pendergrast 1996). They trace this "fad" back to Freud through the concept of repression, invoked by adult survivor therapists in recovered memory cases, and Freud's early methods. Several critics press further, arguing that Freud and his legacy represent an obstacle to more enlightened—that is, scientific—views of the human mind, views that push subjectivity and meaning-making to the periphery. Ofshe and Watters capture a sentiment that runs through some countermovement writing when they argue that with the progressive eclipse of the Freudian paradigm, real scientific progress is being made toward increased "biomedical intervention via drug or gene therapy," and toward the development of a "rehabilitative psychotherapy" that does not require insight but only the "application of applied knowledge" (1994: 298). Revealingly, none of this empiricism is visited on retractors, whose public accounts are highly formulaic and shaped by exposure to false memory syndrome and its interpretive framework (see Davis 1999, 2000).[2]

The paradoxical role of Freud in the memory wars is resolved when we recall the central role of scientific language for both sides. Trauma theorists and antitherapy empiricists are both competing "over our culture's image of the human soul" in positivist discourses of science that obscure the fundamental evaluations embedded within their descriptive vocabularies. For all their other differences, both are working from evaluations of the human person that are pushing in the same direction: for a thinner, less complex view of mental life, for a greater externalization of psychic pain, and even, in important respects, for a reduction of mind to the functions of the brain. Against these, Freud is a symbol. We can be troubled by the objectivist direction of psychiatry and the impoverished view of persons it has been embracing, however, without any particular commitment to Freud or psychoanalysis. Psychoanalytic explanations too, in their own way, tend toward the causal-mechanistic (e.g., see Elliott 1994), and an image of the person as inherently a maker and interpreter of meaning certainly does not rest on them.

Psychiatric conceptualizations of disorder inform as well as enact and reproduce wider social understandings. As Prager notes, contemporary trends in psychiatry interact with a broader cultural movement to replace an emphasis on meaning-making with a view of the self as externally determined. Two decades ago, Christopher Lasch was already arguing in *The Minimal Self* that "[t]he dominant conception of personality sees the self as a helpless victim of external circumstances" (1984: 59). As he wrote, the category of trauma was emerging as a major trope for this view. "We have become a society of trauma survivors," Prager writes, "as we each describe, think, and feel the past traumatically and understand the present in relation to it" (1998: 139). Well beyond a clinical syndrome and outside of any conversation with objectivist psychology, trauma has become an "explanatory tool," an "enabling fiction" for thinking about the interpretation of personal injury and the effects of economic and social dislocations (Farrell 1998). In a time of overwhelming change, Kirby Farrell writes, "people feel, or are prepared to feel, whether they are aware of it or not, as if they have been traumatized" (1998: x). For Lasch, the view of the self as externally determined was encouraged by "our twentieth-century experience of domination," as well as by other features of contemporary life, from consumerism to new technologies. He also adds, importantly, that it has been encouraged "by the many varieties of twentieth-century social thought that reach their climax in behaviorism" (1984: 59). Over the past twenty years, social thought—from postmodernism to posthumanism—has continued down this reductionistic path, toward a view of selfhood as an illusion and away from the view that persons have moral depth and significance.[3]

VICTIM CULTURE

Social observers, of both conservative and liberal persuasions, have argued for some time that claims of victimization have spiraled out of control. Charles Sykes, in his 1992 book *A Nation of Victims,* contends that "society is in the grips of a Revolution of Rising Sensitivities" and that "[p]ortraying oneself as a victim has become an attractive pastime" (1992: 11, xiii). According to Wendy Kaminer, in her broadside on the recovery movement, *I'm Dysfunctional, You're Dysfunctional,* "Like contestants on 'Queen for a Day,' Americans of various persuasions assert competing claims of victimhood, vying for attention and support" (1992: 152). David Rieff, surveying the rhetoric of the recovery movement, asks "victims, all?" and notes that "millions of apparently successful people" now identify themselves as "some sort of psychological cripple" (1991: 49). Robert Hughes, in his *Culture of Complaint,* argues that the "claim to victimhood" has become "all-pervasive." (1993: 14). "It is virtually impossible," writes Alan Dershowitz in *The Abuse Excuse,* "to flip the TV channels during the daytime hours without seeing a bevy of sobbing women and men justifying their failed lives by reference to some past abuse, real or imagined" (1994: 5). Nicholas Lemann, focusing on a "vast new body of work about unhappy childhood in middle-class America," finds "childhood misery" to be a "vogue" (1992: 119). Being a victim has become, according to Eva Moskowitz (2001), "fashionable."

The rights movements of the 1960s and early 1970s are typically identified as a principal source of the trend toward "victim culture." Such "new social movements" as civil rights, feminism, and gay/lesbian rights were in the vanguard of political struggles to self-characterize and gain social recognition. Variously called "identity politics" or "the politics of recognition," these struggles centered on the issue of difference and damaged identities. Activists argued that the identities of marginalized and devalued groups are shaped in part by the definition of "otherness" projected onto them in the construction and ongoing maintenance of the dominant identity. This projection— racism, sexism, and so on—is based on an implicit standard that "reflects the operation of the power of those in charge to dictate the terms by which psychological and social reality will be encountered" (Sampson 1993: 1220). It imposes distinct feelings and experiences of subordination on the marginalized, constricting life chances and, as internalized by individuals, creating a distorted self-image. Injurious and imposed identity definitions, therefore, and the psychological knowledge that supports these subjectivities must be uprooted and replaced with alternative images and frameworks of meaning that give voice and recognition to those who have been condemned to silence (Nelson 2001). Reconstituting identity on a new basis can both change the dominant group's perception of the subgroup and, perhaps most centrally, change the self-perception of subgroup members, giving them their own undistorted voice and a new sense of self-determination, a kind of "psychological liberation" (Herman 1995: 297).

The concern with abusive group relations and the new sensitivity and orientation to victimization that it created has, in turn, fed a wider number of victimization claims that grew alongside and, in some instances, out of the various rights movements. The narratives of adult survivors of sexual abuse are one form of such accounts, but there are many others. The number of collective stories produced about specific types of victimization has, in fact, expanded dramatically over the past thirty years. The ways to "be a victim"—that is, to describe experience in victimization terms—have multiplied. In addition to sexual abuse, categories of victimization like date rape, battering, stalking, and sexual harassment are all of fairly recent collective definition, as are a profusion of new mental disorders and addictions, such as codependency, emotional abuse, and sexual addiction (Loseke 1999: 141). Large numbers of people are now characterized and characterize themselves—in self-help groups, on the confessional talk shows, in autobiographies, and so on—as victims of prejudice and discrimination and abuse and addiction. As with identity politics, the consequences of victimization are held to be in significant part psychological. Negative experiences and interactions external to the self create debilitating psychological reactions and injury. The solution for the victim is to recognize victimization and its conditioning of the self and to appropriate healthy images and positive self-evaluations.

Support for victimization claims has spread among professional groups and across institutional arenas, including law, medicine, psychology, social work, the media, academia, the recovery movement, government agencies, and others (Best 1997). There are many reasons why social movements and key institutions have created new categories of victims. In the matter of sexual abuse, the campaign was clearly directed toward challenging social arrangements, especially with respect to the family, that permitted children to be exploited. As an organizing issue for the feminist movement, it was also part of a larger effort to draw attention to the status of women and to change it. Much the same dynamic is at work in other instances of struggles over psychological knowledge and in the academic focus on victimization. Specific social arrangements are criticized for failing to protect the vulnerable, while social hierarchies are criticized as a politics of domination by which one group categorizes and regulates the identities of marginalized and devalued others. The number of professionals available to help people interpret their experience as victimization has also mushroomed, feeding the expansion of victim types and claims of victim status. Wider cultural changes, including secularization and the shift toward therapeutic approaches to social control, which emphasize "sickness" rather than "sin" or "crime," are also relevant to the promotion of new disorder categories and types of addiction (Conrad and Schneider 1992).

The popular critiques of the "culture of victimization" do not focus on the institutional arrangements that promote victim claims. Rather, they are primarily concerned with the claims themselves and their consequences. Despite differences, these critiques share an essential sameness. They argue that the central theme of victim culture is the evasion of responsibility, that the central dynamic is blaming something outside one's volition—prejudice, past abuse, mental disorder—for personal failures, illnesses, unhappiness, and even crimes. They then chronicle the many ways in which victimization claims are extended and often distorted and trivialized. Not all victim claims are merely evasions or excuses, these observers hasten to emphasize. There is "real" victimization, like that fought by the civil rights movement, and then there are the numerous parasitic claims that feed off the genuine article. A decline of character (Sykes 1992), a sense of powerlessness, and a retreat from the demands of genuine individualism and rational thinking (Kaminer 1992), along with an economic affluence that buffers people "from the real harshness of the world" (Rieff 1991) are among the reasons proffered for this unfortunate proliferation. Its consequences include the "abrogation of societal responsibility" (Dershowitz 1994), the dissolution of a "sense of common citizenship" (Hughes 1993), and the displacement of a "community of interdependent citizens" (Sykes 1992).

These critiques rightly focus on the issue of responsibility. There is no question that victimization accounts involve a denial or diminishment of personal responsibility. As we saw in the case of sexual abuse, innocence is the moral core around which theorizing about its consequences and its treatment is organized. This innocence includes the abuse experiences themselves and extends to all subsequent reactions deemed related to the abuse. Much the same can be said about other forms of victimization. As studies have shown, one of the consequences of medicalization, a process implicated in many of the new forms of victimization, is the dislocation of personal responsibility. According to Peter Conrad and Joseph Schneider in their seminal text on medicalization, "defining behavior as a medical problem removes or profoundly diminishes responsibility from the individual," though taking the "sick role," in turn, creates a responsibility—to get well (1992: 248). Studies of social problems also emphasize that victimization involves the deflection of personal responsibility (Holstein and Miller 1990; Loseke 1999). Victimization accounts, therefore, can serve as an "excuse," a "denial of volition" (Semin and Manstead 1983), or a justification for problematic behavior or experience. Consequently, they can also serve as the basis for appeals for sympathy, special treatment, compensation, insurance reimbursement, or favorable judgments in a court of law. The person-type of the victim is worthy of sympathy, concern, and help.

Critics of victim culture have seen the proliferation of victim claims as a sign of cultural change. The fact that people are so apparently willing to express weakness (a lack of control) and the need for help, they argue, indicates that our culture of individualism, that once esteemed strength and individual responsibility, has undergone a transformation. The sociologist Donileen Loseke argues that the "category of victim is about *weakness* and personal *non-responsibility.*" Therefore, the fact "[t]hat so many people are willing to categorize themselves and others as victims means that our moral climate surrounding the morality of individualism has changed" (1999: 141; emphasis in original). From their various angles, the critics of victim culture reach a similar conclusion. In fundamental ways, they argue, the concept of personal responsibility has been transformed. According to Sykes, our society now refuses "to hold individuals accountable for their own behavior" (1992: 241). We might ask, however, *If individuals are held less accountable for their actions, then why is it that neutralizing blame for matters such as personal failures and unhappiness are so important?* Might it be that, rather than a weakening of personal responsibility, claims of victimization (and the proliferation of psychiatric categories) actually signal cultural conditions that entail an *increased* sense of and unease about moral accountability? The implications of this study strongly suggest this possibility. The proliferation of victim accounts and, more broadly, the political struggles over psychological knowledge, I propose, are driven not by a flight from responsibility but rather by the force of a moral ideal: the ideal of the inwardly generated true self and its moral logic and demands.

ACCOUNTS WORK

In the introduction, I briefly discussed two concepts of accounts. The first, the social interactionist, conceptualizes accounts as explanatory statements made by a social actor to avoid or resist undesired evaluations of an act or its consequences and thus forestall a change in social status. The general categories of accounts are excuses and justifications. This understanding of accounts certainly has some relevance to victim claims and their proliferation. Given the institutional attention, support, and resources made available to victims, some claims to victim status, whether real or invented, are made primarily for the purpose of avoiding culpability, as in a legal setting, or simply to pursue entitlements or reparations. The critics of victim culture give many anecdotal illustrations of such claims.[4] But simple excuses/justifications do not begin to explain why people read self-help books, attend support groups and seminars, see therapists, and in myriad other ways, alone or in concert with others, work hard to understand troubling and stressful personal experiences and give voice to them. People's experience matters to them, and they engage in autobiographical work in order to create and organize meaning for themselves as well as to express it to others. The issue of responsibility is certainly crucial to victimization accounts, but its role is complex, and, as social psychological research on accounts has shown, it is interwoven with definitions of self and projections of the future.

This second, social-psychological concept views accounts as self-narratives or storylike constructions. Accounts emplot description, attributions of responsibility, and affective reactions to problems and stressful life events. The stories that divorced people tell about their marriages and their dissolution are classic examples of this sense of an account. In his 1975 book *Marital Separation,* Robert Weiss used the term *account* for the history of the marital failure that each spouse generates as they come to terms with the events of their marriage and reconstruct their sense of self. Each partner's history, typically centered on a few significant events or themes that dramatize what went wrong, is a story of what each partner did and what happened in consequence. The account, Weiss argued, is of "major psychological importance," because it settles the issue of who was to blame for what in the separation, and because "it imposes on the confused marital events that preceded the separation a plot structure with a beginning, middle, and end and so organizes the events into a conceptually manageable unity. Once understood in this way, the events can be dealt with: They can be seen as outcomes of identifiable causes and, eventually, can be seen as past, over, and external to the individual's present self" (1975: 15). These accounts, Weiss observed, were not some sort of impartial description, but a selection of certain events that "together can constitute an explanation" (16).

Following on Weiss's work, John Harvey, Ann Weber, and other attribution theorists began to examine attributions (the reasons people give for their own behavior and the behavior of others) within the context of the stories that people tell about their lives and close relationships. From this research, they developed a concept of accounts as "packages of attributions" in story form. Accounts, framed in response to problems or stressful life events, involve memories and feelings emplotted in narrative form. They sequence events so as to make retrospective sense of and explain situations and episodes that may have made little sense while they were happening. The principal concern of accounts research, as sociologist Terri Orbuch summarizes, is the "functions and consequences of accounts to a social actor's life" (1997: 458). These functions and consequences, as Weiss observed, include facilitating coping, gaining a greater sense of control, and achieving personal closure. Further, according to Harvey and his colleagues, accounts may function to preserve and protect self-image and identity, to provide catharsis and emotional release, and to promote hope for the future and the will to carry on. In the face of imposing or traumatic experiences, accounts help individuals enhance "meaning, morale, and direction" (Harvey, Weber, and Orbuch 1990: 120; also see Frank 1995).

In helping adult survivors to develop and adopt accounts of their experience, adult survivor therapy aims to promote all of these general functions. In addition, as we saw in the analysis of therapy, the account-making process is designed to serve other purposes. It aims, for instance, to eliminate survivors' guilt and shame and to prove their basic goodness. It aims to alleviate confusion and a sense of "craziness" and to confirm survivors' essential normality. It aims to reduce feelings of isolation and to provide a sense of public recognition.[5]

Settling the issue of responsibility is central to the realization of these functions. Accounts, unlike narratives more generally, always include attributional statements of causality or responsibility. Thus, the personal meaning and order that accounts create is accomplished in part through assessing and ascribing causality and responsibility (Harvey, Orbuch, and Weber 1992; Orbuch 1997). We saw this quite clearly in the case of adult survivors, where establishing responsibility for the early events and the subsequent reactions is fundamental to the account-making process. In this case, as with other forms of victimization accounts, the point is to establish innocence, which, of course, need not be true of other types of accounts, such as those that follow a divorce. The general point, though, is that attributing responsibility in accounts is part of a larger effort to understand the past, to construct a new sense of self, and to situate oneself in relation to the future. Attributions of responsibility are not ends in themselves but means to new self-definitions. So in survivor therapy, the victimization account is the first story of the mediating narrative, but it is not the last. The goal of the subsequent stages is to move beyond it.[6] The victim account shows how the past came to be, but it serves in turn the larger objective of helping the client to take control of her life, her life circumstances, and her future. The larger objective is to reject "victim behavior" in favor of a more individuated and self-responsible life course. It is to live a more authentic and self-determined life.

This moral ideal is by no means unique to the account-making process for adult survivors. It generally animates the way that victim psychological injury and recovery are conceptualized. Seeing its significance helps us to understand the role of innocence and the function of victim accounts.

THE TRUE SELF AND MORAL ACCOUNTABILITY

As the philosopher Charles Taylor has argued, the moral ideal of authenticity is a powerful force in modern culture and a crucial element of modern identity (also see Trilling 1980). Authenticity is being true to oneself. This means, Taylor writes, that "[t]here is a certain way of being human that is *my* way. I am called upon to live my life in this way, and not in imitation of anyone else's" (1991: 28–29; emphasis in original). "Being true to myself," he continues, "means being true to my own originality, and that is something only I can articulate and discover. In articulating it, I am also defining myself. I am realizing a potentiality that is properly my own" (29). In referring to authenticity as an ideal, Taylor is emphasizing that people feel *called* to shape their lives in its terms; that for them living an authentic life represents a higher, more fulfilled life. If I am not true to myself, according to this ideal, "I miss the point of my life, I miss what being human is for *me*" (29; emphasis in original). Taylor's writings seek to define and defend authenticity as a valid ideal against both critics who view self-fulfillment as merely a form of self-indulgence and supporters who, because of their commitment to a "soft" relativism, cannot vigorously defend any moral ideal (see Taylor 1989, 1991, 1992). His effort at "retrieval" of the ideal is crucially important. However, as Taylor notes, authenticity is often debased in contemporary discourse and practice. It is typically joined to a subjectivism of values, an affirmation of choice itself as conferring worth, and a distancing from the demands of society and our obligations to others. Much that passes for authenticity in contemporary culture is in fact antithetical to the ideal rightly understood.

A further problem with the dominant modes of authenticity, and one particularly relevant for present purposes, is the view that an authentic identity is inwardly generated. To be true to oneself is to be directed according to largely internal criteria. The true self is self-determining; it is not shaped by external influences.[7] In this view, individuals must engage in an isolated struggle for self-definition, one in which they are effectively responsible to be their own moral source. Indeed, as we saw in chapter 7, the notion of a "true self," or the "inner child," or "the child within," as used in self-help books and other forms of therapy, often refers to an inviolate, core self that is good, creative, and energetic. This inner self is presented as a moral source, perhaps even the only genuine and trustworthy moral source.

The struggle for self-discovery, to get in touch with and be guided by the true self, however, is not without its problems. Combined with the wider cultural erosion of traditional moral frameworks, it generates inchoate and troublesome feelings of moral accountability. The religion scholar Frederick Bird captures this dynamic with what he has called the "modern dilemma of moral accountability." The core of this dilemma, Bird argues, "is that diffuse feelings of moral accountability have been aggravated, somewhat ironically, by a cultural situation in which multiple, relativistic and comparatively permissive moral expectations have supplanted a fairly unified system of more strict moral standards" (1979: 344). While an increased relativity of moral standards eases some of the sense of accountability, the demand to be one's own moral guide, the normative expectations of the various institutions in which people participate, as well as a continuing sense of accountability to parents and their values, create conflicts between competing moral standards (also see Taylor 1989). Feelings of moral accountability and unease are further increased in a cultural context that makes people feel they are "responsible for the condition of their own health and personal well-being, as well as for how they act in relation to particular norms" (345). Bird continues as follows:

> The personal sense of failing, confusion, or disapproval, therefore, cannot be blamed on institutional norms or role expectations. As a result, persons experience moral unease not only by occasionally violating some traditional and absolutist moral standards which they only partially honor but also by violating their own intentions or personal promises, by trespassing on the feelings of their

friends or associates, by failing to live up to their expected performance in various roles or institutions, and by failing to make into a coherent whole the various, often disordered aspects of their lives. (345)

This moral unease, Bird argues, leads people to adopt different strategies to reduce the sense of personal accountability, including various efforts to augment a "sense of innocence."

As Bird emphasizes, in the contemporary culture of authenticity, people have a unique responsibility for themselves. Their health and well-being are in their hands. They must discover and give expression to their true selves, set their own priorities, be in touch with their feelings, live up to their potential, make their mark. As subjects, in the words of sociologist Nikolas Rose, they "are not merely 'free to choose,' but *obligated to be free,* to understand and enact their lives in terms of choice. . . . Their choices are, in their turn, seen as realization of the attributes of the choosing self—expressions of personality—and reflect back upon the individual who has made them" (1996: 17; emphasis in original). The catch, he continues, is that they "must interpret their past, and dream their future, as outcomes of personal choices made or choices still to make" but "under conditions that systematically limit the capacities of so many to shape their own destiny" (17). And they must do this amongst other people who have no a priori commitment to recognize their self-definitions or identity projects (Taylor 1991. 48).

The promises of this "regime of the self" can generate powerful anxieties. The risks of failure and disappointment are significant, creating the conditions for disillusionment and the diffuse moral unease that Bird describes. A victim account is certainly one way in which these feelings can be managed and reduced, and a kind of coherence introduced to the life narrative. To shrink these burdens of selfhood, people might seek out a victim account, despite its other status implications; interpreting problematical personal experience in causal-mechanistic terms comes as a relief (cf. Goffman 1961). Certainly accounts by adult survivors and other victims (e.g., see Rice 1996, 2002) suggest such an effort.[8]

There is a more fundamental issue here, however, that concerns how the inner, inviolate, true self is conceived. By definition, threats to this self come from the outside. The source of experiences of failure, disappointment, anomie, or disconnectedness *must* be external. They cannot implicate the true self. They must arise from childhood socialization, victimization, social conformity, or nature.[9] Accounts of innocence, then, with their origin story of external determination, serve a very basic and important function within the culture of authenticity. They show, in the face of failure and disappointment, that the inner self is not tainted after all: it is good, and autonomous, and creative. It can, in fact, be the foundation for a new and better and, paradoxically, more morally responsible life. In this sense, accounts of innocence redeem the notion of the true self and reassert a radical moral individualism. In this sense, the notion of the true self *requires* accounts of innocence. Victim culture and the culture of authenticity go hand-in-hand.

The inviolate true self, like the mechanistic concept of the false self, is an illusion. We are selves, as Taylor among many others observes, only in relation to certain interlocutors, both those who were essential to our achieving self-definition, and to those who are now crucial to our "continuing grasp of languages of self-understanding" (1989: 36). A person cannot be a "self" outside these "webs of interlocution" or, as sociologist Margaret Somers (1994) calls them, "public narratives," for the language through which we articulate our moral frameworks and self-understandings is always relating us to others. Taylor notes that "[w]e may sharply shift the balance in our definition of identity, dethrone the given historic community as a pole of identity, and relate only to the community defined by adherence to the good (of the saved, or the true believers, or the wise). But this doesn't sever our dependence on webs of interlocution. It only changes the webs, and the nature of our dependence" (1989: 39). A conception of ourselves, therefore, as finding our bearings within, as drawing our "purposes, goals, and life-plans" out of ourselves, is based on ignoring or denying the dialogue, both internal and in direct conversation with others, through which our identity is formed and maintained and the significance of our personal choices made meaningful.

°❦°°❦°°❦°

If accounts of innocence ultimately fail, then are there other, more genuinely humane ways to tell the story of actual victimization? The answer is certainly yes. Just as certainly, however, telling alternative stories will require resisting the two contemporary trends I have been discussing: the trends toward a mechanistic view of mental life and toward a distorted form of authenticity. These trends foster a passive, helpless view of persons on the one hand and a sentimental, subjectivist view on the other. We are determined from the outside in the mechanistic model, while in the sentimental-subjectivist model we are pure, and little that stands independent of our desires and aspirations can have significance for our fulfillment. Neither of these views takes us toward an empathetic understanding of victims—who are encouraged to display pathology—or toward a perspective that helps us to see the real complexity of victimization, both as a social phenomenon and as a personal hardship. For this, we need a richer and subtler picture of our world and ourselves.

This book is based on published sources. I conducted a few interviews with psychotherapists and therapy clients. While these interviews contributed to a sense of what transpires in adult survivor therapy and the sorts of issues confronted there, they are not formally represented here. Rather, I relied on a wide variety of published materials. Near the beginning of each chapter, I list the types of data used in that chapter. I do not repeat that information here, but briefly elaborate on the method of selecting the data and, for chapters 6 and 7, the method of analyzing it.

For the first three chapters I sought an exhaustive review of the relevant material. Before the mid-1970s, the research and clinical literatures on incest and child offenses are large but circumscribed. For chapter 1, I tried to locate every major research and clinical study in English as identified in Medline searches and the bibliographies of relevant books and articles as they were identified. For the media coverage of the sex-crime panics beginning in the late 1930s and late 1940s, I relied on the *Reader's Guide to Periodical Literature*. For chapters 2 and 3, I also attempted an exhaustive review of the relevant literatures and media coverage appearing from the late 1950s to the early 1980s. I identified sources by searching indexes of the professional and popular literature, as well as the bibliographies of previously identified publications. For the section of chapter 3 on adult survivors, I also collected a large number of adult survivors' accounts published in books, magazines, and newsletters up to the mid-1990s. The point was not to find every such account, an impossible task, but a wide and representative sample.

For chapter 4, the exhaustive approach was simply no longer feasible. The research and clinical literatures were simply too large. Since the goal was to trace the developments that shaped the major clinical approaches being formulated in the 1980s and early 1990s, I selected those sources that were most widely cited in the literature for their formative influences. The appellate court cases were identified through a search of the LEXIS legal database.

For the part of chapter 5 that deals with the survivor rationale and self-help books, and for chapters 6 and 7, which deal with the structure of survivor therapy, the principal data are the treatment books for adult survivors, both professional and self-help, from their initial appearance in the 1980s through 1995. I describe these in more detail below. I stop at 1995 because the basic approach to survivor therapy was codified by that date.

For chapter 8, an exhaustive review of the recovered memory/false memory debate was also not feasible. The literature is vast and much of it repeats a number of fundamental criticisms and countercriticisms. Because of the key role played by the False Memory Syndrome Foundation, I drew heavily on works authored by professionals who served either on its scientific and advisory board or were closely associated.

THE TREATMENT BOOKS STUDY

The specific treatment books were chosen from among an extensive professional literature concerned with treating various aspects of childhood trauma and disorders that are believed to be caused by childhood trauma. Of course, much writing has been concerned with the treatment of children and families. Among works dealing with adult survivors, some focus strictly on child sexual abuse, while others deal also with physical abuse or emotional abuse, or some combination of the three (e.g., Gil 1988). Some literature deals with specific diagnostic categories, for example, multiple personality (e.g., Putnam 1989), post-traumatic stress disorder (e.g., Herman 1992), and borderline personality disorder (e.g., Kroll 1993), and includes treatment considerations for all those suffering from the disorder. These sufferers include adult survivors of child sexual abuse as well as others. Some books are concerned primarily with individual psychotherapy and some primarily with group psychotherapy.

Given the focus of the study and the extensive treatment literature, I selected only those professional treatment books that concentrate on individual psychotherapy with adult survivors. I located these books by searching *Global Books in Print Plus* under combinations of the subject headings of sexual abuse, incest, psychotherapy, and trauma; by reviewing the bibliographies of all of the books that met the selection criteria; and by reviewing the bibliographies of other theme-related books as well. My goal was to locate every book that was published until 1995. To compare the treatment process in the self-help books with the professional approaches, I selected a small sample of self-help titles on the basis of the frequency of their citation in the sexual abuse clinical and research literatures.

The professional and self-help books used in the study are listed in the following tables.

PROFESSIONAL TREATMENT BOOKS

Book	Therapeutic orientation	Profession
Males at Risk Bolton et al. 1989	eclectic (behavioral and cognitive-behavioral)	psychotherapist; clinical psychologist; professor of social work
Therapy for Adults Molested as Children Briere 1989	eclectic (abuse-focused)	clinical psychologist
Healing the Incest Wound Courtois 1988	eclectic (feminist, traumatic stress, self-development, loss)	clinical psychologist
Opening the Door Crowder 1993	eclectic[a]	social worker
Treating the Adult Survivor of Childhood Sexual Abuse Davies and Frawley 1994	psychoanalytic, relational	clinical psychologists
Resolving Sexual Abuse Dolan 1991	solution-focused, Ericksonian hypnosis	psychotherapist
Counselling Survivors of Childhood Sexual Abuse Draucker 1992	eclectic	professor of nursing

a. Based on interviews with forty-one therapists who work with male survivors of childhood sexual abuse. All use an eclectic approach.

(*Continued*)

PROFESSIONAL TREATMENT BOOKS

Book	Therapeutic orientation	Profession
Surviving Child Sexual Abuse Hall and Lloyd 1989	psychoanalytic, feminist	clinical psychologist; lecturer in social work
Working with Adult Survivors of Child Sexual Abuse Jones 1991	systemic family, feminist	family therapist
Working with Adult Incest Survivors Kirschner, et al. 1993	family therapy (cognitive-behavioral, psychodynamic, family system)	clinical psychologists
Resolving the Trauma of Incest Meiselman 1990	eclectic (psychoanalytic and post-trauma)	clinical psychologist
Treating Adult Survivors of Childhood Sexual Abuse Nichols 1992	eclectic (?)	psychologist, marriage counselor
Integrating the Shattered Self Roth 1993	eclectic	clinical psychologist (?)
Counselling Adult Survivors of Child Sexual Abuse Sanderson 1990	eclectic (survivor-focused)	clinical psychologist
Shattered Innocence Weiner and Kurpius 1995	eclectic	psychologists

SELF-HELP BOOKS

Book	Therapeutic orientation	Profession
The Courage to Heal Bass and Davis 1988	eclectic	counselor, lecturer; author
Adults Molested as Children Bear and Dimock 1988	eclectic	writer; social worker
Reclaiming Our Lives Poston and Lison 1989	eclectic	English professor; psychotherapist
Victims No Longer Lew 1988	eclectic	psychotherapist

Note: These works do not identify a specific therapeutic orientation. Bass and Davis present their work as atheoretical: "none of what is presented [in the book] is based on psychological theories. The process described, the suggestions, the exercises, the analysis, the conclusions, all come from the experiences of survivors" (1988:14).

METHOD

In order to conceptualize the treatment models, I analyzed the adult survivor treatment books following the grounded theory approach developed by Barney Glaser and Anselm Strauss (1967; see also Strauss 1987). In this qualitative, inductive approach, conceptual specification is achieved by coding conceptual categories and their dimensions from empirical indicators in the data. The dimensions are of four basic types: (1) conditions, (2) interactions, (3) strategies and tactics, and (4) consequences. The coding proceeded in three phases. In the initial step of "open coding," each book was scrutinized in detail for the concepts that seemed to organize the information being presented. The categories of "victim," "survivor," and "thriver" emerged as the three central stages in the change process, following the diagnosis. The elements of the therapeutic relationship, as well as the major elements of each stage (memory and emotion work, disclosure, letting go, and so on) were also identified. In the second step of "axial coding," the emerging central categories were studied one at a time in order to consider their relationship to other categories and subcategories and to fill out their dimensions in greater detail. The key therapeutic tasks of each stage were considered in their relationship to the total process, and the logic of the survivor rationale was elaborated. A first description of the treatment process was written. In a final step of "selective coding," the focus was on the central categories and their subcategories. The place of story construction and deconstruction emerged in this phase, as well as the notion of the treatment sequence as a "mediating narrative." Books were reread in an effort to produce further conceptual clarity and systematization. The final written description was then prepared.

INTRODUCTION

1. In making their claims for a social problem, recovered memory critics regularly refer to an "epidemic" of false accusations and to a large hidden incidence of the condition. One influential critic argued in the mid-1990s that there are more than one million recovered memory cases per year (Pendergrast 1996: 504).

2. In an earlier study, I briefly looked at the origins of a "mind control" or "coercive persuasion" framework—drawn from older studies of concentration and reeducation camp detainees—and how it was retooled to explain why young people joined various of the so-called cult groups, such as the Unification Church, Children of God, or Hare Krishna. I also explored how that framework was being applied to converts to a wider number of restrictive religious groups and adopted by individuals who subsequently left these groups as an account of why they joined and stayed (Davis 1993).

3. There are exceptions to this point, though the exceptions prove the rule (see chapter 3). For example, in 1998, Psychological Bulletin published an article by Bruce Rind, Philip Tromovitch, and Robert Bauserman, called "A Meta-Analytic Examination of Assumed Properties of Child Sexual Abuse Using College Samples." The authors reviewed the data from fifty-nine studies based on college samples and found that "[s]elf-reported reactions to and effects from CSA [child sexual abuse] indicated that negative effects were neither pervasive nor typically intense, and that men reacted much less negatively than women" (1998: 22). The authors also questioned the scientific validity of the term *child sexual abuse* and "related terms such as *victim* and *perpetrator*" (22). Though they conclude by saying that "the findings of the current review do not imply that moral or legal definitions of or views on behaviors currently classified as CSA should be abandoned or even altered" (47), the article generated considerable public protest, including a unanimous condemnation by the U.S. House of Representatives, and a rejection of the article's conclusions by the American Psychological Association itself, the publisher of *Psychological Bulletin.* See the discussion and sources in McNally (2003: 22–26).

4. A sexual abuse survivor identity is not unique in this respect. An account in terms of codependency, for instance, might be desired for the same reasons. "Memory work" and "history work" are common themes in the movement, where they mean consciously searching for memories of childhood experiences that, in light of present understandings, might be recharacterized as abusive and fitted within a codependent self-narrative (see, for instance, Rice 2002). I suspect this practice has not generated any great public

conflict because there has been no emphasis in the codependency movement on confronting and accusing one's parents of abuse.

5. I want to be clear. Victimization claims can take many different forms. Making a police report following an assault, for instance, or taking offense at a racially insensitive remark, invoking in court a disorder as causative of illegal actions, or constructing a personal account after—perhaps long after—the experience(s) of victimization are obviously different things. The purposes of claims differ, as do their social contexts, their audiences, and their consequences. I am concerned here with accounts, like those of adult survivors, given not in the immediate aftermath of victimization but later, when the victim is seeking to make sense of his or her experience (and perhaps only then identifying it as victimization). These accounts are accounts of the self, and they presuppose some sort of theory of recovery or healing or "getting on with life."

6. *Construction,* in its implication of a planned building of a structure from parts, is certainly an imperfect metaphor for what is always a complex, interactive, and never final process. Ian Hacking (1991) has offered the alternative metaphor "making and molding," which better captures this malleability and flux.

7. From the extensive literature, see, for example, Best (1995); Loseke (1999); Miller and Holstein (1989); Spector and Kitsuse (1987).

8. Best (1995) distinguishes between two approaches to the social construction of social problems. The initial approach, formulated by Malcolm Spector and John Kitsuse, he calls "strict constructionism." In this approach, only the social definitions are of interest. Strict constructionists bracket the idea that there is a reality prior to definition. Best calls the alternative approach "contextual constructionism." Here the focus remains on definitions, but more weight and credibility is accorded to the actual problem and its context. The alternative strikes me as only sensible, as I cannot see why recognizing that condition-categories are socially constructed by claims should prevent us from acknowledging the actual behavior that is the object of the claims. Still, the "putative" is important, because while most claims of harmful conditions have a foundation in actual practices, occasionally they do not. For example, as I will note in a later chapter, claims of sexual abuse conducted in the context of Satanic cult activities do not appear to have any factual basis.

9. Neither the harmed nor the agent of harm is necessarily human in social problems claims. The problem might be harm to the environment, animals, the economy, and so on. The agent of harm might be an amorphous and impersonal force, such as capitalism, bureaucracy, or racism. However, even when the harmed or the agent of harm is nonhuman, claims-makers may still personify it with concrete human actors who are victimized or act as victimizers. A similar personification process has been observed in the ways that social movements construct their collective action frames.

10. Two other approaches in social movement research might also be mentioned. The "new social movement" (NSM) approach originated in Europe in the 1980s. It has two principal dimensions. One is a causal argument about the connection of contemporary social movements to the broad structural changes of postindustrial society. The second dimension is an argument about features of contemporary movements (of the 1960s and after) that distinguish them from the working-class (labor) movements

of the industrial period. A key task for NSM scholars has been to identify these features and to develop analytical tools to study them. For overviews, see Pichardo (1997) and Buechler (2000). Another approach to social movements is embodied in the literature on identity politics, which is concerned with the constitution of collective identities and the political implications that result from group struggles to self-characterize and claim social franchise. The analytical focus in identity politics has centered on the issue of difference and the interrelated problems of social recognition and self-recognition. Writers frame identity in terms of group or category membership. These social identities in turn serve as common bases for making moral and political claims on the state and for seeking recognition and legitimacy in the wider culture. For an overview and analysis, see Dunn (1998).

11. See, for example, Benford and Snow (2000); Gamson (1992, 1995); Johnston, Laraña, and Gusfield (1994); Snow et al. (1986); Snow and Benford (1988, 1992).

12. In developing their frames of meaning, scholars argue, social movements "proffer, buttress, and embellish" identities by locating movement-relevant sets of actors in time and space and by "attributing characteristics to them" (Hunt, Benford, and Snow 1994: 185). These "identity fields" are constellations of identity attributions for categories of persons and collectivities. As in social problems theory, fields may be framed for movement protagonists (such as "innocent victims") and movement antagonists (such as "victimizers," personified as immoral and devoid of compassion), among others. Again, these identity attributions specify new meanings, a new reality, for the social category.

13. See, for example, Brown (1995); Freidson (1970); Horwitz (2002). Social constructionism in medicine also deals with illness experience. Analysis concentrates on the subjective experience of people facing their own and others' illnesses (e.g., Karp 1996, 2002). As I explain more fully below, this book is about victim subjectivity as a cultural construct and not about the personal experience of individual victims. The construct and the experience are related, of course, as people draw on the psychological knowledge—in therapy, through self-help books and groups, and so on—to make sense of their experience. But the stories individuals tell are not determined by this knowledge, and interpretive tension and divergence are always possible.

14. See, for example, Foucault (1965); Horwitz (1982, 2002); Kirk and Kutchins (1992); Scheff (1966); Zola (1966).

15. See, generally, Conrad (1992); Conrad and Potter (2000); Conrad and Schneider (1992); Riessman (1983).

16. Ian Hacking (1986) has used the phrase "making up people" to name the feedback process by which people may change because of how they are classified and may, in turn, effect change in the meaning and boundaries of the original classification. His books, *Rewriting the Soul* (1995) and *Mad Travelers* (1998), are compelling case studies of this process.

17. I do not for a moment question that victims can suffer, often grievously so. Thinking specifically of sexual abuse, I would want to add my voice, however, to those who strongly reject a consequentialist ethic in this case. Research purporting to find that adult-child sexual relations have no adverse psychological consequences for some

adolescents, as conducted in the past (see chapter 1) and still published today (see note 3 above), seems to me to have no bearing whatsoever on whether these acts are morally wrong or should be illegal. Indeed, the tendency to equate wrongness with psychological harm has certainly contributed to the tendency to define victims in terms of psychological problems.

18. In a study of the typification of "battered women," Loseke notes a similar process: "Since each such morally contaminating characteristic [e.g., drinking, drug-taking] is constructed as a reaction to victimization, they support rather than threaten the evaluation of a 'battered woman' as a morally deserving person" (1992: 46).

19. See, for example, Bruner (1987); Kerby (1991); MacIntyre (1984); Taylor (1989).

20. See also, in this regard, Berger (1965); Gergen (1994); Gubrium and Holstein (2001); Hacking (1986); Holstein and Gubrium (2000); Mason-Schrock (1996); Mattingly (1998); Prager (1998); Shotter (1984); Somers (1994); Taylor (1989).

21. Except for some analysis of the role of public survivor accounts in shaping and confirming the emerging movement construction of the new meaning of sexual abuse, I am concerned with institutional and not individual narratives in this book, and therefore do not analyze the stories of individual survivors.

22. On the social movement construction of identities through story-telling, see Benford (1993); Fine (1995); Hunt and Benford (1994); Irvine (1999); Nolan (2001); Polletta (1998, 2002); Rice (1996, 2002). In social problems studies, see Bromley, Shupe, and Ventimiglia (1979); Gusfield (1981); Johnson (1989); Loseke (1992); Rose (1977a).

23. Whereas justifications and excuses follow a potentially offensive act, Hewitt and Stokes (1975) defined "disclaimers" as a class of neutralization techniques that anticipate a challenge or reproach before the act and try to obviate it. Harold Garfinkel (1967), and the ethnomethodological approach he initiated, emphasizes that individuals lead their daily lives so as to be accountable to others for all their behavior, not just that which is potentially problematic. Accounting practices render behavior intelligible; they serve to make meaningful what the social member is doing or has done. They are, in other words, an aid to perception, functioning to constitute otherwise indeterminate action as explainable and recognizable within the familiar frameworks of daily life (Shotter 1984: 3).

24. Given the emphasis in this conceptualization on neutralizing the effects of untoward behavior, research has focused on the use of accounts and related concepts to disavow deviance. Studies have investigated the discursive efforts of child molesters (McCaghy 1968), rapists (Scully and Marolla 1984), illicit drug users (Weinstein 1980), clergy sex offenders (Thompson, Marolla, and Bromley 1998), and others to excuse or justify their behavior and so deflect stigma, manage strained social interaction, and maintain an identity as a "normal" social member.

25. For representative works in this tradition, see, Harvey, Orbuch, and Weber (1992); Harvey et al. (1986); Harvey, Weber, and Orbuch (1990); Weber, Harvey, and Orbuch (1992); Weber, Harvey, and Stanley (1987). For an overview, see Orbuch (1997); Davis (2000).

26. Although not under the concept of accounts, per se, research on the importance of stories for dealing with illness and traumatic experience overlaps considerably and

reaches many similar conclusions about their importance and consequences (e.g., Brody 2003; Frank 1995; Kleinman 1988).

27. In their survey of psychologists, Melissa Polusny and Victoria Follette note that those with more recent clinical training "were more likely to ask adult clients about sexual abuse, to rate adults' memories of CSA [child sexual abuse] as more accurate, and to agree that there is a constellation of presenting symptoms indicative of a history of sexual abuse" (1996: 50). They suggest these findings may be due to greater exposure to information about sexual abuse during the training of recent graduates. They cite another survey of psychologists that found that recent graduates gave higher ratings to their training with regard to addressing abuse issues.

CHAPTER ONE

1. Another support and advocacy group, The Linkup-Survivors of Clergy Abuse, formed in 1991, and its president, Susan Archibald, were also regularly mentioned in press stories.

2. Michigan enacted such a law in 1937, but it was declared unconstitutional. A revised law was enacted in 1939 (Sutherland 1950). On the public concern and media coverage of sex crimes in the late 1930s, see Freedman (1987). She notes, for instance, that "[i]n 1937 the *New York Times* ... created a new index category, 'Sex Crimes,' to encompass the 143 articles it published on the subject that year" (1987: 83). See also Jenkins (1998).

3. Howard Whitman, "The Biggest Taboo," *Collier's*, Feb. 15, 1947, p. 24; David G. Wittels, "What Can We Do about Sex Crimes?" *Saturday Evening Post*, Dec. 11, 1948, p. 30; "The Unknown Sex Fiend," *Time*, Feb. 13, 1950, p. 85; D. Diamond and F. Tenenbaum, "To Protect Your Child from Sex Offenders," *Better Homes & Gardens*, May 1953, p. 160; E. M. Stern, "Facts on Sex Offenses against Children," *Parents*, Oct. 1954, p. 42. Also see Levy (1951); 4–6; Freedman (1987); and Jenkins (1998).

4. "How Safe Is Your Daughter?" *American Magazine*, July 1947, p. 32; "How Safe Is Your Youngster?" *American Magazine*, March 1955, p. 19.

5. Even as late as 1978, and using a definition of incest as broad as any that had appeared in the earlier literature, Karin Meiselman could write of incest, "Although its incidence is much higher than many people would guess, it still qualifies as a relatively rare event, much more rare than most other forms of stigmatized sexual behavior" (1978: 31).

6. However, compare the comment by Kinsey and his colleagues that "some psycho-analysts ... contend that they have never had a patient who has not had incestuous relations" (1948: 558).

7. The 2–4 percent range is calculated from percentages reported in Kinsey et al. (1953: 118). Greater precision is not possible. The higher figure assumes little or no overlap between those who had an experience with a father, grandfather, uncle, or older brother (in fact, there almost certainly was overlap, since the authors report that 15 percent of the girls were sexually approached by more than one adult male). Since only about half (609 cases) of those who reported a preadolescent sexual approach (1,075 cases) also identified who the adult male was (stranger, friend, father, etc.), the higher figure also assumes that those who reported were representative of all cases. If we make

the first assumption about no overlap, but just report the percentage of respondents who actually indicated a sexual approach by father, grandfather, uncle, or older brother, the percentage stands at 2.5.

8. The studies by Hamilton (1929), Landis et al. (1940), and Landis (1956) (see discussion below) found that 20–35 percent of the reported sexual incidents involved a family member or close relative. Like the Kinsey study, however, these do not focus on incest, and it is not possible from the reported data to determine what percentage of cases involved incest.

9. See Howard Whitman, "The Biggest Taboo," *Collier's,* Feb. 15, 1947, p. 24; and Howard Whitman, "The City That Does Something about Sex Crime," *Collier's,* Jan. 21, 1950, p. 20. For a children's bedtime story warning of potential "sex perverts," see H. C. McDonald, *Playtime with Patty and Wilbur* (Culver City, CA: Murray & Gee, 1952). On a cartoon booklet distributed to school children in Long Beach, California, see Jeree Crowther, "Answer to Sex Fiends," *American City,* April 1950, p. 119. On similar booklets distributed in several other states in the 1950s and on the educational films, see Beatrice Schapper, "The Best Defense against Sex Perverts," *Today's Health,* Nov. 1958, p. 28. Also see Thaddeus P. Krush and Nancy L. Dorner, "Ten-Point Protection against Molesters," *National Parent-Teacher,* Oct. 1957, p. 7; and Marjorie Holmes, "How to Protect Your Children from Sex Offenders," *Better Homes and Gardens,* Jan. 1959, p. 25.

10. A more precise percentage of subjects reporting an aggression is not possible since Landis et al. report on incidents, not individuals, and some individuals had more than one type of experience (1940: 278).

11. The exceptions include the marriage study by Hamilton (1929) and a German study of 1932 by Moses (reported in Burton 1968). The percentages presented by Hamilton for inadequate orgasm capacity in adult women and a "pre-marital sex aggression" suggests a significant correlation (1929: 343). The Moses study traced the development several years later of 60 children sexually assaulted by an adult, and concluded that well over half had suffered (mostly in sexual acting out) as a result of their experience. However, 50 of the 60 cases involved complete intercourse, an extremely high percentage for a study of this kind, and only one-third of the children were believed to be "normal" before the assault. Burton, who reported this study, therefore, discounts its contrary findings (1968: 102–3). Similarly, De Francis (1969) reported that two-thirds of the 263 child-victims in his study were emotionally harmed by the experience, with 14 percent found to be severely disturbed. This harm was expressed in various hostile and delinquent behaviors and school problems. However, in this study of cases known to the police in two New York counties, noncontact and other cases unlikely to be prosecuted were excluded, and half of the cases involved rape or attempted rape. Fifty percent of the cases involved direct force, and another 10 percent involved the threat of bodily harm. About two-thirds of the cases were criminally prosecuted. Moreover, De Francis reported that more than half of the children in his study were emotionally disturbed before the sexual offense occurred. The De Francis study, like that of Moses, involved a much higher percentage of serious cases. Indeed, the majority of his cases involved just the features that other studies predicted would lead to a negative outcome for the child victim.

Psychodynamically oriented clinicians disagreed on the question of effects. C. Landis (1940) reports that "[t]here is, at the present time, a good deal of controversy over the significance of sexual aggressions in childhood. [Melanie] Klein and [Susan] Isaacs ... emphasize their importance, while Rasmussen and Bender and Blau believe that such incidents have not very much significance" (1940: 32; see also Weiner 1962: 615).

12. An added and potentially confounding effect, noted by many studies, concerned the possible harm to the child victim caused by the reaction of the child's parents or her need to testify in legal proceedings (e.g., De Francis 1969; Schultz 1973).

13. Kinsey and his colleagues, for instance, write that "in many instances, the experience was repeated because the children had become interested in the sexual activity and had more or less actively sought repetitions of their experience" (1953: 118). De Francis (1969: 61) identified 14 percent of the victims in his study as complying or participating in the offense and another 22 percent as placing themselves in the hazardous situation. See also Burton (1968); Mangus (1953); Mohr (1962: 258); O'Neal et al. (1960); Schultz (1973).

14. Some researchers identified "internal deficiencies" in the victim, most especially mental deficiency, as contributing to impaired judgment about the sexual activity (e.g., French studies reported in Burton 1968; Bender and Blau 1937; Weiss et al. 1955).

15. The sexual offender literature also made this point; see, for example, Gebhard (1965); Karpman (1954); Mohr (1962).

16. Researchers did not argue that the child's personality needs were sufficient to account for the sexual experience, for they observed that other children with similar backgrounds did not become victims of a sexual offense (see Weiss et al. 1955).

17. Based on his own cases, Abraham (1927) argued that a child's participation in a sexual seduction causes intense guilt feelings. Because of this guilt, the child fails to report the seduction and may seek to deal with the guilt by mentally eliminating the "displeasurable recollections." "They are split off," he wrote, "from the rest of the contents of consciousness and thenceforward lead a separate existence as a 'complex' " (1927: 55).

18. For findings from lesser-known studies, see Meiselman's (1978: chap. 6) extensive literature review and the results of her study of fifty-eight former child participants. See also Karpman: "A psychic trauma represented by early incestuous experiences lies at the root of a variety of psychosexual disturbances" (1954: 345).

19. In a similar vein, Masters writes, in a note on a case report from Louis London's 1957 book, *Abnormal Sexual Behavior,* that "[p]robably a father's sexual approach to a nine-year-old girl would almost always be damaging. It is, in fact, a 'betrayal'—an exploitation of the parent-child relationship and a violation of the trust the child reposes in the father" (1963: 216–17).

20. Against this general picture, an occasional study reported "no-effect" findings. The 1934 Rasmussen study (reported in Bender and Blau 1937; Burton 1968), which included fourteen cases of father-daughter or father-stepdaughter incest, falls into this category and was occasionally cited in the early incest literature as such. Later, Yorukoglu and Kemph (1966) reported on two incest cases which involved prolonged

sexual contact. Within two years of the incest, they found neither child participant to be "manifestly seriously disturbed emotionally" (1966: 112). They were sharply aware, however, that their findings were inconsistent with the incest literature and added numerous qualifications, including suggestions that the child participants might experience developmental problems later in life, such as in marriage. Rascovsky and Rascovsky (1950) presented a single case of incest that began with a touch incident at age ten. Later, when the daughter was in her early twenties, she developed an erotic relationship with her father that eventually led to oral sex with him and finally intercourse. Comparing her case with similar cases in which an erotic relationship had formed between father and daughter but had not been consummated, they theorized that the incest may have diminished "the subject's chance of psychosis and allow[ed] better adjustment to the external world" (1950: 45). I mention this study because it was later cited in the sexual abuse literature as suggesting that some earlier researchers believed incest might be beneficial. I found no general evidence for such a belief. Even the conclusions of the Rascovsky and Rascovsky paper need to be read in the larger context of the disordered family relations that they describe.

21. According to Young, early in his career, Freud distinguished between two kinds of neuroses, both of which he then theorized to originate in traumatic experiences. Psychoneurosis was his term for a neurotic formation that originated in early childhood trauma—which he initially believed was always sexual in nature—while "actual neurosis" developed due to traumatic events later in life (1995: 36–38).

22. The incest literature before the mid-1970s is concerned with all possible incest arrangements (father-daughter, mother-son, brother-sister, etc.), although the father-daughter case gets by far the most attention. My concern here, however, is limited to the discussion in the literature involving an adult or significantly older sibling and a minor child. Since the most commonly discussed case is father-daughter or stepfather-stepdaughter, I essentially limit the discussion to that case, though much of what comes under the father category also applies to other family males, and much of what comes under the daughter category could also apply to other family children (son, grandchild).

23. Some researchers reported changes in the child-daughter's attitude that occurred after the relationship had been initiated. Maisch (1972), influenced by family systems thought, believed that the incest brought about a progressive sexualization of some daughters. He reported that the great majority of daughters were passive at the beginning, but classified them after the incest had begun into two categories: "passive, tolerating" (57%) and "provocative and encouraging" (23%).

24. Breaks in thought, of course, are never clean. Some of the influential studies of the mid- to late-1970s might best be described as transitional with respect to their approach to the older literature (e.g., Justice and Justice 1979; Meiselman 1978; Peters 1976).

CHAPTER TWO

1. This figure presumably comes from Kinsey (1953). Brady (1979: 175) cites the same percentage, but likewise without citing its source.

2. By one count, more than thirty books on child sexual abuse appeared between 1978 and 1982 (see list in Summit 1983).

3. In the 1980s, concerns with sexual abuse and adult survivors spread to many other developed nations. These categories, however, were formulated in the United States and then gradually exported elsewhere. Miller, for instance, in the American edition of her book on sexual abuse, states that when the book first appeared in German in 1981, "I was virtually alone in my thinking, for the sexual abuse of children was still a forbidden subject in Europe" (1984: 309).

4. The retypifications of the 1970s are perhaps best described as a remoralization of the offender category. Prior to the rise of the psychiatric/legal framework, incest in England, for instance, was a matter of church law (Manchester 1979); this was also true in the United States until statutes were enacted by the various states (Weinberg 1955: chap. 2). Also see Gordon (1988) on the view of sexual molesters held by the child savers of the Victorian period.

5. Information on the Santa Clara program comes primarily from Giarretto (1976a, 1981, 1982); Giarretto, Giarretto, and Sgroi (1978); and Kroth (1979).

6. The original recommendation to the Santa Clara Juvenile Probation Department to use family therapy in the management of incestuous families was made by Robert Spitzer, a consulting psychiatrist to the department, cofounder of the program, and a close colleague of Virginia Satir. On Satir's philosophy and method, see Satir (1964).

7. The Assembly Bill is reprinted in NOW Child Sexual Abuse Task Force 1976 (hereafter cited as NOW 1976).

8. For example, Judith Anderson, "The Trauma of Incest: Everyone in the Family Suffers," *San Francisco Chronicle,* April 15, 1974, p. 15, and "The Trauma of Incest: When the Whole Family Breaks Down," *San Francisco Chronicle,* April 16, 1974, p. 18; Rasa Gustaitis, "Incest: Help for the Victim … and the Offender," *Washington Post,* June 16, 1974, p. K4; Michael McBride, "Incest: It's Time to Turn Over the Rock," *Sacramento Union,* Feb. 6, 1977, p. D1; Judith Ramsey, "My Husband Broke the Ultimate Taboo," *Family Circle,* March 8, 1977, p. 42; Ellen Weber, "Incest: Sexual Abuse Begins at Home," *Ms.,* April 1977, p. 64; Ann Landers, "More Incest Treatment Centers Needed," *Daily News,* Aug. 26, 1977, p. B-2; Gwen Kinkead, "The Family Secret," *Boston,* Oct. 1977, p. 100; Roul Tunley, "Incest: Facing the Ultimate Taboo," *Reader's Digest,* Jan. 1981, p. 137; NBC *Weekend Show,* May 7, 1977; *Phil Donahue Show,* March 20, 1978; *Tomorrow Show,* Oct. 6, 1978.

9. The CSATP was also recommended in the advocacy literature that began to appear in the mid-1970s. See, for example, *Sexual Abuse of Children: A Guide for Parents* (San Francisco: Queens Bench Foundation, 1977); NOW (1976), which reprinted an article by Giarretto and the program description circulated by Parents United; Butler (1978); Forward and Buck (1978); Geiser (1979); Herman and Hirschman (1977); Kempe (1978); MacFarlane (1978).

10. See the discussion of the broadening of the incest category below. Like the child protection advocates, family-therapy oriented mental health professionals like Giarretto also radically extended the definition of incest. For other examples, see Browning and Boatman 1977 and Henderson 1975.

11. In time, according to Giarretto, the daughter in the program would typically "confide that she was not entirely a helpless victim" and would be "gently encouraged to explore this self-revelation" (1976a: 153). Given the emphasis on abuse, incest believed to be consensual—such as brother-sister where there existed little age difference or adult-adult—was excluded from concern.

12. The child protection movement has been called by various names, including the child advocacy movement, the child welfare movement, the child abuse movement, and the child maltreatment movement.

13. " 'When They're Angry ... ,' " *Newsweek*, April 16, 1962, p. 74; "Battered-Child Syndrome," *Time*, July 20, 1962, p. 60; Charles Flato, "Parents Who Beat Children," *Saturday Evening Post*, Oct. 6, 1962, p. 30. For other early press and television coverage of battered child syndrome, see Paulsen, Parker, and Adelman (1966: 488–90).

14. The child protection movement that emerged in the 1960s was not the first such movement. For discussions of the concern with child cruelty at the end of the Victorian era in the United States and England, see Antler 1981; Costin, Karger, and Stoesz 1996; Hacking 1991; and Pfohl 1977, esp. the citations to the historical literature.

15. On the background of De Francis and the Children's Division of the AHA, see De Francis's statement and accompanying attachments in U.S. Senate Committee (1973: 293–332).

16. Kempe and his colleagues in Denver went on to found the National Center for the Prevention and Treatment of Child Abuse and Neglect in 1972 and figured prominently in both Senate and House hearings leading to the passage of the federal Child Abuse Prevention and Treatment Act of 1974. They also turned out numerous influential books. These medical doctors, too, eventually adopted a much broader and more psychological definition of child abuse, and the services they offered through their Denver Center, the model for other hospital-based programs, mirrored in most respects the emphases of child welfare services.

17. On the contrast between a "medical view" and a "child welfare service view," see the statement of William G. Lunsford of the Child Welfare League in U.S. House Committee (1973: 143–44). For a fuller description of the child welfare model and its history, see Kadushin 1974.

18. In addition to David Gil, important family violence research in the 1970s included studies by Richard Gelles, Murray Straus, and Suzanne Steinmetz. In the late 1970s, scholars in this camp began to write about sexual victimization, the most prominent being David Finkelhor, a student of Straus. Unlike the child protection advocates, family violence researchers like Finkelhor tended to avoid the categorization of sexual abuse together with physical child abuse (see Finkelhor 1979).

19. The AHA version, it should be noted, did take exception to the focus of the Children's Bureau's model statute on physical abuse only and its failure to mention neglect (American Humane Association 1966).

20. A little-noticed article summarizing some of the early findings from the study was also published; see Chaneles (1967).

21. See, for example, Burgess et al. (1978); Sgroi (1975); Peters (1973). The study findings received much wider public attention when they formed the core of a 1977

Ms. magazine article (Weber 1977). See also, for example, Michael McBride, "Incest: It's Time to Turn Over the Rock," *Sacramento Union,* Feb. 6, 1977, p. D1; and Sherry Angel, "Don't Be Afraid to Say No," *Redbook,* July 1978, p. 40.

22. See Hoffman (1978) on the history leading up to these hearings.

23. See De Francis's statement in U.S. Senate Committee (1973: 293, 312).

24. See the statements by Dr. Frederick C. Green and Peter J. Costigen in U.S. House Committee (1973: 122, 160).

25. See, for example, the responses by Brian Fraser and Dr. Annette Heiser in U.S. House Committee (1973: 21, 61).

26. " 'Child abuse and neglect' means the physical or mental injury, sexual abuse, negligent treatment, or maltreatment of any child under the age of eighteen by a person who is responsible for the child's welfare under circumstances which indicate the child's health or welfare is harmed or threatened thereby" (PL 93-247, 1974, sec. 2). What acts constitute sexual abuse, however, were not defined. Nor was sexual abuse defined in the vast majority of state reporting laws that were enacted in order to meet the funding requirements of the act (Fraser 1981). When CAPTA was amended in 1978, however, the term *sexual abuse* was given greater specificity, and the original focus on "a person who is responsible for the child's welfare" was greatly expanded. In the amended act, sexual abuse included "the obscene or pornographic photographing, filming, or depiction of children for commercial purposes, or the rape, molestation, incest, prostitution, or other such forms of sexual exploitation of children under circumstances which indicate that the child's health or welfare is harmed or threatened thereby" (*Congressional Record–House,* April 10, 1978, Proceedings and Debates of the 95th Cong., 2nd sess., vol. 124, pt.7, pp. 9301–9306).

27. Kempe and his long-time colleague Ray Helfer announced in a 1976 book that they were finally dropping the phrase "the battered child" because the "problem is clearly not just one of *physical* battering." They adopted the more inclusive category of "child abuse and neglect"(Helfer and Kempe 1976: xix).

28. Other new programs dealing with child abuse were started in hospitals, clinics, volunteer programs, day care centers, and whole communities (see sources in Johnson 1986: 298).

29. See the NCCAN paper, "Intra-family Sexual Abuse of Children," cited in Justice and Justice (1979: 27). NCCAN also released a report in August 1978, whose title, "Child Sexual Abuse: Incest, Assault, and Sexual Exploitation," indicates the broad territory covered by the sexual abuse category (DHEW Publication No. [OHDS] 79-30166; hereafter cited as 1978 NCCAN Report). The report summarized the new knowledge about sexual abuse, drawing on the findings of De Francis (1969), among others, and highlighting the success of the CSATP with abuse treatment. Many other NCCAN publications and incidence studies were to follow.

30. In addition to prevention training, several national movement organizations came into being in the 1980s, providing legal advocacy, information, counseling referrals, and the like.

31. 1978 NCCAN Report, p. 3.

32. There were limits, however, such as the effort to characterize all forms of corporal punishment as child abuse. See, for example, the interchange between David Gil,

who argued that spanking was child abuse, and Senator Randolph, one of the sponsors of CAPTA, in U.S. Senate Committee (1973: 42–46).

33. As with the older incest and sexual offense literature, however, some physical child abuse researchers did suggest that certain characteristics of the child—for example, a physical or mental handicap, premature birth, certain temperaments—might precipitate parental stress and abusive behavior (see the review in Friedrich and Boriskin 1976).

34. It seems fair to say, judging from the legislative debates and advocacy literature, that it was especially a concern with the enduring effects of abuse, including the possibility of later antisocial behavior on the part of child victims, that animated the urgency of getting prevention and treatment programs into place.

35. A partial exception in the case of sexual abuse is the national campaign against the production and sale of child pornography, spearheaded by Judianne Densen-Gerber of the Odyssey Institute, that quickly led to new federal (Protection of Children against Sexual Exploitation Act, 1977) and state legislation. This campaign broadened the focus of sexual abuse to children involved in pornography, though parents were alleged to be the perpetrators in the cases involving young children. See U.S. House Committee (1977); Judianne Densen-Gerber, "What Pornographers Are Doing to Children: A Shocking Report," *Redbook*, Aug. 1977, p. 86; and Geiser (1979). A second partial exception is the concern with child prostitution. In 1977, the Mann Act, which made it a federal crime to transport females across state lines for the purpose of prostitution, was amended to criminalize the transport of any minor, male or female, across state lines for the purpose of prostitution or any other prohibited sexual contact. This too is a partial exception because parents were alleged to be involved in some cases of child prostitution.

36. U.S. Senate Committee (1973: 55, 53). Also see U.S. House Committee (1973: 39–44). The high percentage claiming abuse as a child suggests that this explanation for one's behavior had been institutionalized within PA as an "excuse" for abusive parents. In this instance, the "excuse" is an "appeal to defeasibility" (Scott and Lyman 1968). The parents admit that their behavior was wrong but deny full responsibility by explaining that their actions were not truly free: their childhood experiences impaired their free will. Self-help groups both supply such standardized accounts and expect them from their members (e.g., Rice 1996).

37. Indeed, the early success reports coming from the first treatment centers, including Kempe's in Denver, helped fuel the wave of legislation in the 1970s. Child abuse was a big problem, the centers reported, yet solvable: In most cases abusers could be treated and children safely returned to their homes.

38. For treatment approaches to physical child abuse, see, for example, Martin (1976); Beezley, Martin, and Alexander (1976); treatment papers in *Child Abuse and Neglect: Issues on Innovation and Implementation,* vol. 2, NCCAN, 1978, pp. 305–70 (DHEW Publication No. [OHDS] 78-30148); and Harold P. Martin, "Treatment for Abused and Neglected Children," NCCAN, 1979 (DHEW Publication No. [OHDS] 79-30199).

CHAPTER THREE

1. On the rape speak-out, see also the report by Sheehy (1971) and discussion in Brownmiller (1999).

2. Many antirape groups, however, critical of the way the criminal justice system handled rape and of the Law Enforcement Assistance Administration's desire to see more dignified treatment of victims for the sake of increasing convictions, refused to apply for these monies (Matthews 1994: 107).

3. For example, in response to the dramatic rise in reported rapes and agitation from women's groups, the New York Police Department created an all-female section in 1972 called the Sex Crimes Analysis Unit (Keefe and O'Reilly 1976). This highly publicized special unit became a model for other police departments that also established special sexual-assault and rape sections to ease victim reporting and processing in rape cases. Hospitals also made changes in response to the new activism, including the establishment of rape treatment centers and new emergency room procedures (e.g., see Gager and Schurr 1976: chap. 4; Hicks and Platt 1976; "'Code R'—for Rape," *Newsweek*, Nov. 13, 1972, p. 75).

4. Like the group in Detroit mentioned above, many of the early antirape groups took the name Women Against Rape—WAR (Gager and Schurr 1976: 260). Retaliatory measures from harassment to physical attacks were sometimes used against accused rapists. See, for example, Rose (1977b: 184–85); Russell (1975: 286–87); "The Rape Wave," *Newsweek*, Jan. 29, 1973, p. 59; and "Women against Rape," *Time*, April 23, 1973, p. 104.

5. The features of rape laws that feminists worked hardest to change—corroboration of rape charges by witnesses, investigation of victims' past sex lives, and proof of penetration—were put in place in the 1950s, advocated by, among others, influential psychiatrists concerned with the treatment of sexual psychopaths (Freedman 1987: 102).

6. However, according to Mary Ann Largen, who was coordinator of the National NOW Rape Task Force from 1973 to 1976, many antirape activists did not have the requisite bureaucratic skills or credentials to secure center funding. Victim service providers, therefore, "were effectively excluded from the programs and priorities of the Center" (1981: 50).

7. By the early 1970s, feminism had developed into two major branches: a liberal branch concerned with gaining access to rights and opportunities held by men, and a radical and socialist branch, concerned not only with rights but with broader issues of women's liberation and calling for a fundamental restructuring of society, including male/female relationships (Echols 1989; Schechter 1982: chap. 2). The more radical branch (itself anything but monolithic), with its emphasis on women gaining control over their bodies and their sexuality, and its challenge to the privacy of the home, set the stage for feminist activism on sexual abuse. However, both wings were active on the sexual abuse issue, and in the following analysis I do not distinguish among feminist activists on this question.

8. The center was also known as the Sex Offender and Rape Victim Center. Information about the center and the rape victim study is taken from Peters (1975, 1976, 1977).

9. Information on the beginning of the counseling program and victim study is taken from Burgess and Holmstrom (1974b). Burgess later served as the chairperson of the National Rape Prevention and Control Advisory Committee of DHEW and NIMH. Some later writers count the work of Burgess and Holmstrom as part of the feminist literature of this period. Their early work, however, is not written from a feminist viewpoint, and so I class them separately.

10. Brownmiller (1975), for instance, both chastises Freud for avoiding the subject of rape (177) and for asserting that women are masochistic by nature, a theme elaborated by others, notably Helen Deutsch (315–22). Brownmiller argues that the notion of female masochism is the root of the myth that rape is something women desire.

11. The notion of rape as a political act was derived from the Communist Party, which defined rape of blacks by whites as an act of subjugation. In feminist hands, the idea was broadened to all rapes as the axis of subjugation became men over women (Brownmiller 1975: 211).

12. A new social problem might be identified because the problem itself is actually new; it simply did not exist or existed in a much less significant way earlier. While a feminist writer occasionally asserted that the incidence of child molestation had risen (e.g., Russell 1986), the more general feminist opinion was that it had been going on at continually high rates for a long time (Herman 1981; Rush 1980). In this view, the great increase in molestation reports stems from people's new willingness to talk about their experience rather than an actual increase in its incidence. A second possibility, then, is that the social problem has been present but has not been the focus of concern because its incidence has been hidden from public view. This second possibility was the argument of the feminist advocates, who fingered psychiatry for keeping the problem of abuse out of public consciousness.

13. Freud's term for his shift from an emphasis on infantile sexual trauma to infantile sexual fantasies was a "correction" (Freud 1962b: 168).

14. The Freudian cover-up thesis was later worked out in even greater detail by Masson (1984); see also Miller (1984: chap. 10).

15. In the 1980s, an explicitly feminist family therapy emerged (Philipson 1993).

16. Weisberg (1984) documents a shift in the 1980s away from rehabilitation and treatment, and back to punitive approaches in sex offender legislation, approaches that have, if anything, intensified in the 1990s, spurred again by sensational sex crime cases, such as the 1994 rape-murder of Megan Kanka, which led to the rapid adoption of so-called Megan's Laws in both local and national versions (see Jenkins 1998).

17. New prevalence studies, based on adult self-reports, which first began to appear in 1979 with Finkelhor's (1979) survey of college students and with great rapidity after that, generally used a broad definition of incest.

18. One of the earliest and most influential of such programs was the Harborview Sexual Assault Center in Seattle, Washington.

19. The public success of the construction of sexual abuse as a social problem is perhaps best evidenced by its inclusion in CAPTA and the subsequent involvement of the federal government in the issue. In a 1982 decision, the U.S. Supreme Court made a particularly strong case that, due to the harm caused by child abuse—the inability to

"develop healthy, affectionate relationships in later life," later "sexual dysfunctions," and a "tendency to become sexual abusers as adults"—"the prevention of sexual exploitation and abuse of children constitutes a government objective of surpassing importance" (*New York v. Ferber,* quoted in Tate 1990: 80). In order to measure middle-class attitudes toward various forms of sexual deviance (forcible rape, bestiality, necrophilia, etc.), French and Wailes undertook a student survey at two large state universities. Their most significant finding was the consistent ranking of child molestation by all sample groups "as constituting the most serious form of sexual deviance in the United States today" (1982: 247). Reporting on a survey by Finkelhor reported in 1981, Summit notes that "almost all American respondents recalled some media discussion of child sexual abuse during the previous year" (1983: 178). A national public opinion poll conducted by the *Los Angeles Times* in July 1985 "found that Americans are very interested in the problem of child sexual abuse," with 69 percent reporting that they had read or talked about it in the previous month. Some 50 percent agreed that "sexual assault within families is very common." Ninety-five percent of respondents said that they believed that a ten-year-old sexually abused by an adult would suffer "very great harm" (79 percent) or "a lot of harm" (18 percent). Seventy-three percent said that sexual abuse would have "great permanent effect" on the child victim (Best 1990: 152–53; Timnick 1985: 1).

20. This mainstream orthodox position did not go unchallenged. A small number of academics, the so-called pro-incest lobby, and pedophile organizations (e.g., the North American Man-Boy Love Association) publicly advocated counter-opinions about the morality of adult-child sexual contacts. A stream of research studies also continued to conclude that some adolescents willingly engage in sexual activities with adults. Moreover, a number of researchers reviewing outcome studies came to the conclusion that while adult-child sexual relations could cause appreciable harm, this was by no means an inevitable outcome if no force was used. On all these points, see the discussion and citations in Li, West, and Woodhouse (1990: chap. 7), as well as the later review by Rind, Tromovitch, and Bauserman (1998). When I refer to the "sexual abuse literature," I am referring only to the mainstream position and excluding this other research.

21. Researchers conducted at least fifteen studies between 1976 and 1986 that sought to determine the prevalence of child sexual abuse by surveying individuals. According to Peters, Wyatt, and Finkelhor (1986), these studies reported prevalence rates that ranged from 6 to 62 percent of women, with half of the studies showing a prevalence rate of 6 to 15 percent. Among males, the estimates ranged from 3 to 31 percent, with a median of 6 percent. While some of the variance in findings is the result of different sampling and data-gathering methods, the most telling factor for such widely discrepant rates, according to Berrick and Gilbert, "is each investigator's working definition of child sexual abuse" (1991: 5). As one might guess, the highest prevalence rates were found when very broad definitions of sexual abuse were utilized, such as those including unwanted hugs and kisses and incidents that involved no touch (for example, sexual propositions). When survey respondents are, in effect, asked to define sexual abuse themselves by being asked if they regard themselves as victims of sexual abuse, the prevalence rates are at the low end of the spectrum. In a 1984 general population survey in Texas, for instance, 7.4 percent of respondents (11 percent female, 3 percent male)

indicated that they considered themselves to have been sexually abused as children (Kercher and McShane 1984). More recently, in a 1996 national survey, 5 percent of respondents (9 percent female, 2 percent male) indicated that they felt they had been victims of sexual abuse (see the *Survey of American Political Culture* [Charlottesville, VA: The Post-Modernity Project/Gallup, 1996], vol. 2, table 82D).

For the most reliable numbers on adult and adolescent (over age fourteen) sexual contacts with children (under age thirteen) based on retrospective self-reports by adults, see the findings of the massive National Health and Social Life Survey in Laumann et al. (1994: 339–47). That study does not attempt to define or measure "abuse." It found that 12 percent of women reported having a physical sexual contact before age thirteen with a partner who was at least four years older (but not younger than fourteen).

22. Susan Forward, for instance, a therapist trained in social work, who took a family-systems approach to incest in her popular *Betrayal of Innocence* (Forward and Buck 1978), became a very public figure. Her work with incest victims was covered in the press (*Betrayal of Innocence* was excerpted in *Ladies' Home Journal,* Nov. 1978, p. 116) and on TV (*Merv Griffin Show,* 1980). She hosted a national call-in radio program from 1982 to 1987 on ABC Talkradio and testified as an expert witness in numerous trials.

23. The same author notes that in his own private practice the number of women who had reported an incestuous relationship had jumped in the previous three or four years to over 30 percent of his female patient caseload (Woodbury and Schwartz 1971: v).

24. It may be that part of the initial impetus for the turn to child sexual experiences was that in the shared subculture where rape was under discussion, women needed a story to share. If they had not been raped, then childhood molestation and even embarrassing incidents at the hands of other children provided a story (a feminist journalist covering the 1971 NYRF rape speak-out describes such a sequence in Sheehy 1971: 28). Scholars studying self-help groups have noted the requirement of having a story to tell (Denzin 1987; Rice 1996).

25. The quotation is from a brochure for the film released by the J. Gary Mitchell Film Co., Sausalito, CA.

26. For example, *The Last Taboo,* Cavalcade Productions, 1977; *Shatter the Silence,* S-L Film Productions, Los Angeles, 1979; and *Breaking Silence,* Future Educational Films, San Francisco, 1984. The last film was narrated by Michelle Morris, who was molested at the home where she was baby-sitting and who wrote a novel about father-daughter incest (1982).

27. The woman in the film and in the *Ms.* article is not actually identified. However, the details of the two accounts clearly point to the same person.

CHAPTER FOUR

1. Judith Herman notes, "Perhaps the most impressive finding [of clinical studies] is the sheer length of the list of symptoms correlated with a history of childhood abuse" (1992: 122).

2. C. K. Li charges that, given their a priori rejection of the notion of victim participation and their value judgments regarding victim harm, Browne and Finkelhor left

out studies that were not favorable to their position. He lists seventeen such studies (see Li, West, and Woodhouse 1990: 172).

3. Trimble (1985), for instance, describes a late nineteenth-century condition known as "railway spine," an injury, in the words of its first investigator, resulting from the "violent shock of railway collision." Like "shell shock" (see below), railway spine was originally conceived as an organic condition—symptoms arising from actual spinal injury—but was later argued to be essentially psychological in origin, with some cases described as hysteria. The identification of this disorder followed the introduction of compensation laws for railway injuries, and the debate over its origins centered in part on the question of whether compensation claimants were "malingering"—the deliberate imitation of disease symptoms—for their own personal gain. After the introduction of workman's compensation laws, the issue of malingering came to be tied up with a whole range of injuries ostensibly caused by workplace accidents. As I note below, the same issue was long the center of concern about battlefield neuroses.

4. The concept of trauma was originally limited to physical injury and then progressively "psychologized." For discussions of this change, see Hacking (1995) and Leys (2000).

5. The first edition of the *Diagnostic and Statistical Manual of Mental Disorders (DSM-I)*, published in 1952, included the entry "gross stress reaction," which was based on the work of Kardiner and other psychiatrists who had worked with the military in World War II. The editors of *DSM-I*, in the words of Scott, "distinguished [this disorder] from a neurosis or psychosis and described it as a temporary condition," which "should disappear after the individual was removed from the stressful situation" (1990: 295). The stressful situation, as the name of the disorder suggests, included not only war but disasters, earthquakes, explosions, and so on. Gross stress reaction was dropped from the *DSM-II*, published in 1968, and thus no specific psychiatric disorder connected to combat was included in that edition, though "temporary situational disorder" defined a reaction, again temporary, to an unusual stress (Gersons and Carlier 1992).

6. I have filled out this brief description of the political struggles with details from Scott's (1990) account of how PTSD entered the *DSM-III*.

7. After publication of the *DSM-III*, other formulations of the etiology of rape-induced problems were often abandoned in favor of the PTSD framework (e.g., Kilpatrick, Veronen, and Best 1985).

8. In the *DSM-III-R*, published in 1987, an idea that appeared in the discussion of PTSD in the *DSM-III* was used to further specify the formal criteria for the trauma as "an event that is outside the range of usual human experience" (American Psychiatric Association 1987: 250). The *DSM-IV*, published in 1994, revised the definition again (American Psychiatric Association 1994: 424, 427–28); see the discussion below.

9. The three symptom groups are somewhat reconceptualized in the *DSM-III-R*, and their connection to the traumatic event made more explicit (American Psychiatric Association 1987: 247–51). The second group is redefined to include not only a numbing of responsiveness but signs of persistent attempts to avoid anything likely to bring the trauma to mind. The third group is pared down, with avoidance behavior and memory loss moved to the second group, and survivor guilt removed as a formal criterial

feature (it is mentioned as an associated feature). The third group, then, is unified as comprising signs of an underlying physiological reaction, "autonomic arousal," seen in such behaviors as hypervigilance, sleep disturbances, and irritability. See also the discussion in Young (1995: 114–17).

10. According to the *DSM-III* editors, "Because *DSM-III* is generally atheoretical with regard to etiology, it attempts to describe comprehensively what the manifestations of the mental disorders are, and only rarely attempts to account for how the disturbances come about, unless the mechanism is included in the definition of the disorder" (American Psychiatric Association 1980: 7).

11. A common theoretical model used to explain PTSD was Horowitz's (1976) conceptualization of "stress response syndrome" (e.g., Donaldson and Gardner 1985; Gelinas 1983). In oversimplified terms, this information-processing model posits the mind as unable to integrate the overwhelming experience, the memory and meaning of which is then consciously or unconsciously warded off to reduce anxiety. However, due to the mind's "completion tendency"—a repetitive effort to assimilate the thoughts and feelings associated with the event—these thoughts and feelings, which remain in active memory storage, push toward release and are experienced as intrusive, emotionally upsetting, and uncontrolled representations of the event. Hence, a cycle of numbing and intrusive thought representations continues until such time as the thoughts and feelings are integrated and thus "completed."

The notion of a physical component to the trauma was gradually deleted from the *DSM*. The *DSM-III* notes that "[f]requently there is a concomitant physical component to the trauma which may even involve direct damage to the central nervous system (e.g., malnutrition, head trauma)" (American Psychiatric Association 1980: 236). In the *DSM-III-R*, the same sentence appears, but "sometimes" has replaced "frequently." The *DSM-IV* makes no reference to a physical component.

12. It also seems likely that Finkelhor was influenced by the fact that he and Browne, in their review of the clinical and research literature, found little unanimity as to which variables believed to produce greater trauma actually did so (Browne and Finkelhor 1986).

13. *Splitting* was another, and somewhat confusing, "survival mechanism" term. J. A. Brook (1992) argues that Freud used the term in at least three different ways, one of which was for dissociation. Roland Summit cites a 1979 paper by Leonard Shengold, who distinguished the term from the sense in which it is used with schizophrenia *(split personality),* a disconnection of a person's thoughts, emotions, and physical reactions. Rather, by *splitting,* Shengold referred to a vertical split in reality testing, the "establishment of isolated divisions of the mind that provides the mechanism for a pattern in which contradictory images of the self and of the parents are never permitted to coalesce" (Summit 1983: 184). In this use, the term would seem to be the same as *dissociation,* and in the clinical literature I surveyed the two terms were regularly used interchangeably. In at least one other use, however, *splitting* was used in the sense it has in borderline personality disorder, as designating a process by which people view themselves or others, perhaps alternately, as either all good or all bad. Yet an additional term occasionally employed was *suppression,* a term used by Freud and often interchanged

with *repression*, meaning the intentional avoidance of thinking about the trauma. When some writers spoke of *repression* as a voluntary process, such intentional avoidance seems to be what they had in mind. For others (e.g., Herman 1992: 46), *suppression* meant conscious acts of dissociation.

14. Psychoanalysts continue to debate the question of distinguishing empirical inci dents from fantasy. David Spence (1982), in connection with psychoanalysis, distin- guishes between "historical truth," or the "what really happened," and "narrative truth," the weaving of an interpretative narrative that helps to illuminate the client's life in a way that "makes sense" and is useful to her. Spence argues that psychoanalysis is con- cerned with achieving the latter but has no special capacity to establish the former. Janet Malcolm (1983), in a critique of Spence, argues that psychoanalysis is neither concerned with "historical truth" nor "narrative truth" but with what she calls "psychoanalytical truth." What the analyst is really after, according to Malcolm, is "the story behind the story—the story that the patient is not telling him" (1983: 103). This story cannot be dis- covered through the client's own account; rather, it emerges in the interactions between client and analyst, in which the important conflicts and dramas of the client's past re- enact themselves. Both Spence and Malcolm grant that discovering some external his- torical truth is not what analysts do. They may discover conflict and pain during the course of therapy, and they may help to interpret it meaningfully, but they cannot estab- lish whether specific incidents did or did not happen. Psychoanalysts more orthodox than Spence or Malcolm (e.g., Lear 1995; Shengold 1989) insist that separating fact from fantasy is crucial to therapy. However, they also note, as Freud did, that fantasy has path- ogenic power by itself. Thus, those who were not actually molested as children can express psychological problems just like those experienced by actual molestation vic- tims. Knowing what really happened, even though clinically important, may remain beyond reach.

15. If the trauma event could not be recovered or its recovery did not provide relief, Janet would suggest to the patient, under hypnosis, that the trauma never in fact occurred. He reported good results in symptom reduction from this practice of creating false memories (see Hacking 1995: 195–96).

16. Several cases of repression or partial repression are reprinted from the older clin- ical literature in Masters (1963). See also Landis (1940).

17. For example, in a 1987 paper, Herman and Schatzow (1987) use the terms "repres- sion" and "massive repression" to account for varying levels of memory deficit in adults molested as children. Later, however, Herman (1992) uses the concept of dissociation to account for such deficits.

18. When the first multiple was identified is a matter of debate. I follow Hacking (1995: 171), who argues that the concept of multiple personality came into being in 1885.

19. In the *DSM-III-R*, "multiple personality" became "multiple personality disorder." In the *DSM-IV*, the name was changed again to "dissociative identity disorder."

20. The professional society was founded in 1983, called the International Society for the Study of Multiple Personality and Dissociation until 1994, when the name was changed to International Society for the Study of Dissociation following the renaming of multiple personality in the *DSM-IV*. The mission of the society, which had more than

three thousand members in the mid-1990s, is, in the words of its newsletter, "to promote education, training, and research in the dissociative disorders" (*ISSMP&D News,* August 1993, p. 13). Annual conferences sponsored by the society are four-to-five day intensive training events and touch on virtually all aspects of dissociative disorders, including theory, diagnosis, treatment, hypnosis, new research, child abuse, "ritual abuse," family issues, spirituality, legal issues, post-traumatic stress, and, beginning in 1993, at the tenth annual conference, the claims of the False Memory Syndrome Foundation and other skeptics. The society's initial academic journal was *Dissociation: Progress in the Dissociative Disorders.* It was followed in 2000 by the *Journal of Trauma and Dissociation.*

21. Like multiple personality, most of the other dissociative disorders were relabeled in the *DSM-IV.* The criterial features for each disorder were also adjusted somewhat in the *DSM-III-R* and the *DSM-IV.* Most significant of these changes with regard to multiple personality is the shift in the major criterial feature from "two or more distinct personalities" in the *DSM-III* to "two or more distinct identities or personality states" in the *DSM-IV.* This shift represents a change in the conceptualization of the alters; rather than whole personalities, they are reconceived as fragments.

22. Putnam (1989: 35), in his major textbook on multiple personality, argues that one of the features of the book *Sybil* that made it a paradigm for later cases was its graphic treatment of child abuse. Cornelia Wilbur credits another 1970s pioneer, Richard Kluft, with making a firm connection between multiple personality and child abuse in 1979 (Wilbur 1984: 3).

23. Because dissociation was believed to occur simultaneously with the trauma, some professionals theorized that it was the defense most likely to be employed (especially by those with high dissociative capacity) for more severe traumas. For lesser traumas, victims resorted to other defenses that arose after the experience, such as denial and repression.

24. Summit cites the rape trauma model of Burgess and Holmstrom, including their concept of a "silent reaction," in support of this point (see discussion in chapter 3).

25. David Corwin and colleagues presented another model, "sexually abused child's disorder," at the National Summit Conference on Diagnosing Child Sexual Abuse in 1985 and subsequently redrafted it (Corwin 1988). Unlike Summit's model, the goal of Corwin's model was diagnostic, a tool for identifying the signs and symptoms of a valid child sexual abuse case. Long lists of such signs and symptoms were developed for varying age groups. Like the Summit model, however, it emphasized the reluctance of children to disclose abuse and the tendency to recant previous disclosures. It was proposed for inclusion in the appendix of the *DSM-III-R*, but the proposal was rejected.

26. Not all of the new and influential formulations of PTSD theory centered on the role of dissociation. For example, Ronnie Janoff-Bulman (1985) theorized that PTSD was brought on by a "shattering of basic assumptions" that victims hold about themselves and their world, and that self-blame is one of the core coping strategies for reestablishing those assumptions.

27. "For children," according to the *DSM-IV,* "sexually traumatic events may include developmentally inappropriate sexual experiences without threatened or actual violence or injury" (American Psychiatric Association 1994: 424).

28. As briefly noted above, some clinicians began to conceptualize borderline personality disorder as a post-traumatic syndrome following from childhood sexual abuse (e.g., Herman, Perry, and van der Kolk 1989; Herman and van der Kolk 1987; Stone 1990). Briere (1989) argued that his "post sexual abuse trauma" model covered the borderline symptoms. The borderline symptoms included, among others, an unstable sense of identity, unstable and intense interpersonal relationships, impulsive behavior, mood instability, and uncontrolled anger.

29. A linking of these *DSM* categories amounts to a kind of reconstruction of the long-defunct category of hysteria. Herman's (1992) work, especially, would seem to be aimed at a resurrection of Freud's seduction theory in virtually all the details of its original formulation.

30. Some early cases similarly led to rulings that repression of memories did not constitute delayed discovery or "insanity" (an exception which also tolls the statute of limitations). See, for example, *Kaiser v. Milliman* (747 P.2d 1130 [Wash. Ct. App. 1988]); *Lindabury v. Lindabury* (552 So.2d 1117 [Fla. Dist. Ct. App. 1989]); *Whatcott v. Whatcott* (790 P.2d 578 [Utah Ct. App. 1990]); *Baily v. Lewis* (763 F. Supp. 802 [E. D. Pa. 1991]); *Farris v. Compton* (802 F. Supp. 487 [D.D.C. 1992]).

31. See, for example, *DeRose v. Carswell* (242 Cal. Rptr. 368 [Cal. Ct. App. 1987]); *E. W. v. D. C. H.* (231 Mont 481 [1988]); *Hildebrand v. Hildebrand* (736 F. Supp. 1512 [S.D. Ind. 1990]); *Marsha v. Gardner* (281 Cal.Rptr. 473 [Cal. Ct. App. 1991]); *E. J. M. v. Archdiocese of Philadelphia* (622 A.2d. 1388 [Pa. Super. Ct. 1993]); *Messina v. Bonner* (813 F. Supp. 346 [E.D. Pa. 1993]); *Schwestka v. Hocevar* (1994 U.S. Dist. LEXIS 6730 [N.D. Cal. 1994]).

32. See, for example, *Meiers-Post v. Schafer* (170 Mich. App 174 [Mich. Ct. App. 1988]), which was based on an insanity exception and included a corroboration requirement; *Mary D. v. John D* (264 Cal.Rptr. 633 [Cal. Ct. App. 1989]); *Nicolette v. Carey* (751 F. Supp. 695 [W.D. Mich. 1990]); *Evans v. Eckelman* (265 Cal. Rptr. 605 [Cal. Ct. App. 1990]); *Hewczuk v. Sambor* (803 F. Supp. 1063 [E.D. Pa. 1992]); *Phillips v. Johnson* (599 N.E.2d 4 [Ill. Ct. App. 1992])

33. Activists also worked to change statutes of limitations with respect to criminal cases, and a number of states subsequently did so. Unlike their approach to civil cases, very few courts took this approach (Ernsdorff and Loftus 1993: 147–53).

34. Aided by court rulings and legislative changes, civil litigation brought by adult survivors rose dramatically in the early 1990s, growing to hundreds of cases (reported in Evans 1992; Gross 1994; Loftus 1996). In some cases, judgments or settlements of more than $1 million were awarded to individuals bringing suits after memory of abuse was later recovered. However, with the emergence of the False Memory Syndrome Foundation in 1992 and a broader debate over the validity of recovered memories in the mental health professions, litigation declined, and the legal environment became less receptive. Anita Lipton of the False Memory Syndrome Foundation, which tracks legal cases, reported at the FMSF conference in March 1997 that the highest number of cases was filed in 1992–94, after which the number of new filings dropped off dramatically (author's notes).

35. By the late 1970s, a related category, rape trauma syndrome, was also in use in civil litigation cases to validate the occurrence of psychological injuries (Benedek 1985: 12).

36. Besides facilitating legal remedy for individuals, the court and legislative activity was also important for establishing another source of legitimation for professional claims. In the type 1 instance, the therapist was given standing as one who could establish a legally relevant connection between childhood trauma and adult psychological injury. In the type 2 case, legal endorsement was given to the contention that memories of childhood sexual abuse could be hidden from the conscious mind by internal psychological mechanisms and then later accurately retrieved.

CHAPTER FIVE

1. In the memory wars that erupted in the early 1990s (see chapter 8), *The Courage to Heal* was vilified by critics of "recovered memory therapy" as "dangerous" and even compared to *Mein Kampf* (Wakefield and Underwager 1994: 136). Its authors were accused of being purveyors of hate; they were sued and were sent threatening letters.

2. For example, practice informed by family therapy continued to be utilized (e.g., Deighton and McPeek 1985). Other practitioners modified conventional modalities for application to former victims by incorporating an emphasis on abuse-related themes (e.g., Shengold 1989).

3. In subsequent chapters, I present a composite picture of the treatment approaches explained in the professional textbooks describing individual psychotherapy for survivors. These books provide the clearest and most complete description of the adult survivor rationale, and the brief synopsis that follows is drawn from these sources.

4. While some authors raise the issue of making distinctions between problem causes, they do not spell out how these distinctions are actually made.

5. The treatment literature generally regards sexual abuse as including behaviors covering a spectrum from overt physical touching to subtle and not-so-subtle forms of nontouching behaviors, including, for example, verbal innuendo, exhibitionism, or voyeurism. It might involve a single incident or many.

6. Four of the books analyzed for this study focus exclusively on incest, broadly defined (Courtois 1988; Kirschner, Kirschner, and Rappaport 1993; Meiselman 1990; Roth 1993). The balance of the books deal with the general category of child sexual abuse, with incest as the paradigm case.

The treatment of male survivors follows on the same general model. The literature emphasizes some tendency differences between males and females in the way they cope with sexual contacts, but overall it treats gender differences as unknown or fairly minimal with regard to both abuse aftereffects and treatment procedures. As one text asserts, "[T]he clinical differences between male and female victims of sexual abuse are few compared to the similarities" (Crowder 1993: 32). The treatment approaches for both males and females work from the same trauma model built on the father-daughter incest paradigm.

7. Some of the survivor treatment books draw on family-systems approaches (e.g., Courtois 1988; Kirschner, Kirschner, and Rappaport 1993; Roth 1993). These works observe that in cases of incest a variety of family patterns are possible. The male may be dominant, with the woman and children ordered in a dependency relationship to him, or he may be passive and dependent. In cases of "chaotic" families, authority has been

abdicated to the children. More thoroughly feminist treatments (e.g., Hall and Lloyd 1989; Sanderson 1990), on the other hand, tend to focus on the male-dominated family. Both approaches, however, stress the abuser's responsibility for the abuse and reject any tendency to diminish that responsibility by implicating other family members.

8. A 1983 self-help book by Eliana Gil (1983) covered "all forms of child abuse," including sexual abuse.

9. As Jerome Frank and Julia Frank note, the healing agent in psychotherapy need not be a professional. An agent might be "a fellow sufferer, a group of fellow sufferers with or without a trained leader, or even a book or audiotape invested by the sufferer with healing powers" (1991: 2).

10. For example, Bass and Davis (1988: 34–39) list 74 symptoms; Blume (1990: xviii–xxi) lists 34, and Fredrickson (1992: 48–51) lists 63.

11. In the third edition, Bass and Davis tone down this controversial statement: "It is rare that someone thinks she was sexually abused and then later discovers she wasn't. The progression usually goes the other way, from suspicion to confirmation. If you genuinely think you were abused and your life shows the symptoms, there's a strong likelihood that you were" (1994: 15).

12. On the emergence of the recovery movement, see Rice 1996, Haaken 1993, and Irvine 1999.

13. "The I. S. A. Twelve Traditions," no. 3. www.lafn.org/medical/isa/index.html.

14. "The Welcome: An Introduction to Survivors of Incest Anonymous." www.siawso.org.

15. Both the original and revised lists of the twelve steps are given on the SIA website.

16. Pharmacological intervention (i.e., prescribing medications) has largely replaced psychotherapy in psychiatry.

17. Researchers since the 1950s have challenged the view that affective neutrality is even possible, uncovering the features of therapists' personalities, such as empathy, warmth, and sincerity, that contribute to therapeutic effect (see reviews in Dent and Furse 1978; Torrey 1986: 41–45). One prominent researcher, Hans Strupp, argues that "any meaningful definition of psychotherapy would have to accommodate personal qualities of the therapist. ... [T]o describe psychotherapy in terms of its theoretical orientation or techniques, as was common then and still is now, provides a truncated view of what is always a complex human relationship" (quoted in Torrey 1986: 43).

18. Not everything that might be called "psychotherapeutic" by therapists deals with changing client assumptions. A *pure* support (providing emotional support but advocating no change) or nondirective therapy (studies suggest that nondirection is seldom, if ever, achieved, see Efran, Lukens, and Lukens 1990; Frank and Frank 1991: 176–81; Mahoney 1995) would not do so. Nor would any "therapy" that is not voluntary—forced indoctrination, for instance, such as in Communist reeducation camps (Lifton 1961)— or does not try to effect change through symbolic persuasion, such as drug therapies or physical therapies. And efforts to change assumptions would apply only in a very limited sense to treatment of people with severe mental disorders. Psychotherapy is based on exploring and changing the meaning of experience, and if that meaning cannot be assessed, as it cannot be in the case of some seriously mentally ill patients, then it cannot

be changed. Treatments that help patients to adjust to living with their disorder are the only possible type of psychotherapy in these cases (see Torrey 1986: 2–3).

19. The concept of norms of emotion and expression is drawn from Hochschild (1979).

20. Studies have found that some of the differences between the various therapeutic orientations are less important than practitioners suggest. Lester Luborsky and colleagues (1982), for example, found that "giving support," while the hallmark of support therapy, was virtually identical among the three psychotherapies they evaluated (drug counseling, supportive-expressive, and cognitive-behavioral). Further, in their speech-content analysis, they found that "use of clarification and interpretation" was as common with cognitive-behavioral approaches as it was with supportive-expressive approaches. R. Bruce Sloane and colleagues (1975), in a comparison of psychoanalytic and behavioral therapies, found that while the techniques differed, there was considerable overlap, many of the differences being matters of emphasis. Sharon Brunink and Harold Schroeder, in a comparison of psychoanalytically oriented, Gestalt, and behavior therapists, found that communicating empathy was a central characteristic of each and that, contrary to expectation, "the technique of interpretation appears not to be determined by theoretical orientation" (1979: 572), at least early in therapy. Overall, behavior and psychoanalytically oriented therapists "were surprisingly similar in their styles of therapy, with the interesting exceptions that behavior therapists provided more direct guidance and greater emotional support" (572). In addition, many therapists freely borrow theory and techniques from the various schools. As a number of studies have shown, there has been a strong and growing trend in recent years toward eclecticism in theoretical preference (see review in Garfield and Bergin 1986: 7–11), a tendency that is very clear in adult survivor therapies. Additionally, there is also an eclecticism that involves the mixing of various relational postures of the therapist toward the client. These postures include such matters as the degree of directiveness, intimacy, and self-disclosure (see Rappaport 1991). Such convergence of theoretical and relational approaches further diminishes the treatment-specific differences between therapies.

21. According to prominent psychiatrist Robert Lifton, "Psychiatrists ... extend the concept of reality to suggest something on the order of the way things are, as opposed to the way that the patient imagines them to be. In fact, we regard the therapeutic relationship as a means of enhancing the patient's reality-testing, of helping him to recognize his own distortions." He adds, however: "All of these usages [of the concept of reality] have validity; but the therapist's notion of reality is nonetheless highly colored by his own ideological convictions about such matters as psychological health and illness, social conformity and rebelliousness, commitment and detachment, and especially about what constitutes wise or mature attitudes and behavior" (1961: 451).

22. Assessing effectiveness raises tricky questions of whose perspective and what variation you measure. These are issues of considerable subjectivity. One option for measuring effectiveness is simply to ask clients, at some time during or after treatment, if they experienced being helped and how. In the large national survey conducted by Joseph Veroff, and colleagues (1981), respondents who had sought professional help were asked just these questions. A large percentage said they had been helped and gave

various answers as to how this help came about. While such subjective judgments would seem to indicate that some change has been experienced, the question of whether this indicates that therapy has been "effective" is not so readily obvious. On what basis was the subjective judgment made? Since people normally come to therapy with some sort of problem for which they seek help, changes in this regard would be a logical basis. While this cannot be established with any accuracy in the Michigan study (the questions do not tie help received directly to the original symptoms), Hans Strupp and colleagues (1969) found in their study that those who benefited from psychotherapy tended to give reasons that were not at all closely tied to the symptoms that brought them to therapy in the first place. They expressed greater personal "adjustment" but typically in areas that they did not earlier express as a deficiency, while improvements in the problems that did bring them to therapy were less frequently used to assess therapy success. Further, subjective judgments by the client may in part simply reflect the diagnosis and goals of treatment set by the therapist. As has often been asserted, psychotherapeutic schools, at least in part, "unwittingly foster the phenomena which they cure" (Jaspers, quoted in Frank and Frank 1991: 9). If a client is told what her "real" problem is and then is told after a course of treatment that she has overcome the problem, she may very well evaluate her treatment favorably, again quite apart from symptom improvement or external criteria. Or the client may simply be encouraged to accept the symptoms rather than attempt to overcome them. As Sloane and his colleagues note, "[I]f a therapist can convince a patient that masturbation, say, or occasional anger at his mother, is perfectly normal, he may entirely cure the problem without altering the symptom in the least" (1975: 5). Similarly, depending on the treatment expectations set by the therapist, the standard against which help is measured can vary widely.

Additional perspectives on treatment effectiveness could be found by asking the therapist or a close friend or relative of the client. Again, subjective standards of improvement enter in. For instance, the therapist, due to a view about an underlying cause, may not see particular symptom improvement as genuine improvement. A relative, on the other hand, may see nothing but symptom improvement, and thus any evaluation would focus on perceived changes in the symptoms of the client. In addition to matters of perspective, there is also the question of what change to measure. I have already noted this problem with respect to symptoms, but it could also be illustrated with reference to measures of social adjustment, the breadth and durability of improvement, a cost-benefit calculus, and so on. Psychotherapeutic effectiveness requires many subjective judgments.

23. This summary draws on the work of Gergen (1994), Kerby (1991), and Bruner (1987) on self-narratives. See also Davis (2002a).

CHAPTER SIX

1. In constructivist or narrativist approaches, no argument is made for the truth of new self-narratives, only for their utility. Old self-narratives are altered or discarded not because they are wrong in some overarching sense, but because they are undesirable under present circumstances (Gergen 1994: 245). The interpretations offered by survivor therapists, in contrast, are cast within a scientifically argued theory about the

nature of sexual abuse and the determinative effects of psychological trauma. The therapist draws sharp distinctions between proper and improper development, and the effort to reconstruct childhood is in part an effort to correct development that has departed from predefined and fixed standards. Further, survivor therapy is deeply involved with oppositions between health/normalcy on the one hand and disorder/deviancy on the other. Distinctly normative and non-negotiable orientations to old self-understandings mandate and specify the identity change.

2. As noted in chapter 4, Janet saw "fixed ideas" as memories that individuals could not incorporate into their life stories and thus dissociated. Janet saw memory as "the action of telling a story. . . . The teller must not only know how to do it, but must also know how to associate the happenings with the other events of his life, how to put it in its place in that life history which for each of us is an essential element of his personality" (quoted in Young 1995: 35). Building on Janet's conception, Herman (1992: 37–38) argues that the difference between normal memories and traumatic memories is that traumatic memories lack "verbal narrative and context." The therapeutic task is conceived, then, as putting these "wordless" memories into a narrative form.

3. The idea of the connection between some adult experiences or problems and childhood sexual experience along with coaching in how to make that connection is readily available in the survivor self-help literature. Survivor groups and survivor autobiographical accounts, now widely disseminated, also emphasize it. People are thus equipped to self-label.

4. Many contemporary psychotherapists avoid making diagnoses, at least in the formal sense of naming a client's distress or disability as a particular disorder within a formal nosology, such as the *DSM* (though, of course, they likely do so for insurance purposes). But the notion of diagnosis can be understood in a broader sense as the interpretation that links the client's experience to that of others. Psychotherapy demands comparisons across cases. The "diagnosis" is the making of such comparisons, whatever labels they are given or however implicit they remain. It is a name for a category in a system of categories, official or otherwise, for distinguishing one problem or disorder from another and so determining the appropriate therapy or therapeutic technique. Each problem/disorder category demarcates a pattern of symptoms that are believed to share some common features and (or) arise from a common root cause (for example, a specific stressor). Categories are generalized narratives of recurring symptoms, and they are stories about their resolution. They represent possibilities for change. In making a diagnosis or diagnoses, therapists draw from their stock of generalized narratives to classify a specific client's "episodes" as similar in kind to the experience of others. Until at least implicitly classified, the client's distress or disability cannot be dealt with, since the experience of others is what the therapist draws on to indicate what therapeutic steps or strategies are appropriate to the case. With a diagnosis, therapists can interpret the client's experience, even if very tentatively, as symptomatic of a known problem/disorder. They can then offer their therapy or specific resolution technique.

5. Additionally, therapists argue, before beginning intensive treatment, the client needs to be basically ready. Some immediate crisis that has the potential to undermine or prevent therapeutic engagement may need to be dealt with first. Most therapists, for

instance, will not begin therapy until the client has been free of serious substance addictions for a period of time, usually six months to one year. Therapists may require that suicidal or psychotic conditions, if present at the beginning of therapy, be given crisis intervention before regular treatment begins. Further, they may require that immediate relational crises, such as a divorce, which could seriously distract the client from focusing on her deeper personal problems, be resolved prior to fuller therapeutic engagement.

6. In the case of multiple personality clients, therapists conceive of this task as building rapport with each of the client's alternative personalities.

7. For instance, "If the therapist is male and the client was molested by her father, then the therapist may be perceived as a potential perpetrator of abuse. On the other hand, the female therapist may be experienced by the survivor in the transferential projection as the weak, nonprotecting mother" (Kirschner, Kirschner, and Rappaport 1993: 79).

8. Some authors of self-help books recount personal stories of childhood molestation, including Laura Davis (Bass and Davis 1988) and Carol Poston (Poston and Lison 1989). "Although an under-researched area, it is well known by those of us working in the field that a good many 'abuse therapists' grew up in incestuous families and were the victims of sexual abuse" (Trepper and Barrett 1989: 5). In a survey of psychologists by Shirley Feldman-Summers and Kenneth Pope (1994), 21.8 percent of the respondents (25.9 percent of the women and 16.5 percent of the men) described themselves as having been sexually abused in childhood. Although the authors did not report whether these respondents practice survivor therapy, they did find that many have participated in it. Forty percent of those who reported abuse also reported periods of forgetting, and of these more than half "identified therapy— alone or with other events or conditions— as being related to recall" (638). In another survey of psychologists, 32 percent of the respondents (42 percent of the women and 23 percent of the men) reported experiencing some form of child sexual abuse (Polusny and Follette 1996)

9. With regard to gender, no ideal combination is seen. Male therapists may work effectively with females, and female therapists may work effectively with males. The treatment models do not differentiate between male and female therapists. "The only rule that must be followed is that a client must never be forced to work with a clinician they [sic] don't feel safe with, be this gender-based or otherwise, because this replicates the original abuse dynamic" (Crowder 1993: 91).

10. In the treatment literature, therapists suggest talking about their reactions with a supervising therapist, undergoing personal, perhaps survivor, psychotherapy, or even referring a client to another therapist when problems arise.

11. The adult survivor treatment books explicitly reject the idea of maintaining relational distance and affective neutrality. All the treatment models, including those in a psychoanalytic framework, use a relational model.

12. The same author argues that the therapist need not believe that everything the client says is historically accurate. However, "the counsellor must guard against conveying doubts about the veracity of the survivor's childhood experiences" (Sanderson 1990: 106).

13. The professional treatment texts used in this study include limited discussion of the use of memory enhancement techniques. A wide range of techniques, however, is discussed in the broader survivor literature and referenced in court testimony. In addition

to hypnosis and age regression, these techniques include body massage (as I note below, some therapists believe abuse memories are "stored" in the body), dream analysis, guided imagery, free association, and, at least for multiple personality patients, drugs such as sodium Amytal. In a random survey of members of clinical divisions of the American Psychological Association, Melissa Polusny and Victoria Follette (1996) found that 25 percent of the respondents reported using some of these memory retrieval techniques with clients who had no specific memories of child sexual abuse. In another survey of clinicians, Debra Poole and her colleagues found that 71 percent of respondents reported using memory enhancement techniques in the previous two years "to help clients remember childhood sexual abuse" (1995: 430). In a similar survey, J. Waltz and Lucy Berliner (1994) found that approximately 20 percent of respondents reported using guided imagery, inner child work, and referral to group therapy to facilitate recall of abuse memories. However, both Waltz and Berliner and Polusny and Follette reported that the majority of therapists surveyed indicated that "only a small percentage of clients were completely unaware of their abuse when they entered therapy" (Polusny and Follette 1996: 49).

14. They might also then serve to trigger similar feelings in the audience, such as prosurvivors, who hear the client's victim account.

15. In a less personal but perhaps very important way, self-help books, survivor accounts, TV documentaries, and other sources that might encourage the client to believe her victimization account function in the same prosurvivor role.

CHAPTER SEVEN

1. Therapists who use the concept of an "inner child" or "the child within" differ in the way they understand and describe it. As in this instance, some use the notion of an inner child to describe the root of the self as a vulnerable but inviolate core that is childlike in being playful, innocent, creative, and energetic. This core, the "true self," is regarded as the wellspring for positive self-esteem and is emphasized in inner child work that aims to address negative, internalized attitudes that the client has carried forward into adulthood. Therapists externalize the self by having the client address the inner child as though she is speaking to someone else, an abused child with whom she can empathize and whose innocence she can easily recognize. Two other uses of the inner child are relevant to the issue of identity fragmentation (discussed below). Some use the concept to mean that an individual's development has been uneven. Some of the client's behaviors and ways of thinking reflect "childlike needs." For therapists, she is in need of a more consistent or "integrated" developmental level. Yet others use the concept of the inner child as a way to describe the split in the individual that is believed to result from dissociative processes. The traumatic effects of abuse are treated as located within one or more "child self" parts of the client, but not in their "adult self" part or parts. The therapist's inner child work in this case is aimed to lead the client to become aware of the child-adult split and, putting the trauma in a more contemporary frame of reference, resolve the underlying tensions in her experience of self.

2. "Self-esteem" is a complex notion that is used in the psychological literature, including the adult survivor literature, in many and various ways. It can mean or span

several different concepts, including self-worth, self-image, and ego-strength. I make no effort to sort out these uses.

3. Although the treatment books do not specify, presumably if the client alleges more than one abuser, she might engage in more than one confrontation.

4. The strength of her new survivor story and her readiness to face denial are also key therapeutic issues at stake in any further confrontations, such as legal action against the alleged abuser and (or) nonprotecting others. In the therapeutic literature, legal action is discussed only in terms of the potential therapeutic gains and losses. If the client is ready, a civil suit, even if lost, can attest to the reality of abuse. It can express the themes of the survivor story in dramatic fashion, as the client can publicly assert that she is one who is autonomous, assertive, no longer a victim, and so on. On the other hand, a court case, even if won, could undermine rather than affirm the new identity. Courts are not safe places, in the survivor therapy sense, but openly adversarial. Even more care is advised in considering legal action than in the personal confrontation.

5. The issue of the sexual abuser is an interesting instance of this paradox. Survivor therapists argue that clients who have abused their own children do so because they were abused themselves. Although the client is in some sense responsible, or at least required to immediately stop, her abusive behavior is not interpreted as a product of her agency, but of her abuse as a child. When faced with the question of the client's alleged abuser, however, therapists run into problems. The technique of assigning responsibility to the alleged abuser loses much of its ability to generate a sense of injustice and moral indignation if the agency of the abuser is called into question due to some possible personal abuse in his past. The textbooks suggest avoiding discussions of the abuser's past.

6. The concepts of narrative rightness and fit are from Goodman (1978); see especially chapter 7, "Of Rightness of Rendering." For Goodman, "rightness" does not mean ethical or moral rightness. While standards for distinguishing right from wrong can be stated, there is no single right version of a self-narrative, as various ways of rendering a right version are possible.

7. I derive these criteria from Polonoff (1987), who in a conceptualization of self-deception, outlines three criteria for judging the rightness or wrongness of any particular version of a self-narrative. First, a right story about the self is one that is internally coherent. The constituent elements of the story hold together, exhibiting both unity and continuity with one another. An incoherent story is wrong. A coherent story, however, can still be wrong. It must also be believable. To be believable, a self-narrative must not only be internally coherent but externally coherent as well. The individual's version must hold together "in some degree both with the versions that others in the culture form of themselves and with the versions that others form of him" (50). A self-narrative radically at odds with these versions is very difficult to demonstrate and probably wrong. To be believable, and this is the second criteria of a good story, the self-narrative must also be one that the teller can live by. The self-narrative is an ordering of the self and thus a commitment to a course of action. Action consistent with the commitment promotes greater coherence and endorses the rightness of the self-narrative, but if the person cannot or does not act consistently, he may, in fact, be "living a lie." Finally,

a right story is empirically adequate. For Polonoff, "it is the ordering of experiences which is constructed in a narrative of self, not the content of those experiences, though the content is given different interpretations depending on its place in the ordering" (51). A right version of the self-narrative cannot be constructed from made-up experiences. A version of the self-narrative that achieves its coherence by deleting or ignoring crucial experiences—" 'unforgettable' experiences, recurrent experiences, 'learning' experiences, emblematic experiences, etc.,—which must be assimilated to any narrative version" (52), is therefore wrong.

8. Berger and Luckmann (1966: 157–63) argue that significant identity transformations ("alterations") involve a biographical rupture in which the earlier identity is subsumed under a negative category. In this process, old identities are not merely discounted but "annihilated." Linking pre-therapy orientations with externally induced pathology certainly accomplishes such an annihilation.

CHAPTER EIGHT

1. False Memory Syndrome Foundation conference, "Memory and Reality: Next Steps," BWI Marriott, Baltimore, MD, March 22–23, 1997.

2. A research literature about retractors, which includes case reports and survey findings, has also emerged; see de Rivera (1997, 2000); Lief and Fetkewicz (1995); McElroy and Keck (1995); Nelson and Simpson (1994); Ost, Costall, and Bull (2001, 2002).

3. Immediately after its founding, the foundation publicly announced the names of a fifteen-member board of scientific and professional advisors. That list of prominent psychiatrists, psychologists, and other researchers and clinicians would grow to more than forty in the following years, with new members often recruited from the personal and professional networks of the original group.

4. By the late 1990s, according to the foundation, more than twenty thousand families had made contact, and local groups were meeting throughout the United States and Canada. Affiliated groups were also organized in several other countries. A British False Memory Society was formed in 1993, an Australian False Memory Society was formed in 1994, a New Zealand group, "Casualties of Sexual Allegations," was established in 1994, and a Swedish FMS Society, "Families against False Incest Memories," was founded in 1996. Additional groups were meeting in Israel, the Netherlands, and elsewhere.

5. Most of the cases involved daughters. In its survey of member families in 1997, the FMS Foundation found that 92 percent of the reported accusers were female (*FMSF Newsletter,* April 1, 1997).

6. The term *false memory syndrome* was coined in 1991 by the parents and professionals who created the FMS Foundation (Wakefield and Underwager 1994: 96). However, the definition subsequently used by the foundation was drawn from a paper presented in 1993 by John Kihlstrom, then an advisory board member (the paper was eventually published; see Kihlstrom 1998). Kihlstrom argued that FMS was not a psychiatric diagnosis but the description of a social phenomenon; he was using "syndrome" not in a medical sense but in the more general sense of a collection of attributes that tend to co-occur. There are differences among the foundation advisors on this

point, but the foundation has never attempted to get FMS included in the official *Diagnostic and Statistical Manual of Mental Disorders*.

7. For an analysis of the adoption of this collective story as an account by retractors, see Davis (1999, 2000).

8. For an encyclopedic overview of the psychological literature, see McNally (2003).

9. An especially clear example of this division was the task force impaneled in 1993 by the American Psychological Association to look into the question of repressed memories of sexual abuse. Half of the six-member committee were research psychologists, the other half were therapists. Reportedly split very sharply along these lines, the committee was for some time unable to issue a statement, and such statements as were published at that time were quite self-consciously middle-of-the-road (American Psychological Association 1994; Alpert 1995).

10. As noted briefly in chapter 5, some of those targeted by the FMS Foundation define themselves as participants in a movement, which they variously label the "incest-survivor movement," the "sexual abuse recovery movement," or the "adult survivors movement."

11. Some feminist critics of recovered memory therapy echo the concern of the countermovement that victim claims are being manufactured (e.g., Acocella 1998; Kaminer 1993; Showalter 1997; Tavris 1993).

12. The decline of insurance coverage for mental health problems and the broader shift toward managed care have certainly "pushed" the decline of the multiple personality diagnoses, which took several years and large sums of money to treat.

13. For a powerful theoretical articulation of the intersubjective nature of memory, see Prager (1998).

14. Some false memory critics not only suggest that therapists are implanting deceptive memories but also allege that they are naively giving credence to clients' accounts of victimization. See, for example, Wakefield and Underwager (1994).

15. Gondolf first told her story to *D Magazine* in January 1992 (Whitley 1992) and in many media outlets after that, including *Donahue*, *The Maury Povich Show*, *Tom Snyder*, and *Hard Copy*, as well as *McCall's*, *Insight*, and *Mother Jones*. Her account also appears in Gondolf (1992) and Goldstein and Farmer (1993), and an excerpted version is given in Wakefield and Underwager (1994: 107–12). Gondolf's story is the subject of a whole chapter, complete with extensive verbatim quotes attributed to her therapist, in Elizabeth Loftus and Katherine Ketcham's influential *The Myth of Repressed Memory* (1994: 8–19).

16. Religious and political conservatives became claims-makers about sexual abuse and satanic cults in the 1980s, framing their arguments in terms of pernicious threats to the nuclear family, including some from the state (Nathan and Snedeker 1995). Allegations of satanic ritual abuse, however, have not been limited to religious contexts.

CHAPTER NINE

1. The book title is a reference to a 1982 article by Armstrong, in which she defined incest as the "cradle of sexual politics."

2. Public retractors say they encountered the notion of false memory syndrome and its interpretive framework through various intermediaries. Some heard about it

through the media; some through FMS literature provided by parents, siblings, or an attorney; some through a "retractor therapist" (a number of therapists, including several of the FMS Foundation's advisory board members, do "exit counseling" with retractor clients); and some through direct contact with other retractors.

While retractor accounts provide few if any details of the interpretive process, an exchange I witnessed at the 1997 FMS Foundation national conference suggests the interactional process by which the meanings of an individual's experience and the FMS framework are coordinated. The exchange involved a retractor I will call Anne and took place during a roundtable "conversation with retractors" at the conference. The dozen or so of us participating in the session had just heard a horrific account of three years of hospitalization from another retractor, Mary, who told her story in essentially the FMS terms. Then came Anne, who prefaced her narrative by announcing that she was "totally responsible" for her false memories of sexual abuse. Unlike the previous speaker, she argued, no therapist told her that she had been abused. Rather, depressed by some business deals that had gone sour, she had attended a weekend "understanding yourself and other people" seminar at which child sexual abuse was discussed. During the weekend, she had a "visual" that she interpreted as a memory of childhood sexual experience. She subsequently attended a workshop for incest survivors and participated in an outpatient program for women molested as children, where she heard others' stories and soon began to have "flashbacks" of her own, eventually accusing "all the men in my life of abuse." Later, under the guidance of a helpful therapist, she came to see how she had confabulated troubling and painful memories, such as one of a miscarriage, into images of abuse that had never occurred.

The parents and other retractors listening to Anne's account did not respond favorably to her suggestion that she was "totally responsible" for her "memories" of abuse. "I just can't accept that," said one parent, assuring her that she was not responsible. Another asked if, at the original seminar, anyone had suggested that she might have been sexually abused? Knowing nods greeted Anne when she responded affirmatively. "What happened in the workshop was the same as therapy," concluded a third participant. Others concurred, noting that the outpatient program was effectively a form of group therapy, and likewise reassured Anne that she was not to blame for what happened to her. As time had run out, the session was forced to end. Whether Anne later adopted an FMS account or not, I do not know, but the interaction indicates the process by which the diverse and heterogeneous experiences of retractors can be interpreted and redescribed in the homogeneous categories of FMS.

3. As I have argued elsewhere (Davis 2002b), while postmodernism and posthumanism proceed along different lines and have their origins in very different fields of study, both reach strikingly similar conclusions about human subjectivity.

4. These anecdotes, however, may add up to less than the critics assert. As sociologist Saundra Davis Westervelt has shown, for example, social victimization (injury resulting from the actions of other people) is now recognized as an exculpatory condition within criminal law but only in very specific and limited circumstances. The "free-will model of behavior," she argues, "is still the working hypothesis of the legal system" (1998: 10).

5. As Judith Herman writes, "Naming the syndrome of complex post-traumatic stress disorder represents an essential step toward granting those who have endured prolonged exploitation a measure of the recognition they deserve" (1992: 122). The original introduction of post-traumatic stress disorder and its application to war veterans and concentration camp survivors was similarly seen to represent a form of public recognition (see Gersons and Carlier 1992).

6. In survivor therapy, being a "victim" is a condition to be overcome, not celebrated or wallowed in. Self-help groups also emphasize this. According to Incest Survivors Anonymous, the "only requirement" for membership "is a desire to stop being an incest victim and become an incest survivor." As commentators have observed with respect to other campaigns on behalf of victims, being defined as a "victim" carries negative implications of "being damaged, passive, and powerless" (Best 1997: 13; see also Holstein and Miller 1990: 120). The social problems scholar Donileen Loseke writes, "Sure, by the cultural equation, a victim deserves 'sympathy' from others, but this comes at a cost of admitting individual failure of one or another sort, even if this failure isn't the fault of the victim" (1999: 141). There is stigma attached to victimization and status *loss*. This is why, for instance, adults molested as children first preferred the term *survivor* to *victim*, and many others have similarly sought to avoid the victim label.

7. In academic circles, as briefly noted above, the notions of self or self-discovery are now considered passé. The emphasis is on performance not authenticity. In summarizing this view, the philosopher Carl Elliott writes, "We no longer have identities; we 'perform' them. We do not live lives; we follow social 'scripts.' The concept of a 'true self' has become entrenched in popular culture, but it has abandoned the scholarly journals" (2003: 48). This is correct, yet perhaps not quite the whole story. Taylor argues that the postmodern critique advanced by writers such as Jacques Derrida and Michel Foucault draws from "the same sources as the ideal of authenticity." "In the end," he writes, this critique "leaves the agent, even with all his or her doubts about the category of the 'self,' with a sense of untrammeled power and freedom before a world that imposes no standards, ready to enjoy 'free play,' or to indulge in an aesthetics of the self" (1991: 61).

8. One retractor told a researcher that: "In the role of survivor I had an excuse to not be perfect anymore, and this is what I needed" (de Rivera 2000: 383).

9. The notion that nature can be at odds with the true self is implicit in the authenticity language that surrounds cosmetic surgery, sex-reassignment surgery, body building "apotemnophilia" (attraction to the idea of being an amputee), and other procedures and practices. Generally, on enhancement technologies and the self, see the insightful work of Elliott (2003).

Abraham, Karl. 1927. "The Experiencing of Sexual Traumas as a Form of Sexual Activity." In *Selected Papers of Karl Abraham, M.D.,* 47–63. London: Hogarth Press.

Acocella, Joan. 1998. "The Politics of Hysteria." *New Yorker,* April 6, 64.

Allen, Charlotte Vale. 1980. *Daddy's Girl.* New York: Wyndham Books.

Allen, Margaret J. 1983. "Tort Remedies for Incestuous Abuse." *Golden Gate University Law Review* 13: 609–38.

Alpert, Judith L., ed. 1995. *Sexual Abuse Recalled: Treating Trauma in the Era of the Recovered Memory Debate.* Northvale, NJ: Jason Aronson.

———, Laura S. Brown, and Christine A. Courtois. 1998. "Reply to Ornstein, Ceci, and Loftus (1998): The Politics of Memory." *Psychology, Public Policy, and Law* 4: 1011–24.

American Humane Association. 1966. *Child Abuse Legislation.* Denver, CO: American Humane Association Children's Division.

American Psychiatric Association. 1980. *Diagnostic and Statistical Manual of Mental Disorders,* 3d ed. Washington, DC: American Psychiatric Association.

———. 1987. *Diagnostic and Statistical Manual of Mental Disorders.* 3d rev. ed. Washington, DC: American Psychiatric Association.

———. 1994. *Diagnostic and Statistical Manual of Mental Disorders.* 4th ed. Washington, DC: American Psychiatric Association.

American Psychological Association. 1994. *Working Group on Investigation of Memories of Childhood Abuse, Interim Report.* Washington, DC: American Psychological Association.

Amir, Menachem. 1971. *Patterns in Forcible Rape.* Chicago: University of Chicago Press.

Antler, Stephen. 1981. "The Rediscovery of Child Abuse." In *The Social Context of Child Abuse and Neglect,* ed. Leroy H. Pelton, 39–53. New York: Human Sciences Press.

Apfelberg, Benjamin, Carl Sugar, and Arnold Z. Pfeffer. 1944. "A Psychiatric Study of 250 Sex Offenders." *American Journal of Psychiatry* 100: 762–69.

Armstrong, Louise. 1978. *Kiss Daddy Goodnight: A Speak-Out on Incest.* New York: Hawthorn Books.

———. 1979. "Kiss Daddy Good-Night." *Cosmopolitan,* February, 168.

———. 1982. "The Cradle of Sexual Politics: Incest." In *Women's Sexual Experience: Explorations of the Dark Continent,* ed. Martha Kirkpatrick, 110–25. New York: Plenum Press.

———. 1994. *Rocking the Cradle of Sexual Politics: What Happened When Women Said Incest.* Reading, MA: Addison-Wesley.

Atkinson, Roland M., Robin G. Henderson, Landy F. Sparr, and Shirley Deale. 1982. "Assessment of Viet Nam Veterans for Posttraumatic Stress Disorder in Veterans Administration Disability Claims." *American Journal of Psychiatry* 139: 1118–21.

Bass, Ellen. 1983. "Introduction: In the Truth Itself, There Is Healing." In *I Never Told Anyone: Writings by Women Survivors of Child Sexual Abuse,* ed. Ellen Bass and Louise Thornton, 23–60. New York: Harper & Row.

———, and Laura Davis. 1988. *The Courage to Heal: A Guide for Women Survivors of Child Sexual Abuse.* New York: HarperCollins.

———. 1993. "Letter to the Editor." *New York Times Book Review,* February 14, 3.

———. 1994. *The Courage to Heal: A Guide for Women Survivors of Child Sexual Abuse.* 3d ed. New York: HarperCollins.

———, and Louise Thornton, eds. 1983. *I Never Told Anyone: Writings by Women Survivors of Child Sexual Abuse.* New York: Harper & Row.

Bear, Euan, and Peter T. Dimock. 1988. *Adults Molested as Children.* Orwell, VT: Safer Society Press.

Beezley, Patricia, Harold Martin, and Helen Alexander. 1976. "Comprehensive Family Oriented Therapy." In *Child Abuse and Neglect: The Family and the Community,* ed. Ray E. Helfer and C. Henry Kempe, 169–94. Cambridge, MA: Ballinger.

Bender, Lauretta, and Abram Blau. 1937. "The Reaction of Children to Sexual Relations with Adults." *American Journal of Orthopsychiatry* 7: 500–18.

———, and Alvin Eldridge Grugett Jr. 1952. "A Follow-Up Report on Children Who Had Atypical Sexual Experience." *American Journal of Orthopsychiatry* 22: 825–37.

Benedek, Elissa P. 1985. "Children and Psychic Trauma: A Brief Review of Contemporary Thinking." In *Post-Traumatic Stress Disorder in Children,* ed. Spencer Eth and Robert S. Pynoos, 1–16. Washington, DC: American Psychiatric Press.

Benford, Robert D. 1993. " 'You Could Be the Hundredth Monkey': Collective Action Frames and Vocabularies of Motive within the Nuclear Disarmament Movement." *Sociological Quarterly* 34: 195–216.

———, and David A. Snow. 2000. "Framing Processes and Social Movements: An Overview and Assessment." *Annual Review of Sociology* 26: 611–39.

Berger, Arthur Asa. 1997. *Narratives in Popular Culture, Media, and Everyday Life.* Thousand Oaks, CA: Sage.

Berger, Peter L. 1965. "Toward a Sociological Understanding of Psychoanalysis." *Social Research* 32: 26–41.

———, and Thomas Luckmann. 1966. *The Social Construction of Reality.* New York: Anchor Books.

Berliner, Lucy, and Linda Meyer Williams. 1994. "Memories of Child Sexual Abuse: A Response to Lindsay and Read." *Applied Cognitive Psychology* 8: 379–87.

Berrick, Jill Duerr, and Neil Gilbert. 1991. *With the Best of Intentions: The Child Sexual Abuse Prevention Movement.* New York: Guilford Press.

Best, Joel. 1990. *Threatened Children: Rhetoric and Concern about Child-Victims.* Chicago: University of Chicago Press.

———. 1995. "Typification and Social Problem Construction." In *Images of Issues: Typifying Contemporary Social Problems,* 2d ed., ed. Joel Best, 3–10. New York: Aldine de Gruyter.

———. 1997. "Victimization and the Victim Industry." *Society* 34 (4): 9–17.

———. 2001. *Damned Lies and Statistics.* Berkeley and Los Angeles: University of California Press.

Beutler, L. E., M. Crago, and T. G. Arizmendi. 1986. "Therapist Variables in Psychotherapy Process and Outcome." In *Handbook of Psychotherapy and Behavior Change,* 3d ed., ed. Sol L. Garfield and Allen E. Bergin, 257–310. New York: John Wiley & Sons.

Bird, Frederick. 1979. "The Pursuit of Innocence: New Religious Movements and Moral Accountability." *Sociological Analysis* 40: 335–46.

Blake-White, Jill, and Christine Madeline Kline. 1985. "Treating the Dissociative Process in Adult Victims of Childhood Incest." *Social Casework* 66: 394–402.

Blum, Jeffrey D. 1978. "On Changes in Psychiatric Diagnosis over Time." *American Psychologist* 33: 1017–31.

Blume, E. Sue. 1990. *Secret Survivors: Uncovering Incest and Its Aftereffects in Women.* New York: John Wiley & Sons.

———. 1993. "Letter to the Editor." *New York Times Book Review,* February 14, 27.

Bolton, Frank G., Jr., Larry A. Morris, and Ann E. MacEachron. 1989. *Males at Risk.* Newbury Park, CA: Sage.

Boodman, Sandra G. 2002. "How Deep the Scars of Abuse?" *Washington Post,* July 29, A1.

Bowman, Karl M., ed. 1953. *California Sexual Deviation Research.* Sacramento: Assembly of the State of California.

Bradshaw, John. 1988. *Bradshaw On: The Family.* Deerfield Beach, FL: Health Communications.

———. 1992. "Incest: When You Wonder If It Happened to You." *Lear's,* August, 43–44.

Brady, Katherine. 1979. *Father's Days: A True Story of Incest.* New York: Seaview.

Braun, Bennett G. 1986. "Issues in the Psychotherapy of Multiple Personality Disorder." In *Treatment of Multiple Personality Disorder,* ed. Bennett G. Braun, 1–28. Washington, DC: American Psychiatric Press.

Briere, John. 1989. *Therapy for Adults Molested as Children.* New York: Springer.

———, and Marsha Runtz. 1988. "Post Sexual Abuse Trauma." In *Lasting Effects of Child Sexual Abuse,* ed. Gail Elizabeth Wyatt and Gloria Johnson Powell, 85–99. Newbury Park, CA: Sage.

———, and Jon Conte. 1993. "Self-Reported Amnesia for Abuse in Adults Molested as Children." *Journal of Traumatic Stress* 6: 21–31.

Brody, Howard. 2003. *Stories of Sickness.* 2d ed. New York: Oxford University Press.

Bromley, David G., Anson D. Shupe, Jr., and J. C. Ventimiglia. 1979. "Atrocity Tales, the Unification Church, and the Social Construction of Evil." *Journal of Communication* 29: 42–53.

Brook, J. A. 1992. "Freud and Splitting." *International Review of Psycho-Analysis* 19: 335–50.

Brown, Daniel P., Alan W. Scheflin, and D. Corydon Hammond. 1998. *Memory, Trauma Treatment, and the Law.* New York: W. W. Norton.

Brown, Phil. 1995. "Naming and Framing: The Social Construction of Diagnosis and Illness." *Journal of Health and Social Behavior* 33: 267–81.

Browne, Angela, and David Finkelhor. 1986. "Impact of Child Sexual Abuse: A Review of the Research." *Psychological Bulletin* 99: 66–77.

Browning, Diane H., and Bonny Boatman. 1977. "Incest: Children at Risk." *American Journal of Psychiatry* 134: 69–72.

Brownmiller, Susan. 1975. *Against Our Will: Men, Women, and Rape.* New York: Simon & Schuster.

———. 1999. *In Our Time: Memoir of a Revolution.* New York: Dial Press.

Bruner, Jerome. 1987. "Life as Narrative." *Social Research* 54: 11–32.

Brunink, Sharon A., and Harold E. Schroeder. 1979. "Verbal Therapeutic Behavior of Expert Psychoanalytically Oriented, Gestalt, and Behavior Therapists." *Journal of Consulting and Clinical Psychology* 47: 567–74.

Buechler, Steven M. 2000. *Social Movements in Advanced Capitalism.* New York: Oxford University Press.

Burgess, Ann Wolbert, A. Nicholas Groth, Lynda Lytle Holmstrom, and Suzanne M. Sgroi, eds. 1978. *Sexual Assault of Children and Adolescents.* Lexington, MA: Lexington Books.

———, and Lynda Lytle Holmstrom. 1974a. "Rape Trauma Syndrome." *American Journal of Psychiatry* 131: 981–86.

———. 1974b. *Rape: Victims of Crisis.* Bowie, MD: Robert J. Brady.

Burton, Lindy. 1968. *Vulnerable Children.* London: Routledge & Kegan Paul.

Butler, Sandra. 1978. *Conspiracy of Silence: The Trauma of Incest.* San Francisco: New Glide Publications.

———. 1980. "Incest: Whose Reality, Whose Theory?" *Aegis: Magazine on Ending Violence against Women* (summer/autumn): 48–55.

Calestro, Kenneth M. 1972. "Psychotherapy, Faith Healing, and Suggestion." *International Journal of Psychiatry* 10: 83–113.

Calof, David. 1993. "Facing the Truth about False Memory." *Family Therapy Networker* (September/October): 39–45.

Cavallin, Hector. 1966. "Incestuous Fathers: A Clinical Report." *American Journal of Psychiatry* 122: 1132–38.

Chaneles, Sol. 1967. "Child Victims of Sexual Offenses." *Federal Probation* (June): 52–56.

Chesler, Phyllis. 1972. *Women and Madness.* Garden City, NY: Doubleday.

Cimons, Marlene. 1974. "Rape Concern Reaches the Federal Level." *Los Angeles Times,* May 9, sec. 4.

Clark, Candace. 1987. "Sympathy Biography and Sympathy Margin." *American Journal of Sociology* 93: 290–321.

Connell, Noreen, and Cassandra Wilson, eds. 1974. *Rape: The First Sourcebook for Women.* New York: New American Library.

Conrad, Peter. 1992. "Medicalization and Social Control." *Annual Review of Sociology* 18: 209–32.

————, and Deborah Potter. 2000. "From Hyperactive Children to ADHD Adults: Observations on the Expansion of Medical Categories. *Social Problems* 47: 559–82.

————, and Joseph W. Schneider. 1992. *Deviance and Medicalization: From Badness to Sickness.* Expanded ed. Philadelphia, PA: Temple University Press.

Cormier, Bruno M., Miriam Kennedy, and Jadwiga Sangowicz. 1962. "Psychodynamics of Father-Daughter Incest." *Canadian Psychiatric Association Journal* 7: 203–17.

Corwin, David L. 1988. "Early Diagnosis of Child Sexual Abuse: Diminishing the Lasting Effects." In *Lasting Effects of Child Sexual Abuse,* ed. Gail Elizabeth Wyatt and Gloria Johnson Powell, 251–69. Newbury Park, CA: Sage.

Costin, Lela B., Howard Jacob Karger, and David Stoesz. 1996. *The Politics of Child Abuse in America.* New York: Oxford University Press.

Courtois, Christine A. 1988. *Healing the Incest Wound: Adult Survivors in Therapy.* New York: W. W. Norton.

————. 1995. "Forward." In *Sexual Abuse Recalled: Treating Trauma in the Era of the Recovered Memory Debate,* ed. Judith L. Alpert, vii–xiv. Northvale, NJ: Jason Aronson.

Crews, Frederick. 1995. *The Memory Wars: Freud's Legacy in Dispute.* New York: New York Review of Books.

Crowder, Adrienne. 1993. *Opening the Door: A Treatment Model for Therapy with Male Survivors of Sexual Abuse.* Ottawa: National Clearinghouse on Family Violence.

Csida, June Bundy, and Joseph Csida. 1974. *Rape: How to Avoid It, and What to Do about It If You Can't.* Chatsworth, CA: Books for Better Living.

Cushman, Philip. 1993. "Psychotherapy as Moral Discourse." *Journal of Theoretical and Philosophical Psychology* 13: 103–13.

Daugherty, Lynn B. 1984. *Why Me? Help for Victims of Child Sexual Abuse.* Racine, WI: Mother Courage Press.

Davies, Jody Messler, and Mary Gail Frawley. 1994. *Treating the Adult Survivor of Childhood Sexual Abuse: A Psychoanalytic Perspective.* New York: Basic Books.

Davis, Joseph E. 1993. *Thought Control, Totalism, and the Extension of the Anti-Cult Critique Beyond the "Cults."* Ann Arbor, MI: Tabor House. Available online at http://religiousmovements.lib.virginia.edu/cultsect/brainwash/davis.htm.

————. 1999. "'Retractor' Accounts of False Memories: A Countermovement's Strategic Use of Narrative." Paper presented at the 94th annual meeting of the American Sociological Association, Chicago, August 6–10.

————. 2000. "Accounts of False Memory Syndrome: Parents, 'Retractors,' and the Role of Institutions in Account Making." *Qualitative Sociology* 23: 29–56.

————. 2002a. "Narrative and Social Movements: The Power of Stories." In *Stories of Change: Narrative and Social Movements,* ed. Joseph E. Davis, 3–29. Albany: State University of New York Press.

————. 2002b. "If the 'Human' Is Finished, What Comes Next? A Review Essay," *Hedgehog Review* 4 (3): 110–25.

————. 2003. "Strangers in the Chancery." *Society* 40 (3): 25–34.

De Francis, Vincent. 1963a. *Child Abuse: Preview of a Nationwide Survey.* Denver: Children's Division, American Humane Association.

———. 1963b. "Parents Who Abuse Children." *PTA Magazine*, 16.

———. 1969. *Protecting the Child Victim of Sex Crimes Committed by Adults*. Denver, CO: American Humane Association Children's Division.

———. 1971. "Protecting the Child Victim of Sex Crimes Committed by Adults." *Federal Probation* (September): 15–20.

Deighton, Joan, and Phil McPeek. 1985. "Group Treatment: Adult Victims of Childhood Sexual Abuse." *Social Casework* 66: 403–10.

DeMott, Benjamin. 1980. "The Pro-Incest Lobby." *Psychology Today*, March, 11.

Dent, James K., and George A. Furse. 1978. *Exploring the Psycho-Social Therapies Through the Personalities of Effective Therapists*. Rockville, MD: Department of Health, Education and Welfare.

Denzin, Norman K. 1987. *The Alcoholic Self*. Newbury Park, CA: Sage.

de Rivera, Joseph. 1997. "The Construction of False Memory Syndrome: The Experience of Retractors." *Psychological Inquiry* 8: 271–92.

———. 2000. "Understanding Persons Who Repudiate Memories Recovered in Therapy." *Professional Psychology: Research and Practice* 31: 378–86.

Dershowitz, Alan M. 1994. *The Abuse Excuse*. Boston: Little, Brown.

Deutsch, Albert. 1950. "Sober Facts about Sex Crimes." *Collier's*, November 25, 15.

Dinter, Paul. 2003. "A Catholic Crisis, Bestowed from Above." *New York Times*, January 1, A15.

Dolan, Yvonne M. 1991. *Resolving Sexual Abuse: Solution-Focused Therapy and Ericksonian Hypnosis for Adult Survivors*. New York: W. W. Norton.

Donaldson, Mary Ann, and Russell Gardner Jr. 1985. "Diagnosis and Treatment of Traumatic Stress among Women after Childhood Incest." In *Trauma and Its Wake: The Study and Treatment of Post-Traumatic Stress Disorder*, ed. Charles R. Figley, 356–77. New York: Brunner/Mazel.

Douglas, Jack D. 1970. "Deviance and Respectability: The Social Construction of Moral Meanings." In *Deviance and Respectability: The Social Construction of Moral Meanings*, ed. Jack D. Douglas, 3–30. New York: Basic Books.

Douglas, Mary. 1970. *Natural Symbols: Explorations in Cosmology*. New York: Pantheon.

Draucker, Claire Burke. 1992. *Counselling Survivors of Childhood Sexual Abuse*. Newbury Park, CA: Sage.

Dunn, Robert G. 1998. *Identity Crises: A Social Critique of Postmodernity*. Minneapolis: University of Minnesota Press.

Echols, Alice. 1989. *Daring to Be Bad: Radical Feminism in America, 1967–1975*. Minneapolis: University of Minnesota Press.

Efran, Jay S., Michael D. Lukens, and Robert J. Lukens. 1990. *Language, Structure, and Change: Frameworks of Meaning in Psychotherapy*. New York: W. W. Norton.

Eist, Harold I., and Adeline U. Mandel. 1968. "Family Treatment of Ongoing Incest Behavior." *Family Process* 7: 216–32.

Ellenberger, Henri F. 1970. *The Discovery of the Unconscious*. New York: Basic Books.

Elliott, Carl. 1994. "Puppetmasters and Personality Disorders: Wittgenstein, Mechanism, and Moral Responsibility." *Philosophy, Psychiatry and Psychology* 1 (2): 91–100.

———. 2003. *Better Than Well: American Medicine Meets the American Dream.* New York: W. W. Norton.

Engel, Beverly. 1989. *The Right to Innocence: Healing the Trauma of Childhood Sexual Abuse.* Los Angeles: Jeremy P. Tarcher.

Engler, Jack, and Daniel Goleman. 1992. *The Consumer's Guide to Psychotherapy* New York: Simon & Schuster/Fireside.

Erdelyi, Matthew Hugh. 1990. "Repression, Reconstruction, and Defense: History and Integration of the Psychoanalytic and Experimental Frameworks." In *Repression and Dissociation: Implications for Personality, Theory, Psychopathology, and Health,* ed. Jerome L. Singer, 1–31. Chicago: University of Chicago Press.

Ernsdorff, Gary M., and Elizabeth F. Loftus. 1993. "Let Sleeping Memories Lie? Words of Caution about Tolling the Statute of Limitations in Cases of Memory Repression." *Journal of Criminal Law and Criminology* 84: 129–74.

Eth, Spencer, and Robert S. Pynoos. 1985. "Developmental Perspective on Psychic Trauma in Childhood." In *Trauma and Its Wake: The Study and Treatment of Post-Traumatic Stress Disorder,* ed. Charles R. Figley, 36–52. New York: Brunner/Mazel

Evans, Sandra. 1992. "Docket of Child Sex Abuse Cases Is Growing in Civil Courts." *Washington Post,* March 15, B5.

Ewick, Patricia, and Susan S. Silbey. 1995. "Subversive Stories and Hegemonic Tales: Toward a Sociology of Narrative." *Law and Society Review* 29: 197–226.

Farrell, Kirby. 1998. *Post-Traumatic Culture: Injury and Interpretation in the Nineties.* Baltimore, MD: Johns Hopkins University Press.

Feldman-Summers, Shirley, and Kenneth S. Pope. 1994. "The Experience of 'Forgetting' Childhood Abuse: A National Survey of Psychologists." *Journal of Consulting and Clinical Psychology* 62: 636–39.

Fine, Gary Alan. 1995. "Public Narration and Group Culture: Discerning Discourse in Social Movements." In *Social Movements and Culture,* ed. Hank Johnston and Bert Klandermans, 127–43. Minneapolis: University of Minnesota Press.

Finkelhor, David. 1979. *Sexually Victimized Children.* New York: Free Press.

———. 1988. "The Trauma of Child Sexual Abuse: Two Models." In *Lasting Effects of Child Sexual Abuse,* ed. Gail Elizabeth Wyatt and Gloria Johnson Powell, 61–82. Newbury Park, CA: Sage.

———, and Angela Browne. 1985. "The Traumatic Impact of Child Sexual Abuse: A Conceptualization." *American Journal of Orthopsychiatry* 55: 530–41.

Fleck, Stephen, Theodore Lidz, Alice Cornelison, Sarah Schafer, and Dorothy Terry. 1959. "The Intrafamilial Environment of the Schizophrenic Patient." In *Science and Psychoanalysis.* Vol. 2. *Individual and Familial Dynamics,* ed. Jules H. Masserman, 142–59. New York: Grune & Stratton.

Fogarty, Faith. 1977. "A Selective Bibliography." In *Forcible Rape: The Crime, the Victim, and the Offender,* ed. Duncan Chappell, Robley Geis, and Gilbert Geis, 356–82. New York: Columbia University Press.

Forward, Susan, and Craig Buck. 1978. *Betrayal of Innocence: Incest and Its Devastation.* Los Angeles: Jeremy P. Tarcher.

Foucault, Michel. 1965. *Madness and Civilization.* New York: Pantheon.

————. 1988. "Technologies of the Self." In *Technologies of the Self*, ed. Luther H. Martin, Huck Gutman, and Patrick H. Hutton, 16–49. Amherst: University of Massachusetts Press.

Fox, Renee. 1977. "The Medicalization and Demedicalization of American Society." *Daedalus* 106 (1): 9–22.

Frank, Arthur W. 1995. *The Wounded Storyteller: Body, Illness, and Ethics*. Chicago: University of Chicago Press.

————. 1998. "Stories of Illness as Care of the Self: A Foucauldian Dialogue." *Health* 2 (3): 329–48.

Frank, Jerome D., and Julia B. Frank. 1991. *Persuasion and Healing: A Comparative Study of Psychotherapy*. 3d ed. Baltimore, MD: Johns Hopkins University Press.

Fraser, Brian G. 1981. "Sexual Child Abuse: The Legislation and the Law in the United States." In *Sexually Abused Children and their Families*, ed. Patricia Beezley Mrazek and C. Henry Kempe, 55–73. Oxford: Pergamon Press.

Fredrickson, Renee. 1992. *Repressed Memories: A Journey to Recovery from Sexual Abuse*. New York: Simon & Schuster/Fireside.

Freedman, Estelle B. 1987. " 'Uncontrolled Desires': The Response to the Sexual Psychopath, 1920–1960." *Journal of American History* 74: 83–106.

Freidson, Eliot. 1970. *Profession of Medicine: A Study of the Sociology of Applied Knowledge*. Chicago: University of Chicago Press.

French, Laurence A., and S. N. Wailes. 1982. "Perceptions of Sexual Deviance: A Bi-racial Analysis." *International Journal of Offender Therapy and Comparative Criminology* 26: 242–49.

Freud, Sigmund. 1962a. "The Aetiology of Hysteria." In *Standard Edition of the Complete Psychological Works of Sigmund Freud*, ed. James Strachey, 3: 191–221. London: Hogarth Press.

————. 1962b. "Further Remarks on the Neuro-Psychoses of Defense." In *Standard Edition of the Complete Psychological Works of Sigmund Freud*, ed. James Strachey, 3: 162–85. London: Hogarth Press.

Friedrich, William N., and Jerry A. Boriskin. 1976. "The Role of the Child in Abuse: A Review of the Literature." *American Journal of Orthopsychiatry* 46: 580–90.

Gager, Nancy, and Cathleen Schurr. 1976. *Sexual Assault: Confronting Rape in America*. New York: Grosset & Dunlap.

Gagnon, John H. 1965. "Female Child Victims of Sex Offenses." *Social Problems* 13: 176–92.

Gamson, William A. 1992. *Talking Politics*. Cambridge, MA: Cambridge University Press.

————. 1995. "Constructing Social Protest." In *Social Movements and Culture*, ed. Hank Johnston and Bert Klandermans, 85–106. Minneapolis: University of Minnesota Press.

Garfield, Sol L., and Allen E. Bergin, eds. 1986. *Handbook of Psychotherapy and Behavior Change*. New York: John Wiley & Sons.

Garfinkel, Harold. 1956. "Conditions of Successful Degradation Ceremonies." *American Journal of Sociology* 61: 420–24.

————. 1967. *Studies in Ethnomethodology.* Englewood Cliffs, NJ: Prentice Hall.

Gebhard, Paul H., John H. Gagnon, Wardell B. Pomeroy, and Cornelia V. Christenson. 1965. *Sex Offenders: An Analysis of Types.* New York: Harper & Row.

Geiser, Robert L. 1979. *Hidden Victims: The Sexual Abuse of Children.* Boston: Beacon Press.

Gelinas, Denise J. 1983. "The Persisting Negative Effects of Incest." *Psychiatry* 46: 312–32.

Gergen, Kenneth J. 1994. *Realities and Relationships: Soundings in Social Construction.* Cambridge, MA: Harvard University Press.

Gersons, Berthold P. R., and Ingrid V. E. Carlier. 1992. "Post-Traumatic Stress Disorder: The History of a Recent Concept." *British Journal of Psychiatry* 161: 742–48.

Giarretto, Henry. 1976a. "Humanistic Treatment of Father-Daughter Incest." In *Child Abuse and Neglect: The Family and the Community,* ed. Ray E. Helfer and C. Henry Kempe, 143–58. Cambridge, MA: Ballinger.

————. 1976b. "The Treatment of Father-Daughter Incest: A Psycho-Social Approach." *Children Today,* July–Aug., 2.

————. 1981. "A Comprehensive Child Sexual Abuse Treatment Program." In *Sexually Abused Children and their Families,* ed. Patricia Beezley Mrazek and C. Henry Kempe, 179–98. Oxford: Pergamon Press.

————. 1982. *Integrated Treatment of Child Sexual Abuse: A Treatment and Training Manual.* Palo Alto, CA: Science and Behavior Books.

————, Anna Giarretto, and Suzanne M. Sgroi. 1978. "Coordinated Community Treatment of Incest." In *Sexual Assault of Children and Adolescents,* ed. Ann Wolbert Burgess, A. Nicholas Groth, Lynda Lytle Holmstrom, and Suzanne M. Sgroi, 231–40. Lexington, MA: Lexington Books.

Gibbens, T. C. N., and Joyce Prince. 1963. *Child Victims of Sex Offenses.* London: Institute for the Study and Treatment of Delinquency.

Giddens, Anthony. 1991. *Modernity and Self-Identity.* Stanford, CA: Stanford University Press.

Gil, David G. 1970. *Violence against Children. Physical Child Abuse in the United States.* Cambridge, MA: Harvard University Press.

Gil, Eliana. 1983. *Outgrowing the Pain: A Book for and about Adults Abused as Children.* New York: Dell.

————. 1988. *Treatment of Adult Survivors of Child Abuse.* Walnut Creek, CA: Launch Press.

Gilbert, Neil. 1994. "Miscounting Social Ills." *Society* 31 (3): 26–34.

Glaser, Barney G., and Anselm L. Strauss. 1967. *The Discovery of Grounded Theory.* Chicago: Aldine.

Goffman, Erving. 1961. *Asylums.* New York: Anchor Books.

Goldstein, Eleanor. 1992. *Confabulations: Creating False Memories, Destroying Families.* Boca Raton, FL: SIRS Books.

————, and Kevin Farmer. 1993. *True Stories of False Memories.* Boca Raton, FL: SIRS Books.

Goleman, Daniel. 1992. "Childhood Trauma: Memory or Invention?" *New York Times,* July 21, C1.

Gondolf, Lynn Price. 1992. "Traumatic Therapy." *Issues in Child Abuse Accusations* 4: 239–45.

Goodman, Nelson. 1978. *Ways of Worldmaking.* Indianapolis, IN: Hackett.

Goodwin, Jean. 1985. "Post-Traumatic Symptoms in Incest Victims." In *Post-Traumatic Stress Disorder in Children,* ed. Spencer Eth and Robert S. Pynoos, 155–68. Washington, DC: American Psychiatric Press.

Gordon, Lillian. 1955. "Incest as Revenge against the Pre-Oedipal Mother." *Psychoanalytic Review* 42: 284–92.

Gordon, Linda. 1988. "The Politics of Child Sexual Abuse: Notes from American History." *Feminist Review,* January: 56–64.

Green, Arthur H. 1983. "Child Abuse: Dimension of Psychological Trauma in Abused Children." *Journal of the American Academy of Child Psychiatry* 22: 231–37.

———. 1985. "Children Traumatized by Physical Abuse." In *Post-Traumatic Stress Disorder in Children,* ed. Spencer Eth and Robert S. Pynoos, 133–54. Washington, DC: American Psychiatric Press.

Greenland, Cyril. 1958. "Incest." *British Journal of Delinquency* 9: 62–65.

Grob, Gerald N. 1994. *The Mad among Us.* New York: Free Press.

Gross, Jane. 1994. "Suit Asks, Does 'Memory Therapy' Heal or Harm?" *New York Times,* April 8, A1.

Gubrium, Jaber F., and James A. Holstein, eds. 2001. *Institutional Selves: Troubled Identities in a Postmodern World.* New York: Oxford University Press.

Gusfield, Joseph R. 1981. *The Culture of Public Problems.* Chicago: University of Chicago Press.

Guttmacher, Manfred S. 1951. *Sex Offenses: The Problem, Causes, and Prevention.* New York: W. W. Norton.

Haaken, Janice. 1993. "From Al-Anon to ACOA: Codependence and the Reconstruction of Caregiving." *Signs* 18: 321–45.

———. 1994. "Sexual Abuse, Recovered Memory, and Therapeutic Practice: A Feminist-Psychoanalytic Perspective." *Social Text* 40: 115–45.

———. 1996. "The Recovery of Memory, Fantasy, and Desire: Approaches to Sexual Abuse and Psychic Trauma." *Signs* 21: 1069–94.

Hacking, Ian. 1986. "Making Up People." In *Reconstructing Individualism: Autonomy, Individuality, and the Self in Western Thought,* ed. Thomas C. Heller, Morton Sosna, and David E. Wellbery, 222–36. Stanford, CA: Stanford University Press.

———. 1991. "The Making and Molding of Child Abuse." *Critical Inquiry* 17: 253–88.

———. 1992. "World-Making by Kind-Making: Child Abuse for Example." In *How Classification Works: Nelson Goodman among the Social Sciences,* ed. Mary Douglas and David Hull, 180–238. Edinburgh, Scotland: Edinburgh University Press.

———. 1995. *Rewriting the Soul: Multiple Personality and the Sciences of Memory.* Princeton, NJ: Princeton University Press.

———. 1997. "Taking Bad Arguments Seriously." *London Review of Books,* August 21, 14–16.

———. 1998. *Mad Travelers: Reflections on the Reality of Transient Mental Illnesses.* Charlottesville: University Press of Virginia.

Haley, Jay. 1971a. "A Review of the Family Therapy Field." In *Changing Families: A Family Therapy Reader,* ed. Jay Haley, 1–12. New York: Grune & Stratton.

———. 1971b. "Family Therapy: A Radical Change." In *Changing Families: A Family Therapy Reader,* ed. Jay Haley, 272–84. New York: Grune & Stratton.

Hall, Liz, and Siobhan Lloyd. 1989. *Surviving Child Sexual Abuse: A Handbook for Helping Women Challenge their Past.* New York: Falmer Press.

Hamilton, G. V. 1929. *A Research in Marriage.* New York: Albert & Charles Boni.

Harvey, John H., Terri L. Orbuch, and Ann L. Weber. 1992. "Introduction: Convergence of the Attribution and Accounts Concepts in the Study of Close Relationships." In *Attributions, Accounts, and Close Relationships,* ed. John H. Harvey, Terri L. Orbuch and Ann L. Weber, 1–18. New York: Springer-Verlag.

———, Ann L. Weber, K. S. Galvin, H. C. Huszti, and N. N. Garnick. 1986. "Attribution in the Termination of Close Relationships: A Special Focus on the Account." In *The Emerging Field of Personal Relationships,* ed. Robin Gilmour and Steve Duck, 189–201. Hillsdale, NJ: Lawrence Erlbaum Associates.

———, Ann L. Weber, and Terri L. Orbuch. 1990. *Interpersonal Accounts: A Social Psychological Perspective.* Cambridge, MA: Basil Blackwell.

Haugaard, Jeffrey J., and N. Dickon Reppucci. 1988. *The Sexual Abuse of Children: A Comprehensive Guide to Current Knowledge and Intervention Strategies.* San Francisco: Jossey-Bass.

Hechler, David. 1988. *The Battle and the Backlash: The Child Sexual Abuse War.* Lexington, MA: Lexington Books.

Helfer, Ray E., and C. Henry Kempe, eds. 1976. *Child Abuse and Neglect: The Family and the Community.* Cambridge, MA: Ballinger.

Henderson, D. James. 1975. "Incest." In *Comprehensive Textbook of Psychiatry,* 2nd ed., ed. Alfred M. Freedman, Harold I. Kaplan, and Benjamin J. Sadock, 1530–39. Baltimore, MD: Williams and Wilkins.

Herman, Ellen. 1995. *The Romance of American Psychology: Political Culture in the Age of Experts.* Berkeley and Los Angeles: University of California Press.

Herman, Judith Lewis. 1981. *Father-Daughter Incest.* Cambridge, MA: Harvard University Press.

———. 1992. *Trauma and Recovery: The Aftermath of Violence: From Domestic Abuse to Political Terror.* New York: Basic Books.

———. 1994. "Presuming to Know the Truth." *Moving Forward* (September/October): 12–13.

———. 1997. *Trauma and Recovery: The Aftermath of Violence—From Domestic Abuse to Political Terror.* Reprint ed. New York: Basic Books.

———, and Bessel A. van der Kolk. 1987. "Traumatic Antecedents of Borderline Personality Disorder." In *Psychological Trauma,* ed. Bessel A. van der Kolk, 111–26. Washington, DC: American Psychiatric Press.

———, and Emily Schatzow. 1987. "Recovery and Verification of Memories of Childhood Sexual Trauma." *Psychoanalytic Psychology* 4: 1–14.

———, J. Christopher Perry, and Bessel A. van der Kolk. 1989. "Childhood Trauma in Borderline Personality Disorder." *American Journal of Psychiatry* 146: 490–95.

————, and Lisa Hirschman. 1977. "Father-Daughter Incest." *Signs* 2: 735–56.

Hicks, Dorothy J., and Charlotte R. Platt. 1976. "Medical Treatment for the Victim: The Development of a Rape Treatment Center." In *Sexual Assault: The Victim and the Rapist,* ed. Marcia J. Walker and Stanley L. Brodsky, 53–59. Lexington, MA: D.C. Heath.

Hilgard, Ernest R. 1977. *Divided Consciousness: Multiple Controls in Human Thought and Action.* New York: John Wiley & Sons.

Hinchman, Lewis P., and Sandra K. Hinchman, eds. 1997. *Memory, Identity, Community: The Idea of Narrative in the Human Sciences.* Albany: State University of New York Press.

Hochschild, Arlie Russell. 1979. "Emotion Work, Feeling Rules, and Social Structure." *American Journal of Sociology* 85: 551–75.

Hoffman, Ellen. 1978. "Policy and Politics: The Child Abuse Prevention and Treatment Act." *Public Policy* 26: 71–88.

Holstein, James A., and Gale Miller. 1990. "Rethinking Victimization: An Interactional Approach to Victimology." *Symbolic Interaction* 13: 103–22.

————, and Jaber F. Gubrium. 2000. *The Self We Live By: Narrative Identity in a Postmodern World.* New York: Oxford University Press.

Horowitz, Mardi Jon. 1976. *Stress Response Syndromes.* New York: Jason Aronson.

Horwitz, Allan V. 1982. *The Social Control of Mental Illness.* New York: Academic Press.

————. 2002. *Creating Mental Illness.* Chicago: University of Chicago Press.

Howard, George S. 1990. "Narrative Psychotherapy." In *What Is Psychotherapy?* ed. Jeffrey K. Zeig and W. Michael Munion, 199–201. San Francisco: Jossey-Bass.

Hughes, Robert. 1993. *Culture of Complaint: The Fraying of America.* New York: Warner Books.

Hunt, Scott A., and Robert D. Benford. 1994. "Identity Talk in the Peace and Justice Movement." *Journal of Contemporary Ethnography* 22: 488–517.

————, Robert D. Benford, and David A. Snow. 1994. "Identity Fields: Framing Processes and the Social Construction of Movement Identities." In *New Social Movements,* ed. Enrique Laraña, Hank Johnston, and Joseph R. Gusfield, 185–208. Philadelphia: Temple University Press.

Irvine, Leslie. 1999. *Codependent Forevermore: The Invention of Self in a Twelve-Step Group.* Chicago: University of Chicago Press.

JAMA. 1962. "The Battered-Child Syndrome." Editorial. *Journal of the American Medical Association* 181 (1): 42.

Janoff-Bulman, Ronnie. 1985. "The Aftermath of Victimization: Rebuilding Shattered Assumptions." In *Trauma and Its Wake: The Study and Treatment of Post-Traumatic Stress Disorder,* ed. Charles R. Figley, 15–35. New York: Brunner/Mazel.

Jehu, Derek. 1988. *Beyond Sexual Abuse: Therapy with Women Who Were Childhood Victims.* New York: John Wiley & Sons.

Jenkins, Philip. 1998. *Moral Panic: Changing Concepts of the Child Molester in Modern America.* New Haven, CT: Yale University Press.

Johnson, John M. 1986. "Symbolic Salvation: The Changing Meanings of the Child Maltreatment Movement." *Studies in Symbolic Interaction* 6: 289–305.

———. 1989. "Horror Stories and the Construction of Child Abuse." In *Images of Issues: Typifying Contemporary Social Problems*, 2d ed., ed. Joel Best, 17–31. New York: Aldine de Gruyter.

Johnston, Hank, Enrique Laraña, and Joseph R. Gusfield. 1994. "Identities, Grievances, and New Social Movements." In *New Social Movements: From Ideology to Identity*, ed. Enrique Laraña, Hank Johnston, and Joseph R. Gusfield, 3–35. Philadelphia, PA: Temple University Press.

Jones, Elsa. 1991. *Working with Adult Survivors of Child Sexual Abuse*. London: Karnac Books.

Justice, Blair, and Rita Justice. 1979. *The Broken Taboo: Sex in the Family*. New York: Human Sciences Press.

Kadushin, Alfred. 1974. *Child Welfare Services*. 2nd ed. New York: Macmillan.

Kaminer, Wendy. 1992. *I'm Dysfunctional, You're Dysfunctional: The Recovery Movement and Other Self-Help Fashions*. Reading, MA: Addison-Wesley.

———. 1993. "Feminism's Identity Crisis." *Atlantic Monthly*, October, 51–68.

Karp, David A. 1996. *Speaking of Sadness: Depression, Disconnection, and the Meanings of Illness*. New York: Oxford University Press.

———. 2002. *The Burden of Sympathy: How Families Cope with Mental Illness*. New York: Oxford University Press.

Karpman, Benjamin. 1954. *The Sexual Offender and His Offenses: Etiology, Pathology, Psychodynamics, and Treatment*. New York: Julian Press.

Kaufman, Irving, Alice L. Peck, and Consuelo K. Tagiuri. 1954. "The Family Constellation and Overt Incestuous Relations between Father and Daughter." *American Journal of Orthopsychiatry* 24: 266–77.

Keefe, Mary L., and Henry T. O'Reilly. 1976. "The Police and the Rape Victim in New York." *Victimology* 1: 272–83.

Kelly, Timothy A, and Hans H. Strupp. 1992. "Patient and Therapist Values in Psychotherapy: Perceived Changes, Assimilation, Similarity, and Outcome." *Journal of Consulting and Clinical Psychology* 60: 34–40.

Kempe, C. Henry. 1978. "Sexual Abuse, Another Hidden Pediatric Problem: The 1977 C. Anderson Aldrich Lecture." *Pediatrics* 62: 382–89.

———, and Ray E. Helfer, eds. 1972. *Helping the Battered Child and His Family*. Philadelphia, PA: J. B. Lippincott.

———, Frederic N. Silverman, Brandt F. Steele, William Droegemueller, and Henry K. Silver. 1962. "The Battered-Child Syndrome." *Journal of the American Medical Association* 181 (1): 17–24.

Kerby, Paul Anthony. 1991. *Narrative and the Self*. Bloomington: Indiana University Press.

Kercher, Glen A., and Marilyn McShane. 1984. "The Prevalence of Child Sexual Abuse Victimization in an Adult Sample of Texas Residents." *Child Abuse and Neglect* 8: 495–501.

Kihlstrom, John F. 1996. "The Trauma-Memory Argument and Recovered Memory Therapy." In *The Recovered Memory/False Memory Debate*, ed. Kathy Pezdek and William P. Banks, 297–311. San Diego, CA: Academic Press.

———. 1998. "Exhumed Memory." In *Truth in Memory*, ed. Steven Jay Lynn and Kevin M. McConkey, 3–31. New York: Guilford Press.

Kilpatrick, Allie C. 1987. "Childhood Sexual Experiences: Problems and Issues in Studying Long-Range Effects." *Journal of Sex Research* 23: 173–96.

Kilpatrick, Dean G., Lois J. Veronen, and Connie L. Best. 1985. "Factors Predicting Psychological Stress Among Rape Victims." In *Trauma and Its Wake: The Study and Treatment of Post-traumatic Stress Disorder*, ed. Charles R. Figley, 113–41. New York: Brunner/Mazel.

Kinsey, Alfred C., Wardell B. Pomeroy, and Clyde E. Martin. 1948. *Sexual Behavior in the Human Male*. Philadelphia, PA: W. B. Saunders.

———, Wardell B. Pomeroy, Clyde E. Martin, and Paul H. Gebhard. 1953. *Sexual Behavior in the Human Female*. Philadelphia, PA: W. B. Saunders.

Kirk, Stuart A., and Herb Kutchins. 1992. *The Selling of DSM: The Rhetoric of Science in Psychiatry*. New York: Aldine de Gruyter.

Kirschner, Sam, Diana Adile Kirschner, and Richard L. Rappaport. 1993. *Working with Adult Incest Survivors: The Healing Journey*. New York: Brunner/Mazel.

Klein, Melanie. 1932. *The Psychoanalysis of Children*. London: Hogarth Press.

Kleinman, Arthur. 1988. *Rethinking Psychiatry: From Cultural Category to Personal Experience*. New York: Free Press.

Kluft, Richard P., ed. 1985. *Childhood Antecedents of Multiple Personality*. Washington, DC: American Psychiatric Press.

Kroll, Jerome. 1993. *PTSD/Borderlines in Therapy: Finding the Balance*. New York: W. W. Norton.

Kroth, Jerome A. 1979. *Child Sexual Abuse: Analysis of a Family Therapy Approach*. Springfield, IL: Charles C Thomas.

Landis, Carney, et al. 1940. *Sex in Development*. New York: Paul B. Hoeber.

Landis, Judson T. 1956. "Experiences of 500 Children with Adult Sexual Deviation." *Psychiatric Quarterly* 30 (supp.): 91–109.

Lanning, Kenneth V. 1992. *Investigator's Guide to Allegations of "Ritual" Child Abuse*. Quantico, VA: National Center for the Analysis of Violent Crime, FBI Academy.

Largen, Mary Ann. 1976. "History of Women's Movement in Changing Attitudes, Laws, and Treatment toward Rape Victims." In *Sexual Assault: The Victim and the Rapist*, ed. Marcia J. Walker and Stanley L. Brodsky, 69–73. Lexington, MA: DC Heath.

———. 1981. "Grassroots Centers and National Task Forces: A Herstory of the Anti-Rape Movement." *Aegis: Magazine on Ending Violence against Women* (autumn): 46–52.

Lasch, Christopher. 1984. *The Minimal Self: Psychic Survival in Troubled Times*. New York: W. W. Norton.

Laumann, Edward O., John H. Gagnon, Robert T. Michael, and Stuart Michaels. 1994. *The Social Organization of Sexuality: Sexual Practices in the United States*. Chicago: University of Chicago Press.

Law, Bernard Cardinal. 2002. " 'My Apology ... Comes from a Grieving Heart.' " *Boston Globe*, January 10, A19.

Lear, Jonathan. 1995. "The Shrink Is In." *The New Republic*, December 25, 18–25.

Lemann, Nicholas. 1992. "The Vogue of Childhood Misery." *Atlantic Monthly*, March, 119–24.

Levy, Sheldon S. 1951. "Interaction of Institutions and Policy Groups: The Origin of Sex Crime Legislation." *Lawyer and Law Notes* 5 (1): 3–12.

Lew, Mike. 1990. *Victims No Longer: Men Recovering from Incest and Other Sexual Child Abuse*. New York: HarperCollins.

Leys, Ruth. 2000. *Trauma: A Genealogy*. Chicago: University of Chicago Press.

Li, C. K., D. J. West, and T. P. Woodhouse. 1990. *Children's Sexual Encounters with Adults*. London: Duckworth.

Liberman, Bernard L. 1978. "The Role of Mastery in Psychotherapy: Maintenance of Improvement and Prescriptive Change." In *Effective Ingredients of Successful Psychotherapy*, ed. Jerome D. Frank et al., 35–72. New York: Brunner/Mazel.

Lief, Harold I., and Janet Fetkewicz. 1995. "Retractors of False Memories: The Evolution of Pseudomemories." *Journal of Psychiatry and Law* 23: 411–35.

Lifton, Robert Jay. 1961. *Thought Reform and the Psychology of Totalism*. New York: W. W. Norton.

Lindberg, Frederick H., and Lois J. Distad. 1985. "Post-Traumatic Stress Disorders in Women Who Experienced Childhood Incest." *Child Abuse and Neglect* 9: 329–34.

Loewenstein, Richard J. 1990. "Somatoform Disorders in Victims of Incest and Child Abuse." In *Incest-Related Syndromes of Adult Psychopathology*, ed. Richard P. Kluft, 75–107. Washington, DC: American Psychiatric Press.

Loftus, Elizabeth F. 1993a. "The Reality of Repressed Memories." *American Psychologist* 48: 518–37.

———. 1993b. "You Must Remember This ... Or Do You? How Real Are Repressed Memories?" *Washington Post*, June 27, C1.

———. 1996. "Repressed Memory Litigation: Court Cases and Scientific Findings on Illusory Memory." *Washington State Bar News*, January, 15–25.

———, and Katherine Ketcham. 1994. *The Myth of Repressed Memory*. New York. St. Martin's Press.

London, Perry. 1964. *The Modes and Morals of Psychotherapy*. New York: Holt, Rinehart and Winston.

Loseke, Donileen R. 1992. *The Battered Woman and Shelters: The Social Construction of Wife Abuse*. Albany: State University of New York Press.

———. 1993. "Constructing Conditions, People, Morality, and Emotion: Expanding the Agenda of Constructionism." In *Constructionist Controversies: Issues in Social Problems Theory*, ed. Gale Miller and James A. Holstein, 207–16. New York: Aldine de Gruyter.

———. 1999. *Thinking about Social Problems: An Introduction to Constructionist Perspectives*. New York: Aldine de Gruyter.

———. 2001. "Lived Realities and Formula Stories of "Battered Women."" In *Institutional Selves: Troubled Identities in a Postmodern World*, ed. Jaber F. Gubrium and James A. Holstein, 107–26. New York: Oxford University Press.

Lowney, Kathleen S., and Joel Best. 1995. "Stalking Strangers and Lovers: Changing Media Typifications of a New Crime Problem." In *Images of Issues: Typifying*

Contemporary Social Problems, 2nd ed., ed. Joel Best, 33–57. New York: Aldine de Gruyter.

Luborsky, Lester, George E. Woody, A. Thomas McLellan, Charles P. O'Brien, and Jerry Rosenzweig. 1982. "Can Independent Judges Recognize Different Psychotherapies? An Experience with Manual-Guided Therapies." *Journal of Consulting and Clinical Psychology* 50: 49–62.

Lukianowicz, Narcyz. 1972. "Incest." *The British Journal of Psychiatry* 120: 301–13.

Lustig, Noel, John W. Dresser, Seth W. Spellman, and Thomas B. Murray. 1966. "Incest: A Family Group Survival Pattern." *Archives of General Psychiatry* 14: 31–40.

MacFarlane, Kee. 1978. "Sexual Abuse of Children." In *The Victimization of Women*, ed. Jane Roberts Chapman and Margaret Gates, 81–109. Beverly Hills, CA: Sage.

Machotka, Pavel, Frank S. Pittman III, and Kalman Flomenhaft. 1967. "Incest as a Family Affair." *Family Process* 6: 98–116.

MacIntyre, Alasdair. 1984. *After Virtue: A Study in Moral Theory*. 2d ed. Notre Dame, IN: University of Notre Dame Press.

Mack, John. E. 1994. *Abduction: Human Encounters with Aliens*. New York: Charles Scribner's Sons.

Mahoney, Michael J. 1995. "The Psychological Demands of Being a Constructive Psychotherapist." In *Constructivism in Psychotherapy*, ed. Robert A. Neimeyer and Michael J. Mahoney, 385–99. Washington, DC: American Psychological Association.

Maisch, Herbert. 1972. *Incest*. New York: Stein and Day.

Malcolm, Janet. 1983. "Six Roses ou Cirrhose?" *New Yorker*, January 24, 96.

Manchester, Anthony Hugh. 1979. "The Law of Incest in England and Wales." *Child Abuse and Neglect* 3: 679–82.

Mangus, A. R. 1952. "Sex Crimes against Children." In *Sexual Deviation Research*, ed. Karl M. Bowman, 45–66. Sacramento: Assembly of the State of California.

———. 1953. "Sex Crimes in California." In *California Sexual Deviation Research*, ed. Karl M. Bowman, 9–46. Sacramento: Assembly of the State of California.

Martin, Harold P., ed. 1976. *The Abused Child: A Multidisciplinary Approach to Development Issues and Treatment*. Cambridge, MA: Ballinger.

Mason-Schrock, Douglas. 1996. "Transsexuals' Narrative Construction of the 'True Self.' " *Social Psychology Quarterly* 59: 176–92.

Masson, Jeffrey Moussaieff. 1984. *The Assault on Truth: Freud's Suppression of the Seduction Theory*. New York: Farrar, Straus & Giroux.

Masters, Robert E. L. 1963. *Patterns of Incest: A Psycho-Social Study of Incest Based on Clinical and Historic Data*. New York: Julian Press.

Mathews, Joan. 1974. "Rape Bibliography." In *Rape: The First Sourcebook for Women*, ed. Noreen Connell and Cassandra Wilson, 113–22. New York: New American Library.

Matthews, Nancy A. 1994. *Confronting Rape: The Feminist Anti-Rape Movement and the State*. New York: Routledge.

Mattingly, Cheryl. 1998. *Healing Dramas and Clinical Plots: The Narrative Structure of Experience*. Cambridge: Cambridge University Press.

McCaghy, Charles H. 1968. "Drinking and Deviance Disavowal: The Case of Child Molesters." *Social Problems* 16: 43–49.

McElroy, Susan L., and Paul E. Keck. 1995. "Recovered Memory Therapy: False Memory Syndrome and Other Complications." *Psychiatric Annals* 25: 731–35.

McFarlane, Alexander C., and Bessel A. van der Kolk. 1996. "Trauma and Its Challenge to Society." In *Traumatic Stress: The Effects of Overwhelming Experience on Mind, Body, and Society*, ed. Bessel A. van der Kolk, Alexander C. McFarlane, and Lars Weisaeth, 24–46. New York: Guilford Press.

McHugh, Paul R. 1992. "Psychiatric Misadventures." *American Scholar* 61: 497–510.

———. 1994. "Psychotherapy Awry." *American Scholar* 63: 17–30.

McIntyre, Kevin. 1981. "Role of Mothers in Father-Daughter Incest: A Feminist Analysis." *Social Work* 26: 462–66.

McNally, Richard J. 2003. *Remembering Trauma.* Cambridge, MA: Harvard University Press.

McNaron, Toni A. H., and Yarrow Morgan, eds. 1982. *Voices in the Night: Women Speaking About Incest.* Pittsburgh, PA: Cleis Press.

Medea, Andra, and Kathleen Thompson. 1974. *Against Rape.* New York: Farrar, Straus & Giroux.

Meiselman, Karin C. 1978. *Incest: A Psychological Study of Causes and Effects with Treatment Recommendations.* San Francisco: Jossey-Bass.

———. 1990. *Resolving the Trauma of Incest: Reintegration Therapy with Survivors.* San Francisco: Jossey-Bass.

Merskey, H. 1992. "The Manufacture of Personalities: The Production of Multiple Personality Disorder." *British Journal of Psychiatry* 160: 327–40.

Miller, Alice. 1984. *Thou Shalt Not Be Aware: Society's Betrayal of the Child.* New York: Farrar, Straus & Giroux.

Miller, Gale, and James A. Holstein. 1989. "On the Sociology of Social Problems." In *Perspectives on Social Problems*, ed. James A. Holstein and Gale Miller, 1–16. Greenwich, CT: JAI Press.

Mithers, Carol Lynn. 1990. "Incest and the Law." *New York Times Magazine*, October 21, 44.

Mohr, Johann W. 1962. "The Pedophilias: Their Clinical, Social and Legal Implications." *Canadian Psychiatric Association Journal* 7: 255–60.

Morris, Michelle. 1982. *If I Should Die Before I Wake.* Los Angeles: J. P. Tarcher.

Morris, M. 1992. " 'False Memory Syndrome' Taking Its Toll on Families." *Utah County Journal*, April 21, A-8.

Moskowitz, Eva S. 2001. *In Therapy We Trust: America's Obsession with Self-Fulfillment.* Baltimore, MD: Johns Hopkins University Press.

Mrazek, Patricia Beezley, and Arnon Bentovim. 1981. "Incest and the Dysfunctional Family System." In *Sexually Abused Children and Their Families*, ed. Patricia Beezley Mrazek and C. Henry Kempe, 167–78. Oxford: Pergamon Press.

———, and David A. Mrazek. 1981. "The Effects of Child Sexual Abuse: Methodological Considerations." In *Sexually Abused Children and Their Families*, ed. Patricia Beezley Mrazek and C. Henry Kempe, 235–45. Oxford: Pergamon Press.

Mulhern, Sherrill. 1991. "Satanism and Psychotherapy: A Rumor in Search of an Inquisition." In *The Satanism Scare*, ed. James T. Richardson, Joel Best, and David G. Bromley, 145–72. New York: Aldine de Gruyter.

Murdock, George P. 1949. *Social Structure.* New York: Macmillan.

Nathan, Debbie. 1991. *Women and Other Aliens: Essays from the U.S.-Mexico Border.* El Paso: Cinco Puntos Press.

————, and Michael Snedeker. 1995. *Satan's Silence: Ritual Abuse and the Making of a Modern American Witch Hunt.* New York: Basic Books.

Neimeyer, Robert A. 1995. "Client-Generated Narratives in Psychotherapy." In *Constructivism in Psychotherapy,* ed. Robert A. Neimeyer and Michael J. Mahoney, 231–46. Washington, DC: American Psychological Association.

————, and Michael J. Mahoney, eds. 1995. *Constructivism in Psychotherapy.* Washington, DC: American Psychological Association.

Nelson, Barbara J. 1984. *Making an Issue of Child Abuse: Political Agenda Setting for Social Problems.* Chicago: University of Chicago Press.

Nelson, Eric L., and Paul Simpson. 1994. "First Glimpse: An Initial Examination of Subjects Who Have Rejected Their Recovered Visualizations as False Memories." *Issues in Child Abuse Accusations* 6: 123–33.

Nelson, Hilde Lindemann. 2001. *Damaged Identities, Narrative Repair.* Ithaca, NY: Cornell University Press.

Nichols, William C. 1992. *Treating Adult Survivors of Childhood Sexual Abuse.* Sarasota, FL: Professional Resource Press.

Nolan, Jr., James L. 2001. *Reinventing Justice: The American Drug Court Movement.* Princeton, NJ: Princeton University Press.

NOW Child Sexual Abuse Task Force. 1976. *Child Sexual Abuse.* San Jose, CA: California NOW.

Ofshe, Richard, and Ethan Watters. 1994. *Making Monsters: False Memories, Psychotherapy, and Sexual Hysteria.* New York: Charles Scribner's Sons.

O'Neal, Patricia, Jeanette Schaefer, John Bergmann, and Lee N. Robins. 1960. "A Psychiatric Evaluation of Adults Who Had Sexual Problems as Children: A Thirty-Year Follow-Up Study." *Human Organization* 19: 32–39.

Orbuch, Terri L. 1997. "People's Accounts Count: The Sociology of Accounts." *Annual Review of Sociology* 23: 455–78.

Ost, James, Alan Costall, and Ray Bull. 2001. "False Confessions and False Memories: A Model for Understanding Retractors' Experiences." *Journal of Forensic Psychiatry* 12: 549–79.

————. 2002. "A Perfect Symmetry? A Study of Retractors' Experiences of Making and Then Repudiating Claims of Early Sexual Abuse." *Psychology, Crime and Law* 8: 155–81.

Pande, Shashi K. 1968. "The Mystique of 'Western' Psychotherapy: An Eastern Interpretation." *Journal of Nervous and Mental Disease* 146: 425–32.

Parton, Nigel. 1985. *The Politics of Child Abuse.* New York: St. Martin's Press.

Paulsen, Monrad, Graham Parker, and Lynn Adelman. 1966. "Child Abuse Reporting Laws: Some Legislative History." *George Washington Law Review* 34: 482–506.

Pendergrast, Mark. 1996. *Victims of Memory: Incest Accusations and Shattered Lives.* 2d ed. Hinesburg, VT: Upper Access.

Peters, Joseph J. 1973. "Child Rape: Defusing a Psychological Time Bomb." *Hospital Physician* 9 (2): 46–49.

————. 1974. "The Psychological Effects of Childhood Rape." *World Journal of Psychosynthesis* 6 (May): 11–14.

————. 1975. "The Philadelphia Rape Victim Study." In *Victimology: A New Focus*, ed. Israel Drapkin and Emilio Viano, 181–99. Lexington, MA: D. C. Heath.

————. 1976. "Children Who Are Victims of Sexual Assault and the Psychology of Offenders." *American Journal of Psychotherapy* 30: 398–421.

————. 1977. "The Philadelphia Rape Victim Project." In *Forcible Rape: The Crime, the Victim, and the Offender*, ed. Duncan Chappell, Robley Geis, and Gilbert Geis, 339–55. New York: Columbia University Press.

Peters, Stefanie Doyle, Gail Elizabeth Wyatt, and David Finkelhor. 1986. "Prevalence." In *A Sourcebook on Child Sexual Abuse*, ed. David Finkelhor, 15–59. Beverly Hills, CA: Sage.

Pfeiffer, Sacha. 2002a. "Geoghan Preferred Preying on Poorer Children." *Boston Globe*, January 7, A1.

————. 2002b. "Famed 'Street Priest' Preyed Upon Boys." *Boston Globe*, January 31, A21.

Pfohl, Stephen J. 1977. "The 'Discovery' of Child Abuse." *Social Problems* 24: 310–23.

Philipson, Ilene J. 1993. *On the Shoulders of Women: The Feminization of Psychotherapy.* New York: Guilford Press.

Pichardo, Nelson A. 1997. "New Social Movements: A Critical Review." *Annual Review of Sociology* 23: 411–30.

Piper, August. 1997. *Hoax and Reality: The Bizarre World of Multiple Personality Disorder.* Northvale, NJ: Jason Aronson.

Plummer, Carol A. 1986. "Prevention Education in Perspective." In *The Educator's Guide to Preventing Child Sexual Abuse*, ed. Mary Nelson and Kay Clark, 5–26. Santa Cruz, CA: Network.

Polletta, Francesca. 1998. " 'It Was Like a Fever...': Narrative and Identity in Social Protest." *Social Problems* 45: 137–59.

————. 2002. "Plotting Protest: Mobilizing Stories in the 1960 Student Sit Ins." In *Stories of Change: Narrative and Social Movements*, ed. Joseph E. Davis, 31–51. Albany: State University of New York Press.

Polonoff, David. 1987. "Self-Deception." *Social Research* 54: 45–53.

Polusny, Melissa A., and Victoria M. Follette. 1996. "Remembering Childhood Sexual Abuse: A National Survey of Psychologist's Clinical Practices, Beliefs, and Personal Experiences." *Professional Psychology* 27: 41–52.

Poole, Debra A., D. Stephen Lindsay, Amina Memon, and Ray Bull. 1995. "Psychotherapy and the Recovery of Memories of Childhood Sexual Abuse: U.S. and British Practitioners' Opinions, Practices, and Experiences." *Journal of Consulting and Clinical Psychology* 63: 426–37.

Pope, Harrison G., Jr. 1995. *Psychology Astray: Fallacies in Studies of "Repressed Memory" and Childhood Trauma.* Boca Raton, FL: Upton Books.

Poston, Carol, and Karen Lison. 1989. *Reclaiming Our Lives: Hope for Adult Survivors of Incest.* New York: Bantam Books.

Prager, Jeffrey. 1998. *Presenting the Past: Psychoanalysis and the Sociology of Misremembering.* Cambridge, MA: Harvard University Press.

Putnam, Frank W. 1985. "Dissociation as a Response to Extreme Trauma." In *Childhood Antecedents of Multiple Personality*, ed. Richard P. Kluft, 65–97. Washington, DC: American Psychiatric Press.

———. 1989. *Diagnosis and Treatment of Multiple Personality Disorder*. New York: Guilford Press.

Raphling, David L., Bob L. Carpenter, and Allen Davis. 1967. "Incest: A Genealogical Study." *Archives of General Psychiatry* 16: 505–11.

Rappaport, Richard L. 1991. "When Eclecticism Is the Integration of Therapeutic Postures, Not Theories." *Journal of Integrative and Eclectic Psychotherapy* 10: 164–72.

Rascovsky, Matilde Wencelblat De, and Arnaldo Rascovsky. 1950. "On Consummated Incest." *International Journal of Psycho-Analysis* 31: 42–47.

Rezendes, Michael. 2002. "Church Allowed Abuse by Priest for Years." *Boston Globe*, January 6, A1.

Rhinehart, John W. 1961. "Genesis of Overt Incest." *Comprehensive Psychiatry* 2: 338–49.

Rice, John Steadman. 1996. *A Disease of One's Own: Psychotherapy, Addiction, and the Emergence of Co-Dependency*. New Brunswick, NJ: Transaction.

———. 2002. " 'Getting Our Histories Straight': Culture, Narrative, and Identity in the Self-Help Movement." In *Stories of Change: Narrative and Social Movements*, ed. Joseph E. Davis, 79–99. Albany: State University of New York Press.

Richardson, Laurel. 1990. "Narrative and Sociology." *Journal of Contemporary Ethnography* 19: 116–35.

Ricks, Chip. 1981. *Carol's Story*. Wheaton, IL: Tyndale House.

Rieff, David. 1991. "Victims, All?" *Harper's*, October, 49–56.

Rieker, Patricia Perri, and Elaine (Hilberman) Carmen. 1986. "The Victim-to-Patient Process: The Disconfirmation and Transformation of Abuse." *American Journal of Orthopsychiatry* 56: 360–70.

Riemer, Svend. 1940. "A Research Note on Incest." *American Journal of Sociology* 45: 566–75.

Riessman, Catherine Kohler. 1983. "Women and Medicalization: A New Perspective." *Social Policy* 14 (summer): 3–18.

Rind, Bruce, Philip Tromovitch, and Robert Bauserman. 1998. "A Meta-Analytic Examination of Assumed Properties of Child Sexual Abuse Using College Samples." *Psychological Bulletin* 124 (1): 22–53.

Rogers, Estelle, Joseph Weiss, Miriam R. Darwin, and Charles E. Dutton. 1953. "Study of Sex Crimes against Children." In *California Sexual Deviation Research*, ed. Karl M. Bowman, 47–84. Sacramento: Assembly of the State of California.

Rose, Elizabeth S. 1993. "Surviving the Unbelievable." *Ms.*, January/February, 40–45.

Rose, Nikolas. 1996. *Inventing Our Selves: Psychology, Power, and Personhood*. Cambridge: Cambridge University Press.

———. 1999. *Governing the Soul: The Shaping of the Private Self*. 2d ed. London: Free Association Books.

Rose, Vicki McNickle. 1977a. "Rape as a Social Problem: A By-Product of the Feminist Movement." *Social Problems* 25: 75–89.

———. 1977b. "The Rise of the Rape Problem." In *This Land of Promises: The Rise and Fall of Social Problems in America*, ed. Armand L. Mauss and Julie Camille Wolfe, 167–95. Philadelphia, PA: J. B. Lippincott.

Ross, Colin A. 1989. *Multiple Personality Disorder: Diagnosis, Clinical Features, and Treatment.* New York: John Wiley & Sons.

Roth, Nicki. 1993. *Integrating the Shattered Self: Psychotherapy with Adult Incest Survivors.* Northvale, NJ: Jason Aronson.

Rothschild, Babette. 2000. *The Body Remembers: The Psychophysiology of Trauma and Trauma Treatment.* New York: W. W. Norton.

Rush, Florence. 1974. "The Sexual Abuse of Children: A Feminist Point of View." In *Rape: The First Sourcebook for Women*, ed. Noreen Connell and Cassandra Wilson, 64–75. New York: New American Library.

———. 1977. "The Freudian Cover-Up." *Chrysalis*: 31–45.

———. 1980. *The Best-Kept Secret: Sexual Abuse of Children.* New York: McGraw-Hill.

Russell, Diana E. H. 1975. *The Politics of Rape: The Victim's Perspective.* New York: Stein and Day.

———. 1983. "The Incidence and Prevalence of Intrafamilial and Extrafamilial Sexual Abuse of Female Children." *Child Abuse and Neglect* 7: 133–46.

———. 1986. *The Secret Trauma: Incest in the Lives of Girls and Women.* New York: Basic Books.

Ryan, William. 1971. *Blaming the Victim.* New York: Pantheon Books.

Sampson, Edward E. 1993. "Identity Politics: Challenges to Psychology's Understanding." *American Psychologist* 48: 1219–30.

Sanderson, Christiane. 1990. *Counselling Adult Survivors of Child Sexual Abuse.* London. Jessica Kingsley.

Santrock, John W., Ann M. Minnett, and Barbara D. Campbell. 1994. *The Authoritative Guide to Self-Help Books.* New York: Guilford Press.

Satir, Virginia M. 1964. *Conjoint Family Therapy: A Guide to Theory and Technique.* Palo Alto, CA: Science and Behavior Books.

———. 1965. "The Family as a Treatment Unit." *Confinia Psychiatrica* 8: 37–42.

Schechter, Susan. 1982. *Women and Male Violence: The Visions and Struggles of the Battered Women's Movement.* Boston: South End Press.

Scheff, Thomas J. 1966. *Being Mentally Ill: A Sociological Theory.* Chicago: Aldine.

Schetky, Diane H. 1990. "A Review of the Literature on the Long-Term Effects of Childhood Sexual Abuse." In *Incest-Related Syndromes of Adult Psychopathology*, ed. Richard P. Kluft, 35–54. Washington, DC: American Psychiatric Press.

Schofield, William. 1964. *Psychotherapy: The Purchase of Friendship.* Englewood Cliffs, NJ: Prentice-Hall.

Schreiber, Flora R. 1973. *Sybil.* Chicago: Henry Regnery.

Schultz, Leroy G. 1973. "The Child Sex Victim: Social, Psychological and Legal Perspectives." *Child Welfare* 52: 147–57.

Scott, Marvin B., and Stanford M. Lyman. 1968. "Accounts." *American Sociological Review* 33: 46–62.

Scott, Wilbur J. 1990. "PTSD in *DSM-III:* A Case in the Politics of Diagnosis and Disease." *Social Problems* 37: 294–310.

Scully, Diana, and Joseph Marolla. 1984. "Convicted Rapists' Vocabulary of Motive: Excuses and Justifications." *Social Problems* 31: 530–44.

Semin, G. R., and A. S. R. Manstead. 1983. *The Accountability of Conduct: A Social Psychological Analysis.* London: Academic Press.

Serrano, Mark Vincent. 2002. "Church Unlikely to Get Tough with All Abusive Priests." *USA Today,* June 3, 13A.

Sgroi, Suzanne M. 1975. "Sexual Molestation of Children: The Last Frontier in Child Abuse." *Children Today,* May–June, 18.

Sheehy, Gail. 1971. "Nice Girls Don't Get Into Trouble." *New York,* February 15, 26.

Shengold, Leonard. 1989. *Soul Murder: The Effects of Childhood Abuse and Deprivation.* New Haven, CT: Yale University Press.

Shobe, Katharine Krause, and John F. Kihlstrom. 1997. "Is Traumatic Memory Special?" *Current Directions in Psychological Science* 6: 70–74.

Shotter, John. 1984. *Social Accountability and Selfhood.* New York: Basil Blackwell.

Showalter, Elaine. 1997. *Hystories: Hysterical Epidemics and Modern Culture.* New York: Columbia University Press.

Sifford, Darrell. 1991. "Accusations of Sex Abuse, Years Later." *Philadelphia Inquirer,* November 24.

———. 1992. "When Tales of Sex Abuse Aren't True." *Philadelphia Inquirer,* January 5, I1.

Sloane, Paul, and Eva Karpinski. 1942. "Effects of Incest on the Participants." *American Journal of Orthopsychiatry* 12: 666–73.

Sloane, R. Bruce, Fred R. Staples, Allan H. Cristol, Neil J. Yorkston, and Katherine Whipple. 1975. *Psychotherapy versus Behavior Therapy.* Cambridge, MA.: Harvard University Press.

Smith, Michelle, and Larry Pazder. 1980. *Michelle Remembers.* New York: Congdon & Lattes.

Snow, David A., and Robert D. Benford. 1988. "Ideology, Frame Resonance, and Participant Mobilization." In *International Social Movement Research: From Structure to Action,* ed. Bert Klandermans, Hanspeter Kriesi, and Sidney Tarrow, 197–217. Greenwich, CT: JAI Press.

———. 1992. "Master Frames and Cycles of Protest." In *Frontiers in Social Movement Theory,* ed. Aldon Morris and Carol McClurg Mueller, 133–55. New Haven, CT: Yale University Press.

———, E. Burke Rochford Jr., Steven K. Worden, and Robert D. Benford. 1986. "Frame Alignment Processes, Micromobilization, and Movement Participation." *American Sociological Review* 51: 464–81.

Somers, Margaret R. 1994. "The Narrative Constitution of Identity: A Relational and Network Approach." *Theory and Society* 23: 605–49.

Spector, Malcolm, and John I. Kitsuse. 1987. *Constructing Social Problems.* New York: Aldine de Gruyter.

Spence, David. 1982. *Narrative Truth and Historical Truth.* New York: W. W. Norton.

Spencer, Judith. 1989. *Suffer the Child.* New York: Pocket Books.

Spiegel, David. 1984. "Multiple Personality as a Post-Traumatic Stress Disorder." *Psychiatric Clinics of North America* 7: 101–10.

———. 1988. "Dissociation and Hypnosis in Post-Traumatic Stress Disorders." *Journal of Traumatic Stress* 1: 17–33.

———. 1990. "Trauma, Dissociation, and Hypnosis." In *Incest-Related Syndromes of Adult Psychopathology*, ed. Richard P. Kluft, 247–61. Washington, DC: American Psychiatric Press.

Spinetta, John J., and David Rigler. 1972. "The Child-Abusing Parent: A Psychological Review." *Psychological Bulletin* 77: 296–304.

Staiano, Kathryn Vance. 1986. *Interpreting Signs of Illness: A Case Study in Medical Semiotics*. New York: Mouton de Gruyter.

Steinberg, Marlene, and Maxine Schnall. 2001. *The Stranger in the Mirror. Dissociation: The Hidden Epidemic*. New York: HarperCollins.

Steinmetz, George. 1992. "Reflections on the Role of Social Narratives in Working-Class Formation: Narrative Theory in the Social Sciences." *Social Science History* 16: 489–516.

Stone, Michael H. 1990. "Incest in the Borderline Patient." In *Incest-Related Syndromes of Adult Psychopathology*, ed. Richard P. Kluft, 183–202. Washington, DC: American Psychiatric Press.

Stout, Martha. 2001. *The Myth of Sanity: Divided Consciousness and the Promise of Awareness*. New York: Viking.

Strauss, Anselm L. 1987. *Qualitative Analysis for Social Scientists*. New York: Cambridge University Press.

Strupp, Hans H., Ronald E. Fox, and Ken Lessler. 1969. *Patients View Their Psychotherapy*. Baltimore, MD: Johns Hopkins Press.

Stucker, Jan. 1977. " 'I Tried to Fantasize That *All* Fathers Had Intercourse with Their Daughters': The Story of Mary C." *Ms.*, April, 66.

Sturkie, Kinly. 1986. "Treating Incest Victims and Their Families." In *Incest as Child Abuse*, ed. Brenda J. Vander Mey and Ronald L. Neff, 126–65. New York: Praeger.

Summit, Roland C. 1983. "The Child Sexual Abuse Accommodation Syndrome." *Child Abuse and Neglect* 7: 177–93.

Sutherland, Edwin H. 1950. "The Diffusion of Sexual Psychopath Laws." *American Journal of Sociology* 56: 142–48.

Swanson, David W. 1968. "Adult Sexual Abuse of Children (The Man and Circumstances)." *Diseases of the Nervous System* 29: 677–83.

Sykes, Charles J. 1992. *A Nation of Victims: The Decay of the American Character*. New York: St. Martin's Press.

Szasz, Thomas. 1970. *Ideology and Insanity*. New York: Anchor Books.

Tate, Tim. 1990. *Child Pornography: An Investigation*. London: Methuen.

Tavris, Carol. 1992. *The Mismeasure of Woman*. New York: Touchstone.

———. 1993. "Beware the Incest-Survivor Machine." *New York Times Book Review*, January 3, 1.

Taylor, Bill. 1992. "What If Sexual Abuse Memories Are Wrong?" *Toronto Star*, May 16, G1.

Taylor, Charles. 1989. *Sources of the Self: The Making of the Modern Identity.* Cambridge, MA: Harvard University Press.

———. 1991. *The Ethics of Authenticity.* Cambridge, MA: Harvard University Press.

———. 1992. "The Politics of Recognition." In *Multiculturalism and the 'Politics of Recognition,'* ed. Charles Taylor and Amy Gutmann, 25–73. Princeton, NJ: Princeton University Press.

Terman, Lewis M. 1938. *Psychological Factors in Marital Happiness.* New York: McGraw-Hill.

———. 1951. "Correlates of Orgasm Adequacy in a Group of 556 Wives." *Journal of Psychology* 32: 115–72.

Terr, Lenore C. 1994. *Unchained Memories: True Stories of Traumatic Memories, Lost and Found.* New York: HarperCollins.

Thoits, Peggy A. 1985. "Self-Labeling Processes in Mental Illness: The Role of Emotional Deviance." *American Journal of Sociology* 91: 221–49.

Thompson, James G., Joseph A. Marolla, and David G. Bromley. 1998. "Disclaimers and Accounts in Cases of Catholic Priests Accused of Pedophilia." In *Wolves within the Fold: Religious Leadership and Abuses of Power,* ed. Anson Shupe, 175–90. New Brunswick: Rutgers University Press.

Timnick, Lois. 1985. "22% in Survey Were Child Abuse Victims." *Los Angeles Times,* August 25, 1.

Tormes, Yvonne M. 1968. *Child Victims of Incest.* Denver: American Humane Association Children's Division.

Torrey, E. Fuller. 1986. *Witchdoctors and Psychiatrists: The Common Roots of Psychotherapy and Its Future.* New York: Harper & Row.

Trepper, Terry S., and Mary Jo Barrett. 1989. *Systematic Treatment of Incest.* New York: Brunner/Mazel.

Trilling, Lionel. 1980. *Sincerity and Authenticity.* New York: Harcourt Brace Jovanovich.

Trimble, Michael R. 1985. "Post-Traumatic Stress Disorder: History of a Concept." In *Trauma and Its Wake: The Study and Treatment of Post-Traumatic Stress Disorder,* ed. Charles R. Figley, 5–14. New York: Brunner/Mazel.

Tunley, Roul. 1981. "Incest: Facing the Ultimate Taboo." *Reader's Digest,* January, 137.

U.S. Congress. House. Committee on the Judiciary. 1977. "Sexual Exploitation of Children." *Hearings before the Subcommittee on Crime, Committee on the Judiciary.* 95th Cong., 1st sess.

———. Committee on Education and Labor. 1973. "To Establish a National Center on Child Abuse and Neglect." *Hearings before the Select Subcommittee on Education of the Committee on Education and Labor.* 93rd Cong., 1st sess.

U.S. Congress. Senate. Committee on Labor and Public Welfare. 1973. "Child Abuse Prevention Act, 1973." *Hearings before the Subcommittee on Children and Youth of the Committee on Labor and Public Welfare.* 93rd Cong., 1st sess.

van der Kolk, Bessel A., and William Kadish. 1987. "Amnesia, Dissociation, and the Return of the Repressed." In *Psychological Trauma,* ed. Bessel A. van der Kolk, 173–90. Washington, DC: American Psychiatric Press.

Vander Mey, Brenda J., and Ronald L. Neff. 1986. *Incest as Child Abuse: Research and Applications.* New York: Praeger.

Veroff, Joseph, Richard A. Kulka, and Elizabeth Douvan. 1981. *Mental Health in America: Patterns of Help-Seeking from 1957 to 1976.* New York: Basic Books.

Wahl, Charles William. 1960. "The Psychodynamics of Consummated Maternal Incest." *Archives of General Psychiatry* 3: 188–93.

Wakefield, Hollida, and Ralph Underwager. 1994. *Return of the Furies: An Investigation into Recovered Memory Therapy.* Chicago: Open Court.

Waltz, J., and Lucy Berliner. 1994. "Community Survey of Therapist Approaches to Delayed Trauma Memories." Presented at the symposium *Delayed Trauma Memories: Victim Experiences and Clinical Practice,* at the annual meeting of the International Society for Traumatic Stress Studies, Chicago, IL (November).

Wasserman, Michelle. 1973. "Rape: Breaking the Silence." *Progressive,* November, 19.

Weber, Ann L., John H. Harvey, and Terri L. Orbuch. 1992. "What Went Wrong: Communicating Accounts of Relationship Conflict." In *Explaining One's Self to Others: Reason-Giving in a Social Context,* ed. Margaret L. McLaughlin, Michael J. Cody, and Stephen J. Read, 261–80. Hillsdale, NJ: Lawrence Erlbaum Associates.

———, John H. Harvey, and M. A. Stanley. 1987. "The Nature and Motivations of Accounts for Failed Relationships." In *Accounting for Relationships: Explanation, Representation, and Knowledge,* ed. Rosalie Burnett, Patrick McGhee, and David D. Clarke, 114–33. London: Methuen.

Weber, Ellen. 1977. "Incest: Sexual Abuse Begins at Home." *Ms.,* April, 64.

Weber, Max. 1958. *The Protestant Ethic and the Spirit of Capitalism.* New York: Charles Scribner's Sons.

Weinberg, S. Kirson. 1955. *Incest Behavior.* New York: Citadel Press.

Weiner, Irving B. 1962. "Father Daughter Incest. A Clinical Report." *Psychiatric Quarterly* 36: 607–32.

Weiner, Neil, and Sharon E. Robinson Kurpius. 1995. *Shattered Innocence: A Practical Guide for Counseling Women Survivors of Childhood Sexual Abuse.* Washington, DC: Taylor & Francis.

Weinstein, Raymond M. 1980. "Vocabularies of Motive for Illicit Drug Use: An Application of the Accounts Framework. *Sociological Quarterly* 21: 577–93.

Weisberg, D. Kelly. 1984. "The 'Discovery' of Sexual Abuse: Experts' Role in Legal Policy Formulation." *U.C. Davis Law Review* 18: 1–57.

Weiss, Joseph, Estelle Rogers, Miriam R. Darwin, and Charles E. Dutton. 1955. "A Study of Girl Sex Victims." *Psychiatric Quarterly* 29: 1–27.

Weiss, Robert S. 1975. *Marital Separation.* New York: Basic Books.

Westervelt, Saundra Davis. 1998. *Shifting the Blame: How Victimization Became a Criminal Defense.* New Brunswick, NJ: Rutgers University Press.

Whitley, Glenna. 1992. "Abuse of Trust." *D Magazine,* January.

Wilbur, Cornelia B. 1984. "Multiple Personality and Child Abuse." *Psychiatric Clinics of North America* 7: 3–7.

Williams, Linda Meyer. 1994. "Recall of Childhood Trauma: A Prospective Study of Women's Memories of Child Sexual Abuse." *Journal of Consulting and Clinical Psychology* 62: 1167–76.

Woodbury, John, and Elroy Schwartz. 1971. *The Silent Sin: A Case History of Incest.* New York: New American Library.

Woolger, Roger J. 1987. *Other Lives, Other Selves: A Jungian Psychotherapist Discovers Past Lives.* Garden City, NY: Doubleday.

Wyatt, Gail Elizabeth. 1985. "The Sexual Abuse of Afro-American and White-American Women in Childhood." *Child Abuse and Neglect* 9: 507–19.

Yorukoglu, Atalay, and John P. Kemph. 1966. "Children Not Severely Damaged by Incest with a Parent." *Journal of Child Psychiatry* 5: 111–24.

Young, Allan. 1995. *The Harmony of Illusions: Inventing Post-Traumatic Stress Disorder.* Princeton, NJ: Princeton University Press.

Zeig, Jeffrey K., and W. Michael Munion, eds. 1990. *What Is Psychotherapy?* San Francisco: Jossey-Bass.

Zola, Irving. 1966. "Culture and Symptoms: An Analysis of Patient's Presenting Complaints." *American Sociological Review* 31: 615–30.

abduction by space aliens, 223, 227

Abraham, Karl, 37, 40, 45, 277n.17

abreaction, 125–26, 128, 183, 184, 230

abuse, 97; cycle of, 76; as defining event, 192; definition, 171; discovering in therapy, 170–72; social causes, 244–45. *See also* child abuse, physical; emotional abuse; psychological abuse; sexual abuse

abuser: abused in childhood, 76; as mentally ill, 77, 97; responsibility of, 195–96, 199, 205; therapy instead of punishment, 77. *See also* offender

"accidental victims," 37–38, 39, 40, 93

accounts, 17–18, 165, 257–59; of innocence, 261–62; in social interactionist tradition, 17, 257; in social psychological tradition, 17, 257. *See also* self-narrative

addiction, 5, 153

Adult Children of Alcoholics, 153

adult survivors, 54, 96, 134; as advocates, 99–108; autobiographical accounts of, 178, 180, 186; pathologized, 245–47; therapies for, 14, 16, 19, 145–49

Adults Molested as Children United, 64

adult survivor therapy. *See* therapy

Against Our Will (Brownmiller), 83

age regression, 298n.13

Alcoholics Anonymous, 152

alcoholism, 10, 46, 47

Allison, Ralph, 126

American Academy of Pediatrics (AAP), 66, 67

American Humane Association (AHA), 65, 66, 67, 68, 70, 78, 98

American Medical Association, 67, 230

American Psychiatric Association, 114, 230

American Psychological Association, 301n.9

Amir, Menachem, 81, 85, 86

amnesia, 112, 126, 128, 131, 132, 172

Angelou, Maya, 103

anger, 130, 170, 184, 187, 194

antirape movement, 29, 80–96, 103

anxiety, 43, 112, 128, 133, 167, 195

Armstrong, Louise, 103, 104, 244–45, 247, 248

attributions, 258–59

"atypical dissociative disorder," 127

authenticity, 259–62, 303n.7, 303n.9. *See also* true self

autonomy, 5, 11, 167, 198–99, 210

avoidance behavior, 118, 159, 172. *See also* denial

Barton, Patti, 138

Bass, Ellen, 143, 237

battered child syndrome, 66–68, 70, 71, 73–74, 77

Bauserman, Robert, 271n.3

Bender, Lauretta, 35, 38–39, 40, 41, 42, 90

Benford, Robert, 9

Berger, Peter, 300n.8

Berliner, Lucy, 298n.13

Best, Joel, 3, 80, 272n.8

Beutler, L. E., 164

bibliotherapy, 20, 149. *See also* self-help books

Bird, Frederick, 260–61

Blaine, Barbara, 25